# The Way I See It

## Henry A. Field

ISBN: 978-1-905553-63-1


Published by Dolman Scott
www.dolmanscott.com

Thank You!

Hey, I'm really grateful to my wife, who was once a school teacher and is from Bonnie Scotland, for all the help given, the grammatical corrections etc and hard work of getting the book ready for publishing regards transferring my hand written copy, sometimes in 'Pidgin English', to the laptop.....and for going the extra mile!

To the publishers for their helpful directives.

To my friends when I was 'out of circulation' for far too long (though no doubt my enemies were well pleased!)

If my three generations of children, family and friends want to know something of what my life was like and answer some of the questions they might have asked - well here it is. So I hope you - and all who are reading this of course - have a good read and find it helpful. It certainly took me long enough to live it and write it!! Things I saw and experienced and the era I lived in, even for the very 'hi de hi' atmosphere, were in one sense unique in the UK so I hope you learn from my mistakes and the positives and perhaps this autobiography will make you think .....laugh..... and cry.....

*My wife, Erika, and I in 2008 visiting friends in Spain*

Front cover picture: Warkworth Castle beside the River Coquet in Northumberland

# *Contents*

# 1
## *Those Earlier Years*

"Why did they have us if they didn't want us?!" exclaimed the older of my two brothers within the last several months. Very stable, hard-working and successful, well over forty years in the same job and house and certainly somewhat pastoral to me in my earlier years, as the first-born often tends to be among siblings. We are both in our sixties now, yet I had no idea that he was thinking so deeply about our early home/school situation. Rejection is a terrible curse for any one of us to cope with. Dealing with it and the like on life's journey to a place of decency, stability, normality and on to victory is what it is about. Let's set the scene then ...

I was born in the Second World War in Jesmond, Newcastle-upon-Tyne, and had two older brothers and, with a gap, two younger sisters. Because 'the boys' were all born quite close to each other during the Second World War and 'the girls' in the early 'fifties, they have their own horror story to tell with differences from ours. Okay, I'll tell you my year of birth from the outset so you don't need to bother working it out ... it was November, 1944. Now, to have a reality check is always a good idea. The more truth you can cope with and face, the better for you. It is always important and good and right that we honour our parents or the memory of them and as parents that we respect and pour encouragement and words of blessings (loving positives) continually over our children and their children - in spite of wrongs. In my own life I have seen so many things, had so much adventure - no wonder I later got burn-out; but battling on was all worth it for the experiences.

Both sets of grandparents were wealthy. My father's side lived in the Cullercoats area, then later in beautiful Warkworth, with its daunting castle, on the Northumbrian coast. My Grandfather Field was an explosives merchant based in Newcastle, linked to the coal-mining industry, and as far as I can ascertain his assets included valuable properties, certainly one being Roxbro House, now a very popular Guest House and Listed Building, in the shadow of Warkworth Castle and in which, as far as I know, my father lived at some point in his life and was the first of six children who all did extremely well in life. My maternal grandparents lived in Monkseaton, near Whitley Bay, but later moved up to Jesmond in Newcastle, probably for the education of my mother and uncle. They had the Wholesale Grocery Firm 'Davison and Pickering' in Newcastle and that included a small sweet factory. My father became a G.P. The status and good standard of living were certainly there. Well, so far so good - doesn't all this sound brill? Born with a silver spoon in one's mouth and all that. Not so! My early years were like hell on earth much of the time.

My mother once told me that my father was virtually a genius and was a very good doctor and I know that when he put his 'plate' up on moving to Carlisle in 1951 and working only on his own he very quickly built up a large practice. Now my father had faults, and whatever his flaws were I can't make excuses for him. He has been gone several years now. As an adult I always desired that I could have had an ongoing normal friendly relationship with him, but this was not to be. Until the age of seventeen, I did relate in this way to my maternal grandfather, the times I saw him, although I had to be careful to always give courtesy and total respect. I took him as my 'paternal role model'. My sisters chose not to turn up at my father's funeral - such was the sadness of rejection from him. He had, I suspect, a very strict upbringing with a 'nanny' and servants, and had a good education. I understand in the little I know of him that his father wanted him to be part of the family business, but he wanted to be a doctor, and so it was his mother who financed him through medical school and he sold Rington's tea whenever! On one of my rare visits to see him in the early 'seventies, I showed him my forces' medal for being in a theatre of war, to which he responded, "Are you insured?" ...! He went away for a few minutes and, returning, showed me a handful of medals awarded to him for his time in the theatre of war in France. I know that one of my father's brothers, the youngest of the six, lost an eye at Dunkirk and was probably not even eighteen. 350,000 of our troops were evacuated from there at the very beginning of June 1940, but an awful lot of our troops and others at that time were also in that general area of France. They were under orders to retreat and get across to St. Nazaire on the Bay of Biscay, where about nineteen ships were waiting to take them to England - mostly Plymouth. Seemingly, the route was from Rouen and area down to Nantes, then to St. Nazaire, with Hitler's armies in hot pursuit to render them useless. Any awards for bravery etc my father would have got at this time and I only remember him ever making one reference to it, and that was about the nature of a certain sexual exploit.

Now one of the ships referred to was a former Cunard Cruise Liner, Lancastria, being used as a troop-ship because of the war. It was anchored five miles from St. Nazaire in the open sea and troops, refugees, RAF personnel and some women and children were being ferried out to her on 16th and 17th June 1940. My father was one of those on board as a RAMC Captain (Royal Army Medical Corps) and would have been 29 years old. Shortly before 1400 hrs, she was ready to sail, but did not do so. There have been many terrible maritime disasters and the Second World War had no shortage of them overall; but some say that what was about to unfold was the worst single-ship maritime disaster ever, even more so than the Titanic. At about 1400 hrs a German bomber came over her - a sitting duck - and bombed her. She was hit below the water line, though accounts say a bomb went down the funnel. She sank in about twenty minutes. The ship was built to hold about 2,000, but for some reason the number on board illegally far exceeded what was allowed. Estimates range from 6,000 ... but it was more likely to have been nearer 9,000 souls. It was 'every man for himself', but not much good for the majority, especially those trapped below decks. It was estimated that about 2,800 were saved. There were acts of heroism, like the person who kept firing at the bomber until all the water had closed in on him as the ship went down, and one or two of cowardice, but no panic. One RAF Officer was smartly dressed and coolly standing on the side of the ship smoking a cigarette, knowing that he had no chance as the ship was just about to go down ... he could not swim. Some of our troops made it into the water, but had been ordered not to lose their kit or rifles, and, although some shouted, "Let your rifles and kit go!", they refused, and drowned. The leaked fuel oil on the freezing water from the ship's ruptured fuel tanks caused some havoc for those trying to swim, as did the German bomber firing at those in the water and trying to set the oil alight. My father told me that he was on the open deck shortly before the ship sank and he became momentarily detached from the situation, observing all the death and horror as if he was not part of it - and then he jumped into the freezing cold water of the open sea and on doing so fractured a rib that punctured one of his lungs. He still managed to get away from the sinking ship. He told me that a man was swimming furiously and pointing menacingly towards him, then stopped and looked at him and swam away. My father was wearing a life-jacket, but blood was gushing out of his mouth. He was rescued, of course, and taken to Plymouth, where he was in hospital for some time. By whichever means he managed to get his discharge from the army ...he got it!

The strange thing about the sinking of Lancastria is that the whole episode was clothed in secrecy and Winston Churchill put a 100-year stop on any of the true and exact details of it all becoming known. Was there something to hide? No official record of it has yet been published. In the interest of public morale, news of the loss was not given out, though the newspapers got hold of it by 26th July 1940 via the USA. I once met someone in the south of England who had been at a primary school in London with a roll of about 500 at the beginning of the war. He was off school one day with a cold and his school was bombed with not one survivor - this too was kept secret, yet resulted in the children in the cities throughout the land being sent to the countryside to live; and such was the national fight against an evil dictator.

A little later that year, my father met my mother and they got married on16th August 1940. I don't think they had known each other very long at all - only days - which was typical of 'live for today', with all the horror of a terrible world war. My father set up in General Practice in Penrith, Cumberland (now Cumbria), and also near the shipyard area of South Hylton, Sunderland. This was where, later on as a baby, I got a bad dose of whooping cough, which seriously affected my health, and also where, at about the age of three, I fell out of the front passenger seat of a car which my mother was driving. Though still scarred on my leg as evidence of this accident, I have no memory of it happening, but my mother told me that, by the time she managed to stop, the back wheel of the car was just about to go over my head. No seat belts or the like in those far-off days and only about a quarter of a turn downwards on the inside chrome door handle was enough to open the door. I know that many of you will have had near-death experiences to tell of and the pain that can come with them makes me think that not only are we so often on borrowed time, but how fragile life really is and worth appreciating.

Well, my father came into a lot of money and I think it must have been on the death of his father, probably in 1948. I think I have an early memory of sitting on a four-poster bed at the time of, or shortly before, my grandfather's death, with family members around; but I have no way of knowing if that's true. Anyway, the family moved up to the beautiful village and area of Humshaugh (not far from Hexham) in the North Tyne Valley, where my father went as a country doctor. The word 'haugh' means the flat land beside a river - not sure whether 'hums' could mean homes - it's anyone's guess! Nearby was Haughton Castle. That general area is richly steeped in history, where the battle was fought by Oswald and his army at the top of Brunton Bank at 'Heavenfield', where he defeated a much larger army under the pagans, Cadwallon and Penda, in 635AD, which cemented Christianity in England. Also, it is on the Roman Wall, started in 122AD by Hadrian, with the fort and barracks of 'Chesters' that the Romans had built just next to the River Tyne, and the layout is still there to this day and is now part of the National Heritage. The crossing over the North Tyne is called Chollerford - it has had a bridge for a long time, of course, and is right next to the George Hotel. That area has to be one of the most picturesque of places, not least because of the shape of one valley, with its stretch of lush green vegetation and the open spaces of the farm fields. Now, much to my delight, it had a single-track railway running by the south side of the Tyne, until 1956 for passengers and 1958 for freight. Parts of where the line ran are still visible. I like trains and planes and for many years whenever I dreamt of that railway line or of its memory, it was always a pleasant dream!

My father bought and owned outright Linden House, towards the top of Humshaugh Village, with its beautiful views across the North Tyne Valley. No doubt that property, with its views, on today's market would be worth an absolute fortune. My mother told me that I used to go down the drive on my 'trike' and straight out onto the road (very quiet in those days) and more than once evidently nearly gave the bus driver a heart attack!

On one occasion my parents left paint and a paint brush beside the large garage doors and for me it was - paint a stroke or two then have a trip down the driveway and back up on my trike and so on until I was discovered, of course. Now that's what I call living dangerously but creatively!! On another occasion, as a pre-schooler, I asked for some money for the village shop and went and bought with my threepenny coin some plums ... stoopid! ... my parents had just *sold* them to the shop from the orchard ... this was much to the mirth of the village!

At one time my mother said I was not eating very well ... only to discover I was visiting old ladies in the village and being fed gingerbread and lemonade or whatever was on the menu for a 'just visiting 4-year-old'! We kept hens and at one time pigs as well. There was an interesting book printed in 2000 entitled Humshaugh, Portrait of a Northumberland Village, giving some good historical background, local information and recent local social history, with a lot of pictures submitted by locals for locals or whoever. My father is mentioned by name in the book, but the year he left is not, on the page where it listed the doctors for most of the last century. Now this is stranger than fiction. Surely my father had a bright, long future as a country doctor in that area - my mother was still only in her late twenties in 1948 - both hard-working with status, wealth, two cars and the best of everything at that time; yet it was cut off after about three years and we moved to Carlisle. I have often wondered why...?

The comparison between the village doctor then and now is quite something. Now they have teams in Health Centres, but in those days they had to be ready for anything on their own, though that was in 1948, about the time the NHS came into being. At that time in Humshaugh, the surgery was on the side of Linden House and, as a toddler, I once got into the 'dispensary part' of it and caused a panic, until I was hurriedly and safely taken out. My father would take medicine around with him in his car boot when on his rounds, i.e. when visiting patients, and if someone, for example, was cut, he would sew them up in their own home. It was a heavy workload and quite some responsibility. In 1991, as a single parent, I took my son to visit the Roman Fort at Chesters and we went up into the village of Humshaugh and into the shop. I explained about the time I had lived there with my family and the shopkeeper said to me, "Well, I don't remember that era, but my mother does and, in fact, the very old ladies in the village still talk about that time." It was as if they were always asking, "What really happened?" To me that said it all.

I have an early childhood memory of visiting a farm and playing by a stream. There was something I wanted to tell my mother, so I ran back to the farmhouse, which had a stable door into the kitchen. I burst in, only to find my mother in the arms of the farmer. I was very surprised, as they were too! Whatever was happening at that time was really serious and sad. Did both of my parents have a moral problem? Was there immorality, family breakdown, suicide, prison even for some farmers, and was it all fuelled by alcohol abuse? I still wonder! When I saw some of those very early episodes of 'All Creatures Great and Small' and 'Hi De Hi' they captured something of what it was like to be a part of those times, whether the vet, doctor or farmers, etc, especially with those   well off in society then.        Even   at   an   early age in Humshaugh I was already witnessing domestic violence, which became steadily worse.

With my brothers I got to know where most of the country pubs were, as we would be given lemonade and crisps in the car while waiting outside. 'Hi De Hi?' Well, a little later on my father bought .... or was he sold? ... cars he really did not like. One of those was an Armstrong Sydney - with a powerful engine, a two-door but large, heavy car. It was in the early 'fifties; one summer holiday the family set off to Butlin's Holiday Camp in Pwllheli, North Wales. Now my father needed a rest, but was he going to get one? ... I think not! Seated on the back seat, we children had to be careful not to put a foot wrong. It was a hot day and over the hills near our destination my mother and father started fighting. He pulled over, stopped the car and started to slap her hard around the face. I can still remember the helplessness and the fear. It wasn't exactly a happy holiday. It was an ex-army camp - and that probably not too long before - regimented even from the early morning and the food was not of a high standard. The holiday was laughable afterwards, especially as some of the early episodes of the TV series were fairly accurate and really recaptured the atmosphere. It belonged to another era, so to actually experience it was quite something.

But something far worse was just around the corner for me. As each of 'the boys' became five years old we were sent off to Boarding School(s).... these were the cruel years...

# 2
# *The 'Fifties - The School Years*

At some point in the early part of 1950, I joined my two brothers, at the tender age of five, at Jesmond Preparatory Boarding School, which had, because of the war, moved out to Spennymoor, County Durham, from Newcastle. It was a medium-sized nice country house with attractive grounds and, although the head teacher and his wife were quite pleasant, in comparison with other teachers later on, the strictness was there and our parents had paid a lot of money, so they had to deliver the goods. Though not everyone agrees, I would never say that boarding schools are right or wise, as they take you out of a hopefully normal family environment into an abnormal situation. Whatever the benefits, it sends the message of rejection. How do you know who or what is really influencing your child? A child will not normally tell a parent or guardian of the abuse suffered. My parents sent me, but my spirit broke within me. No matter in those first hours what the staff did, I was inconsolable, sobbing and sobbing, probably for a whole day or even more. They isolated me (this is always a tactic of the enemy - isolate and destroy), but fortunately for me they were patient and did not use corporal punishment straight away. They brought to me what I thought was a fried egg, but I refused to eat it. I realised in later years that it was, in fact, peaches and cream or Carnation milk! - they were being kind, even though there was still a food shortage, five years after the Second World War ended.

However they achieve it, they mould you into the situation at any cost and do not send you back to your family. A broken spirit weakens the life within you (not to be confused with breaking the will) - it may make you more pliable to obedience - but it will destroy some measure of the creativity within you, the strength to fight and often causes one to go into 'escape mechanism' in order to cope. My parents were making a classic mistake in the way they sent us off to school: a mixture of bowing down at the shrine of knowledge and intellect but at what cost!? ... choosing someone else to instil in their children various disciplines such as courtesy, manners, time-keeping, obedience etc ... even to the stiff British upper lip if you like over and against the health, strength, joy and hopefully fun of the 'place of life' - a proper stable family where correct order and values are all in place but there is acceptance and loving kindness from the father and mother to and amongst the children. It is by example, what they actually are and do, that we follow our parents or guardians and not, in the end, by what they say or tell us to do. If being sent off from home at an early age is simply to get children out from under their parents' feet, a form of rejection, what kind of signal does that send to the children's hearts? Mixed messages bring confusion to the soul. Interestingly enough, the Christian Brethren Denomination had a policy throughout the land that they would never send their children to boarding school ... they got it right! To put a 'you must work in order to be accepted' ethic will also bring confusion as it sends out wrong signals. Only loving kindness and unconditional acceptance and the order they bring will work. In the biography William Grimshaw of Howarth, by Faith Cook, she tells of Grimshaw sending his two children, after his wife had died, to John Wesley's School in Bristol, where there was a strict regime for the children with no recreational time or home visiting during their period of education. The routine must have been punishing, though perhaps not harsh. Jane, William Grimshaw's daughter, became ill and died, aged twelve, in 1750, after being there fifteen months; so I suspect the cause may have been a broken heart and spirit. Grimshaw withdrew his son very soon afterwards and his son was greatly troubled later in life. No doubt the school had a detrimental effect, along with other factors. In my opinion there is no substitute for being with one's own good, healthy, loving family, even though I have met one or two people over the years who actually liked boarding school.

Whatever happened as regards that first boarding school - I don't know the times or reason why - it was fairly short-lived. I think it may have totally closed down in 1951, possibly due to the retirement of the owner. No doubt something to do with my father's move to Carlisle was the reason for my two brothers and myself being moved to Hayton House School, at the top end of Hayton Village, about seven miles east of Carlisle. If I was looking for 'fried eggs' here, I certainly wasn't going to find any!! Nice area though: posh and picturesque. There was a farm immediately to the back of the country house, which was set in its own grounds of lawns and bushes, with fields and woods nearby. Some of the time there was weekly boarding - the great luxury of escaping at weekends to witness the escalating violence at home! But there was a good measure of violence at the school as well - the headmaster ruled with the cane and fear; in fact, it seemed like I never saw him without the cane. I would describe him as an unstable, very sick man game-playing on an ego-trip ... warped and dangerous.

Now I don't have a problem with discipline, even minimal corporal punishment, if administered fairly and genuinely deserved for deliberate rebellion or harm to another and bringing order, peace and equity in its wake, but now at six years old and onward I began to witness and experience corporal punishment at the whim of the powers-that-be, without any check or control; but when it was administered because of not being able to understand or do the school work required, then I drew the line. I would fight back in protest or seek to beat them at their own game if possible. But what of the positive aspects of Hayton House School? The village and countryside walks were of outstanding beauty. I heard Teresa Brewer's 'Music, Music, Music' for the first time in the older boys' common room and I was hooked! I got to do some horse riding as part of lessons - don't think the horse had much life in it, but it was still good fun! I dread to think what they were charging my father! The headmaster had a big American car with a 'dickie' (two seats just above the boot that opened outwards - not part of the inside of the car) and once or twice I got to ride in it! On the infrequent visits allowed into the village itself, I got a sighting of 'Stephanie', and that made my day - she was an attractive mid-teenager with a ponytail!

A young graduate teacher from Wales joined the teaching staff of Hayton House School and he was a fair man who had a teaching gift. As far as I know, Hayton House School bought out Grosvenor College School in Carlisle, a fee-paying school which had enjoyed a good reputation and was in the general area of where my parents had bought a fair-sized Victorian property in St George's Crescent. Hayton House closed and the building was later demolished. For me it was a day school now, rather than boarding, and that was good. There were still some boarders at Grosvenor College School, but mostly day pupils and interestingly enough within a few years the young graduate teacher became the owner and headmaster and the former headmaster was demoted. The change-over of schools would have been in 1952 and the regime was still quite harsh. My father became the school doctor.

Back to St George's Crescent ... No 10 had a bad atmosphere and no doubt the servants' quarters were 'haunted'! By 1952 we had a television with only BBC and that was one part-time channel. We had a Bendix automatic washing machine, which was a real luxury as they weren't even made in the UK at that time. Sadly, despite all the luxuries, at home there was still that increase in parental domestic violence as my father continued to give my mother a rough time. There was a pattern to it during the next few years and, although it could erupt at any time, it nearly always did on a Sunday night. One of us would be ordered by my father to go to the boot of the car and bring bottles of beer up. Later, he might go a bit silly and sing a Tyneside song or something, then suddenly I would get kicked off to bed and he would turn on Mother and words of hate and violence that could last minutes or hours would erupt. When it got really bad, I would put the pillow over my head and sing until it all went quiet. Sometimes, if Father had gone to bed, I would venture down to see Mother, who was in recovery time. If that was late in the night, I would have a drink and something to eat - but was still not allowed to say anything of the situation - not easy to cope with the emotional and mental pain, especially if the next day was a school day. If the phone rang after mid-night, as my father was then back 'on call', everything would change that second. He would be given black coffee to drink and put his suit on, compose himself and go off to the patient's house. 'Oh the games people play now ...'! I soon realised, if she was driving her car with sunglasses on, that my mother was hiding bruises on her face, perhaps around her eyes. On one occasion I came back from an outing to find my mother laid out on the floor between the hallway and dining room, where she must have lain for some time, beaten unconscious. The rules of the game were that I was not allowed to interfere but to keep out of the way and be quiet. Interestingly enough, my mother would never allow any of us to say anything bad about our father - and quite rightly so.

It was probably in early 1953, after one of my mother's suicide attempts, that I visited her in an Edinburgh hospital, for it was compulsory in those days for anyone to be checked out as such after a suicide attempt. There were Social Workers called in and I know that a little later on I was made a 'ward of the court'. My brothers and I were attending day school at Grosvenor College while mother was gone. The elder of my brothers and I decided one morning we would go to the State School, round a couple of corners or so, and this we did that very morning! My father agreed to our request, perhaps because it would save him some pennies. It was so strange to be in a classroom with girls! I have no memory of the exact dates of these happenings, but reckon I had probably turned eight. All I can remember is that one morning my father made me go to school in jodhpurs ... the hard-wearing, horse-riding trousers ... Er ... I liked John Wayne, but this was going a bit too far!! How do you find a corner of the playground and remain inconspicuous in riding breeches?! I got round it somehow, but my self-esteem sure was being tested! It was short-lived anyway - only a few weeks - Mother was coming home and my brother and I were being made ready for yet another boarding school ... no expense spared - the best of wooden tuck boxes made to order, clothes, school uniform, with every item name-labelled, etc, red school blazers - red ... for danger?! I have no recollection of how long I was at this next school, but would hazard a guess that it was just under three years, spanning the years 1953-56, from age eight to eleven.

The school was called 'Holt School' and was situated at Jardine Hall, a large country house, a few miles to the north of Lockerbie in Scotland, not far from the River Annan or the main Glasgow-Carlisle road and railway line. To get there by road from Lockerbie you had to go by 'Devil's Bridge', which kind of said a lot as well! The school was so evil and depraved I doubt whether you would have found much worse in the UK, even at borstals or public schools, apart from the horror of sexual abuse. While the elder of my brothers and I went off to Holt School, my other brother stayed at the day school in Carlisle. I think my sense of adventure was kind of working against me!

My brother could be quite tough when he wanted to be, but as time went by at Holt School, when returning to it after holidays, sometimes my parents would put us on the train in Carlisle Station and my brother would leg it down to the other end of the corridor and jump out! ... and sometimes, when they took us in one of the cars, guess who was in the boot when they set off, alone, for the return journey? - yes, my bro! Pure genius, I call it ... well ... except for the parental wrath bit! My policy was to at least try and keep one lot of the main players on your side and that wasn't the school ... who knows? ... it might just pay off in the end.

It was a harsh regime with total control day and night, apart from some free time on Saturdays. I considered my options to run for it and only on one occasion did so - I ran through the woods for about half a mile or so, then chickened out and ran back. No one knew I had gone. I decided I may not be clever enough to survive at nine years old. There were probably only about thirty pupils in the whole school and I think I was the youngest. Everything was done in regimentation and by the bell. At 8am we would be lined up in the dormitory, the room tidy, us washed and dressed, ready to walk down to the dining room for breakfast. If at this point I was used as a punch bag or spoken to with evil intent, then I knew it was going to be a bad day; but if they picked on someone else ... well ... I would not join in, but just keep things quiet and as low key as possible. I had a lady teacher, not too old, who could generally hold discipline without corporal punishment - but she had a short fuse on anger. Not so the other staff. My brother told me on the first day of term that one of the older boys was told by his teacher to get into the classroom for he had just got a new cane and wanted to try it out - and so it was! The unwritten law was 'no telling tales and no complaining'; good qualities as such, but only if things are normal.

My other brother joined us a bit later on, probably in late 1953 or early '54, around the time of the birth of the younger of my two sisters. He had to take a lot of bullying and cruelty and was not the type to retaliate - damage was done and so life was going to be hard. We each had our own 'corner' to hold and so could not help one another. I longed for there to be fairness and justice. As the weeks and months rolled by, even mealtimes were regimented, like the habit of clearing away whatever at your table, as required, in the middle of a meal. That habit, based on fear, remained with us and later, to the annoyance of wives, we would get up in the middle of a meal and start clearing away in preparation for the next stage of the meal. Being in the countryside was again some compensation and the Sunday afternoon long walks could be okay; also the long holidays - a month at Christmas and at Easter, then eight weeks in summer - complete freedom! - no restrictions, apart from to tell my mother where I was.

There were at least two incidents at the school that brought some change. The regime seemed to have whims to do things, but they didn't work or last. They made me play rugby - no chance, not my scene. It was difficult to avoid having to join in, but somehow I managed it. So then it was football. That was easy .......... take no regard for the rules whatsoever, keep completely away from the other lads at any cost and definitely from the ball, and, when you find a quiet corner of the pitch, enjoy the quiet of it for however long it lasts. If the ball did come my way, I legged it to the other side of the pitch. You see, there was not much else they could do to me, apart from torture unto death - the regime and the bullies knew that. Another time on a Saturday morning I had to scrub stairs and passageways, but I really struggled as I felt near exhaustion, and coping with the constant mental and emotional pain of life was becoming too much.

I liked swimming and cycling and, later in life, tennis. I liked mixing, but would deliberately be a loner as much as I could just to survive, though I was starting to lose my fight for that survival. I was reaching the limit of what a child could take and remain normal. As I look back, I realise that my body was just starting the process of closing itself down, due to all that had happened. I was constantly getting flu and feeling lethargic. I was starting to stoop and have round shoulders. The regime's answer was to treat the symptoms and not the root by putting a book or books on my head in the presence of one of the thugs … whoops, sorry! … masters … giving verbal abuse and fear as I had to walk around a room - and not have the books fall off.

Suddenly, during the middle of a term, I was taken out of lessons up to Lockerbie Railway Station and put on the train to Carlisle. I thought my birthday and Christmas had come in one! They gave me x-rays and various tests at the Cumberland Infirmary and later put me on iron and some other tablets. It was Spring/Summer time and I was taken off with my father on a week's holiday to Edinburgh to stay in a hotel. Much of the time it seemed I was left on my own, but I didn't care - it was a quiet, brill time. That was the time when Norman Wisdom's film 'Man of the Moment' came out. I saw it and it was a good laugh. I was still unable to relate to my father in a genuine friendly way, but at least we both had a rest.

Meanwhile … back at the regime! … a couple of things happened. I was probably about ten, so it was either late 1954 or into '55 when I observed two incidents which had a really bad effect on me. One night in the dormitory, in which there were six of us, two of the lads decided to sort out one of the others after 'lights out' - that alone was asking for trouble! They took one of their dressing gown cords and loosely tied it around his genitals, then each took an end and pulled as hard as they could with great glee, while he writhed in sheer agony. I can still remember where I was standing next to my bed, horrified, looking on. I can also still remember the victim's name. He suffered quite badly at the hands of his persecutors, but was still intact with no blood showing when suddenly Matron burst in, carrying her wide, thick leather strap. Without asking any questions, she beat each one of us several times as hard as she could, so the poor boy had to suffer again at the hand of this wretched woman, instead of receiving the help that he needed. Why did they want to do what they did? Later on in life, I thought it must have been because he constantly wet his bed. I could only describe Matron as an evil, vicious little tyrant, devoid of any love, mercy, feelings, kindness or compassion. She was the black, bitter icing on the regime's cake of evil and wickedness.

The second incident occurred one day in the 'Telephone Room' on the ground floor (servants' area), a sort of small cave with no windows or door. There was a 'Press Button A' on the front of the machine if connected by the operator or 'B' on the side of the machine if no connection was made and you got your money back. It wasn't out of bounds, but I don't know why I was in there at that time. I suddenly heard a great noise and commotion and the rest of the school together walked by in the corridor only a few feet away on a sort of rampage, making a very noisy protest, some beckoning me to join them. 'No way' - and they passed by. I was filled with great fear, knowing there could be a terrible price for us all to pay. After all, the regime was into power and money in a big way and would not easily let it go. I felt so ill. Should I leg it? No, it might make things worse. I felt so weak and decided to report to Matron, who had absolutely no compassion, but at least it got me off the hook. A little later that afternoon, I was outside one of the classrooms on my own when one of the masters, holding a cane, came with one of the older boys - no doubt the ringleader - roughly getting him into the classroom, shutting the door and barricading it with desks and whatever. With the solidity of the building and iron bars on the windows, there was no escape. There were no shouts or words, but as the cane was continuously wielded there was obviously a physical fight going on. I was shouting and banging on the door for them to stop, but to no avail. It raged on for a long time into the late afternoon - over one hour and probably nearly two - that's my memory of it, anyway. Okay, some may thrive on violence and that lad sure must have been tough, but he must have been very badly beaten and marked, to say nothing of the lasting emotional/mental damage to him. By this time I was sinking and thought, "I've got to take some action". What were my options? If I could have told, by telephone, my maternal grandparents in Newcastle, they would have done something no doubt; but I didn't have their number or any money. If I had been a bit older I would have organised myself and run for it - I knew roughly where there was water from the Sunday walks and where the trains would have stopped at signals towards Lockerbie. They wouldn't have found me for some time, but with only some sweets as food I ruled it out. No, I had to get a secret letter to my parents. After all, surely even my father, with all his sexual prowess, had to draw the line at the knowledge that one half of the school could emasculate the other half and that could include his three sons for whose 'privileged education' he was paying a fortune; also that corporal punishment was being administered without bounds.

Now, letters home were written on a Sunday. We were told what to put and they had to be perfect; however, I wrote a letter and what a total mess it was - untidy, etc. Remember, in those days the norm was to use a pencil or a nib-pen that you dipped into ink, so this urgent letter was written, put in an envelope with a stamp, but there was no post box or means of getting to one outside, so I had no choice but to put it in the wooden post box within the school for all letters. I really believed it would be sent off in the mail, but of course it was not. Nobody said anything, but it must have been enough to turn the tables and cause fear in the regime that their game could be up - not only for me to have the school closed down but to get them in the News of The World as well. The holidays would be around sooner or later anyway and so I could have taken some action then. I'm not sure how long it took till I was placed in another dormitory with only three beds and not one bully in sight. I thought I had arrived in Heaven!

I would guess the above took place in the latter half of 1955, and within the early part of 1956 the three of us were pulled out of that school, suddenly … or so it seemed to me. My mother told me later that she fully realised something was wrong when my middle brother, who had always liked school as such, now hated it and that was why she pulled us out. A year or so later, the school closed! Justice? - there always is, sooner or later. About forty years later, I spent a day looking at where the three main schools I attended had been - the one in Carlisle … houses were built there … the one at the top of Hayton Village was now a field; then, after a search for Holt School, that is Jardine Hall, I was told, "The roof fell in - it's been gone a few years". When eventually I found the place, I observed that trees were growing where there had been fields, lawns and bushes and at the place where the actual buildings had stood was quite a large mound that resembled a new grave. I only recognised the place by a wall that was at the back of the school. "It is enough," I thought.

So it was back to Day School at Grosvenor College, Carlisle, and, apart from one nasty incident at the end of a school swimming lesson at Carlisle City Baths, when a much older boy tried to drown me, to the point of me just beginning to take in water, things were quite calm. The regime there could be overly strict, but I did my best and was generally left alone. The former Welsh graduate, as mentioned earlier, was now the 'Head' and the owner of the school and this was for the better. The large 'baby bulge' at the beginning of the Second World War was growing up and around 1956/57 most of them would be leaving school, and there were few, if any, boarders left by 1958. By later in 1959, it was basically a Junior School only, with just four or perhaps five in my class, and that was the entire top end of the school of fourteen years and over. From 1956, vast changes were in store on the home front!

# 3
# *Meanwhile ... Back on the Home Front*

It was probably one day in 1956 that I was standing at the bottom of the steps which led up to the front door at 10 St George's Crescent in Carlisle, when my father came down the steps on his way to take a surgery or whatever and all he said to me loudly and clearly was, "If I catch you smoking I'll kill you!" I gave him eye-contact and never answered him a word, but took an inner vow: "You never will" ... and he never did! I always presumed he was a man who kept his word, so later would not take any chances; but the strange thing was, he had only given up smoking himself a year or so earlier. It was round about that time that he walked out on his whole family. It was suddenly more peaceful at home, but soon there would not be enough money to maintain the standard of living we had been used to, especially in and for the upkeep of a large Victorian property, which he still owned, of course. What were the reasons for his leaving home? My maternal grandmother had died suddenly and I think he had been afraid of her, so he may then have seen the way as clear. Also, I don't think he liked the idea of his three sons growing up, as they might one day soon stand up to him when he was in the wrong.

There was an event one lunchtime before he left home. Only my parents and I were present in the home and my mother had prepared a really nice meal for the three of us. We all had our own chair and place round a large solid dining-room table. Suddenly, my father picked up his whole plateful of food and threw it at my mother. Fortunately, it missed her. Words followed, so I went to push him out of the way from near my mother. It was a protest more than anything else and I certainly was not looking to be aggressive, violent or disrespectful. He easily pushed me to one side against the mantelpiece and left the room. This action of mine that lunchtime went against everything I had been taught and I knew it was wrong as such, but surely somebody had to do something!?

There was a strange emptiness in the home with my father gone - almost an eeriness, with pluses and minuses. It was a lot more peaceful and Sundays became bearable. The timing was right for me as my adjustment from childhood to adulthood was beginning. I had missed out on a normal childhood and was *still* very much a loner, though at heart a 'people person', but survived. Through the schools I had learnt not to look back or wallow in the past, but rather look ahead to the end of a difficult situation as in 'light at the end of the tunnel'. Thinking about role models, parental and same-sex, to get you through those crucial, difficult adolescent years ... if mine, parentally, was not what it should have been - okay, I got through!? As for same-sex ... well, that role modelling was on one or two of the older boys at that last all-male school, and this got me healthily through that stage, leading up to more seriously looking for girls by the time I was thirteen and therefore able to correctly adjust, in spite of what I saw in the bushes behind the shed in the school grounds.

A parental divorce followed, which was a long drawn-out and messy affair, with the unpleasantness divorces generally cause. As time went by, my mother attracted some male friends. It was around this time that I started to enjoy reading a strange combination of Enid Blyton, the Sunday newspapers, comics, and, from the dining room bookshelves, some of my father's medical books ... but with no desire to be a medic through a picture of someone with smallpox! - aargh - it was terrible! Now my desire was to leave school and be grown up. I guess I thought that this would put me more in control of my own life and destiny and that things would therefore be better. It was probably now 1957 and that's when one particular man visited regularly, one or two evenings a week, and we would all play card games. Smoking and drinking were part of the scene, even for me. I went with the flow and felt more 'grown up', though was this wise? By 1958 I was addicted to nicotine. "How stupid can you get?" - taking a lot of my money and not doing my health any good! - and certainly by 1959 would have a drink of whisky or beer, but was never all that bothered about it or ever addicted to alcohol. Then there was another man and a trip in a luxurious Jaguar back to the Humshaugh area and later news of his unpleasant death. Don't dwell on the past unless it can be changed for the better in the future. Take it as it comes, look for the good things and times - keep your peace and don't ask too many questions, if any at all. This was my way of working.

One day, my mother was looking out of the large bay window of the sitting room, which gave a fairly good elevated view of part of 'the crescent'. She beckoned me over and said, "Do you see that man over there?" "Yes," I replied. The man was standing, leaning against a tree, reading a newspaper. "That's a private detective your father has hired so that he can get information against me for the divorce." "Do you want me to do anything?" I asked. "No, we'll just leave it," she replied. A little bit of time went by and one day when at school I was suddenly ordered to go to the headmaster's study. Usually, in times past, that meant there was something wrong and would result in the use of his cane. I knocked on the door and was told to enter, close the door and sit down. Well, guess who was there with the headmaster - it was none other than the private detective! I was introduced and told he was going to ask some questions for me to answer. First of all though, I was impressed by the headmaster's study and had a good look at it! It was the absolute tops in antique leather furniture ... but I was not so impressed by what was to follow. I was grilled for some time on everything that was going on at home, while the questioner made notes of my replies, and he wanted all the details. It was a terrible mental and emotional ordeal. On the one hand, my mother was my friend and I did not want to say anything against her, but I would not tell any lies. On the other hand, to receive the headmaster's, the detective's or my father's wrath would not be a good idea! I gave some information but am sure that in the end I frustrated the detective with my deliberate lack of details as I became more and more disgusted with myself for agreeing to say anything at all! Actually, I felt that the headmaster was appalled at what was happening and would have stopped it taking place had there not been such strong connections with my father to the school socially, financially and as the school doctor. He must have known for some time of the problems that I had had at home - after all, seemingly half of Carlisle knew by then! - but now he had his eyes fully opened. He was a single gentleman and I suspect he did not realise what a dysfunctional family was really like or the extent to which it might affect a child's behaviour and ability to concentrate or learn. From that day on I felt he treated me more respectfully and leniently by making compassionate allowances. He maintained discipline but never again gave me the cane, but I can't say the same for the warped assistant headmaster, although I discovered later he was one of my father's patients, and was really messed up. I went home straight after school on the day of the detective's visit and relayed the entire episode to my mother. She contacted her solicitor like lightning and the detective was soon out of the picture!

An incident at school shortly after that went in my favour. A maths teacher, an 'ex-head' who was fairly old, joined the staff. Nearly all the time he picked his nose and stuck the 'bogey-men' under his desk in full view of us all. One day he was trying to teach me something but I could not grasp what it was and told him politely. His answer was to tell me to put my hand out and he hit it as hard as he could with a ruler. I took it, but said to myself, "That will be the last time you do that to me, for you don't know how to teach." Within a day or so the same thing began to happen again and he told me to put my hand out. At that point I said, "No", turned on my heels, left the classroom, collected my coat and went home, knowing it was a very dangerous thing to do, as it could have resulted in being caned or even expelled. I told my mother, though I was not making an issue of it. Amazingly, nothing was said, but about two weeks later the teacher was gone.

Well, time went by and daily life consisted mostly of school, homework, helping my mother in any way I could with ironing, cleaning or cooking and helping to look after my two younger sisters. The emotional, mental or whatever pain of my childhood was catching up as I entered adolescence. I suffered from frequent bouts of flu-like illness and struggled to cope with my lessons, including learning anything by rote when required. I managed to cope, but it took me a great deal of effort and time, which was not always permitted. I was determined to obtain some GCE 'O-levels', even if that had to be achieved in a place other than school. There were still a few boarders or weekly boarders at the school until boarding stopped, probably early in 1958. School finished at 3.30, but often I would just stay behind and mix with the boarders, do my homework there and after an evening meal with them, by invitation of the headmaster, go home around 6.30 or 7pm. This continued until the summer holiday of '58.

Now I would do any shopping or run any errands my mother asked of me, including going for her drink to a local off-licence attached to a nearby pub. I have no memory of the exact dates of events which followed or even of which year, but would guess late 1957 or into '58. Nobody visited my mother any more. I think the divorce had gone through and, as I understand it, this is when we were made wards of court. The authorities were keeping an eye on the situation until each of us reached the age of sixteen. My mother became much quieter and didn't go out any more. She didn't seem to be taking much care of herself and seemed to be spending most of her time in her dressing gown. Then one day when I was at home, she suddenly shouted to me, "Quick, run. Go and get Dr Raleigh. I need help!" I ran the 150 yards or so to his house and surgery and he was available and immediately came up. I was perplexed and puzzled. The penny had still not dropped. Sometimes we believe what we want to believe and see what we want to see. I semi-hid in the garage with one of the doors slightly open, from where I could just see one side of the bottom of the front steps. An ambulance was called and my mother was taken away - WITH THE BABY! My mother was a little bit plump normally, but how on earth did I miss it? I was angry with myself for a day or two. Why hadn't I realised and I could have helped and supported her more? Being around twelve might be an excuse. As she told me afterwards, she refused to set eyes on the child, even when they brought her to her in hospital, for if she had looked at her baby she knew she would probably not have been able to let her go; so the child was immediately adopted. In those days there was certainly a stigma attached to people being born out of wedlock, whether by society and/or the church. Now that didn't register with me. Surely all babies are lovely and all life is precious. Everyone is worthy of being given a chance. My maternal grandfather was still alive, living in Newcastle, and he sent my mother flowers to the hospital - indicative of the fact that he would stand by her. Well, it was no crime to have a baby, so my mother was back home after a day or two. She said that by giving up the child for adoption she felt that the child would have a better chance in life than with her and that the adopting parents should have the privilege of naming the baby. No, I never ever dared ask my mother who the father of the child was, but sometimes wondered - she did not say. I would have my own private guess - I think I know - but that's all. I think the baby escaped from what might have been a lot of trauma in her childhood. Was that the end of it? No way! There were two things in all of this that almost bordered on the hauntingly supernatural.

To 'fast forward' for a moment. Firstly, about thirty years later, when on one of my quarterly visits to see my mother in Carlisle from my home, at that time in West Yorkshire, she started talking and wondering about the child she had had adopted all those years ago. She was still haunted by what she had done - upset with feelings of guilt and heartache, so I said I would start to pray earnestly that contact would be made and that my mother would find out how her daughter was and the matter would be settled. I think it was within three months that my mother phoned me, excitedly, as a lady called Christine had just phoned her from the south of England. Yes, she was the daughter she had never set eyes on. She had had a good upbringing and was generally doing well in life. Communication by telephone and post followed but, as far as I know, they never actually met. Nevertheless, mother was then content regarding the subject.

The second matter was with regard to my father. I think he may have wanted to blame my mother within their divorce paperwork so as to make it sound good for him. Why bother, when divorces are so horrible and sad anyway? A year or two had passed and I heard he had remarried. More time passed and by then I was married with a daughter and spent a winter in the early to mid-'sixties living between two caravans owned by my father at different locations outside Carlisle. My father had a lady friend, his then wife's best friend, and was visiting her in Carlisle - no problem - nothing to do with me - I'll mind my own business, I thought. Hmmmmm … a bit difficult. Would I drive around in his familiar 'doctor's car' in Carlisle wearing his cap as a decoy, supposedly 'doing his patient visits'?! Not keen, but I agreed … did that once or twice … until I suddenly moved back to Newcastle to live. Yes, there was later a lovely little baby boy, and amazingly he was called Christopher! It was, if you like, balanced up equally on both parental sides, even down to the same root Christian name of my half-sister and half-brother.

My father later left his second wife but never divorced her and spent the last twenty-odd years of his life in a 'common law marriage'. I was even told in later years of another half-brother elsewhere. One could say my father liked his drink, until he had to give it up for health reasons in his old age. He once took me out in about 1964 and got me paralytic drunk … never again … I was not impressed with either one of us! Back to that song 'Oh, the games people play now …'. Couple it with 'Do you want to be in my gang, my gang, my gang?'... and it is interesting how it sums up so much of human relationships, not least when there is so much hypocrisy with game-playing. Does fairness, as in the full sense of equity and truth, really exist? Is life really about joining in the games people play … (or else!) … and joining their 'gangs'? Bad news when all this control upon control leads into a dictatorship of any kind …!?

My school years were drawing to a close. I had a Saturday job at a grocery store in Carlisle for a year from the middle of 1958 and got a ten shilling note (50p) for a whole day's work. I was smoking heavily and my approximate three-year stage of 'transitional rebellion' in growing up was getting underway (at least I had the freedom to think it through for myself, but could have done with wise advice and guidance over major decisions) - some bad language but definitely not blasphemy and, join the rebellion club, with a good measure of stupidity. My mother was managing financially in that big house - not sure how - but the property was not being looked after as it needed to be. Strange really, for all the outward signs of status and wealth, one problem was that I had to wear my brother's 'hand me downs' in clothes, including shoes which didn't fit, which caused lasting problems to my feet. I would still willingly do anything to help my mother with chores and give any help with my two younger sisters. By 1958 my mother and I would share cigarettes, whisky and gin. After the divorce, she got the Vauxhall Velox, the better of the two cars, but 'flogged' it for cash - though I think she was 'taken for a ride'. I don't remember her going out much in those days until 1959, so one important thing at that time was that my mother was available when needed; for example, when I came home from school or whatever. This was beneficial to me and had a stabilising effect.

I was observing then and more recently how life can treat people. You look around at some of your school classmates and other friends and wonder at their potential - of course, nearly all of them in my case were from fairly wealthy backgrounds. Did you ever see that film called 'The Knowledge', where there was a group of people who would be London taxi drivers but on average only three out of the class would make it? It was a comedy and the one who was made to look a bit dithery if not incompetent was always falling off his bicycle as he went around learning all the street names. The ones you would never have thought would make it did so and the man with his bicycle was one of these; yet the ones you might have thought would do so, didn't! Whatever the reasons, life is like that. In the early days of being at Grosvenor College School, I used to mix with a certain lad who was even thinner than I was. That was okay. The years went by and after Holt School, when back at Grosvenor College, one day during a lesson I looked out of the front downstairs bay window of that large suburban house, which over-looked the car-park and grounds, when a Jaguar pulled up. Very slowly being helped out of this car was this same lad: very small in stature and thin, as he had not grown since I remembered him those few years earlier. He was just managing to walk with the help of two walking sticks made to suit his height. He must only have been there for a visit. My heart was deeply saddened - I never saw him again ... you see, he didn't make it. Then there was another lad in my older brother's age group. Life was a laugh - he was easy-going and smiled a lot. Once or twice he visited our home and we would all have fun and fool around. He loved chips; in fact, I don't think he ate anything else! He left school at fifteen and within about a year he got leukaemia and quite soon ... was gone ... he didn't make it. Yet another lad, two or three years older than I was, who had been one of my friends when young and living in St George's Crescent, Carlisle, had me wondering if he too had problems at home and school, due to over-strictness and possibly violence. In the mid-'fifties he called me 'a weed'. Hmmmmmm - not good ... well, that's the way it goes! No doubt he was very strong and extremely intelligent, for he later went to Fettes Public School in Scotland and I would say received one of the best educations that it was possible to receive anywhere. By the end of the 'fifties he would barely, if at all, acknowledge me. Strange though, what happened, despite all his gifting. I think to myself, 'I'm still here in my sixties against all the odds' ... but I heard on the grapevine years ago that that lad didn't make it either. He was an adult, somewhere in Canada ... they weren't sure of the circumstances ... so often those you would never have thought would do so, do extremely well! ... others don't make it! So many do make it, of course, but are emotionally and/or mentally scarred through some kind of abuse and a lack of loving-kindness, so often with an emphasis upon conditional love, and a work ethic linked with acceptance, based only on performance ... but rejection contained within all broken and dysfunctional relationships is one of the most grievous pains to bear. The deep emotional pain we bear, if not sorted out in a right way, will 'kick in' and begin to close our bodies down sooner or later. I am certain that, rightly or wrongly, many have their own 'escape mechanism' into this or that which is, of course, their way of coping or compensating if possible. The middle word in life is 'change' and it is so often unpredictable, but this is reality ... and therefore it's reality we have to face.

By 1958 I had made up my mind to work towards some GCE 'O-Levels' but leave school at fifteen to get out of the place - such was my hatred of it! - and to go to the then Carlisle Technical College to complete them. In those days even to get four could open some quite good doors in the work place or training - this was sort of plan A tied in with another plan in my mind. My 'escapism' was the rock'n'roll music of the later 'fifties. I liked the music of that type in all of the 'fifties anyway. My mother liked some of it too and had a few records in the house - the old '78s'. I was on holiday in 1956 at Allonby on The Solway Firth with its lovely beach, views to Scotland, a café and horses, when I first heard Presley's 'Heartbreak Hotel' on the juke-box. Sixpence got you one play and a shilling got you three! I was smitten, along with the many. I had '6:05 Special' on BBC television on Saturdays (the only part-time channel you could get in Carlisle in the 'fifties) and had a rented radio by my bedside - mainly for Radio Luxembourg '208'. In November 1957, for my thirteenth birthday, I got my own record player. It was a wooden 'Alba', with red and white material on it and had its own 'fragrance' when it used to get very warm. It had four speeds and would play the new records at 45rpm as well as take 78s and the long- playing records. Best of all, it had two diamond styluses - what a novelty not to have to keep changing the needles any more! My first record was Paul Anka's 'I Love You, Baby'. I went on to build up quite a good collection and looked after them even to the extent of keeping the original sleeves, but about thirty years later I got rid of nearly all of them that were left - don't think the man on the stall at Retford Market Square that day could believe his good fortune! For a time I lived for those records.

Now, I would love to have been able to play a musical instrument but it was not my gifting to do so. To work out a one-finger melody of a favourite tune on the piano was about my lot. If most of us have our various types or forms of music that we enjoy – okay, it fills a need or want at various levels of our being and this was so for me - fine, as long as it was not an end in itself or taking the place of relationships. My escapism into the realm of music at this time of growing up with hormones rushing around in my body addressed the need for, not the physical but the emotional and heart-expression from the depth of my being because of all the rejection, violence and stupidity I had experienced. In other words, I was looking to identify with love, acceptance and worth, which came to me through the music. For me this was a healthy expression, as it was an intense heart experience. What did I really want from life? My escapism was not actually into unreality as such, perhaps because of my mother's 'matey' or close type of friendship, and I was free to be me, yet because of her problems there was probably some form of emotional dependence on me. I am trying to honour my parents and be respectful to the memory of them, but the reality was, although everything might have looked okay on the outside, with the status, education, material wealth, etc, on the inside was a poverty of normality and the effects of rejection were causing havoc. I had received an almost total rejection from my father - this was something I would have to overcome later. My mother's life was messed up, hence that measure of emotional dependence on me; but, as mentioned above, I was keen to help her.

If I was a bit of a loner and missed out on having mates or mixing with girls to the extent that it would have been more healthy, I was not really bothered at that time. I was thinking about the future work place. As I think now, looking back to then, I agree with what someone said … that there are three categories with the potential to cause problems if one succumbs to greed in any of them - 'Power, Pennies and Petticoats'. Although I did not articulate it then, I had seen enough by 1958/59 to know that money does not buy happiness, joy or peace and that in fact often the opposite is true … it can so often, in its wake, bring devastation. Yes, we need some money to live, but I was certainly not going to run after the stuff. Power? - no thanks. I believe it corrupts sooner or later in selfishness and within the systems of the world, religion, etc - true friends are too precious to play any power games with and so be the loser. No, what I did was to make a heart, inner vow that I would be happily married! I fitted the music of the 'fifties, which I liked, into the framework … so from Ruby Murray's 'Softly Softly' (turn the key and open up my heart) to Tommy Steele's 'Singin the Blues', 'Handful of Songs' or 'Butterfingers', to Tab Hunter's 'Young Love', Pat Boone's music, Elvis Presley, The Platters, Everly Brothers, etc, etc … but I really got hooked on and idolised Holly and The Crickets. By the middle of 1959, I probably had every record of the latter, separately and together, that had at that time been released in the UK. Yes, I can remember my mother waking me up in the morning of February 4th 1959 with the Daily Express front page to tell me of the tragic plane crash and I told those in my class at school that day - one was fanatical over Holly (and another over Presley) - several of us were devastated. But there was something very strange and it took me years to work it out - because Holly had lost his girlfriend when she was fourteen in a road 'streetcar' accident in Lubbock, Texas, he gave out a strangely passionate type of music of love and was vocally gifted to do so, writing the words and playing some of the music; but contained within some of it was a deep sadness and a death-wish. I could identify with the deep emotional sadness as I'm sure many of you may have done. For then I went with the flow, but later in life would 'sort it out'.

Time was marching on and I got side-tracked! Help! By the end of 1958 and into 1959 my mother started to socialise again. My two sisters were going to 'Red Gables' all girls' school in Carlisle - the female equivalent of Grosvenor College, if you like - for the children of those who had too much money - well, maybe. One of the contacts made through the children being friends together was with the managing director of the Silver Grill Restaurant in the middle of Carlisle. He and his family lived in a village a few miles outside of the city, so my mother began to make visits to the Silver Grill and to his home. The establishment had a bread/cake shop and various bars and eating rooms, along with a large restaurant-cum-function room with a dance floor and a balcony. A lot of money had been spent on the place and the kitchens alone had cost many thousands of pounds in the days when you could buy a good house for one or two thousand. Sometimes I would visit and there was a lot of good treatment, like being waited on, and the coffee, alcohol or whatever flowed. Now this, along with the powerful charismatic personality of the overall boss who could hold a group and tell jokes or stories 'till the cows came home', may all sound very enjoyable.... but ... but ... what was really going on? It seemed good to me ... why? ... I felt more adult and grown-up ... it fed my adolescent rebellion ... careful ... was being sucked in ... but to what? ... 'Oh, the games people play now ... what people say now ...'!

I thought that my middle brother might have had leanings towards something academic but, much to my surprise, he went out to work, probably in the early part of 1959, to the Silver Grill Restaurant as a 'trainee hotel manager'. It all sounded very grand, as he was to spend so many months in each department, then go to work overseas in hotels and have time off to go to catering classes at the local technical college. Mother encouraged or allowed him to do so. So, as 1959 went on, I thought this might be a good idea for me too; but how can you know at fourteen years old what would be suitable as a career to embark on if you have any choice in the matter? If you have been damaged in your childhood, it needs much careful consideration in order for you to become a responsible member of society. I was drawn in in immaturity for the wrong reasons, by a ruthless business man. My mother gave me the green light ... or was it a more positive encouragement? What of getting some GCE 'O-Levels'? I was told, by the managing director, at my interview that they were not that important ... what disgraceful advice! ... as each department, including the office side of things, would be covered and therefore, as a whole, the training would be complete in itself, for that future hotel/catering management position. But it would not have taken a brain surgeon to assess my suitability for particular types of jobs. Listen, I kept accounts of my pocket money at home and my father would use me to do admin work in his surgery now and again, which I really enjoyed … so obviously I liked office work. Physically, I was not built for hard physical labour. I did wonder later on why no-one had had a friendly chat with me to talk me through what I was doing and the possibilities/options for the future so as to point me in the right direction for such a major life decision - a bit of sensible forward-planning. After all, like many other parents, I attempted to do this for my children years later. If my father or maternal grandfather had offered to share with me, would I have listened? I don't know, but I would like to think I would have done so. I had a healthy fear of both of them. Certainly, if the necessary financial help and encouragement had been forthcoming, I would have listened. Just for a parent to pay money for an education at school but not follow it up as to why the child was determined to leave, even though it was supposed to be a privilege, did not make sense, especially if it was not followed through to an acceptable goal. Was this rejection? I left school on my fifteenth birthday, apart from returning one day at the end of term to collect my books, etc, and, having made a decision to start training at the Silver Grill, braced myself to start work on 1st January 1960 ... life was going to be very different!

# 4
# *Learning The Hard Way*

Jimmy Nic (Nicholson) was the head waiter in the large upstairs restaurant/function room of the Silver Grill and he was a hard man. How could it be otherwise, for he had served in the Middle East a few years earlier in the Second World War as an Army Sergeant? People like him had played their part in giving people like me their freedom from Hitler, the evil dictator, and from The Great War. I was fifteen and a half and had just brought him his 'pint of slush' (beer), as ordered to do so - then he looked at me intently and started to laugh and laugh. "Now, what does this mean?" I wondered! Familiarity was not allowed on my part. He stopped laughing and just said, "You've got it all to come!" Well, he was definitely right, but he didn't know I'd already seen quite a lot. Actually, we got on fairly well together - a mutual respect, if you like. A few years later I heard he had a pub in, I think, Appleby, so I went to visit him one evening when I had a car and got a really good welcome.

But back to the dining room … to get there I had to do six months of kitchen portering - the lowest of the low (in social terms, but absolutely necessary in reality) so as to experience what it was like. What rubbish - it was a con! There could be no possible benefit, except to waste precious time when I could have been studying or learning a trade beneficial to me. The schools I went to had already taught me about the importance of 'serving'. I realised later that when I left school the day I was fifteen I was probably well on the way to getting a pass in two or three 'O-Levels'. Of course, there were the qualities of 'serving' and 'humility' that went with this 'portering', but when backed up with my rebellion of mid-teens, at whatever level that was, in this environment which was not exactly 'decent' due to bad language and worse and for me to have hooked in and be influenced by all of this was to really 'stupid yourself'! Cleaning large pans, floors, walls, etc, and dishes for evermore I was, at fifteen, putting in about fifty hours a week and coming out with the princely sum of 19 shillings and 7 pence (almost £1) to begin with. Working overtime made little difference - it was all for 'the cause'. I was being exploited as slave labour - how the bosses must have laughed and laughed as I foolishly played my part in lining their pockets. 'Oh … the games people play now …'! I can't remember details of when it was, but when the authorities came around checking the company finances they were ordered to give me a rise.

I did about a year in the dining room, which included the winter dinner-dance season, so sometimes I would start at 9am and have two or three hours off in the later afternoon, then work through till midnight or 1 or 2am the next morning. On at least one occasion I was putting in around fifty hours for a three-day work period; then I heard that the 'big boss man' had called me 'Creeping Jesus', though it was a shame he never had the backbone to tell me to my face. I would have given him his answer in no uncertain terms. He should have got rid of me and done me a favour! Bullies are so pathetic - they are always cowards. Other members of staff who had some maturity were trying to tell me I was being conned and I started to take it on board. I was not happy and began to realise I had chosen the wrong type of work for me because I was too slow and methodical and was more interested in quality than quantity (possibly some damage from my upbringing). Another lad started as a 'trainee manager' who obviously had good parenting - he was only there a couple of weeks or so and was quickly taken out by his father.

When I went into the kitchen to work as a cook/chef, I realised that having fun trying out recipes at home was vastly different from large busy kitchens within the catering industry; in fact, it spoilt the fun of cooking at home. I think my 'level' would have been owning and running a small B & B - it certainly could have been more fun and more my lifestyle. Now it was reported to me that my other brother and I had been called 'scullions' by our father - not good! I realise now that such a 'spoken negative' would work as a curse, unless dealt with – certainly, if spoken by parents and especially if spoken by one's father. To be fair on him, a few years later he did say to my face that people like me who persistently kept looking and trying for their desired ideal always got what they wanted. I'll definitely buy that 'positive spoken word'. But I had to go beyond the 'kitchen sink!'… not an easy struggle. To either choose or be directed into the right job or vocation at a fairly early age is important if there is any choice. The horrible jobs had to be filled, yet a fulfilment at work would certainly make for a happy and more productive workforce, job capability and satisfaction! Years ago, a lady who had come from a good family told me that she was one day told by her father to report to such and such a bank on the following Monday and that was it and that was that. She worked as a teller … but was not happy or fulfilled in her work. An elderly relative of my first wife once told me that he had to help his father in his preparation for the workplace in a practical way and if he made a mistake his father would dip his hands into near-boiling water. "But that would cause your hands to blister!" I said, aghast. "Exactly!" he said, "the idea was you didn't make a mistake a second time." "Was it survival of the fittest?" was my question.

Hmm … about girls in all of this. My first date was in 1959, I think … she was called Margaret - not unattractive - and I took her to the pictures (cinema). I was terrified and did not have a clue! Her Dad had been a Japanese PoW in the Singapore area in the Second World War and had suffered terribly. When, in the 'fifties, my Grandfather Davison came over to the Carlisle area he would stay in the Crown Hotel in Wetheral - a posh hotel in a beautiful place - of course, there were the steam trains at the back of the gardens just off the station and the 99 steps down to the River Eden - and Joe, as he was called, would serve him drinks, etc. He was still very thin, but must have had a very strong spirit to have survived. He was a very down-to-earth, friendly and cheerful person. My mother would tell me that Joe, as a Prisoner of War, was so starved that any type or scrap of food would be eaten; even a cat or rat or anything like that they had as a delicacy. Later, Joe got his own pub just across the train footbridge from Wetheral at Great Corby and once or twice I went out to see him in my growing up years ... but I didn't get another date with his daughter - I didn't ask! Believe me, though, I had the greatest of respect for Joe - and have even to this day - and those like him.

In, probably, 1959, I was invited to a mainly girls' birthday party in How Mill - a very picturesque village - now that was a good time ... and I know Veronica fancied me! ... but nothing came of it. Looking back, I suppose it was 'equality of looks' and 'keep to your own social class' that was expected, although the all-male schools did not help me to relate to the opposite sex. In 1961, a new family moved in next door to us in St George's Crescent, so there was a new girl next door - and my age group! I soon got to know her and became close friends, even if I was busy at work ... err ... too close! Her father was a dentist and I thought it might not have been a good idea to cross him, least of all regarding his daughter. Now, my mother encouraged me, but I didn't need any encouragement - cold water ... yes! ... but not encouragement!!! I mean, there is a limit to what hormones could take in a sixteen-year-old lad without bursting into flames! I never slept with her, but she sure was temptation! - just in case anyone remembers the Everly Brothers' song. There was some heavy petting ... probably weighed over a ton!! That relationship lasted only about three months - because I think she was wisely directed to mix with other males as she had been to an all-girls' boarding school at some time. My heart was broken and I was devastated, but that's the way it goes! Smoke gets in your eyes - doesn't help your breath much either!?

Back to being taken for a ride at the workplace - one very busy day in the downstairs dining room/buttery bar, when I was working as a waiter, completely non-stop all day, no break given at all for rest, drink or food - I had a number of tables to look after and as soon as a table became vacant it was filled and there was no leader to see fair play. The adult staff around me seemed to be just coping. By late afternoon I 'flipped' and walked out and went home. I foolishly went back; I think it was the next day - not one person said anything to me at all and I continued working. Perhaps that was a shame. Although loyalty and perseverance are excellent qualities, it would have been a good time to re-evaluate and change the direction of my life.

Later, at eighteen months into this so-called training, when back into the kitchens, cooking, it was generally very hot and busy with a lot of work pressure. The second in command was not British. I had been working in there a couple of months or so, and one particular very hot day, late on in the shift, I was in the middle of the kitchen and as I turned around the above-mentioned man had a very sharp, small kitchen knife, one of his own, in his hand and held it close to my face - too close! ... and with foul language threatened to kill me. I just kept very still and let him talk himself out and got out of his way when he let me go. There were no witnesses that I was aware of and to this day I don't know what I was supposed to have done wrong. He never apologised or backed down and thereafter would glare at me with a look of total hatred. They were supposed to be teaching me how to cook to their not all that high standard so that I could manage people like him?! All very strange! And for this I was paid somewhere around the princely sum of £4 per week! Just be nice, do my job as well as I could ... but my mind was fully made up - enough was enough of this stupidity. Because I suffered some shock afterwards, I decided to tell my mother, as I was not going to stay in that environment. My mother told my grandfather in Newcastle and his response of help came quite quickly. Rightly or wrongly, I still felt very much alone in my adolescence - it was now a way of life - I was still left to my own devices and was trying to sort things out by myself, but how could I, for I did not have the wisdom or experience of years? I did not really know where to turn to share my heart and aspirations, for all the adult males that I knew were seemingly not there or not interested or had let me down and I never felt any of them to be genuinely approachable. If this was adulthood it was a strange world - every man for himself. Truly the rat race or survival of the fittest - or should that be 'fat cats'?

About drug-abuse - there was none that I knew of in those days ... although my mother did give me a couple of 'purple hearts' in around 1957! I did not know or want to know that road in any shape or form. I would have a social drink and even got drunk once or twice - but was not really interested in the stuff. I was observing with several different people how alcohol could so easily lead one to be lost in 'A Fool's Paradise'! No, thanks! That was at sixteen. I was still smoking far too heavily in my addiction (they called me 'Sooty'!) - but I had more or less stopped growing and this alarmed me. It took a week or so and my grandfather came back with an offer - I was to report to the Royal Turk's Head Hotel in the centre of Newcastle for an interview on such and such a date and if accepted I could go to live with him in Jesmond of Newcastle and have the attic bedroom and he would arrange to have my bed and personal belongings taken over.

Now my grandfather was high up in the Freemasons, although I didn't really know anything much about them at all - of course (stoopid!) ... it's a secret society! I had no desire to be involved with them - my father was a loner and anti. Freemasonry is a mask - but for what? As I realised later in life, if I couldn't get something due to my own merit then I didn't really want it at all.

The Way I See It

A few years would pass and I would have an experience with Freemasons, but at that time I was grateful for any help I could get, whether I understood or not, and I didn't fully understand what was really happening, for strings were being pulled on my behalf by some of the top business men in Newcastle. Somehow it should have been an opportunity to get out of the catering trade altogether, but I was either unable to communicate or they were unable to 'tune in'. That's the way it goes! You could say I was privileged to have such an opportunity. I felt I had no choice but to go for the interview - I could not fail it, only refuse it! If you say I was fortunate - okay - but life can be a strange mixture. I still never mapped out a plan of action … not wise! Of course, they may not have given it in writing anyway, so on 20th October 1961, I presented myself at the Royal Turk's Head Hotel, part of the Scottish and Newcastle Group, as a trainee hotel manager, for work in the kitchen as a cook/chef. It was one of the best hotels of the group, though the building was time-expired. Nevertheless, a lot of 'stars' did stay there, including The Beatles, as it was opposite the Theatre Royal and not far from the City Hall. In fact, I could have been shot at dawn for daring to sneak up out of the beer cellars, where I was working at that time, in order to try to get a look at The Beatles in the Reception Area, with many thousands of fans outside the main entrance doors!

So what happened to the Silver Grill in Carlisle? Within two or three years the two big bosses left, so there was new management, and some time later I heard there was a serious incident of food poisoning - so that was that. The building was eventually knocked down and I think it was 'Boots' next door who got the ground to expand their store.

Now, I had been about ten years in Carlisle and it seemed strange to be living in Newcastle and back in contact with the elder of my two brothers, who had been living with my grandfather for a couple of years or so before I arrived on the scene. My grandfather was quite old and he had a house-keeper who, along with her husband, lived in the house, and they had been there a few years. I got on well with them. This was a fresh start for me in Newcastle with its yellow trolleybuses and smog.

When I was at work in the kitchens I used to have about three hours off in the afternoons and it was not always convenient to go home to Jesmond, a mile or two away. In those days there was at 'The Monument' - Earl Grey's Monument (as in the 'tea'), right in the centre of Newcastle - a solid and well-furbished building belonging to the YMCA and, as I found out, it was a peaceful place as well. I applied, was accepted and joined, and from that time something happened to me - I started just to be myself again, 'warts and all', like me or lump me, and put any rebellion behind me and started to grow up. Well, after all, you can only be 'you' and do your best - tough if someone doesn't like it. I stopped using any bad language which before I had just used as an act in order to blend in with workmates and to build my ego. I even stopped smoking for several months, though I did go back to it for a year or so.

I got organised on day release to start and get the necessary catering exams for management and, as far as I remember, there were around thirty members of staff in the kitchens alone. I thought I would deliberately be a bit of a loner. This was all when I was turning seventeen.

One evening I said to my grandfather, "Please may I borrow your Bible?" It was in a locked glass book cabinet which was part of his locked desk - lovely antique furniture. Without hesitation, he went and got it and gave it to me - I still have it to this day on my bookshelf. I said, "Thank you" and took it up to my cosy attic bedroom, where there was an open grate for a coal fire which I used to have on in cold weather. The attic was a bit spooky, but that bedroom was okay - though that was not the reason why I got the Bible. I didn't 'know' God, but I believed in Him fully and that He was there … somewhere! Something within me wanted to 'check out', if you like, the spiritual side of life - surely there had to be more. Something had to make sense.

I thought of life as something that one 'survives'. I was a survivor though. On the outside it looked like I was well off financially and materially, yet in spite of all that wealth in the family it profited me very little … well … almost meaningless. But there was damage done to me and I knew I had been severely weakened by all the childhood sicknesses plus the mental and emotional pain I had suffered. Until he left home, my father would treat me himself - usually a massive needle into the buttock as he administered penicillin … oh, was that painful?! Academically, I had to work very hard to achieve an average or above. The reality was I had suffered real rejection but was not willing to voice or face that as such. I was not very DIY/practical, if you like, but could just get by. My stamina and energy levels were not all that high. It seemed like my emotional/mental energies were sapping more than their fair share of my body's given quota of total energy. This of course was due to all the pain and rejection of the earlier years.

The music I enjoyed was a way of calming and sorting it all out, rather than escaping into some sense of unreality … or it may have been an escapism into comfort love, in a sense fulfilling the need to be accepted; but if so I didn't care within the bounds of normality. Something within me wanted to fight back for good against injustice in a non-violent way. Was there such a thing as healthy relationships and loving-kindness or was everyone out there only interested in exploiting everyone else? Was there anything beyond selfishness and greed? I had a sense of adventure and was willing to take some risks and was not easily wanting to be squeezed into 'the mould'. I was a 'people person' really and liked to talk and communicate - so who could you really trust? As I've already said, I was still heavily addicted to smoking and it could not have been doing my health any good. I've often wondered, if I had stopped smoking altogether would I have grown taller and given my brain and other cells a chance to 'breathe'? … to say nothing of saving a few pennies, of course … don't know.

I had had the usual basic C of E thing in my school years with the morning assemblies, etc. When asked to read a psalm out to the whole school at fourteen years old, I remember taking it very seriously as I did so. I had sometimes talked with my mother about spiritual things as she identified herself as a Christian, but I wondered where she really stood. She must have been coping with a lot of emotional pain, or was it the darker side of spiritual things that was somehow affecting her life? Had this in some way held her back and oppressed her and because of what influenced her in her earlier years she never (like many) got herself totally free of this 'whatever', so that there was needless tragedy in her life? She told me of her very middle-class upbringing and good parenting and that she had a Presbyterian upbringing that may have been fairly strict, yet I would guess she was a little spoilt. She was sent to a Roman Catholic Convent Senior Day Girls' School in Newcastle in her teens. She also had a Jewish friend - quite a mixture to sort out. Put Freemasonry into this mix and would it make for a frightening entity?

So the above mentioned Bible was given to my Grandfather Oswald on his 21st birthday by his father, Henry Davison, on 3rd October 1915. Now my Great-Grandfather Davison had been a very strong Christian, an upright man, and in fact with a few other Newcastle business men set up a mission known as Prudhoe Street Mission in the heart of Newcastle to give the poor and homeless food and short-term accommodation. The Bible, a 'revised version', did not look as if it had been used at all. There was no apparent reason why I should have wanted to suddenly start reading a Bible - now 45 years ago as I write - but that was the beginning of much change and new direction in my life!

# 5

# *How to Grow Up Quickly ... and Have Fun! ...*

I opened the Bible and wondered, "Where do I start?" I began to look through it; much of it seemed too difficult or too dry for me, but I was determined to do some searching. Now I soon landed on Proverbs, Psalms and The Gospels. With Psalms I would identify with emotions and situations we find ourselves in and much more of course, and with Proverbs for Godly Wisdom and behaviour 'keys', as it were, for what to do and not to do in your journey through life and make right choices if you want things to go as well as possible. The Gospels started to clarify, bring into 'focus' with some basic teaching of what I already believed and to centre on who is this Jesus that was so blasphemed in the world from day to day - yet I knew of no-one else blasphemed in the same way. What did He do and why did He do it, as laid out in the New Testament? I found that I had got really hooked on the book of Proverbs and was fascinated by it and kept returning to it as the days and weeks of that winter went by. A slow change within me was taking place. I slowly was becoming a secret believer in this Lord Jesus, although I did not know how to express it or even if I wanted to do so or what I was supposed to 'do' or 'join' - so didn't, and think that was right for me for that time. As I read I began to write out sort of 'religious' prayers to the Trinity of God and prayed them, but as I started to absorb Proverbs and found it even more fascinating at the tender age of seventeen as that winter of 1961/62 unfolded, so I would challenge anyone, especially younger people (as against old!), to read Proverbs in a good version of the Bible from beginning to end and for you not to be affected by it, as I'm certain you would start to get a new perspective on life! As for me, it began to give me a fear of God - no bad thing is a healthy fear of God! I don't mean 'cowering in the corner' at that time, but a healthy respect of the awesome Creator we have; bigger than me and my situation, as I was being drawn towards Him as I had begun to acknowledge Him for who He says He is.

Yes, that was the winter that I got a 'Grundig' tape-recorder - a bulky machine which had two large spools of tape and to sort it out you had to thread the loose tape and, for those days, it was quite a novelty just to have one. It was the time of 'Let's Twist Again' by Chubby Checker & co., but I was not buying many records now and was trying to save some money. In fact, I thought the music of the 'fifties was unbeatable, so why bother! Ah well, each to their own era - I mainly kept with the record collection I had. I still had the novelty of going into pubs for a drink occasionally at seventeen, even if at fifteen I had worked with the stuff. If the older of my brothers was possibly sometimes a little bit wild, he would try and draw me into that 'wildness', but not with much success. I clearly remember in a pub in Jesmond one evening someone telling me that a particular horse called 'Sostenuto' was going to win a race and I believed him, so I thought about it and decided to put quite a large portion of my weekly wage, after living expenses, on it - this I did through my grandfather, as he was into some gambling on horses and used a 'bookie's runner' to do so (no betting shops in those days) – well ... the silly horse went and won and I collected several pounds for my winnings, about half of my weekly wage ... and a pound was a pound then. Now if you think I should have been pleased - not so! I saw it as a sort of temptation to go back for more and said to myself, as a vow, "I will not go down that road" - and to this day have not done so.

The day I was seventeen I went to Newcastle Council, as it was in those days, for my provisional driving licence, and started to have weekly driving lessons. Years earlier I had already driven my father's Morris Minor around Crosby Aerodrome, which was built in and for the Second World War but not used and was obsolete (though it is now Carlisle Airport). It was great fun! Also, from about ten years of age I drove on one of my Uncle George's farm fields - Farmer Field! - Hayclose Farm, between Carlisle and Penrith. So, after twelve lessons, I took my test and passed. Shortly afterwards, I had a go at driving my grandfather's Daimler Conquest for a couple of miles down at Whitley Bay with the older of my brothers. When we told him he was furious, as in 'not a happy bunny'! I didn't drive that car again and couldn't afford a car of my own at that time.

By the Spring of 1962 my mother and sisters moved over to live with my grandfather as well, and the housekeeper and her husband moved out. My mother gave back the St George's Crescent property to my father and I heard later that it had dry rot in the basement and the kitchen floor on the first floor was dangerous and started to fall in, no doubt because of one of the first Bendix Automatic washing machines mounted on a very heavy slab of concrete next to the Aga cooker range. It must have taken a fortune to put that property right overall as it had not been maintained for a few years. I applied my mind to these things and realised that, if you do not maintain things, in the physical and spiritual realms, when they first need attention, then it is much harder and more costly later on to deal with them and sort the problems out. I know now that the house definitely needed spiritual cleansing - parts of the house were really creepy and one reason for this may have been because the servants originally in the house would have been virtually little more than slaves - the curses on people and property would have been horrific. The Newcastle Sanderson Road property was also built with servants' quarters, but at least it had no basement and had an open staircase up to the attic, even if it did feel a bit 'eerie' at times. Well, everything was ticking over quite nicely, thank you. Perhaps it could have been that that was that …and lived happily ever after - not so! More sweeping changes to my life during that year were just around the corner!

It was a day in May and I was standing at the side entrance onto Grey Street of the Royal Turk's Head Hotel with two or three of the lads who worked in the kitchens, as we were just about to go in and work the second, that is the evening shift, of the day until about 9pm. People who were finishing work for the day were walking by. As one young female walked by with a 'classy chassis'!! she got a wolf whistle and comments from the lads and tall Jim, a married man, shouted after her, "Hey! He wants to ask you a question!" As I turned around to see who it was, Jim said to me, "You!" "Meeee? I doooo? What question?" "The pictures! A date!", he said, laughing with glee. She turned round and started to walk back towards the group. I was put on the spot but did not want to miss an opportunity for a date as they were in short supply, so I quickly took the few steps towards her and said, rather nervously, "Would you like to go to the pictures on Saturday evening?" She thought for a moment and answered, "Yes", so we arranged a time to meet outside the Odeon Cinema just around a couple of corners from the hotel. On the Saturday I turned up at the cinema and waited outside for a short while. She had hidden herself at a distance, peeping around a corner to see if I had turned up, then decided to walk over the road towards me. She told me her name and age and I told her my name was 'Harry', for that's what everyone called me in those days. I didn't know the name on my birth certificate was 'Henry', ah well! The Odeon was probably the most plush cinema in Newcastle. The film 'Whisky Galore' was showing that week and I don't know about the 'date', but that first time I saw that film I just laughed until the tears were coming down my face - no problem, for it looked like everyone else was as well, except I didn't know when to stop! - so I had to forget trying to make any kind of polite impression. All I can remember is asking her if I could see her again and she said, "Yes!" I think that was the following weekend, when we went to the beach at South Shields … anyhow, the relationship clicked and we were immediately the best of friends and loved to be with each other for each other's company. There was trust from the start. It was only a few days really and the kissing started and we became inseparable - okay, the use of a crowbar to prise us apart might have done so! Now it was not my intention to sleep with her and for a few months I resisted - nearly every day I would see her, even though that meant going up to her home a mile or so away near the Newcastle Football Ground after 9pm on weekdays to spend a couple of hours with her before her bedtime, and I usually managed to miss the last trolleybus into town, which meant up to a couple of miles walk over to Jesmond. Sometimes I think that was a bit dangerous, but those days were so different from today - if you didn't look for trouble with others they would not do so with you. When I got in at home I would have some Hovis bread and Marmite with some cold milk, after avoiding the cockroaches in the dining/kitchen area. It is strange on the old emotions what can be triggered off by taste or smell for us all. Marmite on bread and cold milk will make me think of that time and the smell of toast and seeing a butter dish with a lid makes me think of the first boarding schools I attended.

Now the problem was there was definitely a so-called 'class difference' between us and this meant I was about to go on a very real learning curve. I knew that elements of my background were 'privileged', yet had no desire to play on that. From the terrible things I had seen I wanted reality, truth and justice. I knew I would marry her and never asked her - we both just presumed it would be so, though we thought a year or two would have gone by, possibly tied in with my hotel training. I had found powerful, strong deep and real true love, so this would be the fulfilment of my earlier inner vow for marriage - now that was what you might call 'privileged'! I still believed in God, worshipped Him and believed in Him as a 'Trinity', but put Him on a back burner, as it were, that summer of 1962, because I was so incredibly busy with work … as well as courting.

I came from the posh end of town - she was the total opposite, from the poor side and her home was, in reality, a slum - I say that because the whole area in just a few years from then was levelled to the ground for new homes to be built. Her home was a Victorian downstairs 'Tyneside flat' with an outside toilet down a very small yard, one cold water tap only in a tiny kitchen with a small gas water-heater giving out a tiny stream of hot water in limited amounts. It had a living-room and two bedrooms, one of those being quite small. The males slept in the large bedroom and the females, in one bed, in the small bedroom. It was somewhat dingy, bordering on damp, and unaired at the front of the house. It was a little full or cluttered, although they did their best, of course. The whole family were hard workers, yet I soon realised that her father had a problem with alcohol and was not all that sensible with money; so, along with some gambling on horses, it was all a lethal combination for disaster. His early years sounded horrific, as I later learned; abandoned and barefoot, some time in the 1920s, he was put into a Roman Catholic orphanage which was so bad it would have damaged anyone - very strict with much corporal punishment and worse. He said one punishment for the children was drinking warm melted liquorice with the effects of what that would do to them - not exactly the kindest thing in the world. He later told me there was only one of the priests in the orphanage who had shown some kindness, but when the children were in the sea at a Northumbrian beach, sadly that priest was sucked away by the currents and drowned in front of them. Like many, he escaped into alcohol to deaden the intense mental, emotional and physical pain of the rejection and abuse he had suffered. I also learned later that he had gone to prison in the 'fifties for a short while. Nevertheless, we are all still accountable for our own intolerable behaviour. I got on well with her mother, though I realised later she was a man-hater - not surprising, with all the abuse and suffering she must have seen. She was a very hard worker with incredible stamina. She could be quite wise and was creative on occasions. But things were frighteningly against her. Her father was a very hard man, if not cruel, going back to Victorian times - the conditions of living were not exactly what you would normally vote for. I met him several times before he died and he seemed oblivious to other people's situations. Though she would give him a meal and tolerate him for a few minutes, her intense dislike of him came through - I later learned that he had been quite cruel to his wife and that she ended up in a mental institution. So my first wife's mother had to go into 'service ' - not living in, in the 1920s, at either 12 or 14 years old - she said it was hard. She got married quite young and had a son, then a daughter, and their relationship must have been fine with some prosperity, but her husband died and that, in those days, put her into poverty. She was fair and kind and a very good money manager, but even to get the basics for living would have been hard. She said she had been Roman Catholic, but when the two children were still quite young, and that must have been around the early part of the Second World War, the priest came demanding some money from her, possibly two shillings (a lot of money then), but such was her plight and anger she literally threw him out of her home and never again made any contact with that organisation. It was into this situation in the Second World War and considerably younger than his spouse that my first wife's father came into the scene, giving his common law wife another son and another daughter, but with their differences and what was to unfold, their relationship was going to be, to put it mildly, difficult!

I once tried to calculate, when thinking of the poor conditions of housing and living, that if all the money spent on drinking, smoking and gambling had been saved it would not have taken many years to buy outright a decent three bed-roomed house or flat. Many years later, one day, out of the blue, my mother-in-law just said quietly to me, "I once met your Grandfather Davison." I was surprised. "Did you?" I replied, obviously wanting the full picture. "Yes," she said, "I was working at the sweet factory and your grandfather came into the room and area where I was. He then ordered me to sweep the floor but I refused - so he sacked me there and then." She gave me no further factual or any emotional info and I think she was testing me for a reaction. All I could say was that I was sorry that that had happened and as I thought about it over the years she was probably right to refuse, from a hygiene point of view, at that particular moment in time. I fully realised now how people and families, etc, in authority can get themselves into a place of being cursed that can cause enormous problems all round when they are on a power or money trip! Okay, this needs further understanding. Vindication? Absolutely! She got a job as a morning cleaner in the Newcastle General Hospital, where she worked for over twenty years until she retired. She was so good at her job that all or most of the staff loved her, including the medical hierarchy. When she retired, she had her picture in the Newcastle Evening Chronicle with several other members of staff around her, the presents given referred to and an excellent write-up! As far as I was aware, the sweet factory closed in the 'sixties! For the last few years of her life, she was non compos mentis and outlived her younger daughter by four months. Her funeral was taken by the leader of Prudhoe Street Mission in Newcastle 4, Tom Leighton, a good man who has been well known and respected in that area since the 'seventies. He had known her and the family quite well and said she had gone to him when she was retired, but before she became ill, to talk to him of Christian spiritual things and there she gave her heart to the Lord Jesus.

So back to the late summer of 1962 and the courtship. Sometimes she would give me a rough time to see if I really wanted her and if I would stay the course. On one occasion I said, "No, I'll leave it" … and meant it! Within 48 hours she was on the phone asking to talk. I said, "Yes", and she got herself across Newcastle on the yellow trolleybuses like lightning in under 40 minutes. So we made up and after that the relationship was on a firm foundation. By the September, and with some encouragement, though if I'm honest I didn't need much, I slept with her and as I would very soon realise, had made her pregnant. Once I had 'known' her, of course, it was going to be that much more difficult to stop, almost impossible. No wonder the human race can get itself into so much trouble over sexual issues … and many have fallen … what's that record that is rather explicit? ….. "once you get it (love, sex) you're in an awful fix, once you've had it, you never want to quit" … it's true for many, but that doesn't make it right and that won't keep you out of the danger zone. As I learnt later in life, there is a way to victory. So it was the physical, pleasurable and emotional side of things versus the facing up to the realities and responsibilities thereof and yet falling below the ideal that I'd set myself, to say nothing of wondering where the Lord God stood in all of this and how He felt about the whole scenario. After some quick thinking, I decided what I would do. The emotional and feeling side, even with the 'buzz' of intercourse, was against the mental/thinking and conscience side of me and I knew at seventeen years old that if I made a certain decision and walked in the way of it and honoured that word, life could be difficult. Which side would win? I had no idea of what was about to take place, but was beginning to realise that I always seemed to land on my feet - or at least quickly get up! So I made up my mind, which I suppose was made up anyway - I will face the actions of my deeds and face up to my responsibilities. It is, all being well, comparatively easy to father a child - but to be a good Dad and get parenting with all its complexities right is another issue. I wanted my child and was determined to do my best to be a good father and also to get married and enjoy my wife's friendship with all the physical delights of the relationship as well. That determination was to walk through 'the whatever'.

In those days you were not an adult until you were 21 years old. The signature of each of the four parents was legally required for consent, otherwise we would not be allowed to get married. If that written permission was going to be withheld, then I would find a way for us to get married in Scotland, where parental consent was not required from 16 years onwards; so I got all the necessary forms from the registry office in Newcastle - the two mothers signed immediately, that was good. Her father was stalling. I wondered why! In fact, he was desperately trying to get rid of me, full stop! - I was determined and was taking his daughter anyway! He was unable to defy a certain 'joint female pressure' and reluctantly signed! For further information, contact the 'Husbands' Union' … err … if you can ever find the address! We went over to see my father in Carlisle, after what I think had been a busy day for him, and explained to him all that was happening, having introduced him to my pregnant girlfriend for the first time, and all I can remember is that he was strangely silent for a little while and then signed. It was all quite formal and there was no other interest shown. I learned later in life that a parental curse (a negative) over their children's marriage will usually cause serious problems - but it can also be dealt with and broken effectively, of course. So in my case the four signatures giving consent worked as a blessing, in spite of any reservations. That was in late October to early November of that year, 1962. Back towards the end of the summer, when courting, we were all having a meal around the table in the kitchen/dining area of the house in 22 Sanderson Road and my grandfather, who was sitting at the top of the table, suddenly in conversation gave his approval of the relationship by saying, "You will be good for Harry", and I took it as an important blessing. But within a few weeks of that time my grandfather got lung cancer - he had been a heavy smoker and he deteriorated very quickly. It was the first time I observed someone slowly dying. With his other illnesses, he must have suffered a lot of pain - I can clearly remember a Macmillan Nurse coming in towards the end and my mother telling me he was on heavy doses of morphine. In the October, with all this happening, at work I was moved from the kitchen down to the cellars - could be a very different kettle of fish indeed. With myself it made up three full-time staff seeing to several bars/outlets and included two separate large cellar rooms full of casks of beer on tap as required. At least it was daytime hours, though it could be very busy at times, but not usually under pressure - the timing of the move was just right. I can't remember the exact date of my grandfather's death, but know it was in late November, as I had just had my 18th birthday. I was 'sad', but there was no 'grief' on my part - I just observed and wondered what it all meant.

My grandfather had given instructions that only men were to attend his funeral, definitely no females! My mother, being my mother! said, "I'm going and no-one is going to stop me!" I got time off work - the first miracle - for the funeral. I was in a very posh funeral car with my mother and the older of my brothers - don't remember if there was anyone else in the car or much about the proceedings - it was held in the Newcastle Westgate Road Crematorium, still just more or less the same and in use to this day - except for this one thing. As we were driven into the driveway of The Crem., to the left-hand side, all the way down on the pavement, spaced in exactly the same distance one to another and standing to attention, dressed smartly in black with I think bowler hats, facing the cortège, stood men mostly older rather than younger. Obviously they were paying their respects to my grandfather by coming to the funeral. Then the penny dropped. They were all Freemasons! But why were no women wanted at the funeral? Don't know! My grandfather had been so important amongst them that I was seeing some of the most influential people in society in Newcastle, if not in the north-east of England and probably from further afield. Several of the men came back to the house afterwards, mainly for drinks and coffee or tea. Now the mother of my child in the womb moved like lightning, saw a need and went out and bought some white buns, ham and pease pudding. She buttered the buns and filled them, put them on plates and put the plates on a tray. "I wouldn't if I were you," said I. "It'll be okay", said she. She got into the large sitting room at the front of the house, of course, but was hastily shown out. "It's a snob thing", I explained back in the kitchen as we tried one of the buns: "it is simply just not done." "But you should have seen their eyes go wide when they saw them and they were ready to pounce on them," she explained wonderingly. "Ah well, good try," I said, … "pass another bun over…"

As it turned out, as far as I know, my mother was to get nearly all of the proceeds from the sale of my grandfather's house, so it was put on the market straight away, which meant I had to find somewhere else to live. To be fair on my boss at work, he gave me, without my asking, a £2 a week rise, yet it was still not going to be enough to keep a family on.

Even before the funeral I had set the date for the registry office wedding in Newcastle city centre for 8th December. The second miracle was that I got three days off work - the Saturday, Sunday and Monday - quite something, as it was so close to Christmas. Now the older of my brothers had met someone local and arranged to get married on the same day - but in a Church of England. I had a few pounds saved up, but of course it soon went and by the time the wedding day came I was worth seven shillings and sixpence … not very enterprising! It was all very strange. I don't think my brother and I were the best of friends at that point. I learned later that my father visited him and his wife the day after their wedding and, as stated above, I know now that that would count as parental blessing and it certainly did. He has now clocked up forty-odd years of marriage and has certainly prospered. My wedding day came and it was like a Saturday morning at the cattle market! There was one group in the registry office, one group waiting to go in and my group forming, ready to go in … well, I say 'group' … the only person who turned up on my side was my mother - along with my two younger sisters, who were brought along without choice. If I did ask anyone else they said they were unable or unwilling to come along - now the bride-to- be was late … no mobile phones in those days, so no communication … being held up in traffic.

So I thought, "I'm not doing very well 'ere." She did turn up in time - only just - and the cattle … sorry! … the people were ushered in and at 18 years and nearly three weeks I was married. The whole clan of her family turned up in full force. I'd never been to a wedding, so I didn't know about them - and to be straightforward, I didn't care. I don't know why, but I saw them as a waste of good money, trying to impress people unnecessarily, and did not understand the celebration side of it. It is interesting how we view things from different perspectives, usually the result of our upbringing. I've learnt since that it is good to celebrate something that is genuine and wholesome. I loved her and had the satisfaction of wanting to honour her, putting the wrongs right in the best way I could in my immaturity - at the least without hypocrisy or sham; but there was one incident that was very embarrassing for me and really knocked my confidence. We had a very simple meal in a hired hall close to where her parents lived. I wanted to try and say a few words at the so-called 'speech time'. The bride's father said something, so I had a go as well, after a small tot of whisky - I had nothing prepared or in my mind and I froze … and froze … and froze … managing to say only a few words (if they heard me!?) and gave up … I blew it! Now that was kind of interesting, with all the public speaking I was to do later in life! Are you still young? You just never know what life has in store for later years as and if granted by God, of course.

There was no communication whatsoever, at that time of our marriages, between my brother and myself. I don't remember any contact with my father either in any shape or form at that time. It was all part of the package of a dysfunctional family - I didn't look for or expect anything different and didn't lose any sleep over it. I still had that determination to get it right with my spouse, child or children. That was one of the things that was going to make life so interesting along with the warfare of good versus evil.

I was told a few years later that one person gave my marriage just three months - so they were to be proved totally wrong. Well, my mother courteously and kindly endured that day - don't think she was particularly happy - and got a taxi home as soon as it was polite to do so. I followed with my wife an hour or two later over to Sanderson Road; soon had a lovely fire going in the corner of that front attic bedroom on that cold December evening, with the flames dancing joyfully in the fireplace. It was warm, so cosy and so very peaceful, unbelievably so … and I still had two full days off work!!

# 6
# *Turning The Page to a New Chapter ...*

It was some time in later January of 1963, if I remember the details correctly, and the Sanderson Road property was sold. Mother had bought a little Victorian two-bedroomed property in Warwick Road, Carlisle (where the serious flooding sometimes happens) and had moved over - my wife and I were the last ones of the family to spend a night in my grandfather's property, sleeping in the downstairs front room, and had been given some odds and ends of furniture, and my mother gave me some help to get me started in a small downstairs 'Tyneside flat' in Thornleigh Road, round a couple of corners two or three hundred yards away - a few weeks' rent and whatever deposit was required. That last night in the Sanderson Road property was creepy ... eerie! At one point through the night the stairs creaked as if someone was walking down them - my grandfather used to walk up and down those stairs very slowly due to arthritis! Many years later, I would have a ministry of 'clearing' and 'cleaning out' of such demonic intrusion, but had no knowledge or understanding of this as such in those days; but the morning came and the end of an era with all the mostly pleasant memories that the house had held for me. I often wondered how the next owners got on and expect they had some fun. I certainly had in my new home!

The 'loo' of the flat was outside, across the back yard. There was a bathroom of sorts with a washbasin and a bath. The hot water system came via a coal-fired back boiler from the living room. The bathroom itself was damp and very cold, but the very old bath ... oh that bath! ... that Victorian bath! ... had been hand-painted a few times at some point and most of the paint was flaking off. Though I tried, it was unusable, useless! It would have to be a tin bath in front of the open fire when on, or go down to the City Baths in Newcastle. I don't remember the cost of the latter, but you were allowed lashings of very hot water and so a very deep bath, for they were exactly as built in Victorian times - I could certainly float and almost swim in it! My mother-in-law would send her coalman over from Newcastle 4: Larry and his horse and cart. Both Larry and his horse were very friendly ... well, I presumed the hard-working horse was as well. Somehow we nearly always had enough coal. It was hard when we ran out and no-one could or would help ... 'those were the days, my friend ... we thought they'd never end'. It took a few years into early 1970 and they did ... almost exactly seven years. I had several house moves with some 'homelessness' during those seven years and knew some appalling, terrible poverty. Yet, somehow, by God's grace, I walked through it to victory.

I kept moving home to and fro between Carlisle and Newcastle, about 60 miles apart. Those moves alone were often traumatic and physically and emotionally exhausting - the average time of a move was, as I remember, just over a year, and throw in three times of 'homelessness' - that is, living in my father's caravans or with the in-laws at the times while looking to find somewhere else to live. With hindsight, I realised that was a strange time in my life - I obviously had a need for some help from parents and was grateful for what they gave, but there was also a 'dependency' ... I would now call it a 'soul-tie' that was not too healthy. I couldn't have put this into words at that time, but it needed to be dealt with in a correct way. I would have to learn to stand on my own two feet, but you were not legally classed as an adult until you were twenty-one and only then entitled to earn a wage that would support a family. That must seem very strange by today's standards. The general consensus used to be that you were not ready for marriage until around the mid-twenties, in other words the maturity of that age group; so it was interesting what happened to me later at 25 years old.

There were several changes in jobs or sometimes lack of them that added to the above problems. With the rekindling of my spiritual search after the mid-'sixties and with family responsibilities, sometimes I wonder however did I survive - there was some fun and I made the best of it, though always hated from 1963 onwards whenever I lived within the city boundaries of Newcastle itself, as I found it somewhat depressing. I don't know why, but it always seemed to go against me. Get through it I somehow did and loved being a husband and father and had the great satisfaction of facing up to things and doing my best, in spite of the mistakes made, character defects and the things that were against me. It was to be much later in life before I would see the whole background 'picture' of what I was up against. So, with all of this general backdrop of these next seven years of the 'sixties and with the often complicated interwoven streams of work, homes and family life, here are just some of the things that happened - good, bad and indifferent!

I remember in those first few weeks of being in that downstairs Victorian flat, decorating the main living room - was that some job with layers of old wallpaper going back to between the world wars! - what a lot of energy it took to remove them, but I managed, a square inch at a time, to sort it out and clean it up a little. The months rolled by, summer came and on 13th June I was the proud father of a little baby girl. Well, it had to be just another day at work of course - I was still in the cellars - but straight after finishing I was up at the Newcastle General Hospital to visit. I'll never forget it! All the men were lined up in an almost military straight row down the corridor, some with flowers, no-one speaking, then at just the second of the time of visiting, as everything was ready, a nurse opened the doors and ushered us into the ward - nothing was out of place; I mean, talk about clinically spotless! Now I was conscious of the fact that I looked younger than my actual age and almost out of place - ah well, that's the way it goes!

When I found wife plus daughter I was shocked. My wife was a tough 'Geordie' and the birth had been about three or four hours earlier, but she looked really rough - nobody warned me that she had had a very difficult time. I was also surprised at how a baby looks shortly after birth, having never seen one up until that time - but she was lovely! My wife was in a state of exhaustion, so I could not stay too long anyway. I was proud in a right way and justly so. I was now a father - but would I make a good 'dad'? Only time would tell!

Now, my in-laws had some strange ideas. A few days later, on discharge from hospital, they were going to take mother and baby home with them! Oh... really! No chance! My wife had to make a quick decision to go with her parents or go with me. She chose me and our flat in Jesmond, even though we only had the basics, virtually all second-hand for, and to look after, the baby. That was okay for a week or two until we decided to have our daughter christened. Well, it seemed a good idea, though I did not have much understanding of what it was really supposed to mean, but would identify with the Church of England, and, after all, St Hilda's Church building was directly opposite our flat.

The Sunday came and all went swimmingly - sorry for the pun ... it was 'sprinkling' and not 'total immersion' baptism, of course ... until back in the flat. There were only a few relatives there, including my in-laws. During that afternoon I went round to Sanderson Road to see my brother and his wife and so started to have some contact with them again, but something in my behaviour apparently really upset my father-in-law, even when in my own home, and he was not pleased. I was grateful for all the help I could get, but it was still 'mind your own business time' as this 'growing up business' might just take a little longer than expected!? The next thing I knew, he was literally 'up the wall' - no longer was this just an expression I used when busy and under pressure at work - my wife and mother-in-law and others pinned him to the wall, off the ground, in the corridor, as he was completely filled with great anger and pure hatred towards me and was out of control as he made no bones about wanting to, and was desperate to, put a quick and definite end to my life. Err ... this was evil ... what had I ever done to the man to be worthy of such treatment? No time to think, though - only one way of escape, through the bedroom at the front of the flat - fortunately the Victorian side-sash bay window opened and I was out in a second and off! Was I a true coward or very wise?! Well, once I had turned the corner, I just walked around the streets for a while, giving certain people a chance to cool down. My out-laws ... sorry, in-laws! ... had gone when I got back. The atmosphere was not too good, with one or two people still around. I tried to reason it through as to what had made him so angry, but was puzzled. My wife stood by me, but I think she struggled for a day or two. A few days later, my in-laws came back round in their old 'banger' and we went on as if it had never happened, but there was no talking it through or out and no apologies on either side, yet I knew, as the years went by, he never changed in his attitude towards me - it was only suppressed and concealed.

Somewhere around that time I had a week's holiday and will never forget it. My in-laws had a very old basic and primitive caravan at Warkworth, situated on a grassy gradient with other similar types of caravans, on the way down to the sand dunes and beach. There were no proper toilets at that time but portable loos in little decrepit huts beside each caravan and decent toilets (still there today) in the village several hundred yards away. Nearby, there was a cold water tap. We hardly had enough food, though Baby was okay, and the only treat we had was one glass of lager each (not the baby!) and an ice-cream each. The weather was sunny and gloriously hot and it was total fun from beginning to end. It rated then and now as one of the best holidays I've ever had, in spite of the simplicity of it. Why? Because there was such love and contentment, peace and appreciation between us of the good things we had. I understood a little then, but fully now, that these things have real value and when you find them they are priceless.

At work during that summer of '63, I was still in the cellars - but when the cellar boss went on his holidays I was put in charge - somewhat nervously – and, much to everyone's surprise, and not least mine, everything went really well! So, the next thing I knew was that I was being quickly trained in the large basement food-store near the cellars and when the man in charge, who was really good at his job, went on his annual holidays, I had to run the store - and again all went well! Later that year they moved me to the general office, which was the hub of the admin. for the hotel. I had to learn to do the checking of the accounts of the dining room and its bar, including all the finances regarding the waiting staff's food orders, etc, etc. I got to eat in a staff dining room and was served at table by a young waiter; then one day the big boss said to me, "I want you to exercise your authority." "Yes, sir," I replied and as I walked away wondered, "What authority?! What is the sphere or level of my authority?" I thought real authority was only with those who could hire and fire. I should have asked him, of course, but he was not exactly 'approachable' and it was very dangerous to cross him. "Okay," I thought, "I have one set of fairly smart dark clothes and white shirt and to this I will add a 'silver' tie and I will start to look the part." Of course, I had access to all the main communal areas that were for the guests. I was having fun and soon walked around as if I owned the joint! It is laughable as I think about it now, but I still managed to make one or two enemies - perhaps there was some jealousy? I was still working towards some higher catering exams for those days and was making slow but definite progress, but, with work and family, was not attending classes as regularly as I should have done and was beginning to lose my grip. The authority needed was within the actual job I was doing, but was very limited. Getting that right balance with authority but not an out-of-bounds 'control' was something that I would seek to get right in later years.

As the year went on I made contact with my father. His main concern was that my wife should take the new oral contraceptive tablets that were just becoming widely available - obviously no more children would give a breathing space or chance to succeed - so he sent over an abundance of free samples he had received and my wife started taking them. She took them for years and years and I still wonder about the long-term effects of those tablets.

Because of the poverty, I started to fall behind a little with the rent of the flat in Jesmond and was dismayed. My in-laws said we could move in with them and store our furniture in their front room and all crowd in somehow! Then my father said he might be able to help me out regarding housing. We discussed the possibility of his help to get me on the housing ladder with a deposit and then he had the idea of buying a pair of 'Tyneside flats' and allowing me to live in one of them, paying either minimal or no rent. Once these parental offers of help were made (after we had lived in the Jesmond flat for about a year), I suddenly made a decision and, as it were, moved 'by moonlight' to the home of my in-laws; however, I took the keys to the estate agent, apologised, and agreed on a sum of money I should pay and went in each week and paid whatever I could afford until it was all fully paid within weeks. A few weeks later my father bought a pair of 'Tyneside flats' in Condercum Road in Newcastle 4 and I lived in the downstairs one first, then later the upstairs. They were quite basic: cold water tap in the kitchen, no bathroom and an outside loo. The upstairs flat still had the very old gas-light fixtures in it and so I had to get it wired for electricity. It was decorating time again and I can remember doing out one room, after scraping the walls, with wallpaper that cost in a sale a total of three shillings and nine pence - and it looked really good and clean!

Some public Victorian Baths were not too far away, but were infected with vermin. I collected the rent from the other flat each week and sent it to my father in Carlisle. This pleased him, so he decided he would buy another pair of 'Tyneside Flats' in the same area, about a mile or so away, and let them. I could see to letting them as and when needs be and collect the rents, etc. I said I would do that, of course, but was horrified and tried to tell him why. It was not a good investment. The properties would soon be life-expired, even if they had been modernised - which none of the four had. Buy one or two good properties in reasonably good areas with a potentially long lifespan and keep them well maintained and the value of your investment would stay sound - but even as I started to speak to him he did not want to know, as he had made up his mind, so for that time I did what was asked of me. On one occasion I was renting a flat out and a prospective tenant offered me a bribe of quite a lot of money for those days if I would give him the tenancy - that was a temptation as I was still in some hardship - but I said "No", yet let him rent the property anyway.

I can't remember the exact month or time of another happening. It may have been the Spring of 1964, for at that general time I was in contact with both of my parents, separately. My mother had sold her Carlisle, Warwick Road, property and moved to a really nice rented property in the pleasant and peaceful village of Cumwhinton, a mile or two outside and more or less to the south of Carlisle. One weekend I took my wife and daughter over to see her and my two sisters, who were probably about 10 and 13 years old, and we were going to stay a couple of nights.

Everything seemed to be okay until the Sunday morning - we all got up and got ready - only mother didn't do so. It was a lovely sunny day. We were, of course, all waiting for her to make a move. The elder of my two sisters went into her room and she was in a deep sleep. My sister then said to me that something was wrong, but I thought Mother must just have been very tired, along with having some alcohol the night before. A little more time went by and I could not take it in that there could be anything wrong and said I'd give her just a few more minutes, then try and wake her. This I did and found that I couldn't wake her and fully realised I'd better take some action very quickly. We found the doctor's phone number and some change and I rushed down the village to find the standard red phone box of those days. Her doctor was at home and came out immediately. He straightaway went out and called an ambulance from the phone box, for she had overdosed on tablets and alcohol. I told the doctor the situation and the details of what had happened that morning and can still remember him sitting on a chair writing one and a half pages, several hundred words, of what he needed to give an account of. When the ambulance came I said I would go with her and see the others whenever I got back. The ambulance made haste, ringing its bell when necessary, to clear the way for itself. On arrival at the Cumberland Infirmary, they saw to her immediately and I sat down to wait … and wait … and wait; for even as late as those days of the mid-'sixties, the medics still did not like or approve of those who attempted suicide, though I doubt if they would have admitted it. My mind was now active and I had realised as I started to think it all through that my two sisters would have to go and live with my father … and our stepmother … and, as wards of court until 16, this would be legally binding for them. I doubted whether my father would really want them and certainly they would not have wanted to go and live there - in fact, there would be 'sides' with little love lost between the two. I think that was to be proved correct, though what sadness to even have to write such a thing. I would have taken custody of them myself, but I was too young and did not have a suitable property, etc. I thought it would have been a nightmare if it had been me who had been in their position and certainly would not have liked to go through what they were about to endure. In our search to be loved and accepted unconditionally, it is so hard to be in a real or perceived loveless environment. I was sitting on my own and everything was very quiet. Eventually, I did ask someone about Mother, only to be told she had been taken up to a ward. Having been totally ignored by the staff, I thought, "Why take it out on me? I'm caught in a situation I'd rather not be in and even if I still look quite young for my age I have my own family responsibilities now." So I went up to see her and she was conscious, though she did look rough. We talked slowly and quietly for a little while and she gave me some instructions. As my parent, I still gave her honour and respect and carefully guarded the words I used.

I contacted my father and he came and collected me at the infirmary and sorted the necessary things out that afternoon and took the girls. I returned with my family on the train to Newcastle. The shock of what had unexpectedly happened was quite traumatic as I came to terms with facing the reality of the events of that weekend and my slowness in wanting to accept the truth of the situation. I had been set up. We believe what we want to believe and act out that belief, though sometimes it may be a product of life's conditioning, but that is still no excuse. I would have to break out of the strictness of my upbringing, but hopefully into maturity and not into rebellion! I wondered why my mother had not simply told my father or the older of my brothers or myself or all three that she was in difficulties and needed help. Any practical help on my part may have been limited, but I certainly would have stood with her to listen and try and encourage her to battle on.

Once she had finished with hospitals she got work in hotel receptions for the next year or two in Gateshead, Kelso and Epsom - these were the three work places, and I visited her at least once in each. I did not understand why, if faced with a difficult situation and decision, anyone would not let the lesser go for the greater as they sorted out values and priorities. I was not being judgemental, at least I hope not, but wondered why. Well, I was soon tested myself on that one.

# 7

# *A New Day Dawns*

In spite of the poverty and some trials, I was happily married, which had brought to me its own joys and security. It was fun to see my daughter grow from the baby to toddler stage, but I was wondering about the situation at work, and, as it turned out, quite rightly so. I had been working in a small bar in the corner of the large dining room that dealt with dispensing drinks, cigarettes, etc, and handled money and the admin. side of things to do with the dining room staff in their dealings with the hotel guests. I liked this job: it was practical and sociable and not uncommon to see one or two famous people of that era. The hours were not long, but they were awkward, being over lunchtime and dinner - as I remember about 27 hours per week - but I was beginning to realise that my wife's heart was not for me to be in the catering trade due to the devotion needed for the job; for example, it could be around 10pm when I arrived home, as I lived two or three miles away in Newcastle 4. One day in the earlier part of 1964, the big boss called me to his office. "I want you to go into 'The American Bar', start on such and such a day." My heart sank. I knew that the staff there were quite happy for me to join them, but for one or two reasons I did not want to got into that department. I had seriously wondered how I would really fit in and be able to cope, because of my personality/character ... not being particularly 'worldly wise'. "Sir, I would rather go into reception," I stated somewhat boldly ... but that was the end of that! He was furious. "Get out!" he said, and it would have been funny if he had said, "Don't pass GO or collect £200 ...!" Life just seems like a game of Monopoly sometimes.

I deserved it, of course, and made the slow journey home to tell my wife and talk it through. She couldn't read or write, except a little to get by, but she could be very wise; not perfect, but generally wise, in spite of her having certain fears. Poverty was nothing new to her and if I brought in enough finance for the basic essentials that was sufficient and she was content. Shopping - of course! - along with her mother and sister she loved to buy second-hand clothes, whereby she thoroughly enjoyed herself and had a good wardrobe. Yet she had made it clear that she of herself did not, as a spouse, want to go into or be involved with the catering trade. She wanted a cosy, normal home and family life. I had my doubts. Now I knew that those hours in the American Bar would have been long and would go into the night as needs-be, but I had made my mind up to get out of the hotel trade altogether and this time I would do it ... with that help just given by the boss! I had had a taste of admin. and it was definitely my scene - desks and paper work. All I needed was the office hours - well, so I thought! It's not that simple! But I was determined to plot a new course, though now unemployed. My time in the catering trade spanned more or less five years, for later on at the end of that year and into the January of 1965 for several weeks I got a menial job in a hotel in Carlisle to get by for a short time. At one point in the summer I had tried to get a job in a hotel in Pooley Bridge, Ullswater, where my father had one of his two caravans, because it was handy for the yacht club where he had his yacht/cabin cruiser moored. The man in the hotel said he might offer me a job for the rest of the season, so I returned there during a very hot few days of that summer and remember being very sunburnt.

My father took me down in his car with my family and left us there for about four days. The trouble was, I didn't have any money, there was virtually no food in the caravan and the offer of a job, even only for a few weeks, was just hot air. I was familiar with the beauty of the lakes as mentioned, but the lovely weather of that week was unsurpassed. Now I was tested and my conscience was working at the age of 19. My wife and I were very thin and yet I know now what I didn't know then: that a few days fasting would do no harm … It was a strange thing to be really hungry and by about the third day we delighted in the last bit of food - a packet of Paxo Stuffing - but we both still smoked - both addicted to the wretched things … I hadn't done my general health any good and had hoped that I'd have grown just a little taller and was sure smoking caused this in part. So, in all of the poverty, I still gave a certain priority to obtaining cigarettes. Was this stupidity or total stupidity? The main concern on one day had been to get the last few pennies together to make around two shillings to buy 10 'fags'. I observed the situation in its reality and applied my mind. What really were my values and priorities? Was it just about self or selfishness and what would I need to do and be prepared to put into action to set an example and be a winner? I loved my family and wanted the best for them and that meant basic provision and to be a good example. Then it happened … midweek on the grass just outside the caravan door in the blazing sunshine in a beautiful setting my daughter took her first step on her own - we couldn't have been more filled with joy and fun if she had just climbed Everest!! But for me that sealed it - I would make that necessary re-alignment and stop smoking. It would have to be 'willpower'.

I don't remember whether I stopped immediately or if I set a date to stop within several days, but stop I did and have never smoked since, thus containing my time of smoking virtually to my teenage years only. My wife followed suit within two or three months. We were both free of that terrible addiction and better for it all round. Meanwhile, back to Ullswater. When my father came to collect us on the Thursday afternoon on his half day off, he asked if there was anything we wanted. "Would love some fish and chips" we sort of casually said, as if not really bothered either way; so we stopped in

Penrith at a Chippie, got some food and fell on it, stuffing it into our mouths ... "When did you last eat?" he asked, as he continued driving; but we were too busy stuffing our faces and gave him an incoherent answer.

My father wanted some items of furniture and some other things moving around, so I suggested he bought me a 'banger' which would get me mobile and do the tasks required while I was looking for work; so I got an old 1954 Hillman Estate, hand-painted black and grey, with brilliant suspension, but could not say that about the brakes! I only had the vehicle a few weeks and did the chores required with it. After trying to sort out the brakes, which definitely needed attention, and a couple of days after putting it into a small garage (for the brake repairs), the brakes completely failed going down a hill - my wife having our daughter in her arms. We were okay as I brought the car to a halt in a very dangerous situation by deliberately running it into a tree, which damaged the nearside front, but still did not stop it at a junction to a main road ... we could so easily have been hurt or killed. There were no safety belts or child seats in those days. I said I would never again have a banger or unreliable car - I'd have a decent vehicle or do without.

Later that year my father said I could stay in one of his caravans at a place called Blackford, a few miles north of Carlisle on the Longtown Road, while I looked around for somewhere to live. My father went out and bought a 1959 Morris Minor 1000, a good little motor, and gave it to me for the use of, though I had to let him have it whenever he wanted. Now the caravan at Blackford could be quite cosy, as it had an anthracite coal fire in it; but if it went out in the cold winter weather, any water in the kitchen sink bowl would freeze! We were in a sort of concrete yard with a wall around it and had access to water and toilets a few feet away. Other caravans were being stored in that location. That was okay until one night there was a terrible storm. The area was rural and very open, as to the west was the Solway Firth. By any standard this storm was bad, with very high winds. It was bitterly cold. We kept the fire on to keep warm and of course there was the Calor gas lighting. As the storm raged on after midnight, I didn't have a clue as to what I should do. I felt there was no-one I could turn to and wasn't going to risk the possibility of my father's wrath by knocking on his door in Carlisle through the night. The van was swaying in the wind. I had nothing by which I could anchor it down and could not have done so onto concrete anyway. It would have been too cold to have gone into the car. Turn off the lights and let the fire go out, slacken off the end window and work out a way of escape if the van went over. If I didn't believe in prayer, this was a good time to start ... but I did, and very quickly reawakened that belief and asked Almighty God for help. Not long after that there was a terrible crashing noise - as we looked out of the window in the dark we could just make out that the touring caravan right next to ours had blown over completely onto its roof. It kinda gave a new meaning to the solidity of bricks and mortar ... to say nothing of life ... for a while anyway ... over death! So the three of us were just cosy in bed until the morning, waiting for the storm to blow itself out. I think the caravan was quite heavy and well-built, though made for towing, but even so it could have been a miracle that it did not go over with serious consequences. My father came out as soon as he could the next morning, surveyed the scene and went away. Later that day we moved to his other caravan that he had put at Newby Grange, near Crosby on Eden, out of sight, at the far side of that beautiful country mansion which stood in an acre or two of pleasant grounds of trees and lawns very close to the River Eden. This was the property that my old school in Carlisle had moved to and they left a back door open fairly close to the caravan, giving access to water and a toilet. Of course, it was now adult to adult with some of the school staff, who I'd known since the early '50s, and we were all courteously friendly the few times I saw them.

The next month or two were quite pleasant going into the Spring. I got a temporary admin. job in the Civil Service in Carlisle. It was fine and could be busy, but I was surprised to find there was no challenge or much job satisfaction in it for me. It was good fun when the tea trolley came round - not on its own! Now they hinted that they might make it permanent - the job … not the tea trolley! - so I thought, "Okay".

About a month went by and my father one day asked me to go down to the yacht club at Ullswater in his Riley Pathfinder with his roof rack on the car (it fitted on the actual roof of the car in two separate pieces) and with a large piece of hardboard strapped on. I was to measure the hardboard against one of the little rowing boats owned and used by some members to go out to where the larger boats were moored on the lake. From the measurements my father was going to make a boat. I had my family with me and we got down in good time, took the measurements and hoped they were what was required, as boat-building was not my scene. I noticed the roof rack was a little bit slack, but there were not many people at the club that evening; so, with no-one able to help me, I had nothing with which to tighten up the nuts. I set off fairly slowly and called in at a filling station, but they had nothing by which to tighten it up either. I was about halfway back to Carlisle on the A6 when the whole thing blew off the car. No damage to the car … PHEW!… or the one behind … but the roof rack had now definitely seen better days! I knew this was not 'good news'!!! I put the piece of hardboard over a dry-built stone wall of a farmer's field next to the main road and put the remains of the roof rack in the car. I noted the exact place. I got to my father's house and he had been out for an evening drink … or few … he was not exactly 'delighted' at what had happened - in fact, he went CRAZY … so I gave him the necessary information and left with my family so as not to subject them to too much of that harsh treatment.

We got back to the caravan and decided enough was enough, as the incident had been really quite a bad experience for the three of us. We agreed we would go back to Newcastle, so why delay? We packed the car full of our belongings, tidied up, left the keys and departed. Back over to Newcastle and my in-laws took us in. Within two or three weeks we found a two-bedroomed property to rent not more than a couple of hundred yards from where they lived. It was another Victorian Newcastle slum, but it was home and similar to the ones previously mentioned, with an outside loo in a very narrow dark yard that was somewhat creepy, one cold water tap in a tiny kitchen and the usual small water heater over a Victorian white pottery sink. Actually, it was a corner property with a shop and an upstairs, though the shop area was locked and not to be used. I couldn't afford to run the car, so reluctantly sold it and used some of the money to pay a deposit on the rented property and advance rent, sought out the furniture, etc, some of which I had put in storage, and used some of the money to live on for a few weeks. My father never asked for the car back nor for any money from its sale and I can't remember if I sent any money to him for it. Anyway, I was able to get a home in my own right and this was good.

At the beginning of that May I got a job in a garage in the centre of Newcastle in their Service Reception, an admin. job that I liked, both the nature of the work and the people. It was a five and a half day working week as it included Saturday mornings - but at least I had the evenings off. The wage was only barely enough to live on for the very basics of life. I stayed there just under a year and never did get any holidays or holiday pay, for they said that before being allowed my two weeks off I'd need to work a full year. The drawback was living in the centre of a large city in the poor area: it made me realise just how much I loved the countryside. If not seeing much of the sun in the winter can have an adverse effect on someone, so can not seeing the sea or the countryside or even having a garden. I wasn't complaining; adjust and make the best of it, as long as there was just enough to eat and still be able regularly to get a bath at the public baths. But family life was fun and my 21st birthday came and went, as did the Christmas of 1965 ... all very quietly. I had some contact with my mother and also briefly with my sisters. By the Spring of 1966 my mother had gone back to live in 'digs' in Carlisle because that gave her better contact with my sisters, of which the elder was then fifteen - perhaps she had left school by then - I don't remember.

My mother had found admin. work in a furniture shop in Carlisle and said she would put a deposit down on a house and we would share paying the mortgage if I could get a sideways move to the main car dealers in Carlisle who I'd worked for in Newcastle. This happened straight away in the Spring of 1966 and I stayed in the same digs as my mother. My wife and daughter went back to live with my in-laws and we gave our home up. Every weekend I travelled back over to Newcastle. I'll never forget that my wife's teeth had got themselves into quite a bad state - so that was the time she decided to have all of them out in one go - at 22 years of age, not a tooth left in her mouth. That weekend she would not let me see her mouth as, of course, she had been in some discomfort. She had quite a good dentist, for the following week she had total false teeth with no problems and looked okay. In fact, she kept her new teeth in day and night and made a point of never letting me see her without them for the rest of our married life and I had to be reminded that she did actually have false teeth. No wonder people who knew her called her 'one in a million', for she rarely complained, which was interesting from what I would much later discover ...

The house I was trying to buy jointly was in Eden Street, Carlisle, and was a nice terraced property in a very pleasant area; but when everything was well on its way to completion, the owners decided they didn't want to sell it, so mother and I looked and immediately found a property to rent for £5 weekly, which was somewhat 'different', and we each agreed to pay half. It was a large suburban mansion, set in an acre or so of land with a driveway of about 100 yards, called Deer Park House, in St Anne's, close to the main railway lines and sheds, etc, still with some steam trains in those days. An old man in his eighties kept hens to one side of the house and grew some vegetables in the high-walled vegetable garden. To one side of the house there had been a sunken lawn used as a tennis court and I had fun trying to get a large rusty roller-type petrol lawnmower to work and cut the lawn ... well, with a scythe as well! With a bit of rope for a net we had some fun games of tennis. There were some large mature trees and fields around the house. We rented all of the downstairs and there were families renting various rooms upstairs. There were two nice large rooms to one side of the property overlooking the tennis court and my mother chose one of them as her bed-sitting-room and we had the other as a lounge. The ceilings were very high and at Christmas we had an enormous tree about eleven feet high that touched the ceiling. There was a bedroom that we used and a spacious kitchen and a bathroom that was somewhat damp and cold and its Victorian bath was a bit scruffy, but just useable.

My mother bought a blue 100E Ford Popular and I saw to the running costs. She gave me use of it during the daytime hours, which meant I got home for lunch. We later changed that to a Ford 105E Anglia and that car was a good little runner. My sisters often either visited or stayed at that time and I remember rigging up a swing from a tall tree in the garden, which gave us all a lot of fun (including myself going as high as I dared!) until it broke one day with the younger of my sisters on it - fortunately she wasn't hurt, but that was definitely the end of that swing! It was a good year and life was fine. I was enjoying work and had enough food as the bills were shared. I even got a part-time evening job collecting and selling 'Provident', which turned out to be more social than selling as people wanted to talk ... enjoyable, but a little difficult when I was pushed for time.

We were at Deer Park House a year and then were offered a really nice council house 'semi' at the other side of Carlisle: 92 Beverley Rise, on the Harraby Estate. It was quite modern and beautifully decorated with a well laid out tidy garden. At that time of 1966 they were building railway bridges in preparation for the M6 Motorway just two or three hundred yards or so, as the crow flies, from that property. Whenever I travel on the M6 to this day in that area I can sometimes just catch a glimpse of the roof of that house.

My mother lived about a mile and a half away by road and again had my two sisters living with her and I would visit whenever. My father lived about a mile or so in the opposite direction, but though I had some contact at the end of the 'sixties, it was limited. Well, everything was fine that year and this could have been the end of the story... but the reality was, it was just beginning!

I was enjoying my work in admin. in the garage when they suddenly moved me to another job, still doing admin., but between two departments, which proved to be difficult to do in the way they were separate and both organised. I certainly wasn't liked by everyone and, as I observed, wondered what was going on. Someone told me many years later that there was corruption in one department … and justice was done. But I was still on a low wage, even though I had managed to run a car during that time.

In the earlier part of 1968 a massive new factory was built and opened in Carlisle as a 'weaving shed', housing very fast and noisy Swiss Sulzer machines. They were recruiting and offering very good money, though the shifts to be worked were based on the 'American Shift System' - that is, as I remember, something like you worked the clock round 8 hour shifts, two of 6 until 2, two of 2 until 10 and two of night shift, then 48 hours off and started over again. I applied, got a job, trained for a week or so and began the actual job. I have to admit I found the shift system really difficult as the changes in the working hours were too constant. A week at a time of each shift gives a pattern to settle into, a rhythm for the body to cope with, yet night shift even then can be difficult to adjust to. I know some who have done a week at a time of each shift over many years but have struggled when it came to night shift. For me my body was saying, "Do you want me awake or asleep at any given hour?", yet I was naturally, for better or worse, an 'owl'! Then I discovered that one of my neighbours, who lived opposite me, was a shift manager for the whole of the factory and I was on his shift. We got on well together, though he made it quite clear that at work he was not my friend. I thought it was good that he had clearly set out the ground rules.

However, there was a 'but'… whenever I went on night shift my wife would barricade herself into the back bedroom with our daughter. I was somewhat surprised as it, of course, involved fear, but had no idea of how fearful she really was just under the surface and it troubled me. As for me, I was probably the world's slowest weaver. I was methodical and wanted to do a good job, but they wanted quality *and* quantity! Those machines were the latest in technology for that time and were incredibly fast; with 6, 9 or 12 machines to look after, depending on the cloth being woven, etc, it could be okay if everything worked well - but if things constantly went wrong it could be a living nightmare. You didn't 'think', you just 'did' as in what needed to be done to keep the machines weaving with hopefully no, or minimal, faults.

One night shift at some unearthly hour of the depth of the night, when I was really tired, I tried to start a machine, only to discover there was someone working underneath it! He had immobilised it, but if I had been able to start the machine, who knows? … maybe I could have killed him. There should have been something to clearly show that the machine was officially out of action for a few minutes. He told me as I apologised that I wasn't the only one, but it made me think 'maybe this job is potentially dangerous and not suitable for me'; yet it was at that time my life changed.

During my time of living in that Carlisle Beverly Rise Council Estate, I had not stopped reading and had continued my spiritual search. I still fully believed in God as stated earlier, but did not want to go on or get involved with Him until I was certain of the way ahead. To me 'The Church' was fairly well hidden and my knowledge of it was still very limited - just buildings where you had to conform to certain beliefs, behave in a certain way and be 'religious'. No doubt the dysfunctional family and the way I perceived my father as a 'father figure' and the other male authority figures in my life made me very cautious in what I was going to commit myself to. I had very little knowledge of the Christian Denominations, but I still had a good marriage, family and home-life and could appreciate some of the simple things in life and God's creation, along with a 'freedom' if you like that I did not want to give away. Well, at least it would have to be something very good in exchange for it. I had a concept of good and evil and the warfare thereof that we are all involved in and I wanted what was good and fair and to see justice.

I knew there was something about God that had to be relevant that would go beyond the natural and the mess of this world and make sense of life, whereby Divine help could become very real. I had seen something of this when I read Proverbs and The Gospels: take a particular course of action and you will be in trouble and take another course of action and it will go well for you. How 'knowable' was God in a pleasing, kind and acceptable way?

It must have been in the middle part of 1968, when on a visit to Carlisle Library, I came across two books by a man called Geoffrey Bull - God Holds The Key and When Iron Gates Yield; so I borrowed one and then the other and immediately took note, as they clearly spoke to me and I began to understand through his testimony of how God intervened in his life. He had been a missionary in China and faced persecution when the communists came to power and was wonderfully and miraculously brought through and out of it. I was fascinated by what he had to say - his testimony and his beliefs - so for me I either had to believe and accept … or reject! Yet it rang true, for it was not contrary to what I had read in the book of Proverbs and The Gospels. Any jargon still meant little or nothing to me, but the positive and life-giving side of it all, along with the fact that God cared and would and could intervene in our lives, got my serious attention.

The summer of '68 came and went and I joined the Working Men's Club in the centre of Carlisle after being asked and, as I remember, that was more for some social life than anything else. I only ever went two or three times anyway. Then one afternoon in the middle of October, I was sitting reading a Christian book at home when there was a knock on the front door. I got up, went and opened it, and standing there was a man with a 'dog collar'. I guessed he was aged somewhere in his early thirties. He came over as somewhat 'charismatic'; indeed, something of a live-wire. He introduced himself as John, the Curate from St Elizabeth's Church of England, which was a fairly new building at the top end of the council estate. Was there a certain person that he named living here, he asked. "No," I said, "my family and I live here now - yet it's strange you should call as I've been reading some Christian books recently and in fact am reading one now. You're welcome to come in and talk for a little while if you would like to" - so he did, for the best part of an hour. He shared about the importance of the Lord Jesus Christ, Salvation and something of his beliefs and life testimony and I asked him some questions. He had been an army physical training instructor at some time in his life. I didn't remember much of the detail of what he said and I would say now that was because I was listening and 'tuning in' with my heart and not so much my mind! When he went I was surprised to hear myself say that I would probably visit the church building one Sunday evening. This I did, on my own, a week on the following Sunday, close to the very end of October itself.

So it was during that particular Sunday evening that things clicked into place; into focus, if you like. The 'religious' side of things was similar to what I'd seen at and connected with at the various schools I'd attended, so though that was limited in my experience it was nothing new for me - but it was at a certain point, when on my knees, like most of the others, that I fully realised the centrality of the Cross and the love and intimacy of the Lord Jesus and very simply gave myself and my life to Him and knew in my heart Father God accepted that - I 'saw the light' and it really was, after all the years of searching, as if a light had been switched on inside of me! It was a revelation, an understanding and a clarity to my heart. I believed in Jesus and the work that He had done and that He was who He said He was.

I had done 'the mind thing', but all this bypassed my mind and was directly 'of my heart', with a warmth inside of me. I knew later on that I had been 'born again'. It just happened, even though I knew so little - I couldn't have explained then what happened at that moment, but I was totally changed and have been so to this day nearly 40 years later. I was overwhelmed by the love of the Lord Jesus. I knew I had a lot to learn - err, that was an understatement!! 'I gotalot of living to do!' (Presley); but what I would also learn later was that, 'I hadalot of forgiving to do!', just as I had been totally forgiven by The Lord. My immediate response to the Lord God was to say then and there that I wanted to serve Him - as in I would not take " No" for an answer! I had in mind that 'serving' would be in some kind of 'leadership' position. I wasn't the first and definitely would not be the last, but it all has to do with 'motive' and what one means by 'serving' and exercising your gifting from God - and so much more. If your motive is just to use God for your own purposes and selfishness or to either replace or cover over the negatives in your life to give you status or worth or power, then it is a dangerous game to play. I'm not saying my motive was wrong, but there was a trap that I could fall into - linked to pride and power. The Lord was very gracious to me over the following years and I was to learn what serving Him really meant, in and out of leadership. Even then I was not frightened to seriously question my own motives at any given stage and simply wanted to please The Lord, and my preparation for that time had been life itself.

# 8
# *Walk on ...*

I still did not apply to my sphere the extent of the warfare we are all in between good and evil, in the physical and spiritual that is all around us. Behind the physical is the spiritual and the spiritual is permanent. Yes, I had seen them, or the results therewith of both sides, but maybe I thought somewhat naively that 'the fight' would be easier or that in some way Satan and his minions would have to fight clean - no chance! The battle (from which at this time there is no escape) was now more intense and I had moved into a spiritual dimension that I had up until then only grasped with my mind, but was now amazed at the heart reality experienced. If this was REALITY and LIFE, then I wanted everything like this that God had to give - and so it was in this direction I set my 'life's compass'... such was my determination to stay that way! I wanted to be part of the solution and not the problem and to make a difference, but with so much opposition to 'good' it is only the loving-kindness and power of our Heavenly Father God that will make any difference. Many adventures lay ahead, much joy and heartache, but in hindsight always the Lord has been with me - of course, I had no idea that God, as my Loving Heavenly Father, will carefully and gently correct, prune and the like at the times you have need of this for your own good.

I went around telling people I was now a Christian, expecting them to be delighted! I thought people might know what had happened on the inside of me, want to find out more and respond accordingly, but I got quite a lot of negatives - "Oh no, he's got religion … what next?" and so on. My wife said within a few days, "If you are going to the church up the road then so am I", and so she did in early November of 1968. It turned out that as a youngster she had been to a small Mission Sunday School near where she had been brought up in Newcastle and her Primary School Headmaster had been an Evangelical Christian. But what had happened to me with The Lord God was something akin to the marriage relationship. "Can two walk together unless they agree?" No, they can't, unless they can walk in harmony, compatibility and agreement. If these qualities of real friendship are not there or part of the mixture, then you have no chance of a real true relationship - this applies to most close relationships in life, of course, and must include trust.  In all of this I carefully took stock of my work situation and reluctantly decided I had no choice but to leave the job in the weaving shed, and this I did at the Christmas time. It took just a few weeks till I found myself in a job in shop- work in the centre of Carlisle selling paint and wallpaper.  The drop in income was a bit hard: back onto a low wage; but at least the hours were good, much more sensible. I bought a bicycle that year to use for work, etc, so it was healthy stuff. As I went into 1969 I started to become really involved in that local Church of England, from the Sunday 'services' (I prefer to call them 'meetings', as it is 'believers' meeting together) to the very successful Youth Club that the Curate had going, plus social events. They said I would have to be 'confirmed' and this could be at Easter by the Bishop if I attended the weekly classes given by the Vicar. I could not understand the meaning or application of the word 'confirmation' or the Biblical significance, though I was told it was required later if I had had infant baptism, which I evidently had.

I went ahead and attended, though I was puzzled as the Vicar seemed to have a bit of a problem with what he believed. I can still remember very clearly one time he was reading out of a Bible about The Lord Jesus walking on the water, but he said He was only walking by the edge of the lakeside, probably with His feet or ankles covered. I can remember firmly but politely questioning him as to what it actually said in the Bible, but to no avail! I thought it was very strange, but soldiered on; big of me, wasn't it?! I would later learn that he would be referred to as a 'liberal theologian'; in other words, he had some strange beliefs and did not necessarily take the Bible at face value and was not so much in agreement with the 'Evangelicals', which was the category you would fit me into. So I was dutifully 'confirmed', but did not 'feel' anything or any different.

They asked me if I would like to carry a wooden cross through the city centre at Easter, leading the Anglican Procession to a 'Service' in the Cathedral. I wondered, "Why me?", but said "Yes." Actually, it was quite an experience and I've never forgotten it. It would have been on the Good Friday and I reckon there were up to 200 in the procession. The cross stood about five feet high and I started off at the bottom of Botchergate; but even by two-thirds of the way to the Cathedral it started to feel quite heavy. It was strange to have people looking and staring and to be the centre of attention. Because I had had a good portion of 'freedom' in my life, I was not really 'pro ritual or liturgy', but there was something spiritually gripping and exacting about that day. It made me think carefully of what The Lord Jesus must have gone through for me, and for all of us, and I realised it was something awesome, even with my limited understanding. It affected me at every level of my being and made me want to find out and have more understanding.

Around that time I found out that the Vicar and Curate would meet in the early mornings most week days for their compulsory early morning prayer time and set Bible readings, etc, as laid out for them in the Anglican Common Prayer Book or wherever. I asked if I could join them sometimes and they agreed. I did so and mostly enjoyed those times because I was concentrating on the Lord and was getting my first real taste of public speaking in the prayers and Bible readings - it was a good training to get started. I did make enquiries about becoming an 'ordinand' in the C. of E. and 'put my name down', but the way in was through university at that time unless, I think, you were over 30 years old. This did not seem very promising as, if I'd been capable of going to uni., I would already have done so. They put an awful lot of emphasis on 'intellect', so I wondered if they only wanted 'super-heroes' in their elite ranks and, if so, then those of us in the 'pheasant', sorry 'peasant', class who were a bit thicker would be blocked, even if already schooled in many of the harsh realities of life. So I started to study and got some GCE O-Levels, but my family was too important to neglect at that time or any time … because they needed time! On my own initiative, because I wanted to, I began to visit an Old People's Care Home on the estate on a regular basis - that could be hard going socially sometimes, but well worth the effort.

One evening in the Spring of 1969 I was about to leave the church building and walk home when another male member of the church asked me if I would like a lift in his car. "No, it's okay," I said, "I'll just walk"; but he insisted, so I got in. He started talking and then told me he was a Freemason and as we talked it through he said that some would be happy for my name to be put forward to join. I was very surprised … my mind was in top gear. The trouble was, I knew so little about them, apart from what I have stated earlier in the book, as my father was a loner and was obviously somewhat anti the likes of it and my grandfather had never directly shared anything of them with me. I thought to myself that at some time later I would check them out a little more thoroughly, but a "No" was in my mind. On my spiritual experience of finding the loving-kindness of the Lord God, I had already said "No" to the Working Men's Club membership because I knew I could not serve both them and the Lord. I wondered, "Why the secrecy and how could the Freemasons possibly improve on what has happened to me?" - I didn't want to 'hide' anything and also wanted to find, in life's situations, my true level and worth - if I was not worthy or capable of whatever, then that should be that. I did not want to exclude anyone from having what I had found.

As time went by, I did do some research, along with information that came to me, and, as I gained a knowledge of the scriptures, applied all of that to my understanding and concluded that those with a determination to go down that road may find themselves in a very dangerous situation, whereby even fear alone could 'lock' them in. So far as the man in the car was concerned, I thanked him for considering me, but said my answer was 'No'.

The summer of 1969 came and went and things 'ticked over'. One day there was an incident at work where the young lad they employed was in trouble, even in danger of losing his job. To liven things up a bit, myself and my colleague mate thought we would have a delegation to the manager that he should not be too hard on the lad. Err …! Why was I the 'mouth-piece' of this delegation? There was no conversation; it was just that I was out the door quite quickly and my colleague and the lad stayed! The only thing in my favour was that the boss had previously told me he hated Christians and could tell me a thing or two about them. Ah well, that's the way it goes. He had no sense of humour. I was in the wrong, of course, for interfering and would have apologised. Within a day or, literally two, I got a job around the corner in a clothes shop as an assistant manager. I got a brilliant reference from my previous boss and so got promotion. Whatever next?

Well, 'next' came at the Christmas time. In the mid-December, I went down with a really bad dose of flu and it lasted about two weeks; it sure did knock me back. I had arranged to go back to work and of course had put in the relevant sick notes and went by bus to visit my mother: just a short visit. It was a freezing cold evening ... Carlisle can be a very cold city ... and I went to catch the bus back home and waited and waited, but none came. By the time I did get home, I was ill again and then the cold hit my chest. I was not able to go back to work. There was no messing about in those days. The boss's answer was simply to 'put my cards' (Nat. Insurance card with stamps, etc) through my letterbox at home - no job and no money. It took me another couple of weeks to surface back into health. I had contact with my father and told him and he said something that totally surprised me, not least because it was the only time I could ever remember a conversation with him which was mutually friendly and unconditional, with nothing in it for him! He said, lowering his voice, "Do you want me to get you your job back?" It was another time I had to think very quickly. The firm had a nice private house that went with the job for the manager, but he wouldn't take it as he was settled in a council house and had no intention of giving it up. He was pushing for me to take it, but I was not so sure that it would be a good idea. If they could so easily dish out this kind of treatment and possibly make you homeless as well, I thought it not to be a sensible thing to do, so I turned my father's offer down, though he never said what he would have done. I applied for other work, of course, but I thought it was time for 'plan B'! The 'seventies had arrived and they ushered in a new era!

# 9

# *The RAF Years*

I'm not sure whether it is always a good idea to have a 'plan B', as it might be somewhat negative and lacking in faith; but it was on a shelf at the back of my mind. In the late 1950s I had seriously thought of joining the Royal Air Force when I was about sixteen years old, as a 'boy entrant', in admin. I never had any desire in my heart to go into the catering trade when thinking about what I would like to do in the workplace - it definitely was not my first or second choice – but, of course, getting married put paid to joining the RAF at eighteen, for me. By 1970, conscription was well finished within the UK. The only thing that had bothered me in the 'fifties when I was trying to decide what to do regarding the RAF was that going in so young would have been similar to going back to Boarding School, so it made me hesitant. Also, as I look back now, I think it would not have been a good idea to have gone in 1961, although a good idea for some, especially if to make a career out of it, but I would have lost some of my identity and freedom as the Forces tend to take you over and put you into their mould – how else could they get the job done? But now to go in as an adult with a family was different. They wanted the volunteers, so the conditions and pay were good.

I applied and the process of application was the most thorough across the board of anything that I've ever applied for: no stone left unturned! They offered me a choice of types of work with training, but I stuck to my first choice of admin. So I joined to serve queen and country in early 1970 and gave up that really nice home in Carlisle, as I thought that if I did not burn my bridges then the temptation to leave and return there if things did not go according to plan might be too enticing. The few times of separation from my family - of which the first was about seven months, during which period they went to live in Newcastle with my wife's parents - I did not find easy.

But there was no doubt about it: joining the RAF was a watershed in my life. In days gone by in the UK they used to class 'being 25 years old' as a time of coming into real maturity after growing up and so a suitable time for marriage, etc, and now I can understand why, and though relative to any given situation, it is wisdom!

Since that time I have never again lived in Carlisle and only briefly in Newcastle's west end and that for less than two years in the mid-'eighties. For me that was good, because I broke free from the ties I'd had with those two places and from any need to live near parents/in-laws. In fact, from that time onwards, neither of my parents ever set foot in any of the properties I've since lived in, though my mother-in-law did so maybe two or three times in other properties, and my in-laws did, of course, visit during that time in Newcastle's west end. If you added up the total time I spent visiting and actually communicating with my father on just the very few occasions I did so during the 24 years of the rest of his life, I reckon it would have only totalled up to the best part of one afternoon. On the last couple or so of those visits to his home he would carefully switch off his hearing aid after a minute or two of conversation - and that was that. I realise it is definitely not good to dishonour parents, even when they have wronged you, and so do not want to fall into that trap. One's reaction as a victim of rejection, and indeed of all the negatives and abuse that may happen to any one of us to whatever extent, may not be helpful, but in my case at that time I had started to sort out the forgiveness issue, which is one of the keys to being free and defusing any wrongs and their effects. A fulfilment of this was to fully and supernaturally happen to me years later in my life. As mentioned before, I always desired to relate as an accepted mutual friend to my father, but it was never to be. I regularly had contact with my mother for the rest of her life and visited her whenever I could.

In my heart the rejection issue puzzled me and occasionally I would try to think and reason it through with my mind and intellect and perhaps make excuses, certainly with regard to my parents, so as not to blame them or be wrongfully judgemental, but I wanted some answers to this 'puzzle' - I had never been afraid of a 'reality check' and would be harsh on myself if needs be. Was there condemnation for dishonouring parents? Yet, I have most certainly 'pulled my punches' in what I have written about them in this book, but the rejection I had experienced and the hypocrisy I had seen was real. I knew I had been damaged to some extent, as many of us are in whatever way, from the boarding school evils to the violence and deprivation I had seen at home, and I know that many reading this will have seen much worse than I have - yet it is all about how we cope and react and set the compass of our life.

We are all looking for loving-kindness, within a family unit, from a father and a mother, with a relaxed, unconditional acceptance and a giving of their time; yes, with some rules and order, but always in the context of affirmations to build your worth and self-esteem. But when this is replaced by betrayal, harsh, callous discipline or cruelty, abuse caused by conditional love and acceptance based only on a performance, work or behavioural ethic, and further, if there is hatred, anger, violence, poverty, and the list goes on, it will certainly not be easy because of that damage done, until it is sorted out; rather than the alternative, which is to have some kind of destructive behaviour or escapism. Now that I was walking as a Christian with the Lord Jesus, and although I couldn't have put it into words then, I had found something beyond 'religion' or the mind or the 'senses' or a 'set of rules' that must be adhered to by trying or striving or else … to a heart relationship that was real, based on the finished work of the Lord Jesus, and this was a free gift that I had gratefully accepted. At last I was beginning to understand and, yes, I would have to do a lot of searching and sifting in that walk. In the co-equal Three-in-One Trinity of God, I had no problem of belief, but as far as my Father God having time for me, even though I was now, and found this incredibly so, His son, His child, was a problem. It was, of course, the way I viewed my earthly father, as I had been conditioned to do, and my perceptions of what a 'father' was like, and thus made the wrong comparison with my Heavenly Father. So, in my view, in what had happened to me, I would have to come last after everyone else was seen to in His sight, unless there was a special reason not to do so. If He was seemingly absent at times, just battle on with whatever. With some self-discipline I had to deprogramme to reprogramme. This principle applies, in several different ways, of course, to many and so we carry the problems of our up-bringing in all their complexity, but they never get correctly dealt with. This applies in various ways regarding parents or the lack of them for nearly all of us. For those who had fathers/authority figures who were over-disciplinarians or were violent, cruel or abusive, it may take more effort or a greater miracle to realise that God was and is not like them. From that time it took a year or two to fully sink into my heart that Father God always has time for me, as He can see to everybody at once and that His loving-kindness is totally unconditional and I can go boldly to Him at any time to speak with Him, get answers and know that in His Precious Son, who is a true Friend, I am fully accepted just as I am. On a positive, because of family wealth and provision, I never had any problem in faith of believing that Father God would always provide food for me and He has. Yes, He may deal with issues to help me as needs be - this is good (as long as you know it's Him) - but I can't find words to describe how wonderful, how amazing is His love, acceptance and freedom that is ours for the asking. If He can do this for me, of comparatively little consequence, then how much more will He do it for you and envelop you in His loving-kindness? Almighty God cares for me … and he cares for YOU!

I was posted to Berkshire after all my training - I certainly got very fit - and put my family up in a private hotel in Reading. After a short while they gave me a married quarter about 50 miles away, so I bought a car and commuted for the next three months, by which time I was allocated a married quarter where I was stationed in a lovely area with a first school close to where I lived, along with some sports facilities and an open-air swimming pool in the summertime - it was good stuff. The RAF was the RAF, of course, but it had left the days of conscription well behind by then and so was changing into what it must be like today - I'd guess that information technology would again greatly change things. If I ever thought the time was going to be mundane for me, that was not to be the case. I even wondered if I would ever do any flying at all! No need to wonder; I ended up flying in several different aircraft. On one occasion, on a beautiful clear day, I got to fly in a small executive jet going up the Antrim coast in Northern Ireland, a coastline which was colourful, rugged and scenic, with its panoramic view changing every few seconds, and then over to Kintyre in Scotland and the area of Campbeltown and, to the west of it, a mile or two of clean-looking, inviting sandy beaches and dunes. Although I have never set foot on that actual part of Scotland, I know it was of course made famous by the Paul McCartney song 'Mull of Kintyre', with its haunting melody which enters into and touches the emotions, creating the strong sense of the beauty and barrenness of the area and the mull - the latter being the approximately 400 feet high hill at the very base of Kintyre, close to the sea. There was an RAF presence near Campbeltown which was built for the Second World War and I once knew someone who was posted there attached to a branch of the Navy in the early 1940s. If the enemy had landed in England, that would most likely have been used as one of the footholds to get the American/allies in.

Once I had to accompany a Commissioned Officer and it was like something out of an adventure story - it was real fun! No warning given. "Field, get your coat on! Get outside immediately and into that waiting Land Rover." We were driven to a certain place and I was told to wait. The officer went away and returned after some time, commanding me to follow him, both of us now on foot - we ran across a road, over some grass, through some trees and into a field, where there was a Wessex helicopter waiting - we ran to it and jumped aboard and, immediately we did so, the blades started and it took off … all exciting stuff! It was a 'bank run' in a theatre of war! It seemed to take ages to get back to base in County Antrim and the only place I recognised from the air was the large lake of Lough Neagh, which was quite spectacular as we flew right over it. This was significant because a few months later I took a day's boat trip to an island on it when helping out in running a youth club within the married quarters attached to that RAF station! Oh what fun it is to ride in a one h…h…helicopter …!?

I spent a month or two or more on the RAF station at Hong Kong; well, the peninsula of Kowloon to be exact. Again, that was fun! "Field, you are expected to volunteer to help in the building of a path for the locals on a small nearby island!" "Yes, Sirs," says I - mainly because there were several 'sirs' present and not of any mean rank - I wanted to go on living, so no point in even discussing it; the choice of 'to crawl or not to crawl' didn't even enter into the equation! Now, this was the height of summer and my main thought was how long, in my time away from normal duties, would I be separated from the large open-air swimming pool on the base that was also part of the international airport, and I was fortunate enough to be billeted near that swimming pool. Well, it was only for a day and was a token of help by the forces to some locals who were very poor and had very little. I went to the place of pick-up as arranged and waiting was a small 4-seater helicopter, which took off, flying low over the Kowloon Harbour, with its stunning view of skyscrapers, etc, and on into the South China Sea for a few miles - that sure was some sight, even back in the early 'seventies, and an unforgettable experience. I spent the day labouring on an incline among some trees, where steps were required to be made. It was strange as the island looked like it was uninhabited - no natives to be seen anywhere! Later, we waited for the return helicopter flight in the only building I saw on the island, and it was open to the elements, as it was lacking some walls. It had a concrete floor and a very large table for eating off, with benches on either side and close by empty Coca-Cola bottles in crates, piled high from the ground - a lot of them, oh, and, of course, the 'proverbial' television, so they must have had a generator somewhere. Where they slept, who knows?! I wondered if they were all working in some sweatshop in Kowloon - but their lot must have been simple and meagre.

The return home to base was in a different make of helicopter, and although I went on the tourist trails of the likes of the 'Peak Tram' on Hong Kong Island - that's the one where you pray all the way to the top that the cable won't 'break'! - and also the train ride and sights into the northern territories - in comparison, that view once again going back over the harbour was quite something. I got the opportunity to go on a helicopter trip into the northern territories. That was some journey and experience - the tops by a hair's breadth! Going around the coastline from Kowloon somewhat low down looking at various inlets, coves and bays, the colours of the sky, sea and land of rich blues and greens, worth drinking in deeply as the door was wide open, and I was sitting with my feet dangling out over space - wearing a safety harness - then suddenly over one hill and coming across a small bay in which a super luxury yacht was anchored and those on board who were sunbathing frantically waving their greetings to us as we circled over them and us waving back and then we were gone - kind of put a new meaning to the song 'I love to go a- wandering along the mountain track ... and they waved back to me'; well, a sort of modern technology and well to do rendering of it anyway! We were soon at a place high up in the hills, close to the Chinese border. The helicopter would go up like a lift - quite high - then fall like a stone for a second or so, and each time this happened I left my tummy behind! ... or so it seemed ... some distance above! - and that was fun, as I wondered if I actually started to turn green - but as I looked out over that incredible view of the very south of China spread out before me, going into the distance as far as the eye could see, into the heat haze, I reflected on the masses of people there and those who had and were suffering under a cruel, harsh regime of a communist dictatorship, where life is cheap and yet where, as is known now, untold numbers of people have come to take the Lord Jesus Christ as their Saviour. So, flying back down to base, we passed over the top of some of the Kowloon skyscrapers, at the same time watching a large American airliner negotiating its difficult turning manoeuvre in order to go in to land at the main runway built out into the sea and, as it did so, I was listening in to the pilot talking to air traffic control.

Back in England at the office, "Field, you're religious!" shouted my Warrant Officer across the room. "You will go up to Charles de Gaulle's Memorial Service in St Paul's Cathedral to represent the RAF ranks with a few others in a couple of days' time." I thought to myself, "I'm not that religious, I'm free!" "Yes, sir!" So I went on the train as required on the day with three other lads and the Corporal from our RAF station. Well, it was a day away from the office and fortunately for me was uneventful … well, only just! The Corporal in charge of us with the train tickets went back to the days of conscription and I'm sure he was a really nice fellow but, to put it mildly and politely, he was none too bright. At the service I went with the flow and sang the hymns, etc. There were thousands there and security was tight. At the end, as the people were milling around and leaving, the Corporal decided he would have a do-it-yourself guided tour. He just did so without even saying, "Follow me". The problem was keeping up with him; first this way, then that - some of the time obviously where we shouldn't even have been. We came in the side entrance for those classed as ordinary folk and were expected to leave by that entrance, but he eventually found his way to the main entrance. Now, you have to understand that all the dignitaries and elite of the land and the leaders of the three forces, etc, had been present and, as I followed, lastly, in hot pursuit, I desperately prayed that they had all left or that we would become invisible, because anyone who knows anything about the military would understand that if we were caught running for it down the steps from the main entrance we would not even have had a court martial - we would just have been shot at dawn! … or so I imagined! As I ran down those steps, I saw a very important man turning round to look my way, but fortunately I made it and disappeared into the crowd! Phew! What a way to spend your 26th birthday! That was one of those horrific nightmare experiences that you're desperate to forget as - you see - from the sideways glance that I had, that man was the Marshal of the Royal Air Force!!

Another time, I was on a short trip to Germany with some of my work colleagues. In the evening we went to a 'pub' near to the RAF station and that was okay as in those far off days I would still have an occasional half glass of lager, very much in moderation, whereas for many years now have been virtually teetotal. Of course, the lads said there was a much better pub down the road - I wasn't interested, so they had to work on me with some gentle persuasion to get me there. "We are not taking 'No' for an answer!" They got me there. "This place looks smart," I thought, "plush carpets, decor, chandeliers and the like" - then two of the quite hefty lads, one on each side of me, suddenly lifted me up and I was carried up some stairs and into a dark room; dark, of course, being the operative word, both from the physical and spiritual point of view. I was in a somewhat seedy German nightclub, dealing with hard pornography in its various forms and it was no doubt leading the way for those days. Words like 'totally depraved' would describe it. So they had set me up and played their joke … now I needed to think this through as to what to do.

I had to work with them and some were of higher rank than I was. They knew what I stood for and part of their fun was to see how I would react, not only at that moment but in the months to come. If I made a loud verbal protest or commotion or became 'holier than thou', then they would have a case against me to reject who I stood for. Whatever I did would become public and I did not want to destroy the links of communication. I thought, "I'll wait a little while and then make haste to get out." Because of life itself, the medical books I'd seen, and being happily married with fun in the marital bedroom, I was able to be detached and cold from what I saw, so that it did not affect me and, of course, I just closed my eyes as needs be. There was only one way of escape from the room and that was via a partly glass soundproofed 'cubicle' with one door into it and its other door leading to the outside. You could call the men in the cubicle 'bouncers'. I was not surprised by what I saw there, but my guess would be, generally speaking, that today there would be a lot worse; yet I was saddened for the dangerous slippery slope downwards it held for some, and probably, because of my contented, fulfilled marriage, I remained protected and immune from those images I did see.

As soon as I felt it right to do so, in the dark, I quietly and quickly got up and went through the two doors to the outside of the building - to be followed immediately by one of the other lads! I was surprised! He had only very recently got married. We both agreed we didn't need or want that which we had seen and realised as we talked we both had good marriages. No-one ever said anything or made any comments afterwards about that night, though I did talk briefly with one friend, who started to share about his marriage and told me that his wife would not even undress in front of him. I could see that much marital counselling was needed and, although some of the lads got together later to organise a 'stripper' to come down from London for an evening, when that happened they kept very silent about it. As the years went by, I was able to go on some really good Christian counselling courses that included, in the '70s, 'Family and Marital courses' using mainly material from the teaching of Selwyn Hughes, along with other books, etc, and this was very valuable in future counselling situations.

During my time on that RAF Station near Wallingford on the Thames in Berkshire and in the married quarter, I kept with the Church of England on the Camp and, with my family, got involved. My daughter joined the Brownies and my wife became 'Brown Owl', so I got the job of anything to do with the admin. side. Strangely enough, I was the only one in 'membership' in that congregation below the rank of corporal - and it was a large RAF Station. On Sundays we were all in 'civvies', of course, as it was just like attending any other church building. Sometimes I would go either on my own or with my family to the RAF and Navy Conference and Retreat Centre, a large country house near Andover called 'Amport House', on week-long courses or family church weekends away, and they were interesting and great fun, totally Anglican-based. All of the 'ordained' C. of E. leaders in the RAF had senior commissioned officer status. I thought it wise to resist any work, such as church warden duties, in case I might cause some jealousy, just because of the low rank - I'm not sure I succeeded in that. The catering on the trips to Amport House was of a very high standard because of the commissioned officers present, as everyone ate together. It was there that I experienced a 'retreat' and at one point a 48-hour silence - now this was kinda hard for me!! Spiritually it was quite interesting; not so the odd cockroach in the building itself. It was there I first came across 'Every Day with Jesus' monthly booklets by Selwyn Hughes, mentioned above, who was just starting to become famous at that time and, for the next nine years or so, greatly influenced my Christian walk and life through his writings and organisation called 'Crusade for World Revival', with his counselling courses, seminars, etc. He was a Pastor-Teacher-Evangelist moving in the power of the Holy Spirit, had been a school teacher and, with a good grasp of 'The Word' and a prophetic insight into the 'End Times', his push was 'how to live the Christian life' and in my opinion was much needed. This was the very beginning of a 'search' I made, or was it more of a 'cry of the heart' in looking objectively at The Church and just what it really is, spiritual warfare and just what was this experience in Acts chapter 2 of the anointing from Heaven at Pentecost? I believed what I read and so started crying out to The Lord in my heart for whatever that was and that time was from early in 1971. A little later on, I also read the classic book Nine O'Clock in the Morning, by Dennis Bennett of the U.S.A., a readable and popular book that greatly influenced me. I also started to gain some understanding about the 'high' and 'low' parts of the Church of England - another way to put it is to say the 'evangelical' and 'liberal', if you like, parts of the church - but it applies to everyone who would call themselves 'Christian'!

To simplify it in my own words now, 'evangelicals/evangelists' means 'messengers' as of good news of what the Lord Jesus has done and they tend to believe the Bible as the authoritative word from God as made in two covenants, the Old or first one and the New or second one and the 66 books of The Bible in their present order, along with an experience of being born again and a commitment to have entered into that relationship with God as one's Heavenly Father, His begotten Son and the Holy Spirit. The only way to Heaven is through Christ, His shed blood and His finished work. On the other hand liberal teaching would say that we have to do works to gain favour with God, appease Him, please Him and keep His rules or whatever and so do your 'religious stuff' and if you believe God accepts that, then pretty much anything goes and anyway, they say all roads will lead to God, His Salvation and Heaven. As the 'Oxford dictionary' says for the word *liberal* 'regarding many traditional beliefs as dispensable, invalidated by modern thought, or liable to change' and as someone has said, "Liberal churches only want a *human Jesus*" which means their doctrine is only based on what their concept of Him is and not the truth and reality of Who He really is and the measure of His spiritual power. We cannot build on the traditions of a church or those of man but only on the foundation of the God/Man, the Lord Jesus Christ. ('Religious traditionalism' is the upholding of the traditions of man, handed down over time, and considered to be the 'truth' and 'above human reason' as such but the elevation of these traditions, especially in a hierarchical system and grouping, is extremely dangerous. Our authority and basis of truth etc must be based on reliable versions of the Bible e.g. Authorized Version and New King James Version.) We can only walk with Him if we confess that He is God and put our trust in Him. A 'human Jesus' alone is not only a form of 'religious humanism' but it would seek to have a powerless Jesus that they would be comfortable with at every level and would be within their sphere of what they would want to control, certainly within the physical worldly realm. In contrast - generally most Evangelical and Pentecostal believers should want God to be in control and His awesome spiritual powers to be manifested.

So I now find myself involved with the RAF 'High Church of England' and certainly at times there was a definite element of liberal theology there. I was puzzled by all the 'garb' that was worn, certainly at 'Communion Time', the taking of the bread and wine, with its order and details of what must take place, which must not be broken at any cost. I thought to myself, "Surely this is Roman Catholicism", which I did not have any knowledge of. Everyone was friendly, of course, but I was trying to discern at a deeper level. This was a far cry from St Elizabeth's in Carlisle, which was very basic and supposed to be mostly evangelical - I was trying to understand what was happening, why it was happening, and which way I wanted to go.

As time went by I asked the Lord if He would make a way out for me and my family, but for that time I got a definite answer in my heart - 'Keep with it for the time being', and so I did. This was very strange, as several months later I briefly met another lad on that RAF Station of the same rank as me who was by trade a joiner and he told me he attended a small evangelical church in Wallingford, more of a 'house-church'. He invited me to go along, but I never did, as I did not have a car at that time. Just recently I met a couple from that fellowship who said they were there at that time and confirmed that it was the church where people I knew in later years from Bradford went and preached and taught.

Now there was an elderly lady, well liked, who used to attend the church on the RAF Station. Miss Young, I was told, was about 94 years old and she had only just a few years earlier stopped riding a bicycle because of knee problems. She was a tall, very intelligent lady with a warm, charismatic personality, the salt of the earth, no doubt. She had been headmistress of a large school in Zimbabwe, then Rhodesia. I got on well with Miss Young and was fascinated to think that she went back as far as the 1870s. She had a beautiful detached house set in its own grounds with an orchard, close to the RAF Station. A few times I found myself offering to help her out, doing some digging in her garden, and my 'reward', apart from her friendship and some vegetables, was to have afternoon tea with her. It was more socialising and talking about Christian things than anything else, but entering her property with its distinctive atmosphere of peace was like stepping back years in time, into the upper middle-class Victorian era; yet she had a certain meekness and humility. She loved the teaching/books of someone from Scotland, I think called John MacKay, a really strong Christian, and she was keen to tell me about him. She had never married, but her intensity and love for the Lord Jesus glowed from her. No need for me to see a hundred or more years back in a film or whatever; I saw and tasted a glimpse of it as it really was. Just recently, I found in one of my Bibles the really nice note she gave to me and my family when we left that area and I thought there is a depth and stability of true friendship based on good, unselfish character that is priceless.

When I first went into that modern church building on the RAF station I thought to myself, 'They have definitely got this place really nice and the colour schemes of blue and purple or whatever are just right'. As time went by, one of my friends in the congregation said to me, "Don't you realise it has been done out like it is deliberately so and for a reason?" "No, I didn't realise." So he told me, "It's for royalty - the carpet and certain other parts are in royal purple. The day may not be far away when the reason why will be revealed." I had seen Her Majesty, Queen Elizabeth 2nd, or at least her car anyway, going through the main gates once or twice from the office I worked in. I wondered what this meant, but the time of understanding was not far away.

Some of my colleagues in admin. were preparing to be involved in carrying a coffin for a funeral. It was in preparation for the return of the body to England of Edward VIII, son of George V, of the House of Windsor, who had, of course, abdicated in 1936 after only a few months, in favour of a more ordinary lifestyle, and spent his years in France. He was given the title of 'Duke of Windsor'. He was first of all to be brought to the RAF station and laid in the Anglican Church building, before being moved on from there for the service and burial. As he did die at that time, all the military preparations that were made were then carried out. Now it was that year I got my first colour television - it was an expensive portable one with a good quality picture and, guess what - yes, you've got it, I was addicted to the thing for about a year; that being the first time I had seen a colour television, let alone owning one - so I would watch anything and everything in my spare time. I saw on that television the lads bearing the coffin from the RAF VC10 onto British soil and the armed guard (not RAF) on each corner of the coffin as it lay in state in the church building for a short time … the colours, lighting, the décor; in fact, the whole thing was very impressive indeed and, of course, was shown nationally and internationally. What was my part? Ah, well, far be it from me not to be in on the action in some small way! Between the actual RAF station and the married quarters, etc, that included the church building, was a public road - and in the late evening I had some guard duty (not armed) just on that road near the main gate and fortunately things were very quiet, except for the 'Boss', as it were, the Group Captain, being driven around in his car to make sure all was well. I made sure that I saluted him very smartly as needs be - though I knew him a little anyway, as I had been called on a couple of times very briefly to stand in as his PA when none of the others who would normally have done so were available! So, what of the television? I severely rationed my viewing time and sold it in the middle of 1974.

The day came, much to my surprise, when I was posted to a theatre of war at Aldergrove in Northern Ireland. This was in May 1973. When I got there on that first night I was billeted in an old building which was quite close to the main runways - ah yes, that was the night they managed to mortar bomb near a runway and not too far away from the building I was in. A day later it was large headlines in the Daily Express; something like, 'RAF Aldergrove bombed'. They never did that again, as security was tightened and that was the only time that I ever did an armed guard duty, though there was one occasion later when, in an RAF vehicle with a local civilian driver, both of us in 'civvies', we both felt we were momentarily in a very dangerous situation not far from Larne, with a possible fake accident - the driver didn't wait to find out, as he sped away. My mother-in-law back in Newcastle 'lost it' a little and had a breakdown at the thought of my wife and daughter coming out eventually to live in a married quarter - I had the situation under review, but would not back down - and that's the way it goes!

On one or two occasions I got to play tennis with some of the lads - the courts overlooked the main runway - now that was a strange game or two! Every time an aeroplane was coming in to land, everything stopped whilst we watched it touch down. On one occasion in the billet (used also as transit accommodation) there was a tall RUC man for one night. As everyone was settling down for the night, we got talking and established that both of us were evangelical Christians; then, suddenly, just before he got into his bed, he got down on his knees beside the bed with several eyes on him. I thought, 'He is not afraid to stand up ... sorry ... kneel down, and be counted' - I told him I was impressed. It showed me that he was more interested in what the Lord thought of him than other mere mortals.

I had more or less made up my mind I would leave the RAF after my five years were up, so had my eyes on looking for possibilities of what I might do. At one point in that billet eyes were on me and questions asked as I started to do a simple Bible Study course! Round the corner was another life-changing event ...

# 10

# Northern Ireland and Goodbye RAF

The summer went on and eventually I got a married quarter at the very end of August 1973, so I took some leave and, by public transport, went to Newcastle to collect my wife and my daughter, who was now 10 years old. But I had arranged first of all to go down with my wife on a long weekend's residential interview lasting until the Tuesday evening at the Church of England Church Army College, which was then at Greenwich in London. Some time previously I had visited a Captain Oxley in Oxford, who ran a hostel for the homeless/destitute, and it was a real labour of love on the cutting edge of helping others whose lives were seriously damaged.

I was impressed by what I saw, but realised that that particular type of work may not be for me; however, they had other 'branches' of work which appealed to me, such as pastoral work in prisons and parishes. Those few days were quite hard going, with all the interviews, etc. On the last night, all the candidates with the wives of the married ones had to collectively put on a 'talent show' of things that were suitably 'Christian' for an hour or so, with only a few hours to prepare. If someone could play the piano or sing a hymn, preach a short word or do a sketch or two, that was the kind of thing they wanted. I got involved in acting in a sketch and my wife had a very small part … she played the part of a 'tart'! … but I thought the whole thing was to a very high standard and really interesting in how it had come together, was of the Lord and lots of fun!

It was when that had finished on the Tuesday evening someone said to me, "Henry, someone's taking the minibus over to St John's Church, Hainault, where Trevor Dearing is Vicar." It took a millionth of a second to click with me. "What…..now?!" I exclaimed. "Yes, it's their Tuesday evening meeting and we should catch the tail end of it," I was told. "Is there room for two?" I excitedly asked. "There should be - ask that person over there." I rushed over and 'yes' there were two places if I got a move on and got my wife and our coats and went to the minibus parked in the car park. I ran and found my wife and without explanation and all a bit military, said, "Follow me, we'll get our coats and get out to the minibus" - and this we did. In the minibus I explained to her, "I read about this in an article in the Selwyn Hughes news material a few months ago. There's a sort of revival and move of God's Holy Spirit and some spectacular things have been happening - like healings and deliverance from demons and things. I haven't by any means given up searching for the Acts chapter 2 experience although nothing has happened yet…..this is from

God!!" I paused and though I was a bit tired after an intensive few days declared, "THIS is gonna be good!"

As I walked into the St John's Church building it was after 9pm and, if I remember correctly, it was 3rd September. The place was still packed, but the people were very free in moving around if they wanted or needed to and casual in what they were wearing. The place was very warm and that partly with hot sweaty bodies, but it was not unpleasant for there was a warmth of love for the Lord Jesus and a joy and freedom that I had never seen before as they sang with all their hearts, "Can you wonder ... can you wonder why it is I love Him so ... when I think of all He's done and for me the guilty one ... can you wonder why it is I love Him so?" I thought, "This is it, I've arrived. This is Heaven!" Well, this place had pews and choir stalls, so I managed to find some seats in the choir stalls. My wife was in the row immediately behind me. Up until that time the presence of God in power, love and peace had been within me, but now that presence and power of God was in that building in an awesome way and I could recognise that fact.

So Trevor Dearing started preaching and exhorting everyone to fully enter in; then he said, "The river of God's Holy Spirit is flowing down the aisle - if you want to be immersed in that river, just go out and do so." Without hesitation, I stepped out into that aisle and waited a while ... and absolutely nothing happened. Eventually, I had to go back to my seat. After a little bit more time the meeting finished and I started talking to one or two people. Suddenly, my wife came up to me from being somewhere and said, "Trevor Dearing said he wants to see you." She told me later that she had gone to him and said, "Whatever my husband went out to receive, I would like that as well." He had asked her a couple of questions and then told her to go and bring me to him. Trevor asked me what I had received earlier. I answered that I knew of the Baptism of the Holy Spirit and had been constantly asking God for this, but nothing had happened when I went out in the aisle - I told him I had felt no different at all. So he put his right hand on my head, gently but firmly, and his left hand upon my wife's head, and he started praying. And he prayed and prayed. It seemed like a few minutes went by. He had a 'dog collar' on, but had taken his jacket off. He was praying in English and taking spiritual authority and then in another language. I thought, "This man's giving it rice - everything!" Beads of sweat were pouring down his face. Then I just noticed that my wife fell backwards to the floor - but suddenly something incredible was beginning to happen in the whole of my being - a total warmth and an unspeakable power surge of pure love; and, as it began to submerge my mind in a glory of light and joy, that then went on through my body from head to toe, something like a powerful water jet of clean pure water which would clean everything in its way. I just felt myself completely surrender all to the Lord and fall backwards as someone caught me before I landed on the floor and the anointing from Heaven just kept on flowing over and into me. I could have 'sobered up', if you like, and taken control with my mind at any moment, or at least started that process, but chose not to do so as God was from His side sorting things out deep within me. That is the only way I can explain what happened; however, when I eventually got to my feet, I felt as if I was paralytic drunk - but it was under the power and control of God, just as it says in Acts chapter 2. I didn't care about anything - no inhibitions - except just praising and giving thanks to the Lord for all the beauty and warmth of His love. When I got out into the car park, at one point I was trying to walk in a straight line - I think it was along the lines of the car park bays - but I couldn't do so. I spent just about all that night praising the Lord. My wife had received an anointing as well, but I had received an awesome anointing of the power of the Baptism of the Holy Spirit from Father God - the first of many! I had now received the full package, as it were, from God, of the foundation He gives on which we can build and the free choice to do so is ours. It is definitely not a question of being 'better' or 'holier than thou', compared to anyone else, but being equipped with power in humility to help and serve others as a channel of God's love. God had definitely touched my mind and emotions and dealt with some of the pain that I had been carrying. My spiritual life's perspective and clarity was really going to get underway from that day forward and, though I did not know it at that time, I was a marked man! It wasn't so much that people did not understand, but more that some thought that any such thing was not of God, but even worse ... to do with the occult.

Since then I've seen a counterfeit of this experience once or twice or just plain human religious nonsense, but the rest of my life in one sense has been going from one to the next move of powerful anointing of God from Heaven and so I've witnessed the most incredible sights and happenings as the power of God has moved in meetings. I have no regrets whatsoever about this. It is a revival life power that is not up to us at all, but up to HIM to give or pour out from His Heaven - the only thing He wants each one of us to do is to be totally real, honest and transparent with Him - nothing is hidden from His sight anyway and He knows all things, and so we fully have to mean business with Him, giving Him ALL of our heart. It's worth repeating several times - God tends to give us over to what we really want and if He is our first choice He will by no means disappoint us. He is no respecter of persons and He knows what we really are.

My next anointing came about a year later because, I believe, one RAF Padre had previously in a general way said, "Anyone married in a register office is not really married." My wife and I looked at each other in amazement but said nothing until later, when we just said, "You know, Lord!" This anointing happened at a day's seminar at Newcastle University that Selwyn Hughes was taking and in those days he called it 'Life in a New Dimension'. In the evening in the lecture hall my wife and I were sitting right in front of him and out of the blue he said he wanted all the married couples to rededicate their marriages and lives to the Lord and he led in a prayer that we spoke out each few words after him. As soon as the words finished, the power of God suddenly came down upon us - well, myself anyway - with an indescribable love, peace and joy that felt so tangible - that love which I felt was totally accepting and unconditional - it is well with my soul and my marriage!

They didn't accept me for the Church of England Church Army, but they did say I could reapply later. The following year I applied to the London City Mission to go full-time with them, but the interview in London, lasting a day, did not fully go my way and they also said I could apply again later, after I had made the choice to leave and actually left the RAF - as it turned out, I never did get back to them.

Back in Northern Ireland, it was lovely to have and be with my family again in a married quarter which was in really good condition and a pleasant homely house to live in. My daughter went to school in Crumlin Village and she said they were very strict. She was soon able to learn and speak the local Irish dialect and, as she told me later in life, this helped her to blend in in order to get through. She had one or two bad experiences, but survived. The RAF would lay on a bus for families to go to either Lisburn or Ballymena on Saturdays for shopping and I found these trips enjoyable, even though once or twice they would be clearing pedestrians off a street which we were walking down as there was a suspected car bomb and so we would head back to the main shopping area - but there were no serious incidents.

But spiritually I went into 'a no man's land'; what I would now call, biblically, a wilderness experience. I still prayed, loved the Lord and read The Word, but having tasted the real power of God, other things by comparison were mundane. Everything seemed dull, and this went on for a few months. Each Sunday we went to the Church of Ireland near the married quarter, but although it was packed it was somewhat dead. In fact, once or twice I got agitated and thought, "No you've got it wrong", but sort of bit my tongue, otherwise I might have shouted it out. There was definitely a 'liberal element' and I did not feel accepted, but with my family just kept going anyway on Sunday mornings. I had touched, in London that evening, something of the reality and wonder of Heaven and was determined to pursue and find more in spite of this wilderness experience. It was around that time in early 1974 that I helped run a youth club in the married quarter, along with two higher-ranking men and my wife. My daughter attended as well, though not strictly old enough, and she enjoyed herself.

As I went into the summer of 1974 I realised there was now an urgency to sort myself out regards leaving the RAF, which would be in about 6 months' time. I was thinking about the possibility of living and working in Carlisle.

Around that time I learned of a Forces' organisation called SASRA - Soldiers and Airmen Scripture Readers Association - that worked alongside the Army and RAF personnel as and when relevant permission was given; so I joined them and received their literature. Then one of their workers in

Northern Ireland, called Len Cooper, made contact with me and from then on for the remaining few months 'took me under his wing' with his friendship and pastoral input. Although not a young person, he was fearless, had wisdom and a warm personality and I would say he was quite well respected in the army establishments he visited - I certainly respected him. Once or twice he took me to some large Sunday morning meetings on the outskirts of Belfast, with Sunday lunch at his home along with his wife afterwards. Those churches were most likely 'Presbyterian' in background and they were large buildings, packed to the door. The singing of hymns just about raised the roof and the preaching was good. Len put me in touch with a 'house group' made up of some army personnel and their wives in some static mobile homes used as married quarters at Aldergrove. They really knew and were close to the Lord Jesus and had life, zest and meant business in their faith, for some of them often faced death. They had their values and priorities sorted out and the things of this life in the right perspective. I only went once, maybe twice, and the teaching and fellowship were really good and the fact that the lads were prepared to give their all if need be in serving their country and their Saviour, with their loved ones standing by them, holding steadfast to the faith, was encouraging and showed their maturity.

One day, Len gave me a little booklet and said, "Have a read of that; it's all about Baptism!" So I dutifully read it and read it again and seriously took note! It was a Brethren/Baptist-based thesis on 'baptism by total immersion', as against 'infant baptism or christening by *sprinkling*'. Then I said, "If this is true there is a cast iron case for believers' baptism by total immersion." I thought to myself, "If this is so, not only will I realign but I will get baptised again, this time by total immersion." I sought to verify this truth in the best way I could, by asking Len some questions and checking out what the Bible actually said. I came to the conclusion the booklet was definitely correct and that I would, as soon as the opportunity arose, be baptised by total immersion. That was to be several months later, early in the following year. I was somewhat bothered and if the truth was not being adhered to by all those who called themselves 'Christians', then what else might be wrong? What other truth was being withheld? How much would I be allowed to 'sift' and 'question' whatever and seek answers for living life itself and to test all things in my walk with the Lord? I had a sound motive in mind to search out truth by observation and questions as much as was right, fair and just to do so. I did not have rebellion in mind. How much could we really 'beat the system', especially when that 'system' went wrong, and yet come under authority to live a normal and peaceful life? I wanted to leave this world a better place.

Truth from Heaven and Godly principles surely are the keys that unlock life's secrets and wisdom. So I clearly made up my mind I would sift and question from that time onwards and keep only that which seemed good. Len gave me a clear warning, with baptism in mind, not to 'play God' but to be gracious. Then Len said to me one day ... I think he was having fun, "Do you know about Bible Colleges …?" "No", I said, "I've never heard of them, but I have heard of Church of England Theological Colleges and even visited one of them." Len went on to explain that they were similar types of places to study, but independent and often interdenominational and normally evangelical and there were several in the UK. The time of study would normally be anything up to three years and would prepare men and women for serving the Lord in different ways, such as going overseas in missionary work. So, in due course, he got me some addresses and I wrote away to several for information and prospectuses.

As I gathered the info, weighed everything up and prayerfully considered the possibility of it happening, such as the leap of faith involved, I felt led to apply to two of them. I said to the Lord, "The first one to accept me I'll attend." That's okay to do this, as long as common sense and Godly wisdom are not discarded.

I took some leave and went for an interview in one of the establishments, but felt very doubtful that it would be right for me! Then, within a short time, I got an interview at the Bible Training Institute - in those far-off days it was right in the heart of Glasgow, in Bothwell Street - and I flew from Aldergrove to Glasgow, got a taxi into the city, had the interview, which was quite hard going, and then had lunch in the college with the resident students. The place was vibrant and I really liked what I saw and had already made some friends during lunch and immediately thought, "This is the place; I would do well here." Just as lunch was nearly over, word was sent to me that I was accepted for a place at the start of the next term, on 10th January 1975. I gave a positive answer as long as I could tie everything in for that date and flew back straightaway to Aldergrove. The next morning I was offered a place in the other college, but turned it down. I had about two months to sort everything out and just managed to do so.

31st December 1974 was the day I said goodbye to the RAF and flew in an Andover from Aldergrove to RAF Lyneham on my own, as my family had gone on ahead of me a week or so earlier. I got the train up to Newcastle for a few days off. Though pleased I'd had that time in the RAF, this was the end of an era and, at thirty years old, a new season was about to unfold … in God's will!!

# 11
# Educate ... The View ...and all that ...

It was a real step of faith as I made my way up to Glasgow to start at the Bible Training Institute College with my RAF income finished, nowhere to live to call 'home' and no furniture, after being in a married quarter. I was worth about £50 and, of course, a pound was a pound in those days: 'some might call it foolishness but ...', as one part of a Christian song goes; but within me I knew it was from Father God and if He got me there and He had His purposes then He was quite capable of keeping me and sustaining me for my time in Glasgow. That's not to say it was not a little daunting at times, but when we are younger and willing to take risks, well ... older sometimes as well ... we do and do so best if it's one step at a time.

I lived in the college building for three or so weeks and everyone who did so had their own private room. It was a large building, purpose-built as a Bible College about, at that time, one hundred years old. Because of its age, the building was going to take quite a lot of upkeep, yet the outside architecture of that place was quite grand. I was in Helensburgh a year or so ago, browsing in a bookshop, and came across a book of Glasgow architecture and there it was - an aerial view of the building with some comments. They played down any Christian emphasis, though the building had various busts of some past evangelical leaders on the outside. It's long gone now, of course, and a glass skyscraper of some kind stands in its place.

Because the training as a whole took account of an individual's conduct and character, as well as that of knowledge, intellect and the spiritual side of life, there was male and female segregation both of the living quarters and in the lecture halls. There was a uniform too, a blazer, tie, etc - but that was stopped by the summer of that year, which was the beginning of many changes. The students were of various ages and from many different walks of life, like teachers, nurses, etc, and even some from dubious backgrounds who had been wonderfully 'born again'. I remember speaking to one couple, at that time coming towards the end of their time there, who told me that they hadn't liked their experience as they said they'd compared it to their time at university which they had enjoyed much more. Fair enough, but the whole ethos was towards the more mature and older person and with some outward disciplines to encourage self-discipline towards serving in the 'Body of Christ' and moving towards Godly wisdom, understanding and knowledge ... for leadership is by serving and example. You were expected to be already established in your faith, walk and trust in the Lord Jesus and therefore know something of your gifting and potential ... in that serving.

It took me all of those three weeks to get things sorted and settle in. I got a downstairs tenement flat in Cardross Street, Dennistoun: a little scruffy, so a step back after the RAF married quarter, but nevertheless it had an inside loo and bathroom and the rent was £26 for three months! One morning, one of the lecturers said in front of all of the students, "Is there anyone in need of some furniture?" "Yes!" I shouted, as I raised my hand. "See me after - there's some furniture going free and it can be delivered next Tuesday." And that is what happened. There was quite a lot of stuff I did use, including a beautiful Victorian double wardrobe with mirrors, highly polished and with carving, in excellent condition. One of my fellow student friends had been a plumber and he fitted a modern sink unit, and so it went on, and all came together. The Lord was with me and very much in all that was happening.

I applied to Carlisle Education Dept for a grant because I had lived in Carlisle prior to going in the forces. I completed all the forms and procedures at the time of leaving the RAF and beginning to attend BTI and quite quickly was granted an interview. Quite a few people were praying for me on that day. While waiting to go in for the interview in Carlisle, there was one other person, a man of about 19 or 20 years. "I wasted my first year," he told me, "and now I regret that and want to continue my university course." He went in first and when he reappeared he commented, "It was hard going and did not go well." I perceived he was very intelligent and capable ... "That's the way it goes", I thought, as my heart sank a notch! I entered the room, which was plush indeed, with a massive boardroom table. Oh, boy, were they thorough?! ... leaving no stone unturned, and rightly so. I don't remember now exactly how many were present, but I think it was around ten persons. Because of my roots and connections in Carlisle over the years, I recognised a couple of them. After a few minutes, the door opened and a man came in, an older rather than younger gentleman, and quietly sat down - though he did not say anything. I recognised him as the Director of Education for Cumberland (now Cumbria). How was that? He had lived in St George's Crescent in Carlisle... er ... next door to me in the other half of the massive Victorian semi owned by my father! In 1951/52, I can remember going into his house once or twice when his children were quite young and that was to play, but that soon stopped when the neighbours realised that my family/home life was not all that it should have been - sort of socially the black sheep of The Crescent, if you like! I can remember that his eldest daughter must have taken after him, for she was extremely intelligent. I had always shown him respect and I certainly got a fair hearing and was conscious that they were aware that the 'boss' had come in possibly to look at me and to view the proceedings. Even so, one or two were quite strict in their dealings with me. So I was dismissed. In recovery time I reckoned I had held my own, but I wasn't sure about this one! But no need to worry, as the

Lord wanted me at this college - within a couple of days I was accepted - and that for a mature student's grant, because of my age and good income in the RAF. Yes, it was on certain conditions and that was a good incentive for me. It was a weight, a concern, lifted off me, so that I could concentrate on my studies, etc.

On the day I brought my wife and daughter up from Newcastle via Carlisle to Glasgow, we travelled in a type of flat-top vehicle with a roof but no sides, used for carrying milk, vegetables or the like, belonging to Mr Cyril Proudfoot, the Brethren man mentioned elsewhere, who had the wholesale fruiterer's business in Carlisle and who had lived in St George's Crescent, but by then had moved to a very large detached house not far away. He offered to encourage and help me and gave me a financial gift to get me started. The showers of the blessings of the Lord were coming so thick and fast I wanted to stop and take stock - but there was no time, except to be grateful and thankful. So I got my family and belongings up there and, as my wife went into the flat, she was not at all pleased ... she did not like it! "This is Glasgow," I said, "they are hard to get and this is brill compared to some." I did not 'twig' that she was not really all that happy as she was not sure how much support she would be able to give me, as in the status quo, if this all led to pastoral Christian leadership. She was a tough 'Geordie' and settled down and we made some good friends over that season of years.

My daughter had it a bit rough in the Glasgow school she went to, as not everyone loved the English; so it was from a Northern Ireland accent back to a Newcastle/Geordie accent and now a Glaswegian accent that she quickly learned to mimic. This way she held her own and got by more or less okay. We soon felt at home, got into a routine and a busy life.

The words 'educate' or 'education' hold a key, along with the word 'educe'; all from Latin, of course. The Oxford Dictionary on the word 'educate' goes along the lines of 'giving instruction or information on a particular subject that is intellectual, moral, social', and so on. Also, the word 'educe' is important and means 'to bring out or develop' (something latent or potential) - from the Latin root 'educare, educat, educere' ... and means literally 'lead out'. Education must contain something of the facts and the information that 'go in', but true education is what is 'led out' of a person; so it all has to do with the learning, thinking through, researching and the creativity involved in that process, so that any subject(s) dealt with can be led out from a person as required, desired or needs be and a contribution to whatever made. Back to the Oxford Dictionary and to the meaning of 'an education' in a general and informal way - it is an 'enlightening experience'. These latter words say it all and literally it should read 'give and bring forth the light' ... bearing all this in mind, regarding what I wanted from Bible College - providing the light is really 'The Light'. The Lord Jesus calls Himself the only Light of The World. I wanted a working knowledge of the Bible and a look at the major doctrines of the evangelical Christian Faith (a massive subject) and any different viewpoints of these doctrines, so as to formulate what one believes and why. We do this all the time with whatever we believe in, though for most in this I.T. age we have simply accepted so much without questioning or thinking through what we've taken on board, where it leads and what any consequences might be. In other words, it is how we apply what we have learned and digested that's important, though this can be for good or evil; but it is the good as in life, with a capital L (from the Lord), that we should desire.

But I wanted to take in the view of the whole Christian scene in the UK, not only with doctrine, Bible knowledge and much more, but the observation and researching for the whatever as well, so that what I was about to learn and apply could be 'drawn out' or 'led forth' from me. Of course, life itself is part of the training. At that time, to learn from all the individual and collective people I would observe and come in contact with then, and ongoing, and especially when there was such a rich diversity of personalities and characters which were in those living and life situations during that period, was quite something indeed, and yet I would never want to forget the rejected, the poor and the hurting.

In one sense we were 'disciples' of the lecturers and the time period to be 'discipled' for me for that season in Glasgow I would say was about the right length. Normally, we never stop learning in this life, but we should be discipled/trained at one stage and then at a later stage go on to disciple and train others. This was certainly biblical at the time of The Lord Jesus and the Apostle Paul. The word 'disciple' means 'a learner' and is tied in with the word 'discipline' in balance and interestingly the word (disciple) is used around 250 times in the New Testament. The rest of the time it is the word 'believers' that is referred to, or actual people who are referred to as believers. It is interesting, as I write, that about ten years ago in Heysham, at a small powerful prayer meeting, someone gave me a 'prophetic prayer' that I would have a group to disciple that would be like a 12-seater aircraft which would 'take off'. The person who gave it was stable and mature and I took this prophecy on board and believed it and know in my heart, in faith, that this will one day happen for a season.

I worked as hard as I could during that time in Glasgow and, by the grace of God, accomplished what I set out to do - a foundation on which to build - it was one of those 'gems' in my life that was certainly worth having. The above is the backdrop to that time - now I will just pick out some of the things I observed, plus some things of interest and one or two things that happened.

Along with my wife, I still wanted to be baptised by total immersion and decided to join a local Baptist Church; and, of course, to be in membership I had to be re-baptised and that by total immersion in order to comply with their doctrine. I had to seek permission from the college in order to change denomination and this was granted. I was trusting the Lord that He would give further 'showers of blessings' if I was being obedient and responding to the 'light' I had received. Quite a lot of people turned up and during the actual baptism it rained so hard the noise could be heard loudly inside the building where the peace and presence of the Lord, as He was exalted, was very real and the whole experience was quite something.

They gave me one or two preaching engagements - my first attempts of preaching - and I made the classic mistake of over-preparing, especially with all the knowledge of the Bible I was obtaining and researching. Each Baptist Church fellowship was autonomous, i.e. self-governing, so was vastly different from the Church of England, with its hierarchical structures. I was surprised to learn that there was a lot of Freemasonry in the Baptist Church in Dennistoun, so once when preaching I spoke out against it, starting to make a comparison between what it said and what the Bible said, though only very briefly. Some were not at all pleased - one person walked out - and some were making their signs and there was a restlessness and a fury - but I was and am convinced that Freemasonry when compared to the Word of God is not only incompatible but dangerous. If I was looking to be popular with man, I would guess I was not off to a very good start! But then to be popular with God as a Heavenly 'Dad' is the greatest prize. I was perplexed when I realised that so few really believed in the power, work and baptism of the Holy Spirit - there were the two sides (on the one the nominal, counterfeit, liberal and even Freemasonry side and on the other the evangelical and Pentecostal believers) and the battle was raging all over.

Generally on Sunday evenings I would go around Glasgow visiting the different church fellowships and this was valuable indeed. George Duncan was at 'The Tron'. He was a powerful preacher and the building would be so full that the balcony was in use. Douglas MacMillan from the Free Church of Scotland had a large fellowship and he also spoke at the BTI - he was a very down to earth man, having been a shepherd among other things, a very clever man and a powerful speaker. I have a copy of his book of his life's testimony - though when visiting his fellowship found it really strange, as they all were only singing psalms and there were no musical instruments whatsoever!

I'll never forget the first time I visited Park Pentecostal - definitely musical instruments there! - and moving towards 'happy clappy'; but when the pastor, the leader, introduced a visiting speaker, little did I realise what was about to unfold. When he had finished speaking, the pastor got to his feet and immediately tore him to pieces, verbally, of course! ... saying they did not agree with certain things he had just said. Well, they didn't mess about, calling a spade a spade, with no compromise or just being nice for the sake of it - and ... mmm ... I didn't really think they were likely to ask that speaker back!

Then there was a little Pentecostal fellowship I liked to visit. I think it was called Calvary Chapel and it was part of the Foursquare Gospel Pentecostal Denomination - sometimes it was predictable, but when they got off into freedom it could be real fun, as you did not know what would happen next; but I can clearly remember now as they sang, sometimes for several minutes, the Spiritual Song from a verse in the Old Testament ... 'and as truly as I live, all the Earth will be filled with the glory of the Lord ... the gloree ... the gloreee ...'. Okay, you'd need to hear the tune ... and maybe we'd all be singing it ...!

I can remember early on speaking to a youth group in a Church of Scotland somewhere in the greater Glasgow area and at least one person started to take notes and I momentarily went into shock as I thought, "What do you want to take notes for? - I'm just learning!" But it was not long after that, probably because of all the notes I made in lectures, I went on to make notes of nearly all the speakers that I've heard in conferences and sermons, etc, in the last thirty-odd years... how much I'm able to read my own writing is something of another issue ...!!

It was in Sauchiehall Street in Glasgow in the early part of 1975 that I first did some open-air evangelism with two or three other students and, although we had no amplification, I really enjoyed the fun, challenge and excitement of it. I later became friendly with old Robert MacRae, a born evangelist and fearless with it and who was part of the 'Brethren Denomination'. He would visit our home regularly for hospitality. He was so full of the Lord Jesus and His Word; he was way ahead of most other believers and in one sense was more 'Pentecostal' than the Pentecostals ... though supposed to be anti! ... and yet he was misunderstood. No one could control or curtail his evangelism or his love for the Lord or squeeze him into their mould, as it were, though a few must have tried. He was quite a character, definitely a one-off, though blinkered in some ways; but he was sold out for Jesus - and it was an honour to be his friend.

It was also in 1975 that I found out about fasting and prayer, which is not only biblical, of course, but can be of great value. I looked for some material on this, but there was precious little that I could find in those days - so I found out the hard way. "If I fast for about 60 hours, do I make it no food and no water? Yes, I thought, why not?!" I have now learned a fair amount about fasting and prayer over the years - but not then. I was active over that couple of days, but was like a rake anyway, and yet the food abstinence did me no harm, but I started to dehydrate as the hours went by and realised you must drink as much as you need! But I had tasted of the spiritual power that came with fasting to the Lord and, for me, realised how important it was from then onwards. There is much more material on the subject today, of course. My fasts got longer and longer over the years and up to 40 days at a time (not completely without a little bit of food). Then I compared myself with Mahesh Chavda, who has done forty 40-day fasts and much more, giving him an incredible power from Heaven; and when I worked out the amount of fasting he did in any one year, I once managed to get to that number of days.

After some time, my daughter developed anorexia, so she did not eat ... and she did not eat ... and she still did not eat ... and I was somewhat perplexed! All I knew was that she had had a very small amount of chocolate. I asked a few friends to pray, but nothing happened immediately. Then I found out about a man called David Black – well, there was more than one 'David Black' in Christian circles in the Glasgow area - this was the one who had previously been the leader of the Baptist Church I attended and he now had an independent Baptist Fellowship in Bishopbriggs, Glasgow, and he was well known because he was running 'Scottish Churches Renewal' at that time - bringing a lot of famous names who were of a Pentecostal/charismatic persuasion to speak in the area. I know he has gone to be with The Lord now, but he did go on to build a community of (private) houses centred around a church fellowship/community building which I once, in later years, visited briefly.

One Sunday, my wife and I took our daughter over to Bishopbriggs, found the building and attended the meeting. It was very 'free' and full of life, and he was a powerful speaker with a strong personality - though I don't think he suffered fools gladly. In that meeting, I explained briefly the circumstances and asked him to pray and so he laid hands on my daughter and prayed a powerful prayer and a command of release - it's called 'taking authority'! Later, when we got home, she sat down with us and ate some food - as I remember, that was a fair portion of a full meal and that was a miracle in itself... and she continued eating. Later in her life, there were some slight recurrences over which she got the victory. So it was that whenever I could I would go over to that fellowship, not always easy by public transport ... but worth it! They were moving in the gifts of the Holy Spirit such as prophecy, tongues, etc, and it was at that time I broadened my outlook of the 'Pentecostal/charismatic churches' in the UK and USA with the likes of Kathryn Kuhlman testimonies, written about her, of the most incredible miracles and healings; likewise Smith Wigglesworth from Bradford and also the 'Florida Five' (Derek Prince, Bob Mumford, Ern Baxter, etc), these three mentioned being the three that I actually saw, live, in the UK. I went on to see Derek Prince at several conferences, etc, over the years. It was their New Wine magazine, sent to me from America regularly for about seven years, which influenced me. They made some mistakes, but were generally able to back up their beliefs and words with a demonstration of power and were keen to get back to some of the basics of the early Church as found in the New Testament. In the south of England, if not the London area, was the southern house church grouping/movement - their magazine was called Fullness and included names like John Noble, Maurice Smith and Terry Virgo. The Bradford Church house movement (generally the house church movement of the north of England) was getting underway at that time, as I would discover later on, and their magazine was called Restoration. The reason for mentioning these groups, and David Black, is that they were seeking the move of the Holy Spirit and Revival and daring to break out of the very denominational 'moulds' with their structures and restrictions and their aim seemed to be to seek, allow, and give God the freedom to move and work in power.

On the final year at the BTI, if you could set it up, you could work with a local church leader of your choice; so, as that time approached, I asked and it was granted to be assigned to David Black at Bishopbriggs Baptist. I was limited in what I could do time-wise with not owning a car and with the work he would give me to do and my own workload – nevertheless, I was given some work to do and observed as much as I could and would not have missed that opportunity.

The BTI had a superb library – well, two really, with thousands and thousands of books. One room covered the expositional or devotional side and the other mainly that of 'exegesis', the literal interpretation of languages, grammar, commentaries on the Bible, doctrine, etc, etc - I was in my element, of course, to be surrounded by those books.

One day I went into the main library and someone said to me, "Have you not heard or considered the work of John Calvin?". "No," says I, "didn't know there was a John Calvin, never heard of him." So, I suppose someone wanted to 'keep me right'! I was to learn he was one of the reformers and something of 'the debate' that rages in its controversy. Well, so what - they didn't get it all right. The reformers made their fair share of mistakes like the rest of us! I thought to myself, "Is this fellow greater than the Lord Jesus? Did he die and shed his blood for your and my sins?" For me, nothing and no-one could ever match up to the Lord Jesus, having tasted of His total grace, mercy and perfect love and the whole package. "No, no," they say, "it's predestination and you were chosen." "Was I?" All I know is that I had previously responded to the Lord with a definite decision with my mind and my heart to seek after Him and His love from that moment onwards.

I understand the equation to be about God's sovereignty over man's responsibility and free will and lastly to throw into this mix 'fatalism', so will give some brief comments. God is totally Sovereign and as such is by us on Earth unreachable, yet knowable, even in an intimate way. His creation is profoundly vast and complex, yet He knows everything about it and that includes you and me - even every thought we have ever had! From man's point of view, if we push God's sovereignty too far it becomes a 'hyper-sovereignty'; that is, so one-sided it leaves us with no free will, freedom of choice or responsibility. If that is so, then it is all fixed and up to Him and nothing much to do with us; therefore, that makes us nothing or little more than 'automated beings'!!!! It is all then some kind of divine chance or 'luck of the draw' if you like to receive divine favour! Definitely not!

With man's responsibility, free will and choice in all things of life, it's where each one of us draws the line as to how much in reality we may or may not have of any choices - these freedoms, of course, could be limited by our sphere of circumstances or conditions, whether slave or free. Yet, if anyone gives emphasis to this issue of man's free will, even to the point of saying it is all up to us and so in some way to leave God out, then God becomes distant, with minimal relationship and seemingly even unknowable. So it then becomes all up to man to try and sort things out and work out his own salvation and try to deal with unrighteousness, evil and the state of his heart - and that is when he gets into trouble with all kinds of rituals, works, laws, legalism, do's and don'ts and all sorts of behavioural problems - not least 'control' in order to try and get relationships 'right' by conformity. This can apply to 'religion', but is definitely the start of 'humanism', which I will deal with in another chapter. But the extremes of the above equation when they go haywire can lead to *fatalism* in the full sense of *what will be will be and that's that* - everything is predetermined; why bother anyway, so let's just submit to all events, to whatever happens! NO! ... fatalism is a deadly poison, as it sends its victims into a coma to work its work of death, so it is to be rejected.

God does have foreknowledge of all events and therefore knows the beginning from the end, so He knows the decisions we will all make here on Earth, within our free will to choose, and therefore He will act accordingly as prophetically laid down in scripture - Roger Price dealt superbly with these issues in the relevant material he left.

For our salvation it is as if the Lord takes nine steps towards us from His side that only He could make, doing everything that is required for us as individuals to come into a right, close and loving relationship with Him, and all that any one of us has to do is to make that commitment in belief, repentance and humility of that one step that is required of our heart's choice towards Him and so complete this process. It is worth noting that there are no conscripts with God, only volunteers.

Another thought is that of democracy - it is better than the blatant 'tyrannical dictatorship', but democracy of itself with its 'majority vote' is no guarantee that the result will be right and fair in every good way. If the leaders of a democracy are deceptive and corrupt, for example, then they too can be tyrannical. This is because what really counts is what emanates from the human heart, which, of course, can be good or evil, in any one of us, and is conditioned by the mind, its thought structures and the emotions as it is channelled towards right or wrong. Love for whatever is active not passive, and comes from the human heart and its source and channelling towards an object; whatever that object is may also be for good or for evil/right or wrong. There are several different kinds of words for our one word 'love', in the Greek. True love will be active and not passive and never fatalistic. This love is the Greek word 'agape' and is God's special, pure, wonderful love from Heaven and when that love has entered, captivated and won your heart it will lead to *life* that will fight with all the armour that is available from Heaven's armoury to destroy the works of darkness, evil and destruction and so bring in the *light* of God's life and amazing love - for God is love!

For most of the summer break of 1975 I drove a van for a furniture shop called The Black Cat, in the Parkhead area of Glasgow, delivering new furniture. Now, that is generally okay, especially to earn a few pennies, until you get a metal-framed sofa/bed to deliver somewhere to a 4th floor tenement flat (no lift!) and when you get to the door with the bed it doesn't want to go in!… we have ways …! ! If I got to know many of the Glasgow roads, then it cannot be denied that they have certainly changed in the past thirty years!

I remember they were demolishing the two or three tenement blocks that still remained just across the road from where we lived. They put a thick steel cable right around the building and then the tractor unit would pull that cable right through the building like slicing cheese with a cheese wire - on one occasion the cable snapped, but the demolition people soon sorted another cable out and continued - and as each building went down there was a large, thick, black cloud of dust or whatever it was. Even before going outside it was wise to wait until it had settled. Eventually that left one side only of tenements still standing and lived in on Cardross Street though someone told me that a few years later on they were emptied, gutted and modernised. That demolition left a large open space right over to what was then a (Tennant?) Lager Factory, which I could then observe from the front of the flat. So it was in the year of the bin or refuse collection strike, the summer of 1976, a lot of the city rubbish, a mountain of it, or so it seemed, was dumped about one or two hundred yards from our home. With the rubbish also in 'the midden' at the back of the tenement for several flats looking onto that small area the smell, the sight … the thought of what 'beasties' were hidden - it was not unusual to see a rat or two - it was just as well in that ground-floor flat that we had Mitzi, our Yorkshire Terrier, on vermin deterrent duty!

In the beautiful summer of that year it seemed like every day was sunny and hot and it just went on and on and on … until September, when it seemed months of rain had been stored up to fall all in one go - and the River Clyde burst its banks!

Early in the summer of that year I went on a 'mission' for a couple of weeks or so; it was one of those times I've never forgotten, as I really enjoyed it. Nearly everyone at BTI had to complete one mission during holiday time as part of their course and, as I remember, the minimum was ten days - yours was the choice of whatever and yours the task to set it up! I prayerfully chose 'Youth With A Mission', which had its base in America in those days and was Pentecostal. They had the use of a large suburban Victorian property in Hawick, in Scotland, near the Borders. (I was in Hawick recently and was told the building is still in Christian hands.) I was to go there for three days, followed by the rest of the time on the beautiful Isle of Cumbrae, a short distance off the Ayrshire coast from the town of Largs. The time came and I got a bus to Hawick and found the place. Most of the group were Americans: lads and lassies in their teens and twenties from an 'Assemblies of God Fellowship' in Eugene in the state of Oregon. Oh boy, were they alive and full of zeal and love for their Saviour!! … and not frightened to demonstrate that fact in their walk with Him and in evangelism. So, when they sang the lively choruses with great gusto they would have actions as well - I'm sure if there were no actions they would have invented some! They were just 'themselves' and free to be so. "I can run through a troop and leap over a wall … Hallelujah, hallelujah, …!!" and so we would run as on the spot and leap as to go over a wall and so on … quite unusual for these days! That was 'us centred' in aspects of our walk with the Lord Jesus, but when worshipping and concentrating on 'Him' with all of our minds and hearts, who He was and what He had done, His presence was awesome and this further set a precedent for me for the rest of my years on Earth. Some of the music and actions which, as far as I'm aware, came out of the Toronto Revival, such as … 'and I will be even more undignified than this … hey!' … and at the 'hey' you would leap for the Lord … this, of course, referred to when King David danced before the Lord regarding the Ark of The Covenant but Michal (1 Samuel, ch 6 v 20), his wife, kind of 'blew it' when she despised him. So, even much later on in life I would find myself joining the younger ones in their exuberance, even if only for a few minutes! The Jewish Dance is something I had a go at, though it was a lot more serious and I would fall around laughing when I couldn't get it right! … ah well, in years gone by at least I had a go!

We did open-air work as a group in Hawick and got some 'YWAM … Youth With A Mission' teaching, as it was called. I had hardly ever seen my Grandma Field - perhaps four or five times in the 'fifties and once briefly in 1970, yet had heard she was in a care home in Hawick, so I made some enquiries and found out she was in a large Roman Catholic house called Stirches (a housing estate I've been told is in that area now) and so obtained the necessary permission and visited for half an hour or so in the afternoon prior to the day I was leaving. She had been a very disciplined and strict lady and would have been in her early nineties. Afternoon tea was laid out for the two of us on one of the sun terraces and, with the views, gardens, mature trees and deep blue sky on that hot summer day, the setting was idyllic. I enjoyed the food that was served with the cup of tea and suddenly she started 'cleaning' the chair she was sitting on with one of the cakes, then threw it away as far as she could! "Well, that sorted that cake out!" I thought to myself as it whizzed through the air, "I couldn't throw it that far!" Although she was non compos mentis, I had a strange feeling that I reminded her of someone she once knew - perhaps a family resemblance came through. I treated her with respect, of course, and quietly prayed for her, but I never saw her again. I heard years later that she went on to be 100 years old - I was not surprised, as she was a very strong lady.

The WYAM Isle of Cumbrae team travelled to Largs and then over on the small ferry to the Isle of Cumbrae and by the bus to Millport. At Largs, we went to a family's home and were given afternoon high tea. I remember talking to the lady of the house and asking her one or two questions, for one of her children had Down's Syndrome; then she just said to me, very clearly and forthrightly, something like, "Do you want to know something … I would not have missed having or bringing up this child for anything because of the love that I've poured in and the love I've received back … it was totally worth it!" Now that, I realised, was the Father Heart of God's love, wisdom and maturity working through her in that situation.

Well, the Isle of Cumbrae seemed to be a very sort of relaxed place - it was, and I'm sure still is, a beautiful small island. There was or had been some kind of religious community at Millport, where we were given living quarters and, for the next several days, reopened a café as the team's focal point for outreach. There were tracts/leaflets for the café work with some street evangelism and one or two meetings of various kinds arranged. I had my eye on the streets - yes! - evangelism!! "You're allocated to the café kitchen in charge of the food!" "Definitely not!" says I. "You're definitely allocated to the kitchen; it's only through the daytime." "Okay, to the kitchen then!" Whatever you do for the Lord, do it to the best of your ability and with all your heart. I groaned. "They'll never throw me out of the kitchen if I do well …!" A day or two later, people were actually coming back for my scones! "I'll experiment," I thought, "I'll try banana cake - and that'll be that!" Oh no, everyone seemed to like my banana cake! (though I would have to admit I've never made it since) … and so I settled into the routine of those few days. But the important thing was that we worked together as a team and this we did not only for the outreach but as a group of friends. The prayer times, prayer walks, meetings and taking spiritual authority as well as the café contacts … made it all worthwhile. I kept contact with one or two of those Americans for three years or so and was invited to go over to Eugene, but never took them up on it.

As the last academic year got underway, I started to look at various possibilities of what suitable Christian work might be available and applied accordingly - my heart was towards pastoral ministry, but there were various 'missions' too. I tried one or two 'doors' and got some interviews, as well as doors beginning to open, e.g. in YMCA management. On writing to someone in England for a 'lead', he put my name forward to a small but lively Baptist Church Fellowship on a council estate in Huddersfield and, although it was a slow and thorough process over several months with varying interviews, the result was the offer of the pastorate from October 1977 - and this I accepted. One of those interviews, at which I was accompanied by my family, lasted from the Friday evening until the Sunday evening, with three speaking engagements, pastoral visits, etc, and was intensive, to put it mildly. On that Saturday night's meeting I gave something of my life's testimony, including my spiritual background and experience just as it had happened, holding nothing back - trouble was that not many turned up that evening, but those who came enjoyed what I had to say.

Now, several in that fellowship were pro the Baptism of the Holy Spirit and some others had been to meetings of a man called Trevor Harpin from Halifax (who had had some contact with Trevor Dearing!), who was very much alive, and so they became somewhat Pentecostal - as in free and fired up, if you like. The structure of the Baptist denomination was that each church fellowship was autonomous with its own elder(s), deacons and members, with everyone in active membership supposedly having a certain equality, having their say and having a vote on whatever as and when needs be in the decision-making process of the issues raised, normally by a majority vote. There was something called 'The Baptist Union', which co-ordinated several areas in England, each under an area superintendent, who would maintain the links between the fellowships and give advice as might be deemed necessary, etc. Funds were involved and various other things as well, though not all local Baptist Fellowships belonged to the Baptist Union. This particular fellowship that I had accepted did belong and was under the North East of England Area, with a superintendent - I had an interview with him and we got on well, though he said he did not want me to teach on the Holy Spirit. When he said this, I thought very deeply and quickly - "This could be a difficult one" - but I agreed. So as not to be or seen to be divisive, I did not divulge this to anyone at that time. A little later, I received Baptist Union Accreditation as the fellowship's leader/pastoral elder.

Just to clarify, some of the other denominations that were similar to the Baptist structure of church government included the Brethren (who were also generally similar in their doctrines), the Congregationalists, Independent Evangelical Fellowships and the Assemblies of God Pentecostal Fellowships. The opposite of that, of course, is the hierarchical structure, with its measure of structured control to give directive and vision from the top downwards, with authority and power and an expected obedience, regardless of whatever happens, and that according to one's given status, and would include hierocracy (rule by priests) or a type of it in essence - and so would include denominations such as the Church of England, the Salvation Army, the Apostolic and the Elim Pentecostals, some of the house churches, such as the original 'Bradford Church House' and 'New Frontiers', and so on. In essence, we seem to have ended up with a choice only between these two types. But in each one, and that would include any democracy, as in a majority vote/decision, it does not mean immunity from unrighteousness in any shape or form. The same applies to leadership anywhere if it too is unrighteous, as Proverbs clearly states. The government of the Baptist denomination should be the safer of the two, as it will certainly give people a say; but I would now seriously question the above and say that radical change is necessary. What is the true Church anyway and what is it supposed to be about? I will refer to this in a later chapter!

As the details of the pastorate in Huddersfield were sorted out, the Fellowship said they should be able to try and get a council house manse for me, and this they did, though not immediately, and when they brought up the issue of salary and certain expenses I simply accepted the figure they said, for I was sure if the Lord was in this He would provide all my needs - and He did! All money I earned e.g. for funerals, etc, I gave to them. I said that my wife would have no kind of upfront ministry, but that she was my back-up and would give hospitality in the manse when necessary. I finished my course at BTI and said goodbye to Glasgow at the end of September of 1977 and put my furniture into somebody's garage in Huddersfield for storage for a few weeks.

On that last Sunday evening meeting at Bishopbriggs, Glasgow, David Black commissioned, blessed and 'sent me out' to Huddersfield. The presence of the Lord was with us and we had a good time, during which he prophesied over me and my wife. He prophesied for quite a long time over me, or so it seemed anyway, and it was good positive stuff ... until he suddenly said, "... and people will not like your fragrance." I thought, "Hang on a minute, this is me you're talking about ..."; then, as he continued, it got worse, as he said, "... and you will be the grandfather of much fruit" ...! I had to just about bite my tongue so as not to interrupt him, thinking, "You've made a big mistake, you're getting me mixed up with someone else ... surely I'll be the father of much fruit, which will suit me fine ... not the grandfather ...!" He finished and turned to my wife, laid hands on her and gave a gentle and profound short prophecy of blessing, of which the centre was simply that she would open like a flower to the Lord, to the warmth of His Sonshine and blossom ..." In response, I said, "Thank You, Lord, that was quite something!" It was not audio-taped and I asked one or two afterwards, but no one could remember the details or had made any notes of the prophecies, so, okay, Lord, Your will be done! Well, it certainly was and, as I glance over my life as a whole, the prophecy given to me looks to be accurate!

There was just one thing regarding my wife ... she had not felt well ... gone to the doctors and had a visit to Glasgow's Duke St Hospital ... but onwards now into another season, with its intensive life training ...

# 12
## *A Season in Huddersfield*

It says in Biblical Proverbs that when a desire comes into fruition it is a tree of life and also that it is sweet to the soul and this was certainly true for me at that time and for most of us in fulfilling a vision and desire. It took a few weeks to settle in and get organised and into 'the driver's seat' and to put my finger on the pulse of the fellowship, as it were, but in that first couple of weeks there was not much to do and that was just as well, as I needed that time. It was a servant role that would require a lifestyle of dedication and would therefore mean that it would virtually engulf my life - and this it did and I gave it my best shot.

The key, of course, is not to be so consumed that you neglect your family and don't give them of yourself as in attention and prime time and not the dregs after you're spent on everyone and everything else (though it's said in a real move of God your family do not miss out anyway). There would be some who would misunderstand, of course. I tried to get one day off a week on a Monday, so perhaps my daughter missed out a little - I'll have to ask her what she remembers of that time as she started her teens!! I wonder if I'll have to apologise!? Ah well ...

I can remember, as the workload built up and I became incredibly busy, I would often work into the night - it was more peaceful at that time and so I could pick up more inspiration from the Lord for all the various preaching/speaking engagements which I had to do every week. My wife would come in and stand quietly to one side, just in case I was deep in thought or needed to write something down before speaking - even up until 2am or later, and more than once she came up with a cooked meal and put it carefully beside me as I'd not got time or had forgotten to eat. So when I slept in, as I sometimes needed to, and the curtains were closed, some complained! They never complained when the light was on till 2 or 3am though! They didn't quite understand - I was something of an owl anyway and needed my sleep at some time. It was getting the results and (good) fruit that would last, which was important to me; not just a 'show' of the present to look good - so I would just open the curtains at an early hour when I was really tired ... I could easily sleep on in daylight anyway!

There were certain basics of what I had to do, such as taking and preaching at the two Sunday 'services' and give a children's talk at the Sunday morning meeting - 25% of my preaching had to be away at other fellowships in that general area and I preached as far away as Leeds and Dewsbury, though later on someone said that I was wrong to give my pulpit to others - but this was laid down by the fellowship as part of the deal of taking up the pastorate and anyway it did my flock good to hear different speakers and I really enjoyed visiting other fellowships! So, apart from meeting the deadlines, I had a total freedom. It was fun and suited me. I had to look after my flock, given on a list of members, between 60 and 70 people, and this I did systematically on a regular basis of visitation. I also had the diaconate leadership and whole church business meetings to chair, along with the Lord's Table of the Bread and Wine on a monthly basis, and these were all speaking engagements needing preparation. Apart from the evangelistic campaigns, open-air preaching work and ministers' fraternals of various kinds and in various places - I was once invited to the Anglican Fraternal at Kirkheaton, Huddersfield, with the leaders and the then diocesan Bishop Richard Hare and he was somewhat 'Pentecostal', to put it mildly, and on my wavelength or … was I on his!! - plus various social outings, the fellowship said it was up to me what further contacts I made, if any (and make them I certainly did), how I organised my time and what other work I wanted to take on.

They, the fellowship, wanted to see fruit and growth and so did I, but my way/vision was slightly different from that of a small but powerful element within the fellowship. They had a midweek meeting in the church building, but I wanted to move it into 'house groups', as in people's homes, giving a certain pastoral leadership to those who would run them - I believed that this was a way of growth - warm and friendly, relaxed, etc, if we could get it right.

I wanted much more emphasis on prayer, as in crying out to the Lord from the heart for revival (a powerful, supernatural move of God). I was not looking just for 'contacts', say, of other leaders as such, but I seemed to make them all over that area, e.g. Pastor Thomas was leader of the Elim Fellowship in Huddersfield and lived in my area - we became good friends and he borrowed the church building for use of the baptismal pool, after permission being given, and I preached once or twice at his fellowship. A colleague in Huddersfield told me not to refuse funerals if I was offered them as it was a way of helping people, making contacts and sharing the love of Jesus, and this eventually became a regular ministry for me; every few weeks I seemed to be offered one and, as far as I remember, I only ever turned one down due to another speaking engagement.

Let me bring this preamble to a precise conclusion as I tie in some loose ends, followed by a brief summary of this shorter-than-expected season in Huddersfield.

It was a brill little fellowship - I liked the area, the people and the work. They were workers and I would say that most were workers in the area of their giftings, which meant good teamwork with minimum control, with the bonus of the people being generally very friendly. We did several 'open airs' and 'campaigns', including one small group from the BTI, and one weekend when a busload from Capernwray Bible College visited; more about that weekend just below. Most of the time it went well for me, as the Lord was with me - I was sold out for Him - yet, so what? - I was just myself, warts and all. But the issue of the place and work of the Holy Spirit would not go away as the months went by. It was a divided fellowship and even silence was not enough to appease or pacify those in a minority who were opposed to anything 'Pentecostal'. The battle has raged in many places with the same pattern and continues to this day. In the end I found it somewhat stressful and it was heartbreaking stuff.

Back at the beginning I had my photograph and an article in the local Huddersfield newspaper, which put me on the map, followed by an induction service. The small building was absolutely packed and there were various speakers that Saturday afternoon, including the Area Superintendent, some colleagues in Huddersfield and Geoffrey Grogan, Principal of the BTI, who came down, spoke, and then went straight back by train to Glasgow, for it was a long journey and his time was at a premium and so much appreciated. I got to speak as well, of course, and was prayed over - ah, yes, and there was food!! ... and the feedback I got of that Saturday at the end of October was very positive.

That little fellowship covered a lot of ground in its 'campaigns' and though most took a fair amount of organising they were great fun. We arranged for a whole weekend to have a single-decker busload of students down from Capernwray Hall Bible College, not far from Carnforth. We had to feed and water them, then put them up in different people's homes: no easy task. The idea was to at least evangelise the entire council estate and to let them take the meetings, giving as many students as possible the opportunity to speak. It went really well and I'd say that most of them enjoyed themselves, though the last meeting on the Sunday went on far too long and they still had their return journey ahead of them. With hindsight, I should have intervened, but I remained silent rather than destroy that young speaker's confidence. Myself and a student went out door-knocking, as we all did, on the Saturday afternoon and I think it was the second house we went to where the lady said she recognised me from the local paper's photo and article - she got her best china out and gave us afternoon tea ... that was an honour and kind of her ... but we still talked about the Lord Jesus and what He had done for each one of us!

Another time we had a sort of evangelistic garden party in the church grounds, with food, of course! ... with loudspeaker amplification for the music and speaking - it seemed to take a lot of organising and we needed police permission. With the balloons, etc, for decoration, it was quite a colourful affair and certainly was a success and we shared the Gospel with several people, including (for me anyway) invites into people's homes for some lengthy talks about the Lord. Another time, I organised a team from around the area in downtown Huddersfield. I was amazed how well it 'flowed' and the impact it had - one lady with a child in a pushchair ran down towards us and said she was a back-slidden believer, and wanted to rededicate her life back to the Lord Jesus, which she did, as some of the others prayed with and for her, and so on …!

I once went on a leaders' get-together; oh, what was the place called? … Coberhill, a Christian Centre a mile or so outside of Scarborough. The accommodation and food were excellent. I needed it more as a 'retreat' replenishment rather than anything else. Now, if you think I would be super-spiritual at this point - no chance! The highlight was a beautiful crisp winter's day and a walk of a couple of miles or so along the trackbed of what had been the railway between Scarborough and Whitby - I was in my element! - yet in every step I simply gave thanks to the Lord for the beauty of His creation, the peace, quiet and rich colours of the scenery.

I had a class come down with their RE teacher from the nearby secondary school in order to have a look at a local 'Baptist Church' and see what we were about! After a look around and a few words, I said that the best way was just to fire questions at me and I would do my best to answer them. The teacher agreed. Oh boy (and oh girl … far be it from me to get strung up!), the questions came fast and furious – well, intense on the last word would be more accurate. I was pretty much able to answer them all. It was informal and fun for them and me! So I was invited a short time after that to take a morning assembly and speak to the whole school - there were about 350 pupils. OK, let's call it 349 ... why? My daughter attended that school and she flatly and absolutely refused to go that morning! At first, I was going to pull rank and insist that she go, then realised that in this situation it would not be the right thing to do and said, "It's okay to stay at home" and so she did. I wasn't happy with what I'd prepared for the age range of that school - the challenge was to keep it very simple and fast moving and give the Gospel. I had quite a lot of people praying for me, but was not pleased with the way it went - I spoke from a narrative in Acts, but afterwards thought it was not simple enough. I felt it was somewhat 'formal' on their ground, but I should have treated it like an open-air meeting and then finished with a short prayer. I and others prayed though that I'd have their attention and I got some feedback from one teenager: "I wanted to turn my head away while you were speaking, but couldn't!"

I was returning home on foot in Dalton from the main road through a 'cut' and onto the council estate at dusk one evening and there was quite a large group of teenagers - mostly lads, that I could make out, talking boisterously and fooling around. I wasn't sure who they were, but thought I'd ignore them, as I was keen to get home … until I discovered my daughter was right in the middle of them … help! … keep calm, play it cool, man … that was around the time she turned 15 ... had she discovered boys? … or was it 'bees around the honey'? … on the inside of me was 'this can't be … is she old enough?'… on the outside it was 'nothing bothers me … well, not much!' … "You okay, C …?" "YES, Dad!" … and I was gone! I suppose she was going to have to start growing up some time ... and I never forgot that moment.

It wasn't long before one from that group was involved in a serious violent crime and his mother, very greatly troubled, asked me to give him some support. I did give some minimal support at the time of the court case and visited him in the Young Offenders' Prison, where he was being held. He would not respond and I felt he was not broken enough to accept the Lord and I therefore was unable to help him further, but it was good to at least have tried.

The first couple or so of funerals I took were small affairs, with only around a handful of people attending. One of the undertakers had no time for me and let it be known - yet for whatever reasons I kept dealing with him or his second-in-command. I didn't seem to have any problems with any of the other undertakers in Huddersfield during that time and got on really well with one or two. I was being driven into Huddersfield Crem. and thought to myself, "My, there's been a big funeral on here." Wrong! I quickly realised, I was taking a big funeral around here! There were cars and people everywhere and in the chapel a good number were having to stand. I had prepared well and got through it, but had misjudged the situation. I realised a few hours later that if I didn't personally know the deceased's family and church connections with Baptists or Evangelicals and if I could not spend a suitable amount of time and follow up with close relatives, then it would and should be more righteous for me to refuse. In other words, I would be fully involved or not at all. I knew the limit of my capabilities, as I've said above, and if I got involved with this ministry (a sort of pastoral caring evangelistic ministry all of its own), I could have made a lot of contacts in that whole area - in fact, I did, as one or two people did stop me on occasions when in down-town Huddersfield to say they were involved or saw me at a funeral I had taken. In serving, after all, my first priority was to Dalton Baptist Church, so as the weeks went by and the undertakers phoned me I tried to refuse - desperately so - giving my reasons as of the above ... but to no avail! ... so, as I remember and have mentioned, I only ever turned one funeral down and that was because of a previous engagement - and one or two of them I even took on my precious day off ... help! It was an honour, of course, and my heart went out to so many people so often in difficult situations. On at least one occasion at that time I started to become emotionally involved with tears as I picked up their pain and tears, but, of course, had to get a grip in order to help them through. Although now a long time ago, I apologise to anyone for that time in that area for any mistakes I unintentionally made.

Time went by and at the start of one week in the Spring it was told to me that there was an evangelist speaking in Huddersfield that week. I didn't know, but did check it out and found that this was so and that several of the members of the fellowship were attending - the venue was the local YMCA. He was only there for around three nights, but I was not able to find out any more information and so decided I would go and have a look for myself and did so the following night - there was a good turnout, probably between 100 and 150 people. When he eventually 'made his entry', he was dressed in a very colourful way: brightly coloured suit with a sheen to it and a somewhat expensive-looking cape of a satin-type material (which he took off as though 'Batman has arrived'!) and his whole style was outlandish and flamboyant. He was totally surrounded by females in his team - not a male in sight - and one of the females seemed to be in charge of the others. He had a charisma that matched his looks and he generally had the people exactly where he wanted them. He preached the Gospel - that I could not deny – and, of course, there was the very proverbial, very powerful appeal for money and many eagerly gave. On the one hand I thought, 'live and let live', and on the other I got a check in my spirit … something was not right, but what was it? I said to myself that if I still felt uneasy about this in a few hours' time I would come back on the last night. This happened and so I did and carefully watched the proceedings again, this time making myself known to one of his entourage, and I had a brief word with him. His name was Cecil Gilbert. He was South African and had a base at that time in Sheffield. "Come down and visit us in Sheffield," he said. "Okay," and we set it up for a few days ahead on a Friday. I made my arrangements to go by train. Late on the Thursday evening before I was due to go, the phone rang and it was one of the females on his team. "Cecil Gilbert has been urgently called over to South Africa so tomorrow's meeting is cancelled. Goodbye." "Okay then, goodbye." I had no further contact. "There is nothing else I can do and I'm too busy anyway," I said to my wife. "Well, that's the end of that!"

Not so! A week or two had gone by and I discovered that one of the young adult ladies in the Fellowship had gone down to see Cecil Gilbert in Sheffield and had stayed at least one night. It was her parents who were concerned and so was I, but she would not share or answer any of the questions I gently put to her - in fact, she was quite 'down' and withdrawn. Well, I knew she struggled at times in her relationship and walk with the Lord, but there is more!! Fast forward, and years have rolled by - possibly some time in the later 'eighties. I was in a newsagent shop somewhere and just happened to glance at the front page headlines of the national newspapers and there it was, on the front page of the Daily Express, loud and clear … I was aghast! Cecil Gilbert found guilty and gets (I think it was) 12 or 14 years in prison. He had committed terrible sexual crimes that involved drugging his victims. I do not deny, of course, that he paid his debt to society. So I had been on the right track all those years ago, but what a shame that I had not been able to obtain any evidence or that that young lady had not spoken out, for she must have suffered. Again, several years later, on a visit to Huddersfield, I was told that the lady concerned had died - I think it was cancer - and would guess that she had only been in her late thirties, leaving young children, which made it even more sad.

The Way I See It

In the summer of 1978, I had three consecutive weeks as summer holiday in order to give myself an opportunity to really unwind and take stock! I had done my best to serve the Lord and He gave me that holiday, which I've never forgotten! I went to the Dales Bible Week near Harrogate for three days and nights - sleeping on the back seat of someone's single-decker bus (with permission, I hasten to add!); surely that was the year Bob Mumford spoke, along with others - excellent meetings with thousands attending them - as there was a real move of God. Mumford's humour was brill!

On the Saturday I met up with my wife, daughter and Mitzi, the dog, and we went with John and Sheila Thomlinson and Bill and Betty Thompson to the holiday bungalow, right next to the sea at Silloth on the Solway Firth, owned by the latter. They had friends and relatives who came out for all or part of that week (and some of that group later formed into the Carlisle Christian Fellowship, which grew quite strong in itself. John and Sheila were very gifted as pastors, having pastors' hearts). The friendship, fellowship, fun, laughter, prayer times, meetings that were powerful and informal, the singing and the way everyone willingly helped with the practicalities of the food and cleaning and whatever made it a very special time. I spoke at one of the evening meetings. It was a beautiful spot (I had been before in the early 'fifties, as the holiday bungalow had been owned by Cyril Proudfoot, mentioned earlier in the book) and it took all of about 40 seconds to get to the water's edge. The air is so fresh at Silloth, the weather was lovely that week, the views over to Bonnie Scotland were spectacular and, of course, Silloth, with its cobbled main front street, had, and has, not changed much since Victorian times. I really enjoyed the walks into Silloth itself, along the front with my family and Mitzi. It was one of those precious moments in life as a whole that you can only keep in your heart, but as they happen they are untouchable and it was such a simple holiday! (Obviously, we had to pay our way for the essentials.) Selfishness, greed, money and the stupidities of life were simply not there - the love of the Lord Jesus was wonderfully in our midst. I needed that time for what was just ahead!

As that year had gone on it was, as it were, 'behind the scenes' that things got steadily worse, then almost unbearable. It was the issue of the Baptism of the Holy Spirit again; that is, the power of God, in or not in, your experience and doctrine. This battle, as I've mentioned before, still rages today, though sometimes subtly, in various places; quite simply, it will not go away. I had still not preached or taught on the subject, kept a unity and thought that that would be enough. My push was, let's get on with the work through teamwork on what we do agree on. But it was at the monthly leadership (diaconate) meetings where I started to have serious problems. There were … ? … five or six of us each time to discuss what we would bring to the next fellowship membership business meeting, and any problems. But an element, a married couple, who had exercised a leadership gifting within the fellowship prior to my call to the pastorate, who were intelligent, with status in society, had their doctrine based or rooted on that similar to the 'Brethren-Baptist movement'. I thought they would leave any issues about me alone as time went by; after all, there was a lot of evangelism and other good things going on that were bearing fruit and which would yet bear more fruit, even in another 'season', and, as already mentioned, it was teamwork and all on a voluntary basis. Freedom and fun was what I wanted as the backdrop to some serious work. It was not my desire to be drawn into 'sides' and 'contentions', especially if they thought I had not been 'up-front' enough. I felt that I had been and my conscience was clear. I refused and resisted being drawn into discussions as to where I stood and my experience of the relevant part of Acts chapter 2 - how could I have been drawn on this, as I would be in trouble the moment I would have done so?

There are certain instances in scripture where the younger had to respect the older to keep favour with Father God - David with Saul was one of these times - so I would not say anything against this other leader in a wrong or abusive way, though I would and was entitled to respectfully have, or choose not to have, my say as I felt it right to do so. It sounds crazy, but our personalities and leadership giftings complemented each other. In fact, all of us in the diaconate had genuine leadership giftings. I might be wrong, but there were only about five in the whole fellowship who adamantly believed that at the point of genuine conversion to Christ you received everything from Heaven then and there to enable you to walk the walk and so mature. As I've clearly stated above, that was not only not my experience but, even before September 1973, I was open and believed for more of His power and love and whatever, ongoing from Heaven. So, as stated, I've gone on to have many experiences in God's Holy Spirit, even to the point of being 'drunk'. Now, we are individually sealed with His Spirit inside of each one of us, like a down payment at the first point of salvation. No-one has the right to tell you of your experience - you will tell others. It is the same with Acts chapter 2's further baptism(s) when the Spirit of God comes upon you, fills you full and overflows from you. You can't rationalise the mechanics of this! The Lord does or doesn't do this at His pleasure, though it helps to wait upon Him and ask Him.

So where does this leave the doctrine of the Brethren and others? They said that some of the things and giftings did happen but stopped after the first twelve apostles; so this, then, in my opinion, stopped them from looking for anything further from the Lord. I know there are counterfeits out there as well, so we have to be on our guard, but the Bible says if I genuinely ask, as His child, for His anointing and blessing, that is what He will give me and not something evil - how we need discernment! Where then does this leave the viewpoint of those who say they have received an anointing and tongues, etc? If those who have known me say I am suspect in some aspects of my fellowship and my ministry and they have no real case against me, then that is both sad and serious. Enough to say, there are two extremely dangerous things that we can do in our lives: knowingly misrepresent the Lord ... and call good evil. I was now under some stress and this made life more difficult, e.g. for a time I started suffering from mouth ulcers. A few weeks after my summer holidays, at a diaconate meeting, another one that went on far too late, the husband of the above-mentioned couple suddenly blurted out that he had written about me and the way he perceived the situation within the fellowship, complaining to Geoffrey Grogan, who was still the Principal of the BTI! "What? ... of your own accord?" I asked. "Yes," he replied. The whole meeting went deadly silent! ... and the minutes ticked away for some time! That is exactly what, as a Baptist, and according to their rules, you did not do, as everything had to be (collectively) agreed on and upfront at every meeting. It was serious and I was in a state of shock. I eventually spoke ... "You had no authority and why did you not just simply go off to another Baptist Church in the area?" Without waiting for an answer, I called a halt to the meeting and said, "We need to pray and seek the Lord further", and we dispersed.

I now felt that my only option was for me to go for a vote of confidence and, as from the Lord, abide by the result. Now this procedure is laid down in the Baptist Union rules as an option if things are not going well, to establish clear leadership or to resign. The rules said that the result of a vote must be 66% or above to be carried. Because I had gone there on a completely unanimous (100%) vote (one man who had declined to vote only did so as he had wanted a private vote rather than a show of hands, but he had told me later that he was absolutely in favour of my going there), I decided I would make it exactly 75% or above rather than the 66%. As the time for the vote approached, towards the end of the year, I still did not say why it was happening, so as still not to be divisive, but that it was to do with the general direction in which I wanted to take the fellowship.

On the night of the church business meeting when we took the vote - there was a handful 'against' and everyone else was 'for'. When someone worked out the exact percentage, it was a fraction over 74%. Some said, "That's near enough, you can stay on!" "No, I didn't make it," I deliberately and sadly stated, "though the Lord was very gracious." Psalm 15 in the NIV says clearly we must honour our word, even when it hurts. The place went up in an uproar with cries of "Oh no!" and weeping and wailing. The pain and emotion of that moment lived in my heart for some time to come. I stated, "I will take my nine months' notice as of today, but I may choose to leave earlier."

As time from that night started to go by, I found myself in a wilderness experience, a no man's land, not a nice place to be. As I viewed that time from later years, I realised I had actually started on the grieving process path. One or two started to leave the fellowship immediately and I groaned within myself; but, of course, they were free to go to whichever fellowship they wanted to go. If the shepherd is in trouble, it's not exactly good news for the sheep! The fellowship could not now lean towards anything of the so-called 'charismatic' or 'Pentecostal' movements of those days. In my opinion, they could only move to something more 'dry' or 'staid' or 'legalistic'. Only a few days had gone by when I received a really nice and fair letter from Geoffrey Grogan, still Principal of BTI, explaining how he had been drawn in towards what was happening and he vindicated me and my character as he had known and observed me. After all, if it had taken around six months to give someone the post of a pastor in a fellowship, would you not think that someone with one of the highest qualifications possible in the land, namely a PhD, could thoroughly check you out to their own satisfaction? That letter gave me much-needed encouragement.

I thought to myself, "Get Christmas over with, it's a busy time anyway". But what were my options, what could I now do and what was the Lord doing in my life? - the latter being the most important, as His ways are not always our ways or what we might want or expect. I entertained the idea of starting up an independent fellowship in Huddersfield - start in a house, then hire somewhere suitable for Sunday, etc, meetings. Even a small independent fellowship that would be sold out for all that the Lord had to give, real, meaningful and in agreement, would be potentially very powerful.

I thought I would go and have a look in the Bradford Church House Fellowship in the centre of Bradford and this I did one Sunday morning. It was quite lively and the music/singing was good. It looked like a wealthy, somewhat middle-class fellowship and that didn't surprise me. I guessed the numbers were about 350 strong. I was invited to a Ministers' Fraternal Meeting one week day, so I went to have a look as there were a lot of good and bad rumours floating around about them. I reckoned there were about thirty male leaders present from quite a wide geographical area; a tasty light lunch was laid on, and there seemed to be a good level of maturity, as might be expected. Bryn Jones, the leader of the Bradford House Church Movement, was temporarily involved in a fellowship at that time in the USA and Kerri Jones was in charge. Arthur Wallace spoke and took the meeting that morning and, of course, he was well known through his books and ministry and was also friends with Derek Prince who, as mentioned, was one of the so-called 'Florida Five'. Arthur Wallace with his wife did, a few months later, move up from the south of England for a while and joined the Bradford Fellowship.

Why have meetings like that anyway? Were they looking to be more accepted in the wider church or did they want to influence that same wider church? Maybe it was a bit of both. As they became very strong and wealthy - maybe it didn't matter much to them anyway. Some were very sympathetic towards my situation and I made one or two contacts that day - one of them being an Assemblies of God Pentecostal Pastor in the Manchester area. He said he was available to talk with me any time and just to make contact with him and go and see him in Manchester for a few hours if I wanted to do so.

Several weeks later, I did so and, as we talked, he strongly advised me to leave Huddersfield altogether. I was carefully considering what he said 'before the Lord'. I had further contact with two of the Bradford leaders - there were several - and they offered to take me in, but not for work or ministry as such; after all, they already had a few men they had taken in from different denominations and one or two had aspired to House Group Leaders, as far as I could ascertain, and some they had brought into the top leadership - so they had no shortage of 'leaders' or potential leaders and, of course, they were in a place for having their own 'home-grown leaders', young men who generally, being younger, were soaked in that fellowship and its ways.

By now I could only think of one step at a time and what was the next step to be? When I had a talk with the Baptist Area Superintendent, he said he might be able to offer me one or two fellowships further up north in the north-east area of England, but they would only be part-time in payment; but I thought 'availability' could therefore be a problem because of having to find other work. On the same lines, he said that the Baptist fellowships in Huddersfield would employ me as their 'Area Evangelist' and I was quite surprised at the offer - I took it as a compliment and it led me to consider, as time went by, was my predominant gift that of the 'pastoral' or was it more towards 'evangelism', though I had always thought it was more pastoral with an overlap of the two, of course. Would I one day change my mind?

My daughter would be ready to leave school in the summer of 1979 - she had no desire to stay on and she wanted to be a hairdresser, so a move on her part would not matter too much. The problem was, my wife was still not well and was not responding to prayer and though in some discomfort she did not complain. On one occasion I accompanied her to see our GP and he had checked her out, though he was not saying much - we were just about to go out of the surgery door and as she turned to say goodbye he exclaimed, "Get back in here! How did I miss this one? Your eyes show you've got a thyroid problem." This was quickly affirmed as a major problem (along with ulcerated colitis) and she was soon waiting for an operation in the Huddersfield Royal Infirmary.

Whatever would happen to me, whatever my ministry was to be in the future, whatever the attacks of the enemy to knock me out (lies and death are the only thing he can deal in) ... one thing I knew was that I could not go through the likes of the last three or so months again - I would have to withdraw, regroup as it were and, always as a survivor against the odds, return to the front-line fight against evil later - I know I am always learning here on Earth, but will never compromise on that gained ground of the truth that I know I've found and won in the fullness of the Lord Jesus Christ. I held no anger, bitterness, hatred or unforgiveness ... there was no 'heavy shepherding' or manipulation, but oh, what a missed opportunity sacrificed on the altar of churchianity limiting God's awesome power, name and who He really is. There are differing times, situations and seasons in our lives that come and go, and it is good to understand them. There are people likewise who enter our lives for however long in time and then they are gone … I had decided to go and join with the Bradford Church House Fellowship! This was definitely going to be a difficult and valuable learning curve, the likes of which hopefully helps one to grow into further maturity. They found me a suitable and pleasant small bungalow to rent in Eccleshill, Bradford. This was in the early Spring of 1979. They came with a large hired van and with around 18 men(!!) and moved my furniture/belongings over.

I left quietly with no fuss. As I handed back my church keys and said goodbye to the one who had not been happy with my standing in the Messiah, we shook hands and a couple of tears rolled down his face … it was so, so strange …

# 13
# *A Difficult Learning Curve*

It took only 24 hours and I was completely settled into the new home - everything put away, etc - time-wise for me it was a record!!

It was a year or two later that I learned that a lot of my friends were earnestly praying that I would come out of the Bradford Fellowship at the time of my going in! How would the Lord answer all the differing prayers that were going up to Him from the various believers? Well, dead easy in hindsight! He would keep me in for only a few years whilst showing me more lessons of this life; yet for me it was three gradual steps downwards in each of three house moves that would eventually lead to my withdrawing. Years later I (and no doubt others) would pray for some of my friends in that fellowship to withdraw too ... and the Lord did answer those prayers.

Things would start off well and then go against me - very peculiar, to say the least. I thought I could only learn from them in that fellowship as a whole and had nothing to give - that was wrong of me. I didn't put them on a pedestal, but realised that the Lord in some ways was with them, e.g. the music and worship, the manifestation of the 1st Corinthians chapter 12 spiritual gifts. The fellowship could be very generous in their giving, yet this hierarchical structure - for that is what it was - was top heavy and not perfect as it first seemed to be. A nurse friend of ours came down from Glasgow to visit and find out what was happening regarding the whole Huddersfield/Bradford move and she simply stated, "Henry, it is as if you have lost a baby", which said it all. For a while I was still geared up for the work of serving and ministry, but there was no outlet and the process of 'winding down' just slowly happened. At the first Sunday morning after the move, they had my family and I up on the platform to be introduced, but my wife would say nothing. It was a shame, they said, as they wanted to hear her Geordie/Newcastle voice over the loudspeaker! I only spoke for a minute or so as I was taken by surprise, as I hadn't really thought about saying anything at all.

As I was musing on those four years or so in that fellowship, and in spite of all my training and work for the Lord, I realised that that Sunday morning was about the sum total of my ministry as part of the fellowship, though there were some odds and ends of ministry in the house groups. My organising and open-air evangelistic giftings were never used. At last I got to relax with some prime family time. They had taken me in, but I soon felt as if I was left high and dry. I could find no way as an outlet for my serving gifts, as I definitely would not put myself forward just for the sake of it. They agreed that the gifts and calling of God are given without repentance from the Lord, but that some had to lay them down within the fellowship as required. Perhaps I should have realised straight away and not joined in membership. I did realise at some point that the conditions for the rank and file members were introverted, inward looking to the 'system' and the 'cause' of the fellowship without deviation (red warning light time! … this is dangerous!) - that was definitely not me as an extrovert, a people person and socially looking at and mixing with other fellowships and believers, and I've never changed on this one. If I'd realised this at the beginning, I would have left immediately. Although the writing was on the wall, I did not perceive it and tried to persevere, go forward and not retreat.

They had said, "You need to get a job and a house with a mortgage, and to become a member you must go through our commitment class of several weekly sessions." I thought to myself, "What do you want me to do that for? Just tell me your doctrine and church government in four or five minutes and I'll tell you if I agree or not"; but I actually asked, "What is the point of that?" "So that you can say publicly that you will be obedient to the leadership," was the reply. I had no choice if I wanted to continue, so I agreed, and they said I could, with my family, attend the Eccleshill House Group in a home very close to where we now lived.

Any desire to see an effective house or home group previously withheld was now given as from the Lord. In fact, I'd say that never before or since have I ever experienced another house group that equalled that one. The leader, who was an elder in the Bradford Fellowship and had formerly been part of the Elim Pentecostal denomination, was called Chris McDermott. The group varied between about 14 and 16 in number and had a healthy mixture of ages, singles, couples, one-parent family, differing social levels and so on, but they really had gelled together with acceptance, openness, respect, good sharing, caring, fellowship, love for the Lord, etc. The meetings were so good that my wife and I could hardly wait for house group night. I had been allowed to see the reality of it - that was exactly the way it should happen, with the right sense of belonging, giving and receiving. I was not happy when they said things like, "Bring your wallpaper scrapers with you next week, because we're going to so and so's house to scrape walls" or "Next week we are going to the main building in Bradford's North Parade, as this house group is on toilet, etc, cleaning duties." "Really!?" I kicked up a fuss: "I'm not interested, can't they afford to employ a cleaner? … It's all a bit military!" But it was, "You're going!" … and so we did! That house group did tolerate some freedom of speech; it didn't get me very far, but at least it was a step in the right direction.

So I went through the commitment class and there was nothing new in it for me. When it came to money, they said, "You must tithe" - that is, give 10% of your salary to the fellowship - "and there will be offerings over and above that." When I said that there was no command to the church to tithe after the Cross, and certainly not in Hebrews, I was told in no uncertain terms in the class itself that in *this fellowship you must agree to tithe*. I decided to continue in the fellowship, so after the course finished at the next Sunday meeting, all those on the course who agreed to make a commitment had to stand up on the platform together and repeat aloud given words, stating their allegiance to the fellowship and their obedience to the leadership. As soon as I had done this, I started to get a check in my spirit. "It must be me" … everybody else seemed to be okay and, after all this, agreement should bring unity and that would bring strength. It took a while for me to put it into words, but it was that we trust the Lord not man and we must never, ever, absolutely not, give man, no matter who he or she is, that 'blank cheque of obedience' for the future, as it were. They or any other leadership have no right to ask … and we have no right to give … total allegiance - it is only to our Father God that we give any 'blank cheque of obedience'; but in my experience, if things are normal, He would rarely 'pull rank' as it were, for we who are His sons and daughters are in a partnership by an intimate sharing and in agreement with Heaven of the heart's love … and His way is never with a big stick or in the dark. "Obey your leaders" is for a right unity and agreement for a purpose and never that they should lord it or take the place of God over you. I was slow to face the reality that this 'mighty' fellowship had a cultish side and influence to it. The issue was not 'salvation', but how much authority and power (to say nothing of greed) of leadership and others could rightly be exercised amongst believers and still leave room for sensible free speech, notwithstanding the place to deal with trouble-makers or leadership that has gone astray.

Some of the things I've now seen on my Christian walk regarding 'control' by leadership have been frightening, to say the least. The Lord will not tolerate this 'spirit of witchcraft' found in His church … I'll come back to this later on. Because of the Brethren denominational influence (though at some point that did soon stop), the women had to wear 'head coverings' and my wife and daughter were not exactly over the moon about it - legalism … yes… but they both suited hats!

I got some admin. agency work to start earning some pennies and this led to quite a good temporary admin. job, but I just couldn't fit into it, so left after a few months. A month or two later, I started in admin. with British Rail and this was more my scene.

Other members of the fellowship were hospitable and could be very generous, which we were all encouraged to be. I had visits from some members of a house group from the other side of Bradford who would visit us to share and pray and they would bring gifts of things like towels. One day a couple visited and as they left to go home they gave me a substantial financial gift (of £1,000... this was 1979 and a pound was a pound!) - I was amazed, as I didn't know them, but was very grateful and our friendship lasted several years into the 'nineties before losing contact. This would have been enough to buy a decent second-hand car or perhaps to help me to get onto the mortgage house-buying ladder. I kept as much of it as I could for the possibility of the latter.

My wife's health though was still a major problem. She went back in the summer of 1979 to Huddersfield Infirmary and had the thyroid gland operation because it was 'overactive'. It was a total success and even the scar was minimal and very neat in its looks, but I was puzzled as to why she had not been healed directly from the Lord. As the months rolled by, her 'colitis' got worse as it became ulcerated and a loss of blood meant that she had to have blood transfusions - and even with 'PMT', she rarely complained, but I always knew when she was poorly and would do my best to help her around the home, etc. Someone in the fellowship was into homeopathic medicine and, without looking into it deeply enough, I gave my agreement with consent, but as it was administered I felt very uneasy and so did my wife. We both felt it was suspect or at least that there was no Biblical warrant for it. She stopped and I repented with apologies to her and to the Lord. Help, was I losing it? I loved the Lord Jesus and I was a man of His Word, though I hope that that was always in loving kindness.

I was beginning to ask questions and would stop at nothing until I got satisfactory answers, though some of these answers would take years to transpire. I started to think that I had been duped over the issue of the demonic and the deliverance ministry/spiritual warfare by nearly all of the church, wherever found. Trevor Dearing, Derek Prince and Don Basham all had powerful deliverance ministries, along with those in days gone by such as Smith Wigglesworth. I had taken on board Selwyn Hughes' doctrine on this issue without asking the right questions and that was a mistake. He believed no true Christian could be demonised. The Anglicans, Brethren, Baptists, Bradford Church House, in fact none of the major denominations were teaching or practising deliverance ministry as such or understood it. If it held a key to freedom from oppression and then on to healing, then why not? Years later, Ellel Ministries would be into deliverance, as would the revival in Toronto. As the years would go by, the Lord would give me understanding on the deliverance ministry, which is part of spiritual warfare - enough for me anyway, in my life, to change my doctrine completely and to have a working knowledge of the same. But my wife was not being miraculously healed at that time.

After my daughter left school, she was chosen for a hairdressing apprenticeship out of eighty applicants by a lady who had moved her business from her home to a small salon on a main road not too far away from our home. Along with the owner, there was only my daughter at sixteen years old with absolutely no experience of hairdressing. By the end of the first week, she had the keys to the shop, was expected to mix 'whatever' for perms, wash ladies' hair without giving them a bath! ... and so on. She totally lost her confidence and would not go back and, although I really tried, I was unable to sort it out between the two of them. The owner should have employed a proper qualified assistant and not a raw apprentice. I tried everything to get my daughter into the Bradford Hairdressing College, but she would not agree to go. Several would say in later years that she has a natural talent, a real hairdressing gift. She went to work in a factory, and that was the once famous Bradford Lister Mill. I wondered about some of the company she mixed with, but I could not live her life for her - I was always available to share and she was very close to her Mum.

After about a year in the Eccleshill House Group, the Bradford leadership suddenly rearranged it, along with other home groups. There was no real choice as such and it was devastating, as the group had bonded into a real spiritual family. At the same time, the landlady of the bungalow I was renting wanted it back, which meant I had to find somewhere else to live with real urgency. Oh what fun it is to ride on a ...!

I thought, "I will obey the leadership"; but still, on a low basic wage, how could I do so? It is strange to think of it now but I got a council mortgage on a small Victorian 'back-to-back' terraced property with real character in Wyke, Bradford - it was between Huddersfield and Bradford. It had a lounge, very small kitchen, two small bedrooms, bathroom and on the second floor an attic room - the cost was around £3,500. I was able to borrow some extra money on it in order to do some further important modernisation work. The trouble was, it was nine miles and two buses into and out of the centre of Bradford to get to my work and I worked shifts. I had been obedient and got on the housing ladder, but it was in the wrong place work-wise and difficult without a car. It was several hundred yards from home to get to the nearest bus stop on the main road. The prices of property were rocketing up at that time. I had made things difficult for myself because of the travel costs and time involved in getting to and from work – ideally, I should have been in the Shipley/Bingley area, but properties were a lot more expensive to buy or rent there. Also, I was really limited in what I could do as regards house group, only attending whenever I could. At times I couldn't risk a late night when I had to be up at 4am for early shift.

Somewhere around the very end of 1980, my wife came to me and said very quietly, "The Lord has told me He has not closed my womb!?" ... Should I be in shock or not?! ... "Okay, I'll have to wait on the Lord," was the gist of my reply. My daughter was now seventeen years old and all but grown up. Apart from my wife's bad health, we were tasting real freedom as a couple. I knew that if my wife claimed to have heard from the Lord, she would have done so. As I sought the Lord, it came to me that I was to have a son and I was given the name to call him. A few weeks later, when in the doctor's surgery with my wife, he confirmed that she was by then already pregnant and I nearly fell off the edge of the chair in surprise, as I thought we could still have been wrong and I was thinking of the responsibility of another child! Then I said to the Lord in my heart, " If You want me to have a son, then I want to have a son. Thank You for the gift." From that moment onwards, I had received the 1 Corinthians chapter 12 gift of faith and from then on was immoveable in my faith and trust in the Lord over this issue.

At that time my wife and I had discussed the sickness that she had and, instead of faith for the Lord to heal her, discussed the possibilities of major surgery, possibly an ileostomy as the most extreme. We were getting on for nearly twenty years of marriage. I said to her, "You must choose, you know what you can take in suffering, etc, so I will abide by whatever you decide." She replied slowly that she didn't want that operation, so would just quietly die unless the Lord did something to intervene. She was lovingly submitting to the Lord. "Fair enough, I will stand with you," I replied. We may as well have been discussing if the moon was made of cheese, as I did not really take it in!

What I did take in was that as the months started to go by into 1981 I did not have enough money to live on and could not easily make ends meet. "So what?" you might say. "Ah, well," I would have answered, "I had to give 10% of my income, legalistically, plus offerings, to the Bradford Fellowship and this now upset me." "Why the upset?" you might ask. I would have replied, "My wife could not get the right food or the vitamins that she needed because of the cost." I did a little overtime whenever possible and I knew that every penny I earned should have been ploughed totally into the home for basic living, so I took my plight to the hierarchy of the fellowship in Bradford and they allocated a man called Martin Dunsford to deal with me. Now Martin and I got on quite well. We had one or two discussions over doctrine: it was deep stuff and fun, a bit like being back at Bible College, but he gave no hint that he would allow me to stop tithing (the 10% giving of your income). He said he would send someone up to my house to look at my home accounts. "Feel free," I said. Even when I explained had they no real grasp of my situation?! Was everything so strict there was no leeway for compassion in this very wealthy fellowship? I was angry because of what my wife was suffering. Did they really think that I was the village idiot and unable to manage my own finances?!

A man came up from the fellowship one evening who, as far as I knew, worked in a tax office and he knew his stuff. He was obviously an executive … After he looked through everything, he simply said, "I can find nothing wrong with the way you have handled your finances, but there is one thing you could claim for as regards work - a tax rebate" - which I did and I think I got £12 back - worth having in those days. Several days later, Martin Dunsford made a very brief visit to my home, laid hands on and prayed over me, a powerful and authoritative prayer for the Lord to sort things out. Okay, the Lord heard that prayer, but the only trouble was it would be answered *later*, in *His* time! Bradford Church Fellowship never even temporarily let me off the hook re tithing during my wife's pregnancy and this astounded me. I came so close to leaving the fellowship, a cut-and-run job back to sanity. The whole fellowship was still growing fast in numbers, bringing its own set of problems to the leadership, no doubt. The worship and praise in the big meetings continued to be excellent. During the time I was in the fellowship they were responsible for the Dales Bible Camp Week each year in the summer holiday at the Harrogate Showground.

Some friends from Huddersfield were with me on Camp Week in 1979 and I visited for one or two days only on the next two years. There were people who said they were healed on at least one occasion as the Lord moved supernaturally in power - one lady sitting next to me in a meeting suddenly said, "I've just been healed!" It happened in an instant and she was totally surprised, as she had had a heart problem. But what I remember most from one of those years was in a morning meeting with about 8,000 people present and Bryn Jones leading. All of a sudden, everything went completely quiet, then ever so faintly and seemingly from the far end of the long building came a sound like that of the drone of bees and this captivating harmonious hum slowly got louder and louder. Suddenly everyone, including myself, erupted simultaneously into high praise, lovely worship and 'singing in the spirit' to our Heavenly Father and this lasted several minutes. It was an awesome sign and wonder to participate in. Bryn Jones at the evening meeting of that day said that everyone thought it started away from them at another part of the building. All the people I spoke to agreed it was some of the Angels from Heaven that we heard and we were allowed to join in with them!

The fellowship needed workers for the various things they were doing, but I obviously could not get involved, so my worth to the fellowship diminished accordingly because of their 'work' and 'giving' ethics. It felt to me as if I was simply hidden within the fellowship!

On 2nd July 1981 my very pregnant-looking wife went for a bus into Bradford for a hospital appointment. She ran the last few yards to catch a bus that was at the bus stop and she tripped and fell on the pavement. She was badly shaken, but managed to continue on to her destination. I was at work in Bingley. Later in the day, she explained to me what happened. She had held her own, but it was not good. Baby in the womb was seven months old. Late that night in bed, we thought she had wet the bed; but then, of course, suddenly realised the 'waters' had broken. It seemed serious, yet we decided to do nothing there and then but to get some rest. I said I would still go to work for the early shift as there was no-one to inform through the night, so that someone could stand in for me. I said she must call the doctor and St Luke's Hospital and an ambulance if need be to be checked out in the morning. The only trouble was that we had friends, Neil and Lesley Morrison, on a rare visit from Glasgow, coming to spend the afternoon with us. She was a school teacher and he had a Christian Counselling Centre in central Glasgow. They later had quite a large fellowship in Kirkintilloch and as far as I know they eventually ended up in pastoral leadership in the USA.

I received a phone call later that morning from my wife, who was by then in hospital and they said the baby was in distress and totally unplaced for normal birth. It was serious and would I give my permission for a Caesarean section? "Absolutely, it goes without saying," and she agreed too. It would have to be done fairly soon, of course. My wife said she had asked our daughter to stay off work to sort out lunch for our guests. I said I would go home first, but get down to the hospital as soon as I could, as they had a car. She said to make sure they had some food. My work colleagues were good as they almost threw me out of the booking office well before the end of my shift to go and sort things out. We had lunch and fellowship, fun and laughter and I felt guilty - surely this was not allowed! But I realised immediately that this was from the Lord in order to help and relax me that day and take my mind off the crisis, as I wouldn't have been allowed to see my wife while she was being prepared for her op. Neil took me to the hospital and we were in a waiting room while my wife was in theatre, around 6.30pm. A nurse put her head round the door and said to me, "Don't worry, you will soon know whether you have a boy or a girl!" "I'm in faith," I stated, "and I'm having a son who will be called ... but I need to know how my wife is." She looked at me somewhat strangely and was gone. I knew if the Lord really promises you something then that something is what you will really have! When the nurse came back, she said, "You have a son and I can let you see your wife and son separately for a few moments each." My wife looked drained and weak - I did my best to reassure and encourage her, but don't know if I did a very good job. Then I went to see my son in an incubator in a special room/ward with a Sister in charge. He was a little over 4lbs and so small at seven months, but looked a bundle of joy! He would have to stay in the incubator until his weight increased to 6lbs and that took about a month. He had jaundice and one or two upsets but, of course, he survived. Years later, my father would briefly see him once, or was it twice, and only observed him, but nicknamed him 'Smiler'. I visited him nearly every day of that month to have a little time of nursing and feeding him and, of course, to pray good things over him. My daughter was only allowed to look through a window to see him during those few weeks, so was a bit 'dis-chuffed' but very patient until he came home.

My wife was in hospital slightly less than two weeks until she regained her strength, but was still not a well person. My daughter agreed to give up work for however long it would take to look after her Mum and baby brother and help in the house. It was a sacrifice and really good of her ... and I did wonder if she enjoyed a break from work! I was grateful to Neil and Lesley, not only for their help the day of the birth, but also for their prayers and encouragement. Someone in the house group we now attended showed their kindness and generosity. Did I want a washing machine that would fit into the very small kitchen? I would not turn that one down ... definitely not ... does a cat drink milk?! I was told to be at home the following Tuesday morning. A brand new Philips Slimline top-loading washing machine was delivered - it was a superb machine and got those Terry nappies really clean! … a real boon, for which I was extremely grateful.

Later in the year, when a health visitor came to see my wife and son, I was in the house that afternoon too - all routine stuff. We ended up talking about my wife's illness and the thoughts she had about an ileostomy op., and she did not stop talking and sharing until my wife was persuaded that she would have the operation. I was included in the conversation and thought it was an interesting development. As I am definitely not a 'medic', I wondered how I would cope from my point of view as time went by. "Well, 'tough' I'll just have to get on with it," I said.

In the November of that year, she went to the Bradford Royal Infirmary for some important tests. The consultant was dismayed, as my wife had still not complained, but was in such a terrible mess inside that she could not possibly live very long. She agreed to the op. and he allowed us Christmas, then later in January of 1982 he called her in for that major surgery - a few days of preparation, then she would be in for a month afterwards. She needed a miracle now, but where was our faith, or what were we really in faith for? I started asking a lot of people all over, to pray.

The time came and during my wife's time in hospital I took approximately three weeks off work to help my daughter at home and look after the little lad and to cope with all the emotional/mental stress of what was happening and the church fellowship kindly offered me the use of their minibus for most of those weeks.

The day my wife went into hospital I can remember observing her some yards away in the ward as they started the preparation procedures and for a moment I felt as if I was detached from the situation. A nurse wanted to talk with me in regard to what would happen to my wife and what it would be like for me and so on. At the house group meeting a week or so earlier, someone gave a 'prophetic word' as from the Lord, saying that He would be 'behind the surgeon's knife'. If there was not to be some miracle healing, then I would 'buy' that one - and received it - it meant she would get through. The op. was to last several hours, but the problem was: would all the work be completed in one go? - because, if not, she would have to return for more of the same. I earnestly prayed that this would not be necessary. So my wife had the op., with everything that had to be done completed in one go - it was totally successful and later a nurse said to her that she had never before seen such a neat job done on this type of operation. When I first saw my wife, she was in much pain and discomfort and very weak. I would say she was wondering if she had done the right thing. I gave her all the encouragement, reassurance and praise that I could. It took some months, but she did bounce back and learned to cope with 'the bag' she now had on her abdomen area. Sometimes she struggled at the beginning to sort things out with it and get into a routine - apart from one or two mishaps, she coped okay. She was still spiritually and mentally the same wife of twenty years of marriage. We made some minor adjustments and simply got on with the rest of our lives.

About four months after the operation, when my wife was getting back to normal with a new lease of life, it was answer to prayer time and the time of a miracle. At work I had made a case to get promotion, as I had helped management out over the training of staff and this was granted and even backdated! Not only was this now a living wage, but, because properties had risen in price and were selling well, I realised I could make about double on the sale of my property - in fact, I sold it within hours of putting it on the market. I would have to pay some money back to the council out of the profit, and that was rightly so.

I moved as fast as I could to look at properties in Bingley within approximately five minutes' walk from where I worked. I was going to view a house in Binns Street, Bingley, one day after work and can remember The Missus saying, "If you like it just buy it". I did so there and then and started the ball rolling to buy it that day! A few days later she did have a look, of course. It was in a cul-de-sac in a lovely quiet spot and had four bedrooms, two of which were spacious attic dormer rooms. It needed some work doing to it and other work I wanted to do, plus I borrowed some money to fit gas central heating throughout and double-glaze one window! Although the house needed a lot of decoration, etc, it was reasonably priced. Part of the kitchen ceiling fell in, causing further work - but once I got it sorted, apart from some of the decoration, it was a superb property with a lovely atmosphere, kind neighbours, a good investment and a happy home. We moved in during midsummer of 1982 and life was much easier living so close to my work.

You might think that should be that, having been obedient to the church leadership, I still had a wife, a daughter, now a son, Mitzi the dog, a nice house, a good job - and by the Grace of God, had, as usual, landed on my feet - so could it be that should be that - 'live happily ever after, goodnight and goodbye!!?' ... well ... not exactly so ... lots more fun was just starting!

The Bradford Church House Fellowship had grown so big that the Keighley/Bingley side was starting to have its own Sunday meetings, etc, in its own right with its own leaders. Sometimes the whole of the fellowship for the Bradford area would meet at St George's Hall in the centre of Bradford and there were some quite good meetings. With working shifts and not having a car, my attendance at various meetings was definitely limited. I made the mistake of asking for help to get a cooker plumbed in at the time of moving into the Bingley house, but as it was leading up to the annual 'Dales Bible Week' and peak holiday time, was told a definite 'No', as no-one was available. Perhaps I was supposed to be giving as a helper and not taking, but I had a need which I did eventually sort out, but was not off to a good start and the bad feeling continued well into 1983 and on into the rest of my time in that fellowship. I was sharing with my 'middle' brother, who lived in Carlisle, about the issue of 'tithing' and 'giving' to the church and he asked me if I had heard of Roger Price and I said I hadn't, so he borrowed and sent me the relevant audio tapes by Roger Price on the doctrine of tithing and I listened to them - they were well used - but the truth he gave of balanced sound doctrine, with revelation, was superb. I weighed it up against the Scriptures and clearly realised that tithing had been required under the 'law' as in a tax, but not so under 'grace'. I realised the fruit of this revelation would be real freedom in giving. Don't misunderstand me ... forget 10% ... I seek to give as much as possible in serving, financially, whatever, and that generously, wisely, secretively, cheerfully within my means. Roger Price gave a testimony of when he was in charge of Chichester Christian Fellowship that when the Lord told him to stop the Fellowship tithing the amount of money given each week increased! I obtained a catalogue of Roger Price's tapes and saw that there was a wealth of material worth tapping into which would build on or clarify all of the teachings I had received over the previous several years, such as my B.T.I. training, and though always sifting and sorting, as stated, have gone down that road ever since, as it has always helped me to keep walking closely with the Lord.

Even when I kept my mouth shut I knew now I was on a collision course with the Bradford Fellowship and others as the truth always sets you free and I still wanted to get free and keep free, whatever the cost. Freedom and truth won't puff you up with knowledge and pride, but will pleasantly and in humility set you free, and its fruit with integrity will lead to peace. No matter how much I tried, I just could not integrate any more with the Bradford Fellowship - I was becoming detached and was powerless, or so it seemed, to stop this happening. I had no intention of changing the truth I had attained, for bondage. Mind you, I really liked living in Bingley, with its famous 'Five Rise Locks' on the canal within short walking distance, the park with the River Aire beside it, etc.

I don't remember the exact date, but guess it was the later part of 1983, when two of the elders of the Fellowship said they wanted to come up to my house to see me. They were much taller and stronger-looking than my wife and I. They had neither mercy nor compassion in the way they dealt with us - it almost seemed to me that they were provoking us in order to get an adverse reaction through a verbal attack, but I gently stood my ground ... though not so my wife. The four of us were all stood up and facing each other. As we talked and we had to face their verbal onslaught, suddenly my wife started to weep and then sobbed deeply as she slowly sank to the floor where she was standing - ending up with her head face downwards, resting on the back of her arm, and in her brokenness continued to sob. They showed no care or emotion, but still talked on. I thought to myself, "*You* think she is just another neurotic female seeking attention or whatever, but you are wrong; she has more courage and love in her heart and being than probably the two of you put together will ever have" ... but inwardly in my heart I was crying out to the Lord, "Help! What do I do?" I realised that just about every man who was a husband that I knew at that point would have set about them with violence, or at least driven them immediately out of their home. I looked at my wife on the floor and then my anger was certainly kindled. I could see to my wife in a minute or two, but I wanted to know or see the full picture of what they were up to. They still could get nothing against me to support their case, so I was now convinced it was provocation. "You will have to go through the commitment class again," they said. "What purpose will that serve?" I asked. "So that you can again give your public word on completion of it to obey the leadership," they answered. "Okay, when is the first meeting?" I asked. They gave me the venue, date and time. Then I was very keen to show these two 'pastors' (of Ezekiel chapter 34 verses 4 and16-22) to the door, and this I did in haste.

I went straight back to apologise and ask my wife's forgiveness, console her and pray for her ... and put the kettle on! My words sounded hollow for a minute or so as I spoke to her and reassured her of my and the Lord's love, but explained that, before the Lord, I had to see what they were really up to, for this was the very hub and heart, the calloused heart, that is, of 'heavy shepherding', which is rampant in the church. "Don't you see, this is man playing at and being 'God' to man and is a total abomination of what the Lord really wants?" I know now it is a forced agreement to get a unity which will bring a measure of power and some strength, but it is not the real way God wants to work - but this type of control, man's control, is rampant everywhere in different forms - in the world and the church, and is a form of witchcraft. It is where the right bounds of control have been passed or transgressed. As stated above, we give our allegiance to Jesus, our commitment and obedience in the ultimate sense, as in a 'blank cheque' to Him alone. God only wants volunteers (from gentle, soft and loving hearts) and *never* conscripts. This applies within the church and in evangelism and became a favourite saying of mine. The one who can only lie, deceive and destroy will only work through 'conscription' and that by fear, force and covert control, wherever it is found. The power and the authority that man has is, or should be, limited.

I was to gain an invaluable insight and discernment that sometimes would get me into all sorts of trouble, but my wife would never again fully integrate into a fellowship or put her trust in man's leadership and control. After another incident at the end of the 'eighties, I could not get her back to any fellowship meetings. Again, it is no wonder that to misrepresent the Lord is such a terrible thing.

I attended the first of the commitment classes of people queueing up to join the Bradford Church Fellowship being held in a house in Keighley and although I was not happy with what I discerned, I still went back to the next one that I was able to attend. I kept my mouth shut - it was a sham and the wrong foundation on which to join or build a fellowship. There was no way on this planet that I would ever have taken that 'oath of obedience' to that group of men or indeed would ever do so again with this cultish type of behaviour. I could still work in a team, serve and do my best and give money, etc, but I would always listen to the Lord and check out what He was saying, and if I was in conflict or disagreement with a group then would quietly withdraw. No-one in the true Church has any right to deny these freedoms of thought, actions or choice to a fellow human being by an adverse control. Various helpful disciplines that we may learn which are given in justice for correction are another issue. Every 'power' and 'authority' here on Earth has, and must have, its limitations. I went home from that second group meeting and wrote a letter to that leadership saying I would withdraw and leave it at that and asked them to destroy all the paperwork/records they had of me and my family. I never did receive any reply.

Several weeks later, I met the man, a leader, in whose house those last two classes I attended in Keighley were held, and not only was he also an ex-B.T.I. student, but he too had left the fellowship. He said he came off worse than I did, for he said they sent him a letter which simply heaped curses on him. He shared with me some of the failings of that leadership and I was not surprised. He later moved to just south of London and, when I went around the Spring of 1984 to a superb Roger Price conference held at Butlins' Holiday Camp in Bognor Regis (the only time I was to see him in action before he went to be with the Lord ), I went to stay a couple of nights with the man who had lived in Keighley and his family. Forgive, forget, pray good things for them and that any further damage will cease, then move on. I went with my family to Guisley Community Church for a while, but not having a car made it very difficult. We also visited a couple of fellowships in Bradford itself and I was given two preaching engagements. At the end of one of them, the little old ladies hugged me and the leaders wouldn't speak to me ... what didn't they like about the book of Amos?!

I don't know the exact date, but it was probably in early January 1984 when, at home and relaxed, my wife whispered in my ear, saying, of course, her name, "Our daughter is pregnant!" There was no eye contact, but silence ... followed by more silence! I wasn't too happy about one or two things regarding my daughter and within the limited authority I now had over her, i.e. to obey the rules of the home, I had previously given her a gentle warning, perhaps too late. I could not reason it through or intellectualise it - we are all sinners and need a Saviour. It is the heart's response of mercy and grace I have received from the Saviour in the past, so on this occasion mercy and grace I will definitely pass on. With eye contact, I said to my wife, "I will totally stand by her and give all the help I can to her and the child." "So will I," she replied. "You two are so close, I knew you would say that anyway", was my reply, as she disappeared out of the door to put the kettle on! Another precious gift of a little life was forming and this time I would get to be a grandad ... still in my thirties ... well ... just ... at 39 years old! I mused before the Lord, it is a blessing to see your children's children ... some might not agree, but I knew it would be! Years later, I was in an enjoyable large conference in Oxford and the leader/speaker was Neil T. Anderson from the USA. He had status, all kinds of qualifications, was gifted and no doubt wealthy, and during one of his seminars he said his unmarried daughter had been made pregnant, so I immediately thought he was going to give the same testimony that I could by then give, but he didn't, much to my surprise. He said she left the family home to go elsewhere to live - I don't remember all the details and am only going by my own experience - but I thought, sadly, "You probably missed out on a lot of love, input, fun and blessings … for me it was to pot with what people think of you!"

1984 rolled on, with big changes once again imminent. In hindsight and with the 'if only' mentality, perhaps what was about to unfold was a tragic mistake, yet in the overall picture of my life's tapestry, I would say it had to be. There were certain signs within that year of what was happening which made me make the decisions I was about to make. Of myself I did on no account want to move from that home and area because, as already stated, I loved Bingley and West Yorkshire. If I had stayed, would it have given myself and family a much needed stability or, in God's plans for me, would it have made no difference anyway? I soaked my motives in self-analysis and decisions in prayer.

I asked the father of the child forming in my daughter's womb if he was going to marry her and his mother put some pressure on him to do so - but he would not. I then offered them the two dormer attic rooms - one as a bedroom, the other as a lounge, and stated there would be some rules of the home to be obeyed, but the answer was "No!" They applied for a council house in that general area and as the time of the birth became very close they were allocated one. I would not normally get into unnecessary debt, but got a bank loan in order to help them buy some furniture, etc, to get them started, as they both were without jobs.

The neighbours on either side complained only once about our Yorkshire terrier barking when it was being left on its own more often than usual. We had had her for twelve years and she'd always been healthy and fit, but I thought there was something wrong with her back end bones and had previously had her to a vet in Bingley, who persuaded me not to have her put down. I did not want to see the dog suffering, so I now took her to another vet with a view to having her put down. He said it was common in this type of dog to get arthritis like Mitzi had on her back bone structure and that it would be fair to put her down if she had always enjoyed a good quality of life. I agreed and said I would hold her - the vet and assistant said, "No, leave her". I said, "Yes, I will hold her." They looked at each other. They guessed what was coming. The vet said to me, "Count to ten," as he injected into her front leg. I only got to nearly four and she was gone. Twelve years of our really good little pet gone in three to four seconds. My emotions welled up and with all the pain of that season I started to weep, then sob - I simply could not get control of my emotions. I tried to talk … but … with no chance. I left to catch a bus, still weeping, with the lead and harness in my hand, and said, "What am I doing?", as I found a bin to throw them into. Yet the weeping was therapeutic, though I had had no idea how deeply attached to her I had become, as such a docile, friendly member of the family. I have had no bad memories of her at all. When I told the neighbours on each side what I had done, they were taken aback as they said, "We loved the little dog!!" ... so did I, yet I never again had a pet.

Within two days of that event, on 27th July 1984, my grand-daughter was born in Bradford Royal Infirmary. Because my daughter had moved out two days before, we were not allowed to visit her - hospital regulations! ... so we went to Morecambe to stay with friends for the weekend. But all was not well in that common-law relationship; things were not good. After six weeks, she turned up at the door with baby in her pram and some of her belongings and asked if she and baby could come back home to live. I was not surprised and said, "Yes", along with my wife, and so they did.

At this point there were two other things that were affecting the situation. There was a lot of reorganisation happening on the railway in that area that would affect me, possibly even a move work-wise to Leeds or somewhere. Also, my mother-in-law, now in her seventies in Newcastle, had the onset of Alzheimer's disease and I thought my wife would want to live near her, so we discussed the possibility of moving back up to Newcastle and agreed I would try to do so. My daughter plus little one would move with us and I guessed it would be a fresh start for her. I applied for a transfer post to Newcastle Central Station and got it, put my house on the market and it sold for a good price immediately, but the transition became difficult. I had to move to start the new job before the sale of the property went through. My father-in-law would have nothing as such to do with me and the only 'digs' I could find were expensive and not ideal. All I could do in desperation to give myself a breathing space was to rent a council house on the then notorious Scotswood Housing Estate in Newcastle, renowned to be one of the worst in Europe ...!

# 14
# When It All Goes Wrong ...

Family life in Scotswood was interesting, to say the least. As we settled in, the place was so bad I groaned to myself, "What on earth do I do?" I wasn't in despair as I was in a situation of being able to buy a property if needs be, but I hadn't realised that there would even be a stigma attached to just living in that area ... also, coming from a lovely home in a beautiful area to that was a culture shock and a lesson in humility - that's an understatement! I can remember going down to have a look at the River Tyne, which was not far away and close to 'Blaydon', as in 'The Races', after 'The Scotswood Road' (hence one of the famous Tyneside songs), but it was so unpleasant I thought, "No thanks, I won't bother!"; so I didn't walk there again. To be fair, as that was around a quarter of a century ago, that area has been or is in the process of being tidied up, including The Tyne and its banks.

Our neighbours ... well, on one side of us, whenever the man came in drunk you could hear the violence and usually it ended up with him throwing the woman down the stairs until one stabbed the other and then it was quieter!! On the other side, an end-terrace property, you would have thought if anyone was going to break in they would have done so through the side door ... not so ... they took out a circle of bricks next to the side door, big enough for someone to easily climb through into what would be the kitchen, in order to steal! "What about their Alsatian dog?" I wondered. It didn't devour the person who broke in, so it was an 'inside job'!! If this was how they treated their friends, who would like to have been their enemy?!! When I had a look at the loft area of our mid-terraced house, I could observe, by replaced bricks, where someone had tunnelled *from both sides* by removing enough bricks to be able to climb through, and a neighbour had informed me they had wanted to go through the row of terraced properties to steal whatever!! When I went to catch the bus to work for early shift, I never saw another soul, so I guessed the people in that area who actually went to work were few and far between.

I found out there was a small house-group a couple of streets away belonging to a large Pentecostal house church fellowship based some distance away, still in the west end near the city centre of Newcastle. I went to a weekly meeting and thought, "Well done for having this small group and to be praying for this area! This is good, I'll go along and give support"; so I arranged to have a talk with a leader at their spacious building with meeting room, offices, etc. All was going well until I mentioned I didn't believe in tithing - may as well clear this up at stage one! Cleared up! ... and cleared out, as I had no choice but to leave and that was that! I was unrepentant on behalf of the poor - did they not have any idea of the poverty on that estate? 'Robin Hoods' were needed to sort it out and please the Lord! I found another large, lively fellowship and got on really well with the pastor ... until ... yes, you've guessed it ... I mentioned tithing and his face instantly clouded over and he never acknowledged or spoke to myself or my family again after saying goodbye. In both of these fellowships you had to tithe to be in membership. What did 'the Church' think? - was it worse than heresy not to worship or be interested in money in their eyes? How could they justify being so strict in their interpretation and obedience to some scriptures, e.g. over the divorce issue and not over the 'financial issue'? If God wanted them to have pots of money, surely He was quite capable of getting it to them one way or another, rather than *demanding* people give?! The Bible clearly states in 1st Timothy chapter 5 verse 8 that if you don't look properly after your family first you are worse than an unbeliever.

There was an Evangelical Mission Hall fairly close by and the leader was an evangelist with pastoral duties. I got on well with him and he had me preach once or twice in the fellowship. He himself did not live in that area, but in Cramlington.

I thought about putting my son into a Jewish Independent School in the Newcastle area and even made contact with them, but I thought I would have had to live in that area to afford to be able to do so ... however, what changed it all was a tiny little insect! I called it a 'spider beetle' ... well, not one, but many of them! This type is evidently found where there have been old birds' nests, which have not been cleared away, and in unclean properties. The Council had decorated that property throughout before we moved in, but it was questionable as to any thoroughness in the necessary cleaning and preparation before painting. Those insects were everywhere: we were invaded by them! My wife said she was even finding them in our baby grand-daughter's cot. She collected quite a lot of them in a matchbox and went up to the Council Housing Offices on the estate (this was the second time of mentioning the problem to them) and emptied them out onto the counter - female office staff scattered at the same time as the beetles ... but she had made her point! By now my reaction was to say, "Enough is enough, we will buy somewhere and move in as soon as possible."

In hindsight, I probably should have moved straight from Bingley to Cramlington, which had originally been a pit village and was then a new town and still growing, being eight miles north of Newcastle, with a railway station and a good bus service to the city. The leader of the Scotswood Mission invited me for lunch at his home in Cramlington and I liked what I saw of the area that day. My motive for moving to Newcastle, of course, was to allow my wife to be fairly close to her mother and I wanted to be on a good bus route as close as possible to my work, around ten minutes' journey time. I quickly found a suitable property in the Benwell area: an upstairs 'Tyneside Flat', fairly modern, as it was built between the wars. I had some work done to it, including putting a new kitchen and bathroom in it, along with my first 'combi boiler', etc, and the flat was clean, light, pleasant, homely, with a good atmosphere, close to shops and a bus stop. At the front was a neat and well laid out rose garden, which I owned and was responsible for. We moved in in the early Spring of 1985 and we all liked the flat. The area, however, was not good for an investment as it was generally deteriorating and would yet face social problems. The year went by and it was certainly better than being in the previous residence. During that time my daughter started getting dates and for a little while was courting. My son went into reception class at the nearby primary school, but some time towards the end of that year his behaviour was not always as good as it had been and he developed asthma. I was concerned, but couldn't find any answers as to why. I was now attending another reasonably close Evangelical Mission Hall, which later closed; not exactly Pentecostal, but I went along anyway.

With my wife and son, I was returning by train on a Sunday in early December after a couple of enjoyable nights at a hotel in the Lake District at Lake Windermere … the weather was very damp and cold. My wife became poorly as the journey progressed … most unlike her, she could hardly walk except with much pain. I wondered if she might collapse. By the time we reached Carlisle, I considered it might be a hospital job, but we managed to change trains and eventually get to Newcastle and home. The next day she was examined by a doctor who at first thought she was pregnant, but after further examination in a day or two they discovered she had large cysts on the ovaries and was told she would require a 'complete' hysterectomy as soon as possible. It would be fortunate that my daughter was living with us, not only to look after the home but two very active little ones when I was at work, as my wife would not be able to lift anything for at least four months.

At the Christmas time my mother overdosed, only this time she did not recover. Up until then she had still lived in the little OAP council bungalow in Carlisle, but towards the end of her life she never went out and rarely got dressed, if at all. She had lost a lot of weight from previous years and had become quite small and thin and had looked several years older than her sixty-six years. She had had a television, but had really liked the radio for such as 'The Archers' and Christian programmes. Her strong personality had still shown through, although she had had very limited energy; but that meant she had made and had been friends with several of her close neighbours. The tragedy was, she never gave up smoking or drinking alcohol and her health had suffered accordingly. I don't remember the date, but think it had been earlier in 1985 that she had been burgled and they had taken her television and whatever else they could from around the bed she was sleeping in - that wickedness was despicable and obviously she had been upset by it. Why had she in reality not been able to cope with the emotional pain in her adult life? I know that some spiritual forces of evil, over which she never got the victory, had left their mark. In the natural realm, I believe it was in part the tragedy of an unhappy marriage due to my parents' unsuitability in relating properly to each other. She liked fast cars, was an excellent cook and knew how to throw a party, was a 'people person', gifted in admin. and liked five-star standard in her home. She was generous and well liked. She was suited to the 'swing seat' in the garden, but hated sport, camping and the great outdoor life. Having said that, she was in the WRNS at the beginning of the Second World War until she got married on 16th August 1940, in haste as far as I know, in those dangerous and very uncertain times. My father was the opposite in a lot of these things, as he was into running, swimming, camping, yachting, etc, and the great outdoors. To put it simply, I believe that my parents were just not compatible. They were not the first and definitely not the last! My mother seemed to believe that you only got one chance of marriage and that was your lot. I know at the time of her divorce she had returned to see the nuns at the Roman Catholic School she had gone to in Newcastle and one had told her, "Of course, you know you can *never* get married again". Also, her childhood strict Presbyterian influence may have been somewhat negative. I clearly remembered the times mentioned earlier when she had seriously attempted suicide at least once in the 'fifties and again in the 'sixties. She once told me that she had had some boyfriends in the time of her growing up when close to adulthood, and she named them ... one in particular she had wished she had married. In other words, I believe there was regret in such a way that her inner pain was unbearable. She sought true love, but did she ever find it?

I ended up taking her funeral at Carlisle Crematorium at the very beginning of January 1986. It was a really cold, crisp sort of a day, with clear blue skies and some winter sunshine. I don't recommend taking a close relative's funeral, in case you become too emotionally involved. I was surprised at the turnout, as there was a good number of people present. My father was determined to attend and so he did. The now elderly Cyril Proudfoot, who I mentioned earlier, was there, flanked by two of his sons. The coffin was brought in with my two brothers, a brother-in-law and one of the undertakers as pall-bearers with myself leading ... but when I turned and faced the coffin and those who were there, the emotional pain suddenly hit me and I started to weep and the tears just kept on streaming down my face. The undertaker was good at his job, but he must have been thinking, "It's *plan* B on this one!" but suddenly I was okay, took control and got through it.

The time given was limited, as normally happens with cremations, and I spoke for around 15 minutes, which was not really long enough. The gist of what I said was to briefly preach the Gospel of what the Lord Jesus had done to make salvation possible for each one of us, that we are *all* sinners, and that included Mother, who had really struggled with addictions as mentioned above and whatever else hindered her and although she believed, for I was sure, after a frank heart-to-heart talk with her a few months earlier, when we shared openly and honestly about our beliefs, and after a short prayer with her, which I believe the Lord accepted as the seal of her salvation (although she was not able to take that decision in her walk with the Lord much further), that she will definitely now be rejoicing in Heaven.

But the reactions of those present were very varied, as I was about to find out. One or two hugged me and some ignored me, and to this day I respect their right to agree or disagree. I would say even now that I had earned the right to say what I said and I loved and respected Mother, although I didn't always understand her. The truth is the truth and it is a precious commodity.

The reality was and is that that 'family tree' was that of a generally dysfunctional family and that while Mother was alive there was a measure of 'peace', as it did not or was not allowed to surface; but once she was gone, it would find another 'level' and that is what happened and has worked out over the years.

Generally, because of all the pain of rejection and everything that had happened over the years, something would have to give and anger and the like would have to surface. So many that day would blame 'religion' and 'the church' and what I stood for; but why would they not accept my love for and relationship with the Lord?

About ten days later, I phoned the elder of my two sisters, but before I was able to get into any conversation I was blasted in no uncertain way by her for who I was, what I had said (with regard to mentioning the suicide, etc, of my mother) and what I stood for and she stated she would never again recognise me as her brother or in any other way and not only has she totally and utterly kept to her word regarding myself and my family, but my younger sister has followed suit even to this day. I have respected that, of course, as their prerogative. As you can imagine, that hurt as it was designed to. I still wanted the best for them, knowing well they had suffered in their early years, as mentioned before. We still had the same mother and father and nothing can change that fact, even if all is now just distant memories.

But hang on a minute, what is this I see …? It's the Carlisle daily newspaper at the time of the funeral … On the front page, in the bottom left-hand corner, as I remember … an article on my mother! It gave some background to her life and to what had happened and listed all the diseases she had had, which, of course, were due to her adverse lifestyle of nicotine and alcohol addictions. It was heart-breaking stuff, but it was the truth for all to see.

Am I being hard-hearted in some way? Okay then, I'll turn things onto myself. Whatever I dish out, can I take it? Mother would quote and usually try and put it into action to 'do unto others as you would have them do unto you!' Since being young I liked that maxim and thought, "I'll buy that, that's a good way to live." So what about my death and funeral? When I die I want a pauper's funeral - no bother, no fuss and no big deal. I've already obtained a plot down at Blyth South Beach, near Blyth in Northumberland. It's not many yards away from the sand dunes and the North Sea and was a special offer economy plot - there's room for another two! All I need is a cheapo coffin and an undertaker to sort out the basics of what is legally required. But you can tell and say it as it is! ... warts and all, the good and the bad, all about 'moi'! Just one thing, though: why should anyone attend who didn't get on with or care about or didn't particularly like me? ... it would be pointless. No professional mourners as in religious nonsense and pharisaicalism and definitely no hypocrites. If anyone turns up, just sing praises and glorify the Lord Jesus with great joy and I'm sure you'll be given a glimpse of some of the angels of Heaven doing the same!! Know this: I will be in Heaven with such ecstasy and jubilation, praising my Wonderful Saviour Messiah for all that He is, has done and will do and it is such indescribable bliss that I want to see you join me later, no matter what the cost!!

Swiftly on the heels of all this, on or just around 22nd January, 1986, my wife was called into hospital to have her hysterectomy. I had asked one or two to pray, but not as many as I'd have liked. I had a bad feeling in my heart about this operation and was at home at the actual time it was taking place; but strangely enough, I just could not pray - everything was a blank and hopeless! A little time went by and, eventually, on my face before the Lord, I committed my wife to the Lord, asking for His mercy and taking some spiritual authority for her life and healing from both the Lord and the medics. So it was that my daughter and I were told afterwards that she had gone through the operation, but it was in the post-operative room that she had haemorrhaged badly and had to be taken back into theatre. Praise God she lived, though she was very poorly and weak; but once again she slowly recovered and most certainly regained her health and strength for a very neat span of time indeed! The terrible suffering of PMT, along with the recent years of menopausal problems, came to a sudden end for her - all of that area of suffering was over for her for the rest of her days, which made a big difference to her quality of life.

By this time and into February and beyond, there was only one word which would describe how I felt, and that word was 'reeling'. I hardly knew what had hit me and my health and work suffered accordingly.

As 1986 progressed, I found myself doing some deep thinking and asking questions to the Lord. I could recognise a serious spiritual attack in the last few months alone and I had missed something, but what on earth was it? I was absolutely determined from that time onwards to get some answers and take some action!... and I meant business! Life was too short for this to be otherwise! What of my last ten years or so and the pattern of all that had happened to me? 'The Church' expected you to be a 'nice Christian' and 'conform', *or else*, to their agenda and interpretation of what that should be, though time and time again they themselves were not fighting the battle and gaining victory against the enemies of God. I had been denied, even robbed of, my ministry, yet now there was no outlet for my giftings to be used in serving in most of 'structured Christianity'. The pattern was, conform, do as you're told or get out! Okay, so you get out, but then it becomes, "You've got a problem, mate; we, the 'proper Church', will block you wherever." We all have our agendas; they have theirs and I have mine. The politicians have *theirs* and the dictators also have *theirs*. Hitler and Stalin had *theirs*, but how many countless millions of people were murdered or killed directly and indirectly by them alone? It depends whether agendas are good or bad! But what about God's agenda - He *certainly* has one and His plans and purposes will most definitely be outworked on this Earth, even at this time. My desire then is to seek to fit in with His agenda.

My response in all of this was to go to the Lord and say, "Okay, Lord, if I'm really that bad You sort me out and correct me - *please!!*" Now, if you know and fear God, that is a very dangerous thing to ask; for, if He takes you at your word, anything could happen, though He will show loving-kindness and be just and right in His dealings. I knew the importance of serving as mentioned earlier, and especially serving the Lord and that I had some giftings for this, though not always the energy required to do so, but certain giftings were in me, e.g. pastoral and evangelistic, and I was not normally afraid to stand out from the crowd if needs be. If an enemy out there was playing havoc in my situation, then I would not passively sit down under it and do nothing, but would 'worry it' for answers to gain a victory!

There were two areas that I wanted to address, either by research or whatever. The first, as I've clearly referred to previously, was that of the issue of 'demonisation' and the 'deliverance ministry' as in spiritual warfare, which by then I knew without a shadow of a doubt held a valuable 'key' and that I personally must address it. A lot of what I had previously taken on board I now fully rejected in favour of recognition of this ministry and so put paid to playing a game of 'cosy and clubby Christianity'. The second was that of the *family unit* and its importance - I knew if you destroyed the family you destroyed society and then, in turn, a nation. To be able to give some teaching and encouragement in this area was of paramount importance.

I started to look at the possibility of going back to a Bible College for two or three terms to do some reading and research on these two subjects and put together a course on the family; and I also learned that at that time the Assemblies of God denomination had quite a lot of fellowships without pastors, so if I went to Mattersey Hall Bible College (of that AOG denomination), near Retford, south of Doncaster, in the October, then I could see where it could lead me as it unfolded. I would need to sell my flat at a fair price in order to carry this through. I received positive encouragement from some friends and my wife said, "Okay", perhaps because her mother was quite far gone with the Alzheimer's Disease and her father was looking after her at home.

My daughter met someone in the June of that year and they immediately decided to get married around three weeks after they had met and so that was into the July of 1986. I asked her to reconsider, or at least postpone it for a few months, as I thought she was making a mistake (as did her Mum), but it was her life and her choice, so she went ahead. It was a very simple and basic wedding day and so they, with my grand-daughter, at almost two years of age, went off to live a few miles north of Morpeth in Northumberland.

# 15

# *Deliverance ... and the Retford Season ...*

The way seemed clear now, although I had not specifically looked for it, to make a move, and I started to 'test the water' and 'start the ball rolling'. Everything seemed to be positive and it all began to come together. I got a buyer for the flat at the asking price, though I questioned the purchaser's suitability with the estate agent, only to be told in so many words that they were doing their job! Just as I was getting ready to actually move to Retford to temporarily rent and share a house with part of the family who owned it, taking some but not all of my furniture, the buyer backed out of buying the property! I thought if they could resell the property straight away I would be okay, but had no choice, other than to go ahead with the move, and did so towards the end of the third week of September. At the start of the academic year, the Bible College said, after I explained to them what happened, that I could still attend some of the lectures and be involved in college life while I waited to see how things worked out. This was kind of them, but if I could not pay my way I would only give it a week or two, as I was not prepared to get into debt and so would back out. I realised it was going to take me a month or two to get back into studying and researching, but knew I would need to be hassle/worry free in order to do so.

It's interesting to note that the total number of students in that college had not really been very high, but from that year the numbers began to increase substantially. Unfortunately, the flat did not sell immediately and so, shortly before the end of October, I withdrew from the college as such. I had made friends there by then and was kindly given permission to borrow books from the college library, which helped me to study at home.

I admitted my mistake and cried out to the Lord, apologising to Him and all concerned, picked myself up, dusted myself down and, trusting the Lord, said, 'What next?!' I would still rather try and fail than not have tried at all. He works all things together for good for those who love Him and are walking with Him, the Bible tells me. As I look back on that time, I have no regrets as to what happened.

In the November the estate agent had a buyer for the flat - it was someone, a close relative, as I remember, connected to one of their office staff, and, yes, they wanted it at a knock-down price! We had no choice but to let it go and the sale went through like lightning ... I was not impressed, especially as we let them have some nice furniture and carpets which we had left in the flat as well!

It was so strange, as in the December everything came right, or one could say 'came back onto an even keel'. That this should be around one whole year, give or take only days, was really strange, so I knew it had to have a spiritual connotation because of the way it suddenly started and just as suddenly ended … but I could not understand what had triggered it off in the first place! The sale of the house went through and all our bills were paid, even if we were left with only a fraction of what we should have had. Some Christians had a three- bedroomed property to rent out in a lovely area to the south of Retford and, though many were after it, they felt led to wait. Friends told them about us and they came to where we were staying. I was out, but my wife was in, so she was highly delighted, as this time she was taken to look at a property and she got to choose to say 'yes' or 'no'! Of course, it was a 'yes' as it was ideal and God- sent and I was equally delighted. We became good friends of that couple for several years until we lost contact. A week or two later, we moved in and the furniture we had was just right to fit into that partly furnished house. That whole area and certainly Retford itself was a lovely place to live in and, with Retford being very flat, everyone, so it seemed, had a push bike. There was a really good primary school for our son not too far away … and a couple of hundred yards away or so from the house was the Grove Road Level Crossing south of Retford Station on the London to Edinburgh main railway line. To go and watch close up some of those fast electrics doing around 140mph was quite something, if you liked trains!!

In the November I had started attending a tiny AOG fellowship - it was held in a very small purpose-built building in Retford and as such had been there for years. I had been two or three times when, on a cold Sunday early in the November, the evening meeting was in progress, led by one of the leaders of the Bible College - the entrance door suddenly opened and with quite a lot of commotion an elderly, very tall gentleman came in, walking with difficulty, and obviously in much pain and discomfort. He was accompanied by his son-in- law, who was probably getting on for retirement age. As the older man found a seat and sat down with some difficulty, the younger man clearly announced that he would not stay but go and sit in his car parked on the street just outside. After a minute or so, the leader stated that the man was called Ernest, was not well and had asked for prayer and invited anyone who wanted to do so to gather round and join him in prayer. Most of those present did so, but I didn't feel led. Not long after the praying had finished, Ernest got up, again with some difficulty, and so was helped outside to the waiting car and the meeting continued.

A day or two later, the phone rang and it was a lady called Aigund from the Retford area who knew old Ernest and his family in Retford and their situation. She said that in a few days' time she was going into the house of the daughter and son-in-law in Retford where Ernest was staying, as there was no improvement, and would I like to go along as well. Not only was Aigund sold out for Jesus, she was bold and fearless in her ministry, regardless of what people thought. I said a definite 'Yes!', so she arranged to collect me outside of where I was staying at the day and time she stated. The daughter and son-in-law had a nice home and we were shown through to the lounge, a small, tastefully decorated and furnished cosy room. The son-in-law said he had to go out and he left. Old Ernest was sitting on the couch, still in a bad way, with his wrists bandaged where he had tried to end it all since I had last seen him. I learned that he still had a wife living in Sheffield and that he was in his mid-eighties. His daughter sat down on one of the single armchairs four or five feet away. Aigund knelt down in front of him and I knelt by the side of the couch, placing my Bible on the arm of it. I started looking through Psalms - now there is normally nothing wrong with looking for some scripture verses, gaining some more information or praying - but not at *this* moment in time. Outright spiritual warfare was needed and that in the form of deliverance ministry, *and that is exactly what Aigund did*, with firmness and without any fuss.

Old Ernie was completely still and quiet. I began looking again in Psalms and Aigund looked at me - she had cast the demons out and said, "They have all gone. There was a whole nest of them." I didn't find the verse I was looking for, so maybe it wasn't relevant anyway! ... and closed my Bible. Ernie remained as still as a statue, so Aigund went over to his daughter and again knelt down in front of her and I stood to the side of the armchair. "I am going to bring my hands down on your head and when I do so you will be baptised with the Holy Spirit," Aigund said to her. She did so and in that fraction of a second when her hands gently touched her head old Ernest, still sitting motionless on the couch, immediately jumped to his feet, raised his arms and shouted with all his heart, "I love Jesus! ... I love Jesus! ... I love Jesus! ..." Aigund and I turned around in utter amazement to look at old Ernie - or should I have then said 'young Ernie'?! He was totally changed for the better ... what a wonderful miracle with the awesome power of God we had just witnessed!! We only stayed a short while after that, then we left. I never did see Ernest or his family again, but I did ask once or twice as time went by as to what happened. I was told he was no longer in any pain, discomfort or torment from that time onwards as his body healed and that he led a normal life and later on went back to live with his wife in Sheffield.

For me, the Lord had honoured my main reason for going to Retford, for *that* day and its ministry definitely changed my mind and doctrinal belief and I was determined from then on to effectively take part in deliverance ministry. I never looked for it, but a ministry later unfolded. Never again would I go with the general flow of the Church over the deliverance issue, as so many were in denial, or at least not wanting to go down that road. During those months I kept on reading about the subject, though never wrote a paper on it.

Around that time, Mattersey Hall Bible College took the two fellowships which respectively met, one in Retford and the other linked with the college that met in Mattersey Village, and made them 'one' and they started to hire and meet on Sundays in one of the school buildings in Retford itself, with home groups, etc. That fellowship became very strong and they eventually bought a building in Retford to meet in, where they opened a successful café and so on. After a few more years I lost contact with the fellowship.

By the beginning of 1987 it was fully evident that my daughter's marriage was a total disaster and that she and my grand-daughter were in an abusive relationship. We had worked it out that he still loved his first wife and was probably only 'getting at her' by marrying again. No doubt the likes of this has been repeated many times. It was a desperate situation and my daughter needed to urgently make her escape with her daughter. She had tried once, but he came down to Retford and took them back. I selectively asked one or two friends to pray into the situation and they did so. Then my wife said to me one day that she would fast and pray for however long it took to get a victory. Because of her ileostomy and possible dehydration, I said, "No!" She said, "Yes!" I said, " Give me a few hours to think about it before the Lord" and I did so and then said to her, "We will have a joint fast. We will each, during every 24 hours, take one twelve-hour fast of either a.m. or p.m. as we agree in advance between ourselves and not over-eat on our time of eating, so that way we are offering up one continuous fast between us and that will be acceptable to the Lord, as long as you keep having liquids, of course, and at times if need be I will fast for the two of us." She agreed, so we fasted and prayed in this way and it went on for, as I remember, exactly three weeks, after which our daughter plus little one made their getaway on the train, with very few belongings, and journeyed down to Retford. We were not on the telephone in that Grove Road house and didn't have a car, so this had made it difficult to communicate. But escaped she had and she saw a solicitor straight away in Retford and started divorce proceedings. We also informed the police of the situation, just in case it turned nasty, but this time he did not pursue them. I soon made arrangements to go up by car for their personal belongings, only to discover he had cut up all my daughter's clothing! However, she was pleased to be safe and free and to have simply walked away from it all. After the time of one full year since the actual marriage ceremony, my daughter was granted her divorce - the fact that he had written to the judge saying he would kill her and my wife as and when must also have helped!!

Another couple of months or so went by and in the middle of April my wife was informed that her father had lung cancer and was in a bad way. Within a day or two, she announced she was going up to Newcastle to look after him until he died. Her mother, still poorly, with her mind gone, was also there, but it was somewhere around that time that she went into a care home. I said to my wife, "No, it is not right that you do so." She said, "I don't care, I'm going anyway." "We, your family, need you, though I realise you will need to visit regularly," I replied. "I'm going!" she stated. I thought it through for a minute or so - I was uneasy - something, I knew not what, was puzzling me. It was not like her and something was not right. If she went there, how much would the authorities and other family members do to help her, if anything at all? Spiritually, I knew it would be dangerous to let her go without some kind of even reluctant blessing/approval from myself and in the natural for her to part without equal agreement between us was not wise. I said, with a heavy heart, something like, "Okay, go and I pray it will be well with you and no harm will come to you." So she was gone within a couple of days, though she did return for a day or two after just a couple of weeks, but her overall time away was three months. None of us went up to visit her or her family members in Newcastle and we felt that was the right thing to have done. None of us in Retford felt happy with the situation, but my son at six years old took it really badly. I think he thought in his little heart that she was not going to return.

On his sixth birthday in early July, my daughter and I thought we would organise a really good birthday party for him to take his mind off his mother. I remember it so clearly, as we put a lot of work and effort into the whole thing - plenty of really good quality food, an expensive, large sponge birthday cake, hand-made to order with writing on it, which looked and tasted delicious, various party games with some excellent prizes. We invited just a few of his friends from close by and they were all well behaved. It was a lovely summer's day and we had the games on the front lawn. One of those games was 'Dead Lions' and the birthday lad, who seemed a bit too quiet on that day, was completely still as he played the game and so won it fairly and squarely - then I realised he had a temperature - he was not on form and at a certain point he just gave up and I discerned that he was trying to enjoy the party, but without his Mum I reckoned he just wanted to die anyway. It was heart-breaking for my daughter and myself to see him like that.

My in-laws were on the phone in Newcastle and it was mostly my daughter who would go to the nearest phone box a few hundred yards away and make contact. My wife's father was all but gone in early July and spent the last week of his life in hospital. At that point I kept monitoring the situation and around the middle of July at one of the times I phoned my wife she said ... "He's gone, and had a lot of morphine at the end." "Did he make his peace with the Lord Jesus?" I asked. "No," she replied, "all he would say was 'it is up to God now'." "What about the funeral - should I come up?" I asked. "It's on such and such a day. Don't come up though, there are some family members who want to kill you!" I couldn't believe what I was hearing!! ... "What kind of nonsense is this? ... What am I supposed to have done?" I haltingly gasped. "Don't come up," she said, "and I will return straight away after the funeral." "Okay, I'll leave it at that and will meet you with the children off the train at Retford Station." When the day and time came, myself with my son and grand-daughter got down to Retford Station far too early, so one of the things I did was to tell them and act out the account of "The Prodigal Son" from the New Testament!! ... so my wife returned home with great rejoicing! I didn't get a proper explanation with regard to what the problem towards me had been, but I did find out that during those three months the family had largely left my wife to get on with things on her own, including lifting, e.g., heavy oxygen bottles up and down stairs by herself.

Living in Retford itself and certainly that summer was a real positive. The straight-through train to the nearest seaside resort was to Cleethorpes and we managed to get there a couple of times for days out. Just going around Retford and area on the push bike with the child-seat was fun, especially going for a mile or two into the countryside and to the nearest farm for fruit picking. The various markets in Retford itself I nearly always found interesting or useful. I had applied for jobs, mostly of a pastoral nature and some were 'Christian', and got some interviews, but they were in the south of England only: this time no door was opening to me. On one occasion I went with my family down to the south coast for a full day's interview and it was almost unbelievable, but everything went wrong, not only on my side but with the interviewer - at a certain point he just gave up and so did I - I knew the Lord had closed the door for whatever reason and that was that, though it was not for the want of trying!

A little later on, some friends who attended the Retford Fellowship said to me, "We visit Ranby Prison on Sunday evenings, along with other prison visitation - would you like to come along to Ranby Prison with us?" I gave a positive "Yes!" to their invitation. One lady in particular was said to be very gifted in her prison ministry. It took a couple of weeks to set up, for security reasons, then I went in with Celia. In total, I went in three or four times. It was a C of E chaplain who took that first evening Sunday meeting in the chapel and it was well attended. During the meeting I spoke for a couple of minutes or so, but as it was all new to me I was keen to observe all that was going on. At the end of the meeting the chaplain asked me if I would like to preach, so I replied, "Yes!", and he gave me the date and time. The day came and I went along well prepared to speak for a specified short period of time. All was well and it came to the time for the preaching slot ... and the chaplain started speaking! "He'll hand over to me in a minute," I thought. He went on speaking ... then I thought, "Pressure of work. I think he's forgotten. Ah well, that's the way it goes!" The meeting came to an end and we were into ministry time. Celia was doing really well, as she got one, or was it two?, for the Lord and one prisoner was wonderfully baptised in the Holy Spirit - guess you could say he got wonderfully 'set free' that night in prison!! I was sitting on a settee and a prisoner came and sat beside me. He started sharing his situation with me, which was straightforward until he told me he was a paedophile. It would be no problem to help him and pray for him, though he would need some deliverance, but I was concerned for him and his safety, as I thought if any of the other prisoners knew or had heard him tell me they would tear him to pieces. I shared with him a little, but I didn't lead him to the Lord, which was the start that he really needed. When I was leaving, the chaplain asked me if he could visit my home to see me. We agreed a day and time later that week. My wife and I were prepared to give him hospitality when he turned up, but the visit was short-lived as he told me, without explanation, that he did not want me to return to any of the meetings at the prison, so that was the end of that! To this day I do not know what I did wrong, but left it with the Lord.

On a day in the late summer at the Grove Road property, I was up some tall step ladders cutting a high hedge with electric trimmers with the lead plugged into a socket in the close-by kitchen. All of a sudden, every bit of strength within me and certainly in my legs started to drain from me and I only just managed to safely get down the ladders and into the house before collapsing on the settee, very weak, but still conscious. After about twenty minutes, I was able to stand up and slowly put the gardening things away, then go and rest for the evening. That was strange, but I just dismissed it after asking the Lord for healing. A few weeks went by and it happened again when I was pedalling my bicycle with my son on the back and so I stopped and we both had to sit on the pavement until I was able to go on. I did not want to give into whatever was going wrong, yet it kept on happening every few weeks or so when I least expected it and then I would need to rest and struggle on.

At the Christmas time of 1987, my wife, daughter and the two children went up to Newcastle for a few days so that they could visit her Mum and some other relatives. I had been praying that my daughter would meet someone else and she did so during those few days. It took a while to develop into a relationship, as some weekends he would visit us in Retford and she and daughter would go and visit to stay in his family home in Gateshead. Later in the summer, they got their own patch in Cramlington and so started a long relationship.

On New Year's Day of 1988, I was on my knees before The Lord and picked up what I believed to be a word for the AOG Retford Fellowship, now doing well in its numbers of probably over 150 strong - so I got pen and paper and wrote it down. I know in Old Testament times they stoned a prophet to death if they got it wrong, so it is kind of a serious matter at any time if you say you have heard from The Lord, therefore surely it is wise not to play any games. At the next meeting I took courage and a risk and delivered it by reading it out from the front. It was not accepted because of the way I received and delivered it and the leadership went silent on me. When talking it over with my landlady, who was part of that fellowship, I said that it was irrelevant to me how it was given out but the content was important and whether or not it would come true. In hindsight, I know parts of that prophetic word did come true in the change and good things that later happened to that fellowship. Years later, the Lord would show me more about public prophecy.

In the early summer of 1988, my landlord and landlady were visiting us and told us that Derek and Ruth Prince were visiting Sheffield Town Hall for one evening only, for a time of deliverance ministry, and did we want to go along? My wife and I said we would and we'd take our son along as well. They said the five of us would go in their car and this we did when the time came. There were about 1,500 people present and Derek and Ruth Prince were very much on form. It was their meeting and they were fully in charge, so did not have to answer to anyone else, as might happen when being asked to speak at other people's conferences or meetings. They worked together well as a team and I guessed at that time he was still in his later sixties. There was very little teaching, but a thorough preparation for a 'mass deliverance' to take place. There were two children present, one of them being my six-year-old lad, and Derek Prince checked to see who had brought them and was satisfied in my case as both of us, his parents, were present. He went slowly and deliberately through a 'salvation prayer' for everyone to speak out aloud and repeat after him the words he gave from the front and also to renounce all evil and occult involvement, etc - then, after a short complete silence, he just commanded every demonic power to leave the people. He was carefully watching the proceedings from the platform and directing a few of his helpers to go to certain people in need of more help, as at the very moment he had made the command, the place erupted into a lot of noise, shouting, screaming and crying as the tormenting and unclean spirits left people - not everyone present was touched by the power of God, of course, but many were. There was a young lady close by to me choking, so Derek Prince told his wife, Ruth, to go over to her, as he just said the word 'abortion', and Ruth helped her to get free. I had heard and read about this kind of ministry and now I had seen it for myself on top of all the other things I had observed and seen and the reading I had done on the whole subject of deliverance, and for that season in Retford and on this foundation, I would now be able to build further.

In the early Spring of 1988, our landlord and landlady came to see us to inform us they wanted the property back and vacant so that they could sell it. I had previously said to them that if they ever wanted it back I would find somewhere else to live, but would ask them to give me the time to do so. This they did and said if I needed a reference to type something out and if they approved they would sign it - so this I did and they signed it, saying it certainly was a glowing reference! "I have a need to find somewhere soon and don't want to be homeless," I replied. If ever I thought it would be easy to find somewhere in Retford to live, that was not to be the case - every avenue and every door closed. I applied to a housing association that had properties in Cramlington and the Newcastle area and, after specifically asking for the Cramlington area and then being interviewed at our home down in Retford, was offered 26 Eastbourne Gardens in Cramlington - I liked the flat, its outlook and the area, though perhaps not all of the estate had a good name; but the reality was it was 'Hobson's choice', midsummer and to Cramlington we would go within a week or so ... as we signed up and were given the keys on that day's visit. My daughter and family got a house on the same estate a few weeks later. I didn't know it, but again there was an overall neat pattern as to what was happening!!

# *16*
# *At Death Do Us Part ... For A While ...*

I can easily remember the date of moving into that modern purpose-built one-up flat in Cramlington, for it was two days before my son's 7th birthday on 3rd July 1988. My family had stayed away for two days, during which time I got some of the basics sorted out. A few friends in Retford had helped me move up by hiring and driving a van, accompanied by friends with a car. They worked really hard all day and I was very grateful, of course. I struggled but got sorted out in a few days with The Missus's speedy help!

There was a park to the back of the flat with young trees planted, as the estate was only around eleven years old. Nearby was a primary school, which my son attended. We soon got settled in and started to get into a routine and I liked Cramlington, not least for the way it was laid out with lots of greenery and trees and part of our estate bordering on farmland.

Several weeks went by and on one hot summer afternoon we found the park where the tennis courts were situated, about a mile away from home, and we had a family game of tennis. I ended up playing against my daughter's partner. He was fit and much stronger than I was, being in his late twenties, and he gave me a thrashing - but not before I gave him a run for his money and put everything I could into that game - it was great fun! Afterwards, the family got a lift in his vehicle, but I decided I would walk home. I was about two-thirds of the way on a cycle track/pavement when suddenly every bit of strength drained from me and I was on my hands and knees, yet refusing to lie down. I was in a bad way, but determined to make it home, walking a step or two at a time, then resting. I never did play tennis again from that day to this, but I had become so weak in my flesh and so lethargic that in spite of asking the Lord to heal me I knew I would need to go and seek medical help. This I did, though they said there was not much they could do, especially if it might be 'M.E.' or something similar, so they gave me all the help they could and said to just let it take its course. All this was not exactly very encouraging or leading anywhere and I needed more and more rest. It was as if each day I had only a small quota of energy to spend and I needed to use it in the right things, for when it was gone, it was gone.

This didn't suit me at all, as I wanted to be part of the action, but I simply could not do so; I felt that something was catching up with me, such as too high a dosage of life's emotional pain, however caused, with many traumatic experiences, and sometimes I thought maybe enough for two lifetimes! Was this 'burnout'? Was I all but totally exhausted? It certainly seemed so, yet I still forced myself to do one or two chores around the home and some shopping and not neglect to give my son some attention. My wife had enough energy for the two of us and was really kind and understanding, a real 'brick'. I apologised to her more than once, but she was tough and just got on with things without complaining, showing love and compassion. She liked Cramlington and settled into her own routine, which included regularly visiting her Mum in the Newcastle care home.

I felt I had let everyone down, including the Lord, as I could not receive healing, but was still close to Him, reading the Bible and listening in my heart as to what He might say. After initially visiting one or two different fellowships in Cramlington, I occasionally went to one of them for a short while.

It was well into 1989, and one day I was in bed and said to the Lord, "This is no good, Lord, leave my wife and look after her and take me off to Heaven, as I'm sure that would be the best thing to do all round." Saying something, indeed anything, like this is a very risky thing to do, as the Lord might just take you at your word and carry it through - I certainly meant it and made sure my house was in order, but the Lord didn't take me up on it - on the contrary, He had another plan and my time will come - but certainly it was not to be then.

It was, as I remember, in the middle of the following year that the secretary of Dalton Baptist Church in Huddersfield made contact with me to say that the fellowship had done a history of the church since it was founded in the 1950s and that the time during which I was the pastor was the time of its greatest growth/activity. I said to him that was because it was teamwork and I had built on what others had done. He said he would visit us with his family for an afternoon, and this he did. Because Huddersfield was far away from the sea and their visit was on a lovely summer's day, we all went down to Blyth South Beach and had an enjoyable time at the seaside. He gave me a copy of the report of the history of the church, including my time there, and we discussed it for a short time.

The outcome of that afternoon was that my wife, self and son were invited to visit and stay with them for a weekend in Huddersfield a month or two later. When this came to pass, we went to the Sunday morning meeting of the fellowship. I only knew one or two people there compared to the old days and there were lots of changes. All was fine until, about half-way through the meeting, my wife started to weep and did so for several minutes. I, with someone else, quietly consoled her and gave her a tissue. At the end of the meeting I went into the anteroom where coffee was being served. The lady serving me greeted me with a derogatory, "Oh, it's *you*, is it?!" "C'est moi! It certainly is," I thought, "and *you* don't have a clue, discernment or understanding." Like King David of old, I had cried out for her and her family in prayer and fasting as if she was a close relative (it's in Psalms) because of her horrific domestic situation all those years ago. I simply looked at her and asked her two questions to which she gave me brief answers. I was aware, of course, that a lot of others over the years had prayed for her as well and I replied, "Well, it was enough then - for the Lord has answered all the prayers in the miraculous and in the positive against all the odds!" I was grateful for the coffee and thanked her, but I thought, "Okay, you can speak to me like that, you are off the hook, but I wouldn't dare speak to my wife this day in the same way or like manner if I were you, as you will find yourself 'on the carpet' before the Lord, quicker than you would ever think!" Perhaps I should have a rubber stamp with 'misunderstood' on it or 'not able or allowed to explain when needed' and so stamp a lot of situations in my life, waiting for the Lord to one day sort them out! I guess that's life and the battle we're in!

It was no mistake for us to have visited the fellowship that day as it was totally from the Lord - my wife was sorting out some deep emotional pain and forgiveness to do with the time we had lived and served there between her, the Lord, and the fellowship - a 'putting of her house in order', if you like.

One day in 1990, when my son would still have been just eight years old, I happened to look out of my bedroom window, only to witness, to my horror, a close-by neighbour, an older lad, sitting on my son's chest, having him pinned to the ground with his knees over the top part of his arms and viciously punching him with both fists continuously on his face, chest and neck area as hard as he could, and it looked like he had no intention of stopping. With a flashback to my own childhood and for justice, I saw red, opened the window and shouted at him that he'd better stop. After a couple more punches he stopped and, true to form for a bully, ran away. As he was one of the lads from my son's school, I wondered if there was any way I could have educated my son at home with my wife's help. I heard there was a family on the estate who were 'home educating' their children, so tracked them down and they allowed me to visit them and ask some questions for half an hour or so. I shelved the idea because I had in mind some sort of 'laid-out course' that my son could follow, but their general method for me would have been a non-starter. I mentioned it to one or two friends and after a few weeks a couple came back to me saying they had found out about a course coming out of America called A.C.E. (Accelerated Christian Education) and they had a South Wales contact telephone number. I eventually found the people running it at their new address near Swindon and obtained all the necessary info. It certainly was 'on a plate', with course booklets which each child, starting at their own level, would work through on a variety of subjects as needs be and according to parental choice, for the younger ones anyway. All answers where applicable were given and if you got stuck you could phone up during office hours for any help required. My wife said she would try to give a little bit of limited help if needed and I thought about others who might be able to help me when I was not well enough to cope, though the supervision required for my son's age group and level would be minimal. It would take some self-discipline on my son's part, but that would be no bad thing. My thinking was, if I could get around one or maybe two years before putting him back into the school system, it would be worth it.

After praying about it, my wife and I decided to go ahead and give it a try; after all, if it all went wrong we would only need to put him back into school. I communicated to my son it would only be for a limited time period, certainly before secondary school education. I had to buy into the A.C.E. system at a cost of £200 plus and purchase the work booklets as we went along, of course.

As I look back, I can see the Lord's hand in it all. As an extra, I also did a successful 'project' with him for over a year on 'Castles and Fortifications in the far north of England' as, after all, there was and is no shortage of them, including Hadrian's Wall; so we made visits to several of those historic sites. From July to September of 1990, I joined A.C.E., got it up and running and, although I struggled health-wise sometimes, did manage to carry it through for a couple of years.

Around that time a new Baptist Church had got underway in Morpeth and within a few months was very successful and I went along once or twice. Also, a FGBMFI (Full Gospel Business Men's Fellowship International) was regularly meeting in Morpeth and doing well - some from that Baptist Church were involved with it. With my daughter looking after my son for an evening in the late summer, my wife and I booked in to attend one of those monthly FGB dinners. A couple who were Methodists kindly gave us a lift from Cramlington.

It was an excellent meeting and time and all went well, with good food, music, speaker, etc. During the ministry time, my wife and I were talking to a couple who were sitting at our table, who we hadn't met before. We learned his wife had cancer and my wife got up to speak to a leader in order to get her some ministry and, as I talked/shared with the couple, he told me he was a Freemason, but he more or less just treated that as a joke or fun. "What if there is a spiritual link because of all the vows and curses made and your wife being poorly?" I asked. We talked on for a short while, by which time it was getting late and time to go home, so they said their goodbyes. I thought, "Where is my wife?" as I looked around, but could see no sign of her and so walked over to the stairs leading to the exit. A lady was standing there. "Is that your wife?" she said. "Where is she? ..." I asked. She pointed towards a settee and looked at me intently to say only one word ... "Incest." She then turned on her heels and was off down the stairs and onto the street. I knew not who she was and am not aware that I have ever seen her since. I was momentarily in a state of shock, as I do not go around thinking evil of folk, but this was a reality check of no small proportions and I immediately thought, "Who could be guilty of the heinous crime within her family?" I did not doubt this was a word of knowledge given out of the gift of discernment/knowledge (see gifts listed in I Corinthians chapter 12). I walked over to the settee and there my wife was lying on her back on the floor in much discomfort. She told me she had gone over to Steve, a good man and obviously powerful in the Lord, to talk to him about the lady needing ministry and he started praying for and ministering to *her* and as he did so the demonic within her started to manifest and surface. I don't know if anyone else had been involved, apart from the lady mentioned above. With difficulty, she told me that one of those demons was 'stuck' just below her throat/neck area. "The problem is," I said to her, "we have to leave the building and I have to get you out of this place and try to get you home and minister to you there. I do not want to push or allow these unclean spirit beings back down into you when/if they are surfacing. You will be okay, but just go very slowly." And she did so, after I helped her up on her feet. The couple were still waiting to give us a lift home and we all got to their car. On the journey back, a strong discussion started and it transpired they did not believe that a Christian could have a demon (remember 'demonised' is correct, not 'possessed'). I told them by default I sort of believed that doctrine once through Selwyn Hughes' teaching, but definitely did not do so any more. I explained further, but they would not budge on their doctrinal belief. Now this meant to them, what on earth was I playing at having a wife who was not a believer and the only important thing was to get her saved and 'put me right' on my doctrine! I pointed out in so many words that this was a desperate moment for action, as my wife could be further damaged by these things, and it was not the time to debate or become upset over doctrine.

In Cramlington, they parked the car and came upstairs into the sitting room of our flat. I sat my wife down on a chair in the middle of the room and got her as comfortable as possible. I told her to keep me informed as to what was happening and if the Lord was speaking to her. I took authority over the evil spirit using the words of scripture and little by little edged it up, as it did not want to leave this body it had made its home for a good few years ... but leave it did! It took me the best part of an hour, as I remember, then my wife said, "There is another one as well". The couple decided to leave at that point and I guessed they thought that we had both lost the plot and had real problems! After thanking them for the lift and saying goodbye, and being the early hours of the morning, I continued on and got the other one out, which took about half an hour. I was exhausted and so was my wife when we finally got to bed about 2.30am. The next day we both agreed that she needed a lot more deliverance.

I knew of a friend having deliverance ministry at Ellel Grange near Lancaster and that, by this time of later 1990, it would have been open around four years. I wrote to Ellel and got my wife booked into a 48-hour healing retreat in the November - accommodation was in the building itself and I accompanied her to look after her.

For the retreat she was assigned to a married couple and though it applied to both, the wife certainly had a very powerful deliverance ministry. I heard later that sadly their marriage did not last, such would have been the onslaught of the enemies of God at the couple's weakest link. On the second evening of the retreat, being a very cold November night, a lovely log fire was lit in the lounge/foyer reception hall and people were sitting around there talking and praying. The couple ministering came to take my wife into one of the rooms a few feet away for ministry, but they said to me, "You stay here and pray." I replied to them, "It is important that I come in with you!" "No," they said, to which I replied, "Then at least take in the training I've had and the serving I've already done." This was to no avail, so I prayed. It was 'treat me like an idiot time' here again! I know that not everyone could handle this kind of situation, but I knew I could and it would have been really helpful for what was to happen as the years went by.

Now the walls (about three feet thick) of that grand country house from where I was sitting and the solid oak(?) double doors between myself and where my wife was being ministered to afforded great sound-proofing ... that is, until they were getting more of those demons out of her, and I could hear the horrific loud screams as they came out of her one after another, even through the wall and those closed doors. It reminded me of horrendous times in my childhood, but I still wanted to get into the 'ministry fight', if you like, that evening. I was grateful, of course, for what they had done, though my wife did not share any details of what they had unearthed. I had by then realised that it was her father who was the main perpetrator of the incest and he must have committed the most horrific sexual crimes against her, at his will, even when she was a young child, of rape and sodomy. But as the demons from all of that were coming out, so the emotional pain of it all was surfacing. She was totally respectful to her parents and the family 'clan' closed ranks, including her, if anyone got too near the truth. Now this is the grace of God, for if my father-in-law had still been alive I would have stopped at nothing to make sure he went to prison, but the strange thing is, it is highly likely it would have cost me my marriage - the family protection, even of evil, was greater than wanting justice ... no wonder they 'loved me to bits'!?!

As we left Ellel later on the following day, my wife simply stated, "It is good what they have done, but it is still not enough." She was exhausted, as is often the case with this kind of ministry. It was my plan to get her back there for more ministry, but that never happened.

Several weeks went by and it was late January 1991. One day my wife came in from visiting her Mum in Newcastle and just sat down on the settee. She admitted to me she had not felt well for a day or two. "It sounds like flu," I said, "but I think it would be a good idea to go and see the Doc." So within a day or two she did, but he just said she had flu and to let it take its course. A week or so went by and she was still not on form, so she went back. "I've got bruises on my arm," she said to the doctor, and he made some comment about domestic violence, but she put the record straight that it was not so; however, he didn't take any notice. (Interestingly enough, that doctor not many years thence was struck off the register, though I did not complain about him.) Near the end of February, my wife saw another doctor in the practice, a lady doctor, and she ended up that day in the old Ashington Hospital. All the family went up to visit and trooped in to the ward to see her that evening and she told us she was being transferred to Newcastle Royal Victoria Infirmary the following morning for some tests. "Okay," I said, "we will go down in the visiting time tomorrow evening to the RVI and bring the things you need." I wondered what it might be this time, but was not overly concerned.

The time came the following evening and my daughter, son, grand-daughter and I went down and found the ward she was in at the RVI and she was sitting on her bed. Immediately, even before I reached the bed, as my family were ahead of me, one of the doctors asked, "Are you the husband?" motioning towards my wife with his hand. "Yes," I replied. "I need to have a word with you," he said, "I'll be back in a minute." My heart sank and I felt numb as I instantly knew this would not be good news. I went over to my family and quietly joined in with the conversation and after a few minutes the doctor returned and beckoned me away to talk privately. "It's not good news, I'm afraid … your wife has one of the worst forms of leukaemia and it is now in its final stages … she should be gone in two to three days." I was in a state of shock and turmoil. My heart, mind and emotions all wanted their say at the same time! It was the suddenness of it all … but "keep cool, calm and collected for my family's sake and be strong for them, as I will have to tell them," I thought.

"Does my wife know?" I asked. "Yes," he replied, "and we can start treatment tomorrow that would bring her round to stop death, then start on chemotherapy, etc, and it is possible she could live for months or even a year or more." "Does she want this?" I asked. "Yes … and we are going to give it a try," he said. "Do I have a say in this?" "No, not really," he replied, and continued, "but if you come down tomorrow afternoon you can be with her and there is a small sort of storeroom with a bed in it that you can use for a couple of nights, maybe three." "Okay, thank you, I'll take you up on that," I replied. I got a minute alone with my wife at the end of the visiting time and told her I knew what was happening and asked her if she wanted to fight the illness. "They're not really taking 'No' for an answer, so I'll just go ahead with it," she replied. "Tomorrow afternoon I'll tell the family at our daughter's home, then I'll be down here to be with you - there's an anteroom with a bed and some other items stored in it for me to get some sleep for one or two nights." I gently kissed her and told her that I loved her, committed her to the Lord Jesus and told her that tomorrow evening I would start to get as many as I could to begin praying for her and our situation, and I was gone before any tears could flow.

The next day, as I remember, it was some time in the afternoon that I gathered my family together in my daughter's sitting room - my daughter, son and grand-daughter (now aged six years) - all eyes were on me. I launched straight in at the 'deep end' and told them exactly what the doctor had said to me the previous evening and, "Your Mum/Nana is not expected to live more than a couple of days and it is extremely serious" - but immediately a terrible great cry and shouts from their hearts' pain went up from the three of them, with weeping and wailing and their lives would never be the same from that moment onwards. After a minute or so, I explained that the medics would be carrying out treatment to extend her life and then give further treatment that might help her, but that would mean a temporary loss of hair - so they could have her around for a little while yet. I don't remember what else we said and like to think that we comforted each other a little ... but for me it was one of the hardest things I have ever had to do, because I was so emotionally involved.

My daughter was looking after my son when I went back to the hospital and stayed, as arranged, to be near my wife. When they were giving her the kidney dialysis (treatment) I was present with her in the room. All of a sudden, at a certain point of receiving the treatment, she sat bolt upright and exclaimed something ... I don't now remember what it was ... then fell back to lying on her back ... I was startled and wondered what it was about! I wondered if that should have been the point of death, but they had brought her round to be on borrowed time?!!

Later that evening, when she was settled in her bed, I started to contact friends and relatives. I was amazed at the positive response and on the Christian 'grapevine' the news literally spread like wildfire, and likewise amongst relatives. One busy Christian friend, Andrew from Heysham, on the following day travelled four hours to see me for an hour or so and give encouragement, prayer and a gift, then travelled the four hours back. The older of my brothers, in Newcastle, came straight down to the RVI and gave me a bagful of change - several pounds worth to make telephone calls, which in those far-off days of coin-operated machines only in the hospital turned out to be a godsend. It kept on happening and I have to admit I was overwhelmed at the way people rallied round, not least because of the age of my wife and the young children involved.

It was later that first night - I was tired, it was all a lot to take in, and I was just settling down for the night, praying and peacefully reading from Psalm 116, when a verse pierced my heart ... about the death of those who belong to Him being precious in His sight ... and the Lord very gently, clearly and firmly spoke to me in my heart, "This time I am calling her Home." Remember, when the Lord speaks, He never wastes words and I *knew* I had heard from Him and for me to receive the scriptural affirmation was a must. Nevertheless, I was stunned for a minute or two and somehow knew it was His final word on the end of her life and so there was no point in asking the Lord to change His mind, as in the sense of asking Him for more time for her; but when I thought of the much pain and suffering she had endured over her 47 years at every level of her being, I knew this was the best option for her and Heaven would be the right place for her to be. We had been together since I was 17 years and I could not really imagine what it would be like without her. I then said to the Lord, "If You want her Home then I will accept it. This is a difficult one, but I give her to You, Lord." I was in total faith and knew from that moment it was final. I was so tired that I fell into a deep sleep.

As the next few days unfolded and I fully came to terms with all that was happening, I knew in my heart there was a lot of prayer power being generated. I was still amazed at the help and kindness of Christian friends, and relatives, as those days progressed - and I later found out that some were praying for my situation though they didn't even know me, such as in Retford.

But my first test came after a week or so with the head medic, an important and no doubt famous man in his field in that Ward 13 of the RVI. There was something different about my wife's case - the type of leukaemia that she had and possibly the fact that she had a rare blood type. Whatever it was, he wanted to do further research for medical science, but I saw her as my wife and not a guinea pig – indeed, she was precious and had suffered greatly, so, as far as I was concerned, enough was enough. This was the point I made as we had some very strong words together, both desperately trying to be polite to each other. He asked my wife what she wanted and she said she would continue on with the treatment, no doubt having the children in mind, and so I was silenced - except I said, "It won't work!"

Week after week she was in that ward and she started receiving chemotherapy and whatever other treatment was given. Her hair all came out in tufts and I said to her just to get it shaved or trimmed off for the children's sake, as they visited regularly. Actually, she had a perfect-shaped head and didn't look too bad at all, though she did have an NHS wig at one point. She put up a really good fight - surely second to none!!

One day, it must have been somewhere in the middle of April - it was a warm sunny Spring day and I went in as usual to visit her. "Anything that is touching my skin is really painful and I can hardly bear it," she said. She had a nightie on, but apart from a sheet had no other bedding over her. "What if I go and get you a couple of soft, silky nighties from M & S - respectable but light in weight?" I asked. "I'll try that," she said; so I made haste the couple of hundred yards or so down to the M & S at the Haymarket, went to the department concerned and straight to a member of staff. After I fully explained what was happening and why, she sorted out some options. I chose two, made payment and went back to the RVI. After trying them for a couple of nights when on my daily visit, she just about all but broke down, saying to me, "I've tried them, but nothing's working. I just can't bear any more of this pain and discomfort." "Then all the treatment must stop," I said, becoming very emotionally involved. "They won't listen to me. It'll have to come from you; but it's okay, you can only take so much and you've gone the extra mile for all of us. You will have to tell one of the doctors or the sister," I continued. It was a living nightmare. As I remember, at that point I went and told someone - I think it was Sister - and within minutes my wife had told them and they agreed they would immediately stop all treatment. This, of course, meant the beginning of the very end for her - the medics knew the pattern but, of course, I didn't!

In those days in that ward there was a lady social worker assigned to check out each patient and their family conditions, to offer help and advice or whatever. This happened and she was kind and helpful to us and gave some good advice and later made one trip up to see our flat in Cramlington. She told my wife to write a 'goodbye letter' to us all and I thought she would never be able to do that, so I started to write one out for the children and thought I would just get her to sign it! WRONG! I was mistaken: she wrote one out to us all and she did mention that fact to me. I'll come back to this later.

The medics/social worker said she would be able to go home for a week or two and then would she like to go into St Oswald's Hospice in Gosforth? ... We both agreed and they set it up at that time.

Just a few days went by and they sent her home in an ambulance. I think it was just under three weeks that she had at home - still in a lot of discomfort, but she was determined to try and make the best of it. When I was out of the flat one afternoon, she got ready and managed to get down the stairs from the flat and walk the 200 yards or so to our daughter's house, where she had a tiny bit of food. She didn't tell me because she knew I wouldn't have let her go; nevertheless, it was a tonic for her. After a week or so, one afternoon we spent nigh on two hours sorting out all of her clothes, etc, and what should go where, after which time she was totally exhausted. I can remember that we both agreed that, just in case the Lord did heal her at this late stage, we 'hid' one set of her clothing in the 'ottoman' in our bedroom. It would be about a month and a half later that, having forgotten all about them, I came across them - and, in shock, wept!

One afternoon on another day, I was on my way to do some shopping and had just walked down the carpeted stairs to the entrance of the flat and my wife was at the top on the landing, but it was a sharp left turn so you could see nothing else of the flat at that point. There was plenty of light in the stairwell from the glass entrance door and the window a few feet above it. But a debate had started - "Just cremate me," she had said. "Never," I replied, "it is right that you are buried and that should be down at Blyth South Beach Cemetery." We talked on for a few minutes and I put my case. "It is biblically correct if at all possible," I said, and continued, "it is right that there is somewhere for the children and us all to visit, even in later years, so we can remember you and come to terms with it all"; at which point, though I did not know he was there and listening, my son put his head around the wall as he was standing next to his Mum out of sight and, looking down at me, boldly stated, "Listen, it doesn't matter, I'll have her next to my bed, okay?" and that put an abrupt end to that discussion, though I did carefully explain to my son what had to happen at death.

The medics knew 'what and when' and gave me the date that she was to go into the hospice and an ambulance was arranged. Before she left home, she gave me clear instructions to, "Forget all about me, get married again and get on with the rest of your life." Though not sure about 'forgetting all about her' and the grieving process for myself, these were kind and wise, selfless words. We also discussed some of what she wanted us to sing at her funeral and who should take it, but not to be me, she had said. "Don't worry, I wouldn't be able to," I replied. We had a choice of several who had been in leadership, but chose our friend, Andrew from Heysham, who had been at Glasgow BTI when we were students there. It was by then later in May and her time was to be about two weeks in St Oswald's Hospice.

When she went in, I visited each day for about three days and a couple of times my son and grand-daughter visited for a short time. In the foyer of the hospice was a large wooden rocking horse for any visiting children to ride on. My son took a liking to it and kept playing on it, sometimes for all he was worth. The next thing I knew, when he was doing some of his schooling he wrote a poem about 'The Rocking Horse' that expressed something of what he was going through and drew a picture of the horse and coloured it in. I was surprised at his gifting in that area, certainly for that time anyway.

After a couple of visits by the family, my wife said to my daughter, "Don't come back - you don't want to see me this way." My daughter was taking it badly, so she did not return or see her mother again. Just then, the housing association were fitting a new kitchen in our flat, so my daughter and partner decorated it for me, which was kind of them.

All of a sudden, my wife could not walk and so had to stay in her bed in the ward. From then on I spent those last eleven days more or less by her bedside, though, of course, I had to quickly visit home every day to make sure all was okay. I slept on a chair or a bed next to her, just to get a few hours' sleep in the depths of the night, as the nursing staff gave permission. Except for one other very poorly lady, the ward was completely empty and they allowed me to use one of the bathrooms. I wasn't bothered about food, yet I did get some, but made sure I got enough to drink. I said to the staff after a day or two, "What can I do to help her?" They said, "You see these little sponges on sticks? ... dip them in this liquid and gently wipe the inside of her mouth"; which I did 'religiously'! Then suddenly, after another day or two with shock, I realised that she was just not 'sleeping' but her ability to communicate was all but gone. Gently, firmly and clearly, I whispered in her ear, "Do you still love the Lord Jesus?" All was very quiet as I put my ear to her mouth and I clearly, but only just, heard her whisper, "Of ... course ... I ... do." They were the last words I ever heard her speak and they must have taken every bit of strength that she had to say them. I was heart broken and yet filled with great joy at the same time, for in her great suffering she still loved the Lord Jesus! I still talked to her and gave her words of reassurance and love and would read some Psalms, etc, to her and tell her what the family were doing. At this point, I asked the staff to give her morphine or anything to help her bear the pain. Friends and relatives were coming in to visit her every day and would take one look at her emaciated body - just skin and bone - a mere shadow of her former self and almost without fail they would burst into tears or just weep and weep. At least one person who had no time for me shook my hand as he wept, before leaving in great distress. Another strong Christian couple who came had travelled some distance and were good friends and, as they wept and wept, could not understand why I was not taking spiritual authority to see her healed. "The Lord wants her Home," I said; but they would not accept it.

On the morning of 3rd June 1991, the medic in charge of the hospice said to me to go and get my son and bring him down and they would move my wife into a private en suite room, put a bed for me and a place for my son to sleep. In the early afternoon, I went home first of all to my flat. I'll never forget sitting down in my sitting room, all in. "I'll allow myself 15 minutes," I said to myself. All was very quiet and then it dawned on me with startling realisation that this was the way it was going to be. For me, at the age of 17 and now at 46 ... we had shared our lives together and now that relationship on Earth would be no more ... Life would be so different.

I sorted myself out, got some of my son's overnight things together and went down to my daughter's to collect him and have a chat. It was later in the afternoon that self and son got back to the hospice on the bus. Of course, the nurses made a fuss of the lad as we settled into the private room and they gave us something to eat - a short while later my son vomited it all back up, so that sorted that out, such was his anguish! A little later on, he said, "Dad," ... "Yes, Old Son," I replied ... "Mum's snoring like a pig." I told him simply that he was right, though it wasn't a very nice thing to say and that it meant she was now in a coma and it was to do with her lungs and breathing and that she would soon be gone.

The evening went by and we were chatting away to each other as usual. He had got himself ready for bed and was sitting on his bed, made up on a wooden seat in a built-in alcove about three feet away from his Mum's bed. "It's just off midnight," I said to him, "we are both shattered, so I'll just get ready and we'll settle down for the night." I took the few steps into the bathroom and froze - I don't know for how long ... was it just tiredness? ....My son said, loud enough for me to hear, "Dad, Mum's gone!" I took the two or three steps back into the room, looked at my wife and realised she had gone. I looked at the lad, still sitting there looking at his mother ... walked slowly over to him, sat down beside him and put an arm around his shoulder, saying, "Well (saying his name, of course), it's just you and me now." "Dad," he said, "I've just seen a beautiful white creature come through the ceiling and I didn't see his head ... I'm frightened ... then I saw Mum leave her body and she was a different colour ... a sort of red ... and she turned to me, smiled and said, 'Bye bye. J..., I'll see you in Heaven' ... and Dad, the two of them went up through the ceiling!!" I explained to him, "This is John 14 verse 3 coming to pass," then continued, "you have been very privileged to see what you've just seen and no doubt because of your Mum's and all the other prayers and all your pain in this situation you have seen into the reality of the spirit world and the Lord, but not His face, and your Mum was allowed to say goodbye to you with a smile ... for the time being ..."

We just sat there in silence for a minute or two, then I said, "We had best go and tell the nursing staff and then you will need to get dressed." This we did and the two nurses went in immediately and took my wife's body away - we sorted ourselves out for going home and I phoned my brother and his wife, who lived about four or five minutes away by car; as we had previously arranged if this should happen through the night, they would run us home to Cramlington, which they did. The nurses said before we left to come into a kind of 'chapel room' and see the body - they had 'laid her out', sitting up in bed looking 'peacefully asleep' ... the only way to describe her. We both walked into the room, looked, absorbed the scene, thanked the nurses, left the room and went to the foyer. They told me the doctor's certificate of death would be ready to collect from mid-morning and I said I would sort out for the undertaker to collect the body in the morning.

On the way back to Cramlington, my brother said, " I will have to go into work for two hours first thing in the morning and then I will come up and collect you and run you around to sort out anything you want, then we will buy you lunch." I thanked them as they were really busy and this was a sacrifice, and said I'd be really grateful for their help and support. They dropped my son and me off at my daughter's house and, when she and her partner came downstairs into their kitchen and opened the door, that was the point I totally broke and just sobbed and sobbed ... I couldn't get the words out ... but then there was no need to ... as I wept on their shoulders in my brokenness, I eventually did get the words out. Later at home, I just wanted to be quiet and rest for a few days but, of course, I could not do so. I got some sleep after thinking I would do as much as possible 'tomorrow' to make the next few days easier.

Next day was somewhat of a miracle really, for after making various necessary phone calls such as to the undertaker, etc, and being run around in the car to do some of the essentials, I got done just about everything that I had to do. When I picked up the necessary paperwork from the hospice, the nurse, much to my surprise, gave me a hug as she said goodbye! Yet this was the warmth of the love of kindness from the hospice staff and not just the professionalism of cold indifference. At the Civic Centre in Newcastle, when obtaining the death certificate from the registrar, I had no idea which side of midnight the departure of my wife was, so settled for just after midnight. I went to the bank, building society, etc, put the joint accounts into my name only, then had a nice meal out, so that by the middle of the afternoon, because we had no assets or property, there was really nothing major left to sort out - it was all very simple and straightforward. I had started to tell some people what had happened, but as soon as I found out the day and time of the funeral, I made all the required phone calls.

So all those arrangements were made for burial in Blyth South Beach Cemetery. I had said to my son and asked my daughter to do the same for my grand-daughter, to give her free choice, which she did. "Whatever you want to do at the time of your Mum's funeral, I will try and sort out - you can come to the funeral and keep close by me or go out for the day or go to the cinema, etc - it's up to you." "I want to go to the funeral," the lad said, and I replied, "That's okay, no problem." My grand-daughter said the same to her Mum, so that settled it. My Aunty Helen on my father's side of the family, who then lived in Warkworth, said to me, "I want to pay for the funeral." I replied that I had a small insurance cover with 'The Man from The Pru', but she said, "You keep that and let me know what the bill is and I'll pay for it." I was really grateful, of course, as it meant I would now be able to buy a gravestone for my family's sake, which I later did. The designated undertaker who was to take the funeral was giving me a lift in his car and I told him of the above and he said, "Everyone should have an Aunty Helen like yours!" "Hmm … I think you're right," I said.

The day of the funeral arrived and I thought that there might be about thirty or forty people turn up … wrong! It was a beautiful warm summer's day. Some ladies I knew came and saw to the catering in the flat for later, then a beautiful bunch of flowers arrived, followed by some more and I lost count of them after a short while and simply left the front door open for them to be delivered and people arriving for the funeral. People were arriving from all over, from places where we'd lived, including Andrew and his wife, who were going to take the funeral. Already there were too many people in the flat for me to talk to them all. I quickly got a handful of mature believers together, went into the large bedroom, closed the door and we spent just a few minutes crying out to the Lord for His Presence and that He would be uplifted and He would take care of all the details of the funeral and the day and immediately the warmth and love of the Lord's Presence was with us.

When we got to the small chapel on the left-hand side of the entrance to the Blyth South Beach Cemetery, it was already packed with people - they were having to stand round the walls, as well as all the seats being filled. I was trying to take it all in, but my emotions were beginning to surface - my wife was certainly being honoured! Of course, I had to say a couple of words of notices at the beginning and to thank everyone for turning up; also to say why we had chosen Andrew from Heysham to take the funeral and he would read out the letter my wife had left to the immediate family. There were a lot of believers there, including several who could have easily taken the funeral, and the singing was strong and meaningful, with a beautiful atmosphere of joy and sadness … "What a Friend we have in Jesus … all our sins and griefs to bear …" I looked over at the coffin as a stream of tears rolled down my face and thought, "I can't go home after this is over to tell you what happened and share with you ... but on the other hand there's no pain or tears where you are now with the Lord Jesus ..."; and when Andrew read out the letter she left and at one point himself was greatly overcome with emotion ... I don't think there was a dry eye in that room!

Here is the transcript of the letter she left - I have slightly tidied up the grammar and spelling for this page. The abuse she had taken, the dyslexia that was never diagnosed, the terrible pain she had known and was suffering in the throes of death, probably about three or four weeks earlier, writing this was no easy task for her.

> Dear Henry, I love you, you have been a good
> husband and Dad and I would never change you.
> Thank you
> for sharing your life with
> me. M_ _ _ _ _ _. XXX

> Dear J_ _ _ _ _, my Son, I love you. I am very proud of
> having you. I would not have missed having you for
> the world. You have made my heart glad to have a boy
> like you.
> Mother. XXX

> Thank you Lord for Your love to me, and what You
> have done so far. I love You. I give You all the
> praise and glory and thank You for the cross and the
> blood. M_ _ _ _ _ _ F_ _ _ _.

> Dear C_ _ _ and C_ _ _ _ _
> I love you both - thank you for your kind hearts - I
> would not have missed having any of you because I
> love you.
> Be strong C_ _ _.
> Mam. XXX  Nana. XXX

> Thank you D_ _ _ for your help and
> love. M_ _ _.

> Thank You Lord for my
> mother, take care of her for
> me.
> I love her so much.
> M_ _ _ _ _ _. XXX

Later, outside, as I prepared to follow the coffin to the graveside with my son on one side and my grand-daughter on the other, holding a hand each, I looked behind me and the amount of people lined up must have stretched over a hundred yards with, I guessed, about 150 people. I couldn't even begin to acknowledge or talk to everyone, so I just had to hope they understood. I would not have changed the way it went as such, but I was very concerned for my daughter and son, as it was so hard for both of them.

Would I practise what I preach and go away for a few days after the funeral? The next day I went on the train down to Morecambe with my son to see Andrew and his family in Heysham and stayed in a really nice B & B on Morecambe Front, with a room overlooking the sea. I was desperate to rest and take stock of all that had happened in the last few weeks and to start to come to terms with being single and a one-parent family … 'precious mem'ries … how they linger … how they ever flood my soul …'

The top end of the picturesque Northumbrian village of Humshaugh near the North Tyne river and 'Chesters' on Hadrian's Wall, showing part of Linden House behind the trees

Where the wall curves round is where I used to cross the road on my trike in the late 40s and visit some elderly folk for the likes of 'gingerbeer' and 'lemonade.'

The house in St Georges Crescent in Carlisle with its many memories for me both pleasant and unpleasant, recently, as seen here, was in the process of having a 'makeover', and I wonder if it may need some spiritual cleansing as well.

The Crescent since the 50s has changed little. The second tree down on the right is where the Private Detective spent hours reading the newspaper. There was an abundance of children living there in the mid 50s. The tree on the left was used mainly for counting to 100 with your eyes closed whilst playing hide and seek.

This is the council house in Carlisle I lived in during the late 60s. It was a happy home and still looks to be so!

Part of 'Talkin Tarn' near Brampton in Cumbria that holds a lot of childhood memories for me… and is a local unspoilt beauty spot

Deer Park House in Carlisle, now demolished – as it was in the mid 60s with my
daughter on the swing

# Records relating to the purchase of Roxbro in 1919

by my Grandfather and the mortgage that he obtained to do so
– in itself a small fortune at that time

Dated *30ᵗ December* 19*19*

*Mr Norman Field*

TO THE

## Grainger   Permanent

## Building   Society.

**Mortgage** of *free* hold
Property situate *Known as "Roxbro"*
*situate at Warkworth in*
*the County of Northumberland*

to secure payment of Subscriptions, &c.,
upon an advance of £ *656 13 4*
on Ordinary Shares.

WATSON, BURTON & CORDER,
NEWCASTLE-UPON-TYNE.

By the 7th September 1925 he had paid off all of the mortgage in spite of those troubled times.

15

Signed Sealed and Delivered by the before-named Mortgagor in the

presence of

*Y. R. Hutchinson*

*Clerk with Messrs Watson Burton Jordan*

*Solicitor*

*Newcastle upon Tyne*

### The Grainger Permanent Building Society

hereby acknowledge to have received all moneys intended to be secured by the within written deed

**In witness** whereof the seal of the Society is hereto affixed this *Seventh* day of *September* one thousand nine hundred and *twenty five*.

**By order** of the Board of Directors in presence of

Directors. Members of

Seal Committee

Secretary.

**STAMP.**

**This Indenture** made the *thirtieth* day of *December* one thousand nine hundred *and nineteen*

**Between** *Norman Field of Park View Killingworth in the County of Northumberland Explosives Merchant*

( *a* Member of the Grainger Permanent Building Society incorporated under the Building Societies' Act, 1874) hereinafter called "the Mortgagor" of the one part

and the said **Grainger Permanent Building Society** hereinafter called "the Society" of the other part.

**Witnesseth** as follows:—

1.—In consideration of the sum of *Six hundred and fifty six pounds thirteen shillings and four pence*

on or before the execution hereof paid out of the funds of the Society to the Mortgagor being the amount to which he *is* entitled in accordance with Column *III* of the Tables for Ordinary Advanced Shares annexed to the Rules of the Society in respect of *eight* ordinary advanced share *s* held by *him* in the Society (the receipt of which sum the Mortgagor hereby acknowledge *s*) And in consideration of the Money if any which may hereafter be paid by the Society to the Mortgagor in respect of any other share or shares held or to be held by *him* therein he the Mortgagor doth hereby

# 17

# *Singleness ... One Parenting ... Education ...*

If ever I thought, and it had crossed my mind, that I would not ever need to do much grieving, I was mistaken! Our reaction to grief is different for each one of us. My ability to cope with 'grief', even from an early age, as stated previously, was to face up to it, put it behind me, get on with 'the now' and look to the future, especially for any good things ahead. This, of course, ties in with what Paul says in Philippians chapter 3. I needed three years of low-level grieving to reach the goal of full acceptance that is normally required. Any genuine grief is not easy.

I continued with my son's education, which had stopped for about three or four weeks, and kept on with it for another sixteen months. If ever I thought in a single-parent family I could 'wear two hats', to be 'fatherly' and 'motherly' to my son, I was mistaken. I was his Dad, full stop. Even if I was in charge of the kitchen, cleaning, etc, I could never take the place of what his Mum was or had done for him.

I can remember going down to the Christian Literature Crusade Bookshop in the heart of Newcastle, looking for books or info on 'single parenting' and in those days finding precious little. I thought to myself that I could keep a journal and in a few years' time I could be armed with some important information that would be useful to others, but decided I should not do this because I wanted nothing to sidetrack my getting the lad into responsible adulthood. As he still had his 'big sis' close by, that would help him somewhat and be a sort of 'Mum' figure to him. Although I did not want anything visible around the flat to remind me of my late wife - there were few photographs of her anyway - my son could have had reminders of his mother in his bedroom, but he chose not to do so. The good memories locked in my heart were enough.

In the October of that year my late wife's mother, in her eighties, was very poorly and I went to visit her in the Newcastle Care Home with my son and grand-daughter. I was surprised at how poorly - being skin and bone - she had become. She seemed to be in great fear, possibly due to her mind having gone, and be in anguish, if not some amount of physical pain - I certainly shouldn't have taken my grand-daughter. We only stayed a few minutes and I prayed very quietly over her and we left. She was gone in two or three days. I explained to the children how poorly and old she was and that she had had a very hard life. They were not involved in the funeral in any shape or form - except I informed my son that the staff of the Home had put a photograph of him in his Nana's coffin because they had been so fond of each other.

My son had one of those football games where the 'men' are on bars with springs at each end, several of them facing each other, a ball and a 'goalie' each, and this game was placed in the middle of the lounge - if anyone came into the flat they were offered a game of it! ... or the small child's snooker game that he had as well and my son and I and others sure did have a lot of fun with those games!!

I decided the best thing I could do was to try and book in for a healing retreat at Ellel Grange to get some strength back into my being and I was allocated one in the September of that year, 1991. I received some good ministry for emotional release with a lot more tears and the place and fellowship were excellent, as usual, but there was a meeting in one of the large lounges on the second evening of the 48-hour retreat. It started off 'normal', but suddenly and powerfully I personally was in the awesome presence of God and flowing into my spirit from above me was a 'waterfall' of pure crystal clear, cool, refreshing water ... the 'WATERS OF LIFE from HEAVEN ABOVE' were anointing my soul and inner being ... and I never wanted it to stop!! I stood up with my hands raised to the Lord in Heaven, receiving this and gently praising Him, oblivious to what was going on around me, except when someone I knew from Heysham, on the leadership team, cast a demon out of someone who had a deaf ear and immediately he was able to hear in that ear, so there was great joy - but for me 'the waterfall' in all its sparkling beauty just kept on falling in my vision of it on the inside of me. When it stopped, I felt totally refreshed and looked around me and then at my watch. It seemed like it had lasted about five or six minutes but, in actual fact, one and a half hours had gone by. I guessed I was about 70% healed at that time, which prepared me for what lay ahead.

My son and I started from that summer of 1991 to regularly go and stay with friends and go to Christian conferences, etc. We went to the A.C.E. School Conference just outside of Swindon for a day or two and made several friends of other home-schooling families, the result of which was, the following year, we ended up visiting a farm in Devon and a smallholding in south Wales and both were in beautiful areas. We certainly had adventures and fun, such as me driving a very old tractor (carefully!) with four children/youths hanging on. On another occasion down on a farm in Devon a stick was put in my hand and I was told to help get the herd of cows down the path to the milking parlour - "What me?" "Yes, you!" the farmer's wife replied, and so I helped ... not really my scene ... but they were lovely animals!

Twice I got the lad to the annual Sevenoaks Scripture Union Adventure Week - all good stuff and he said *adventures and fun* he certainly had! That first one was a couple of months after he lost his Mum and, when I returned to collect him, one of the volunteer helpers who was a nurse told me that at one point in the week something had caused him to break down in tears over the loss of his Mum and she was able to take him aside to help him as she had received training to deal with children who had been bereaved - I was grateful for her help.

At the end of the year I got a preaching engagement just north of Glasgow and at the Sunday morning meeting preached my heart out on Luke chapter 16 verses 19 to 31. That was okay until the evening meeting, after which my son, grand-daughter and I planned going on the train home from Glasgow Central to Newcastle, so I had packed my Bible and my specs away; but when we got to the meeting and I tried to hide, I was asked to go down to the front and read from the Bible. There wasn't enough light in that building for me to read from someone else's Bible with small print and without my specs, but I did not feel free enough to say it as it was – however, of course, I had to after a few minutes, but not without making myself feel like a real 'nana' - a good lesson in humility!! We only just made the train after several miles' journey to Glasgow Central, with only ten seconds to spare! That was the time when I had my first date - she was an attractive female … Temptation? Yes! Fall? No! That relationship didn't come to anything … it was near Christmas time and, of course, not an easy season that year.

I joined one or two Christian Dating Agencies during the time I was single and that was fascinating and sometimes fun, though sometimes desperately sad … it was all an eye-opener … from one's teens to later forties was a different era. I gained valuable insight into the heartaches of many who found themselves in the single state - not always straightforward. One such agency was ahead of the others, led by a lady called Sue Saxon, and her book was helpful. I later totally destroyed all the correspondence, etc, of all the contacts that I had had and was sure this was the correct thing to have done.

I questioned myself as to where I stood with regard to dating a divorcee, so decided at this time I would do some reading on the subject and a study on 'divorce and remarriage', which I did, but didn't record my findings as such. The scripture has some hard words on the subject, yet I started to ask a lot of questions to the scriptures, as to the Lord, such as, "What is divorce in the first covenant? What is marriage in scripture? What is remarriage in scripture?", etc. If we are 'born again', surely that in itself is a complete fresh start. Is divorce really an unforgivable sin, as apparently it is in so many people's eyes? If you really were wronged in a marital relationship, then any further persecution would be a double blow. Yes, there are some hard words given to lead us in wisdom and for our protection and safeguard, but mercy, compassion and loving-kindness also belong to our God.

Someone who had been through two spouse bereavements said to me, "Don't make any major decisions or move home for two years." "Sounds good," I thought, but in the September of 1992, with my son, I was invited down to stay on the farm where the A.C.E. Christian School was, on the outskirts of Swindon. We stayed in a static caravan for a few days and I was given the use of a car. They let my son do his lessons in the school for two or three days and we began to make a new circle of friends and explore the immediate area a little. A week or two after returning home, they contacted me and offered my son, now eleven years old, a place in the senior school called Maranatha and offered us a 'granny flat' at a farmhouse that was rented by two of the teachers, a couple who were ex-missionaries and had one of their children still in Maranatha. My rental of that flat would be a sub-let from that couple. We had been to the house and had seen the flat when we were down there, but I wasn't sure that I would have liked living in the annexe, though the area was nice and was near a main road with buses into Swindon.

On a previous visit to Swindon, when socialising, a lady mentioned in passing that she would be looking in Swindon for an investment property to rent out. I asked her at that time that if I moved down and she did obtain such a property, would she give me first refusal on rental? She agreed to do so. I was desperately trying to weigh everything up on the Swindon issue to make a right decision. I asked people to pray and someone offered to pay the first term's fees without my asking! It was not in doubt that I would now put my son back into a school and if that was to be in Cramlington, okay, but if not, was this whole Swindon issue going to be the right move to make? Was this really from the Lord or was it once again 'man' just manipulating a situation for their own purposes, even if they meant no harm? If those who offered me a school place for my son and accommodation had 'tuned in' more than they did and had openly talked it through with me (yet how could they if they had never been through spouse bereavement, etc?), perhaps they should have said to leave it for another year or so and see if it was then a viable option. Was and is education so important that it was the 'be all and end all'? Education or any gifting is no guarantee of success or that it will of itself go well for you, especially if there is any kind of curse or negative in or on a person or their life. Education of itself and what it can lead to may play its part - especially for those who say that knowledge equals power - even with some disciplines, but it is no guarantee of a peaceful, contented and fulfilled life! Many were the positives and negatives going through my mind as to what to do. If it had been something concerning myself only, I would never even have entertained the thought of moving for one second, but could it really help my son and give him a better opportunity to prepare for and enter adulthood?

I was not 100% certain, yet decided to move - I can remember clearly making the phone call that triggered it off. About three weeks later, I gave up my super little flat in Cramlington and moved to the farmhouse annexe just outside and to the east of Swindon. It was a cold winter's day - I think in the early part of November 1992 – and, as we put our furniture and belongings into the main room, which was small though pleasant enough of itself, even if cold, I knew I had made a tragic mistake - my heart sank! I should have listened to those who were much older and wiser than myself, even though they were not perfect. Once again I should never have moved without being 100% certain and at peace in my heart to have done so. My daughter and grand-daughter were greatly upset for a year or more because my son and I had left from 'around the corner'. I knew my son was not happy, but he didn't say anything. I repented and apologised to my family more than once and took the responsibility for my actions; for, although my motives were not wrong, I still see it as one of life's mistakes, yet the Lord did turn it round to make it a valuable experience for the two of us (Proverbs chapter 16 verse 9). I don't like to 'back-track' as such and would rather go forwards and onwards, but wondered if I should have immediately tried to get back to Cramlington - I did not do so. Suddenly, I was very much alone and lonely. My son was now in the school, having a taste of what it was like to be in an independent, 'middle class' establishment and mixing, making new friends and so on, though he was the youngest in the seniors. But that was no compensation for the loss of his Mum and now the temporary loss of his 'big sis' and niece, as we didn't get to see them very often.

What am I saying that I could put into words now, but not so then? The heart is more important than the head - the things of the heart are more powerful than the mind or intellect or even the will, for they are to do with the spiritual side of our beings. If your heart is sorted in a right way and 'stable', as it were, education is secondary - it may serve a purpose, you say, but it is the wisdom from above and the fear of God that is paramount - all else is, or will soon become, subservient to the heart. Life and Scripture bear this out. Education has its place with the mind and intellect. The will, as a directive, is powerful, but it is out of the heart that the *most* powerful issues of life emanate - what gets your heart gets you! Love and hate, etc, are as strong as death. Real grief that a person is walking through is too strong to be interfered with or disdained; this process that is important of itself will be damaged - but when dealt with in a right way one will be able to walk through it and so back to normality, then hopefully have compassion and wisdom. That move to Swindon did damage to the grieving process to myself and my family. If I had only known then what I was really up against in the whole spectrum of grief! ... but if we harden our hearts as a reaction, who is there to help us? Nevertheless, mistake or not, overall I loved the Lord and bowed my knees to Him, giving Him this mess and receiving into my heart the Scripture in Romans chapter 8 that God will work (as in over-rule, in my experience) all things for good to those that love Him and are called according to His purpose.

Though I was not happy living in that farmhouse 'flat' and Christmas was an unhappy time for the two of us, despite some kindness shown to us, it was pleasant living in the countryside close to the main Oxford Road and railway line ... I got so that I could tell the time by one or two of the trains going by! One family who had encouraged me to move down to the area for the fellowship and social life announced to me, shortly after I moved, that they had decided for their own reasons that they were going to move back to South Wales. Keith Cline, who had worked with Roger Price doing the tape ministry and whatever down in the Bognor Regis area, had moved to the Swindon area with his family, all connected with the A.C.E. and the school; but when I got there I found that Keith and family had moved on to South Wales or wherever … again my heart sank!

In early 1993, the lady (Mrs Kathy Vincent), looking for an investment property said to me she was going to have a look at some and would I like to accompany her and her husband. I said, "Yes", and this came about in the next day or two. When they looked at the first property, they said to me, "Do you like this one, Henry?" "Not really, if I have any choice!" I replied, and they agreed about that anyway. So it was with another one. We then went down to Helmsdale, at Greenmeadow, a lovely area of Swindon, and this property was a middle, two bed-roomed flat, in one of several blocks of flats, and had a garage to go with it. The flat was very clean, well decorated and carpeted, with a pleasant and peaceful atmosphere. I didn't know it then, but there was a strong 'Christian presence' in that area. The kitchen was big enough to be a dining- kitchen. "This is really nice and would be absolutely ideal," I said, but they had already reached that conclusion! Although she had to check a couple of things out, she said she would buy it and as soon as she had the keys I could arrange to move in. The purchase of the property went through very quickly and I moved in just as we were heading towards the Spring. My landlady said some time later that if ever I could not afford to pay the rent then my son and I would live in her property rent-free … now that was the kindness of her heart … I think she prospered … regularly she and her husband would take us out for meals … that was all the favour of Almighty God!!

We settled into that cosy warm flat immediately and we both really enjoyed living there. By the summer I had built up a large circle of friends. I will take the theme of the fellowships, etc, first, of that time, and then deal with the mostly educational side of things while in Swindon.

There was a church fellowship on the farm where the school was situated and with the leaders of the A.C.E. organisation and their family, along with the owners of the farm(s), it was quite well attended and was independent evangelical, though with strong Brethren roots. It was not Pentecostal as such. Interestingly enough, there was a strong 'Pentecostal influence' from many of the families who had put their children into Maranatha School. Anyway, my son and I were given lifts to and from that fellowship during the time we were living in that granny flat and the leaders were certainly kind to us in giving us hospitality, etc, even sometimes being treated as 'family'. I don't remember being allowed to ever help by rolling up my sleeves to wash the dishes after a meal - okay, sometimes it's load the dishwashers, I know - but some of the friendliest and in-depth conversations I've ever had have taken place when helping to sort dishes out, etc, as in chores, after having been given a healthy meal!

When my son and I moved to Greenmeadow, there was a change of fellowship. In those days, about a mile or so from our flat, a large Australian-based Pentecostal fellowship called 'Christian Outreach Centre' met on Sundays in a secondary school hall - as I remember, it could have been as many as 150 who did so. The leadership and others of that fellowship were linked into Maranatha School and more than once they had said to me, "When are you coming to visit us, Henry?" So the Spring of 1993 was my opportunity and I went on to attend, though not always easy without transport. It was a lively fellowship and fun under the leadership of Ian and Sue Spencer and it suited me. My son made friends with a lad called Peter, who lived very near our flat and whose family were Christians and part of the circle of friends I'd already made.

I found out about and got involved with a small group of believers who faithfully prayed for the Jews and Israel in a house on the Greenmeadow Estate and elsewhere, also linking in with another group who lived in the Marlborough area - all I will say is that some of those meetings were awesome and on one occasion, with about a dozen of us meeting in someone's dining room in a detached bungalow when we were 'singing praises in the Spirit to God', there was more sound than we ever could have made - we all agreed that it could have only been the Angels joining in, as part of the sound seemed to be coming downwards from the ceiling area! I discovered there was a small fellowship that met in the Greenmeadow area and later in the summer they asked me to preach ... and so I did, putting a lot of work into it. From then on, every so often they would ask me to preach and they gave me a gift each time for doing so, which was really kind of them.

As the summer of that year went on, a couple with a young family asked the two of us if we would like to go camping with them down in the West Country at a 'Pastor North Conference'. "Yes, okay, thank you, but never heard of him," I said. "He's elderly now, but had a powerful ministry in his time," the husband replied. We did so and enjoyed ourselves and that family were very kind to us. "I'm going to give you a gift of £200," said the husband. "Are you?!" I said, "I would be grateful!" Several weeks later, he kept to his word. All I can remember now about that conference was that the only musical instrument the leadership would allow was a piano, but it was an enjoyable time.

I knew about a large camping/caravanning Christian conference being held annually in the summer holidays on the "Three Counties' Showground", near Malvern, at the foot of the Malvern Hills. This was a massive, highly successful event lasting a few days with two or three thousand attending and was run by the evangelist Don Double, who lived in the West Country, and his organisation was called the 'Good News Crusade'. I booked in for that August of 1993 and my son and I camped before going to visit family in

Cramlington. The lad went to meetings for his age group and made some friends. We actually ended up going those three summers of 1993, '94 and '95. Derek Prince was one of the main speakers in '93, as I remember, and it was all really good stuff and well worth attending. But who was this man speaking on one of those days? - I had never heard of him before and some people were keen to tell me about him. "Mahesh Chavda," they said, spelling his name out to me. At the first meeting that I saw him, he seemed very free, casual and down to earth. In ministry time he said he would pray for everyone who wanted to be prayed for and everybody lined up in rows all over the large hall and he walked down each row, praying over each person; and even when he was several yards away, suddenly I could feel the power and presence of Almighty God working through him - I was powerfully anointed when he prayed over me. I have seen him in action several times in some of his UK meetings over the years. The Lord had called him to do 40 times 40-day fasts and other fasts as well. It was the following year at Malvern that was possibly the most awesome meeting I've ever seen and experienced.

There were probably upwards of 3,000 people present at this morning meeting and I was sitting on my own at the back with a good view of the proceedings. Mahesh Chavda just casually talked on one or two things - it was almost as if it didn't matter what he said, as he was not trying to prove anything (he was not lacking in intelligence), when he suddenly said, "I see the Glory of God hovering above this meeting and as I bring my hands down He will fall on us." As he then did so, the whole place just erupted loudly into shouts of praise, worship and so on, as people were touched by God and delivered, healed, set free from whatever, anointed and filled with the awesome fear of God. I can remember just saying out loud as I observed it all, "Brilliant, Lord!" After about only a minute, Mahesh just said, "Testimonies", and he left the microphone free on the platform. I think someone said later there were immediately about 80 in a line to say what had just happened to them … but first to the microphone was Pat from Retford, who had been my landlady. I had encouraged her and her husband to go that year, but they stayed offsite because they had their little dog with them. Pat testified that about eight years earlier she had fallen off some step ladders at home and had broken and damaged her wrist - she loved and was gifted at sewing - but her wrist was slightly deformed by her accident and had caused her much pain over the years. I had been aware of the state of her wrist and of the discomfort it had given her, as she glowingly testified that it was completely healed - the bones were as they should be and she could move it normally without any pain whatsoever. I would now call this a creative miracle. Several years later, I lost contact with them when they moved from Retford, but for all the time that I knew her she completely kept that miracle healing! What an awesome God we have! There were more testimonies, then at some point the joyful music and high praise started up - "I'm in the wrong place," I said to myself, "it's all happening down at the front." Most people were dancing around and jumping in worship before the Lord, including Pat's husband, George, who was totally free before the Lord that lunchtime, so I joined in immediately to that Heavenly Praise Party till I was just about exhausted - and have done in likewise manner a lot of times since up and down this land and also in Toronto. I made several new friends at that conference in Malvern and some of my friends from Heysham were also there and afterwards they took us up to Heysham, where we stayed for a few days before going up to Cramlington for a week or so.

Back to the September of 1993... . the Christian Outreach Denomination had recently sent a new man from Australia to head up things in this part of the world. They had booked a venue in South Wales for a weekend conference - it may have been for men only, but whatever, it was quite powerfully anointed and I didn't have a problem with it, though I knew one or two folk who did. Generally, the denomination had been enjoying a 'revival' that had started in Australia.

A few weeks later, I don't know the exact date ... but revival power from Heaven hit that fellowship in Swindon. Suddenly, one Sunday, it was supernaturally alive and many were 'slain in the Spirit' and lying on the floor, soaking in good things from Heaven! Just about everyone in the fellowship that I knew was affected by it - in fact, a little later Ian Spencer said that there were about ten couples he knew of whose marriages were greatly helped and strengthened through it. For me, the actual revival lasted ten days. Every meeting and all the fellowship and socialising were *the tops*! I managed to get down to the midweek meeting held in Swindon itself in a hired local council room. We put the chairs to one side and just stood wherever and Ian Spencer came round, praying for everyone individually. I ended up lying on my back on the floor, as were others, and remember thinking, "Okay, Lord, what next?" Famous last thoughts!! Wave after wave of His powerful love just came over and over me - I couldn't have got into the level of my mind, even if I'd tried. Then suddenly, in my mind a picture of someone in my past came up. I don't normally get 'visions' of any kind, though I've had some 'dreams', of course; not too many of importance and they are 'visions of the night'. The Lord spoke to me deep within my being, "Do you forgive that person?" "Yes, Lord, I forgive them"; so the Lord gave me picture after picture of people from my past who had wronged me and each time asked me if I had forgiven them. It was as if He had started with the least first, then the greater wrongs that some had done came later. Eventually, it became so unbelievably painful I wanted to run away from myself and from that deep-down emotional pain - as crazy as that may sound!

Now everything was peaceful, sedate, prim and proper in that room, but I started to shout out loud, "No, oh no! ..." and thrash with my hands to the floor from side to side – inside, I was saying to the Lord, "You *know* I have forgiven them, Lord"; but it was as if He was saying to me, "It's *deeper*,

Henry, *deeper*!" "No, Lord, no, but don't stop!" - for it was almost too painful to face head on - not one in my past was left out, or so it seemed. Suddenly, a hand gently touched my chest and Ian Spencer simply just prayed for "Peace" and instantly, in a fraction of a second, it was over and all was totally quiet and peaceful, but I was upset because the Lord had not totally finished. It was enough for that evening and I later realised that for me I had to go very deep and be thorough in my forgiving; yet, of course, once forgiveness is dealt with as an act of the will, it is dealt with, full stop. Yet it also had to do with letting the other person off the hook as to the Lord. I stood up in that room and other people were still being ministered to and I wondered what to do next, until I looked at my watch ... one and a half hours had gone by yet again and I thought it had only been a few minutes ... help, I needed to get back home quickly for my son!

On the following Sunday morning, I was in the meeting at the back and my son was sitting next to me with his friend, Peter, next to him. The presence of the Lord was powerful indeed and I had felt that presence coming down from Heaven like electricity going through my hands and arms, and when this happened, often I would begin to shake. But that morning, as Ian Spencer preached and as I was sitting down, the 'weight of the Lord God's Glory' came upon me supernaturally in such power I was pressed heavily to the chair and had no choice as I slid to the floor - the Lord was showing me He was totally all powerful and I was subservient to that awesome power; this was His agape love ... It was a wonderful experience and I wanted it to continue, but my son was dismayed, because I ended up on the floor. He was prodding me with his foot saying, "Get up, Dad!" Perhaps he thought I was going to die there and then, I don't know, but I said with difficulty to him, "I'm fine, I'm okay, Old Son, it's the Lord blessing me." Eventually, the anointing stopped and I got back onto my seat. At one of those meetings, Ian Spencer suddenly stopped and from the front faced me and said, "Henry, raise your hands." This I did immediately and Ian began to prophesy over me for two or three minutes of really good things that the Lord still had for me in the future. That word was not recorded or written down by anyone present, but it was enough for me that the word given was from the Lord, positive and important and so would go forth into eternity!! I don't know why the revival ceased in its intensity after, as I saw and experienced it, a week and a half, but it was great fun, as it centred around the Lord, and for me it was an important experience I would not have wanted to miss!

During that later summer of 1993, I looked out of the Greenmeadow's kitchen window at the garage that went with that flat and thought, "It's empty, Lord. I will start praying that You will give me a car to put in it!" Well, He didn't give me the ownership of a car to go in that garage, but He did put a car, on and off, for a few weeks at a time for my use in that garage!! There was a certain situation with an elderly couple, due to one being sick, whereby one of their cars needed to be out of sight. It came about that

The Way I See It

sometimes I would help them out and run them about, usually long distance, and so the wife would give the use of one car to me and this continued for several months; all I had to do was put petrol in it and be available to help out with some driving - it was a good deal on both sides!

At the beginning of March 1994, I was told that my father had died, aged 83 years. My two brothers and I decided we would go to the funeral, so my son and I went up to Cramlington to stay and the elder of my brothers took myself and my other brother to the funeral in his car - our two sisters never went near. With the C. of E. vicar, there were nine of us present, 'in three groups', as it were, with damaged relationships, and although I tried to relate to each one present, it was somewhat awkward and we only just managed to be polite to each other, or so it seemed, with no in-depth conversation. Because of all the rejection, it was somewhat meaningless to me; I went to be respectful, but in a sort of way my father had 'died' to me way back in the 'fifties/'sixties.

A week or two later, I made contact with his solicitor, who was in Carlisle, and asked about his will! In only one telephone conversation, this arrogant snob of a man absolutely wiped the floor with me, telling me in so many words, "Leave things alone, mind your own business and leave his wife (for he had never divorced his second wife) and his 'common law wife' (with whom he spent twenty-odd years at the end of his life) and your half-brother alone." I was indignant and furious. I put pen to paper ... what kind of game was this? I had every right to ask what was happening. My mother was married to my father from 1940 to 1957, if that was the actual year of the divorce, and they had five children ... how could this then not be recognised? ... very strange! I also told him my age and that he had no right whatsoever to lecture me about bereavement, as two years and several months earlier I had buried the wife of my youth. I also said he should check out motives, certainly as to what mine were. Even if my father disliked his own children, it would still have been a nice gesture if he had given each of us one or two hundred pounds to buy a keepsake or have a holiday on him as a 'goodbye', that was all! ... but if the will had been against my half-brother and his mother in any way I would have tried my best to put that right, and, as it turned out, it was, so I told the solicitor I wanted no further part whatsoever to do with the property in that will (which if I understood correctly, was left to us five children if our half- brother and his mother predeceased us - in my opinion it should have been left totally, without conditions, to my half-brother) and never to be contacted again by his firm in this matter. I didn't ever receive an acknowledgement, but simply put it all behind me and kept my peace.

For all my father's genius, for all his incredibly hard work, for the fortune and all the material possessions he had had through his hands, for all the status and power he had had, for all the good, the bad and the indifferent ... was that it? Was that the sum total of his life? Was he really unable to relate to anyone? He could, in the 1970s, have had a well-built pure luxury bungalow in any of the attractive villages just a few miles out of Carlisle and built a large swimming pool at the back and thrown in a tennis court for good measure; but instead did he really enjoy life, live it to the full or did he finish it with a groan? Did he take no thought for life's other side …?

In all of 1993 and into 1994, my son attended Maranatha School; he got on with his work and had some adventures … one of these was a 'jolly' in a large executive jet over the Bay of Biscay. I think it was for a couple of terms in the first part of 1994 that I helped out on four mornings each week in the junior section of the school. Sometimes I would do playground duties as well: the lawn, gardens and view were very pleasant!! The working part of the farm was out of bounds, of course.

Now the school believed in and still had corporal punishment; this was shortly before it was outlawed in this land. In my opinion it was administered in a fair way, and not at the mere whim or anger of a teacher or two, but only with permission, in writing, from a parent/guardian who knew the reason why it was to be given. Because it was so controversial, one of the ITV channels came in and filmed for a day. I was on that programme for several seconds and it was then I realised I was starting to go a little thin on top!

One morning we were getting a lift to school and the local radio station was on in the car - suddenly an interview came on between my son and Derek Tedder, a local journalist who was into radio and television work and was a friend; it was about Maranatha School and corporal punishment and lasted just a few minutes. It came over really well and, of course, it had been recorded a few days earlier, but we didn't know when it would go on air! I still have a copy of that interview on a duplicate audio tape somewhere in my possession.

In the early part of 1994, because of doing that voluntary work in the school, I started to question the method and the application of the way the school and the A.C.E. System was taught and administered. I can remember when, being given a lift one lunch-time back into Swindon so that I could catch a bus home, asking the lady giving me the lift, whose children were in the school and who was very involved there, what she thought as I voiced certain concerns, including a lack of at least some 'normal' classroom interaction and activity, as such. She was not very happy at what I said and I think I became a 'marked man' at that time.

Yet not long after that conversation that whole family totally withdrew from the school! Someone had written a paper against that system of education, explaining how it came about, etc, and its faults. Later, someone from the A.C.E. side wrote a paper counteracting it! I obtained a copy of the first paper and it confirmed some of the doubts I first had and I also read the other paper at a later date. Under certain circumstances, and normally in the early years, it could be helpful if a child was struggling with some subjects to follow an A.C.E.-type of course workbooks, but if there was a good teacher teaching and the children were interested, this would have been a healthier set-up than not being allowed to see another child or what was going on in the room, as was the case when doing 'Paces' (workbooks) in that school, each child being isolated by the recommended classroom furniture, normally with complete silence in the classroom. No doubt 'the debate' raged, but perhaps the A.C.E. system worked best in the family/home situation! I had absolutely no objection to the excellent evangelical and biblical content within the workbooks.

The fees for Maranatha got paid for as I had received some help, but it was a struggle. By the summer I had decided I would put my son back into the ordinary school system and he had asked me if I would do so. The trouble was that the secondary school he would be allocated to in Swindon at that time did not have a very good name. I thought that if I could find somewhere to rent in Morecambe we could move up, as my friends were still living in Heysham and some of their children attended St Thomas's Secondary School in Lancaster, which was a Christian-based C. of E. school with a good reputation, and also my friend, Andrew, and I had discussed the possibility of starting up a fellowship in that area. As mentioned earlier, there were a few similarities in our walks with the Lord through what had influenced both of us. I wondered, though, at just one sentence, and that was uttered only once by my late wife: "If you ever go to live in Heysham, I don't think it will work!"

I thought this out before the Lord and turned it into a prayer: "I will either go back to Cramlington or try to go to Morecambe, because of the school. I will try Morecambe first and if 'the door opens' and it seems right, I will go through it", was what I said to the Lord.

Well, 'the door opened' as it were and I got a flat next to the old funfair (long since gone), close to the sea and the promenade, in a Victorian property. That summer I met someone and later that year got married and, as I had already moved up to Morecambe, she also moved up from the south coast. St Thomas's School was so popular that I could not obtain a place for my son, though it was not for the want of trying, as I had fought and made out a strong case in order to do so! As that season unfolded in Morecambe and Heysham, I never did start up a fellowship with my friends, but more adventures and trials were certainly underway! ...

# 18

# *Relationships ... Marriage ... and Rebellion Underway ...*

The bottom line of all and any wrongdoing - however it happens and whatever the cause - is broken and damaged relationships. What then follows is the inability for us all to relate well and get on together across the board and this affects every type of relationship … with our Maker, each other, and the harmony in our 'make-up' of our inner beings. It also, of course, affects families, tribes, nations and areas, plus towns and cities within them. Whatever you come up with, so far as mankind is concerned, we just cannot get it right as we try to relate to each other. Some relationships may be or appear to be good, but they still fall short of perfection. Nations make treaties and the like, but are they ever fully kept and if so for how long? People make vows, oaths, promises, contracts, etc, but at the end of the day how successful are they anyway?

Oaths and vows may be dangerous in themselves and if they are broken terrible things might happen. This is why the likes of Freemasonry is not good. A year or so ago I went on a one-day course in the Midlands which included ministry for those who had been affected by Freemasonry and learned from an ex-Freemason and his team that what they are doing as they are going through all the 'degrees' is, in the end, cursing every part of their human bodies at the least, because, if they did divulge the Freemasons' secrets, the most violent bloodshed would be the result - talk about fear! I mean, who literally wants their heart ripped out of them? - and they still do not know what is at the end of it all, because it is so conditional, secretive and desperately frightening … like a childhood game gone mad! Interestingly enough, women were receiving ministry as well as men, as they had been indirectly affected by Freemasonry! It has nothing to do with our Heavenly Father God's loving kindness, but it has to do with evil. Don't swear by Heaven or Earth, the Word of God says, or by anything in fact, but just let your 'yes' be 'yes' and your 'no' be 'no'. There is nothing hidden that will not be made known - a sobering thought!

The Lord God is in the business of healing relationships and helping us to maintain that health, first of all with Himself in a deep and loving relationship through the covenants that He made in history, and secondly so that we can then pass on that loving kindness to others - it is only if you have known true love that you are able to pass on true love. For most if not all of us, that is still a process, as we have a lot to undo and a lot of 'baggage' to get rid of, but if the Lord God asks us to do something He will always help us and make a way as needs be. With the Lord there is always freedom to choose, and truth. When the Lord makes a covenant (e.g. the Abramic covenant in Genesis chapter 15), the 'work' in doing that is always done totally by Him and not through any dependence or reliance on mankind whatsoever, except for us to take Him up on it with a right heart. If it was left totally up to us, we would always 'blow it' sooner or later. A willing heart of loving obedience to the Lord is, by grace, for our own benefit, but on His side, as and when you bring Him into the equation, it is never a hard-hearted big stick legalistic approach towards us by Him! (Correction by the Lord is another matter.)

The closer the relationship in any given circumstances the harder it is going to be to make it work really well. The closest relationship of all is the marital or the marital type of relationship and, of course, that of the 'family unit'. There is one main 'key' given in scripture for there to be successful relationships and that is found in Amos chapter 3 verse 3. That key word is 'agreed'! It asks the question 'Can two *walk* together unless they are in agreement?' The answer is a definite 'No!' Of course they can't. For a marriage to work properly, it must envelop love, friendship (as in really good friends), harmony, teamwork, kindness, and the list goes on. But there are seasons within our lives and life brings much change, joy, pain, etc, so at the outset we may have no idea what a given relationship will really hold as time goes by! True love and commitment should get us through, but at what cost in certain circumstances? Relationships based on evil, fear, control, deception, bullying, hate, lack of a balanced 'freedom' - and this list also goes on and on - cannot possibly of themselves win wholesomely in the end because these things are all seeds of destruction. This is all going on in the natural and I have not even touched on what might be going on in the spiritual realm.

I married a second time in good faith that we were in agreement and we verbally stated and agreed as to what these agreements were, but she changed her mind on some of them later. As far as I was concerned, it was teamwork and we were broadly speaking 'in the Lord's will'. Perhaps I did not give her enough space as time went by, yet I had never had a problem with that issue in the past ... strange ... as for me, by then marriage totalled well over 30 years! We were not short of friends anywhere we went. One of the things we agreed to do was to only accept speaking engagements whereby we would share the 'platform' and the Lord certainly honoured that one, as speaking engagements did come our way from time to time and we shared them. We often found ourselves in counselling and ministry situations helping others and sometimes even those in leadership or with a potential leadership gifting. She was highly intelligent and an academic and was a few years older than myself. As with most close relationships, we had shared in depth to each other regarding life's experiences, etc, so it would not be wise or kind to release certain aspects of that personal information. I will, however, say something of two things that happened. Firstly, as she told me a few weeks later, that on the second or third time that I had met her she said she suddenly saw me from a spiritual perspective, a kind of vision really, and my eyes were sort of a flame of fire for the Lord Jesus. I stated I was not aware of any such thing, but simply was just being myself. Secondly, later, on the Wednesday night of the honeymoon she said, "I've got a vision of you." "Well, go on then, tell me," I replied. "You've got the face of a pig," she said. A horrible silence followed. "I don't get the joke," I replied after a minute or two. "It's something to do with your father," she continued. I slowly responded, "I've been called a lot of things in my time, but never a pig, and also my father was responsible for his own sins before God - nothing to do with me, just as I am responsible for my own sins - not anyone else on my behalf." That was the end of the conversation that night and this issue of that evening was never brought up again. Perhaps I should have 'cut and run', but persevered. It is not unusual to find a mixture of the natural and supernatural, whether good or evil, in relationships, but how often is it correctly recognised and dealt with if it *is* of evil or *is* unsavoury?

She said she would take on my son anyway and help him, as in 'no problem' through his growing-up years - but it turned out to be a living nightmare for us both! Her kindness, provision and help towards me and my son is not in doubt, but years later, when it was all over, for it sadly ended in actual divorce in April 2001, my daughter wisely said to me one day, "Dad, it was as if she came into your life for that period of time just to help you get through those difficult years with my bro. and that's all." I agreed with her and that can often be the way the Lord works for whatever purpose He so desires.

Certain aspects of the status and quality of my life over the years that I have often had in the Lord, in my opinion, were second to none, as I lived by such scriptures as 'Godliness with contentment is great gain'. Our lives here on Earth are temporary anyway and all that we have is only on loan to us!

After a few months in that flat in Morecambe, we bought a modern detached property in Heysham, near the Village Green, and made it into tip-top condition. I had put my son into the large comprehensive secondary school in Morecambe, as I seemingly had little choice, since Morecambe and Heysham were both in its catchment area.

I cannot recall all the exact details or date, but it was summer and around his fourteenth birthday. He told me one day that there had been some kind of drug-related incident at the school and a pupil he knew was threatened or actually harmed. He appeared to know all those involved on both sides. I was horrified. We are forced to send our youths to these establishments, but where is discipline, correction and justice? I slept on it, but then decided I would take some action. I quickly obtained an interview with the Head Teacher and wanted to know what action he was going to take and if he was going to call the police in! Help …! I realise now he must have howled with laughter after I had gone ... and wondered which century I was living in! I was not aware of any action that was ever taken, as liberalism, fear, bullying and evil appeared to rule the day. When I told my son, he was really angry!! I asked, "Do you do well to be angry ... should not this God-forsaken society at least give protection to those they force to go to their wretched establishments?" He replied, "I'm not going back to that school!" "Oh yes you are ... you're going back!" "Dad, you don't understand ... if they ever find out ... they'll break both of my legs!!" So the score in Heysham was one to my son and nil to me ... and I had a mega-problem!!

What options did I now have, if any, with regard to my son's schooling? I came up with just one and so I went, cap in hand ... as near as I would normally ever get to it anyway! ... and got an interview appointment with the Head of the large Roman Catholic School in Lancaster. On the day, my wife, son and I all went to the school and had a look around. Someone spent time with the lad while we were with the Head. He was a busy man, yet gave over half an hour of his time, with some good debate involved and my sharing exactly what had happened. I figured there would be a good measure of order and discipline in the school and that was more or less right, even by the very structure and culture of the Roman Catholic Denomination. My son was accepted into the school, even though we agreed there would be no religious teaching as such given to him.

Now, at that time the lad wanted to be an actor! "Move towards being an actor if that's what you really want, but it would be wise to have some kind of 'trade' according to your gifting to get you into adulthood and something to fall back on," was the gist of what I said to him. Time went by and it so happened that, through that school, he was chosen by one of the ITV companies to be involved in one of a series of children's programmes of youth looking at and experiencing the jobs they thought they would like to do. He would share the programme with a girl from the London area who wanted to be an actress and together, at the end of the programme, take a small part as 'extras' in the then 'Brookside' Soap. The programme itself would be a little less than half an hour in length. The three of us were to spend three nights in a large hotel in the middle of Liverpool and the film-makers would also visit us in Heysham for one day filming in the area. Actually, the quality of the filming and the programme was of a high standard and went out round most of the nation on different channels. After it was made and shown, my son was recognised in our area by some who didn't previously know him.

The opening 'shot' showed the open-plan lounge of that detached Heysham property in Berwick Way. My wife and I were sitting on the settee facing the camera and my son was juggling fruit just behind us ... until he dropped a piece of the fruit and it hit one of us ...!! There were some good shots taken and shown of the village area and some of his mates, also of the old Morecambe Funfair, now long since gone, yet it was unfortunate those shots of the latter were never used, for I thought they must have been really good and would have appealed to the youth.

When we stayed in Liverpool we went one lunch-time to the cafeteria within the studio used for the 'Brookside' Soap. The only trouble was, we didn't have a television and so I didn't know who was who and who wasn't 'who'! The lad said, in a loud whisper, "Don't stay around too long, Dad ... you'll show me up!" "Do you know," I said, 'acting' somewhat! "I think you're right, so a little bit of Liverpool sightseeing would beckon us!" I finished my lunch, of course, as slowly as I could, before leaving! We were also given tickets to go and see the Billy Fury story in one of the theatres and the music brought back some memories for me. So my son and the girl mentioned above played their part as 'extras' on the set and it went well.

Some time later, he got a small part in 'The Railway Children', which was being staged in a theatre in Lancaster. Actually, it was a really good production and well acted, except possibly for one older male actor who was almost trying too hard. The lad played the part of the young man running ahead laying the paper trail for the others to follow - he ran into the tunnel where he 'fell and broke his leg' on the railway line. Now my son had said to my wife and me, "Don't tell me which night you're coming to see the show." On the particular night all went well until *his* part ... how on earth can you just have broken your leg and *burst out laughing* ... ?! ... well, *he* did ...! Methinks the young actors had been fooling around behind the scenes until the last minute ... was my son meant to be a comedian instead? ... I don't know, but I do know I'm not asking any questions!! So the acting desire just faded away and his growing-up rebellion started in real earnest.

The real challenge was to get the lad through his 'metamorphosis' rebellious time and into responsible adulthood without destroying him or his ability to be himself and be creative, in spite of all the pain he had had in his childhood and was still carrying - the full extent of which I was about to find out. Of course, many others have gone through the same kind of thing and especially where grandparents are having to take a large part in helping to bring up grand-children. More than once I was to find that they, in a near state of exhaustion, would just need a listening ear, some encouragement and ministry for some peace and they would weep or sob - then they were refreshed and ready to go back into 'the battle'.

Sometimes I wonder if my son despaired even of life itself – anyway, he had the fight and courage to get through. As families so often have become so dysfunctional as there are relentless spiritual attacks on them by the forces of evil, it is only the Lord God who can sort it all out - Malachi chapter 4 verse 6 being an excellent start to do so. It was my job to be a 'shock absorber' to some extent for him and hopefully minimise the consequences of his wrong actions, but I knew I had to stay his friend and in one sense be there for him so as to help him get through and survive into adulthood. I will be selective in giving some of the accounts as to what happened! The Lord spoke to me very clearly in my heart, saying, "Whatever you do, do not speak curses or negatives over your son." I said back to Him in my mind, "Okay, Lord, I understand and take it on board, but I will need your help, Lord!" This meant that at times when he started to curse me, would come against me such as spitting on me (though he was never allowed to harm me) and once tore part of my expensive Bible up, I knew I had to, and did, come back pronouncing God's favour upon him, along with my acceptance of him as my son. Some of the Christians who knew about this just about gave up on me and thought I had totally lost the plot - what about some 'good old-fashioned Biblical Proverbs' discipline?' some inferred, but I thought, "We'll see!"

It was late and dark one evening and Simon, one of his mates in the village, had come with him to our house. "We're just going up to his bedroom," said Simon, facing me, as they went up the stairs - only my son had his back to me and was facing the wall, as he seemed to go slowly up the stairs. I said something like, "It shouldn't be a problem … strange" … After a minute or so, Simon appeared on the stairs. "I'll tell you what happened." I was all ears! "We were all piled into one car with the hatchback open, going round and round Heysham car park, doing around 30 or so miles per hour. Bodies were all layered in the boot area and 'the lad' happened to be on the very top - at a certain point he bounced right out of the car and onto the tarmac and he was bruised and one side of his face was badly scratched." (Superficial, as it turned out.) I went upstairs, heart in mouth, to have a look. I said to the lad, "Okay, get your coat on and go outside. I'll get the car out and take you to A & E at the hospital in Lancaster." I said goodbye to Simon and thanked him for bringing him home. It took a few hours to sort it out, as A & E was busy. It was the first time I had seen such a place, in modern times, in action and I wanted it to be the last!! He was shaken, but they found him to be okay. I'll never forget what happened next, just as we were about to leave … one of the lady nurses who had been attending to him verbally laced into him without mercy and severely rebuked him … What was he playing at?… he only had one neck and if that had been really damaged what would life hold for him … etc?! …

Roughly a year or so later, a couple of his mates brought him home late in the evening - he was limping badly and could hardly walk. "What happened to you then?" I asked. "The Heysham lads were fighting the Morecambe gang and we ended up having to run from them. I jumped off the prom quite a few feet below onto sand but didn't land correctly." (I noticed the last time I was in Morecambe that that area was filled in with sand - though it was quite a drop in those days.) I made a comment that if he had gone out into the bay, even 50 or more yards, and the tide was going out he could have felt the suction down of quicksand - it is a very dangerous bay. "Okay, I'll get the car out ('Thank You, Lord, for that brilliant Citroen ZX!') and we'll go to A and E." We did so and were there hours and hours into the night as they x-rayed his foot etc. It was badly sprained and painful but again he was okay.

Another night his mates brought him home to the front door. I opened it and the lad stumbled into the lounge. It was frightening - his eyes were big and round and he was staring straight ahead, not looking at anyone. I had a mega-problem … what on earth had he been on? If it was horrific drugs, who gave them to him? I thought he didn't appear to know where he was, but seemed menacing. Very peacefully, gently and quietly, I managed to get him up to his bedroom. I lay awake in bed for some time praying with my wife for a miracle and that he would settle - and he did so. Within the next few days, when I was able to talk to him, he would not tell me what had happened, but at some point he did say that alcohol would still be fair game, but he wouldn't take any drugs, and as far as I know in those days he kept to that!

To show that the 'spiritual' is behind the 'physical', I thought, "I know what I'll do, I'll fast a couple of days, anoint and pray over a clean paper tissue and carefully insert it in the pillow slip of my son's top pillow on his bed and see what happens." I asked for a miracle from Heaven for good as soon as his head would touch that pillow. So I put my plan into action. On the set day when his bedtime came and he was ready for bed, he got in and was sitting up in bed. I went to say goodnight to him and was lounging against the doorpost at his open bedroom door. If he did not invite me in I would not go in, for that was his patch (cleaning purposes through the day was a different issue, of course). He didn't invite me in or particularly want to talk. I was slowly saying goodnight and was playing for time - he was just about to lay on his pillow with some force when only a few inches away from the pillow he stopped, sat upright again, picked up the pillow concerned and threw it across the room to the floor. "What did you do that for?" I asked. "I don't want it," he said. "Good night, Old Son," I said, put the light off and quietly closed the door! "Interesting," I thought to myself!!

One dark evening there was a knock on the door. A policeman was standing next to my son. "Are you named so and so and is this your son?" "Yes," I replied. "May I come in?" he asked. "Please do," I said. They came in to the open-plan lounge near the door and the four of us were near enough facing each other. He looked at me then at my wife and then at what he could see of the property. He then turned to my son and without any mercy he verbally laced into him and tore a strip off him in no uncertain way. The gist of it was, "You've got a lovely home, you're being well looked after and cared for, but you would throw it all away … etc, etc!" I didn't say anything, but the lad was not exactly 'happy'. The policeman seemed a fair man and after he had finished talking to my son and with just a few words to me and my wife, excused himself and left.

One afternoon a year or so later, the phone rang. It was a duty policeman at Morecambe Police Station … "Are you so and so?" ….. "Yes," I replied. "Is your son called such and such?"…..."Yes." "Would you come down to the station to pick him up and I would like to have a word with you and your wife." "Okay, but it could be nearly twenty minutes before we arrive," I said.

"I'll see you when you get here," he replied. When we arrived, my son was sitting alone at the entrance to the Police Station with a face like thunder and the place was very quiet. The duty policeman took my wife and me deep into the bowels of the building into an interview room and spent some fifteen minutes or so doing some hard talking about the lad. He seemed to be very angry at my son's cheek, but I managed to only just pacify him, so he agreed to let us take him home. The three of us went back out to the front of the Police Station, where the lad was still sitting and seething. Before any of us could say anything, he immediately started giving the policeman cheek and the policeman was furious - I think he would have happily thrown the three of us into the cells, such was his anger! I didn't even have time to groan or laugh or cry. I would like to have done so, you understand! Like lightning, I intervened before the policeman could say anything and started speaking roughly to my son – well, I tried anyway - my words went something like, "Go and get in the car *now* and don't give any of us cheek and I will speak to you in the car and when we get home." As we hastily went through the door, I thanked the policeman and said I appreciated what he had done and we were gone! Later, I said to the lad, "What's the real problem?" "Me and my mates, we don't like the police!" I groaned. "You show your immaturity," I said. "I'll tell you who and what the police are and how it's supposed to work!" The gist of my lecture to him was that they were just ordinary folk amongst us who applied and trained for the job and hopefully got well paid and were there to protect decent law-abiding citizens against those who were not so and bring the latter to justice, so that decent folk could live peacefully and quietly in the land. Now that sounds good to me, if we want our freedom to choose what is good, etc. But I don't think he was ready to buy anything like this at that time.

I suppose I could laugh now … or do I mean weep? … at the memory of the next happening, but not so then! I plucked up some courage and went to the Social Services Offices in Morecambe. I don't remember which year it was. I went in and up to reception and a man was on duty. "Yes," he said. I looked at him and said, "I'm a failure, I can't control my son any more. I've lost the plot and can't control my son any more." He stopped still and just stared at me intently - we were eyeball to eyeball. After about a minute or more, he changed his gaze to over my shoulder, then I realised he was looking at the door to the outside, so I turned and looked - it was a heavy glass door, but there was no-one there. Then I looked back at him and realised, "I'm a bit thick on this one - " … he was indicating to me that I just go and walk back through it!! Then he spoke some words like, "You're doing okay, go back and go on with it, but I tell you what I'll do, I'll log it - okay?" "Okay, log it!" (He probably felt like saying "Leg it!") He took just the barest of details - I thanked him and left. "I can't even give him away!" I thought to myself; then a scripture came to my mind, "Vain is the help of man but the Lord is a present help in time of trouble." Okay, that was my paraphrase, I know, but I went back into the 'fight', as it were, against all unrighteousness to get him into maturity.

Now, in Heysham around that time amongst the group of lads and lassies that my son was involved with was a 17-year-old lad. He had been at least once to our house, but I don't now remember his name or any details about him. He was attacked and knifed in the chest, in the heart area - someone tried to kill him, but he lived and the medics operated straight away, stating that if the knife had gone in any further he would definitely not have lived. I remember his parents were so pleased he was still alive. The healing was quite fast and he had his picture in the local Morecambe newspaper with his shirt open, showing all the scars and stitching right down the middle of his chest. I saw him once again when he visited our house, but only spoke to him for about a minute. I wondered how this might affect my son - I think he was somewhat shaken because of it, but his behaviour at that time didn't really change.

I had been doing my share of gardening to bring and keep it up to scratch; it was fun - but I looked at my hands one day and thought, "Oh no, I've got some arthritis … not very good." I prayed for my healing, took authority and made sure once again I had forgiven everyone that I needed to forgive. (Some say there is a link between arthritis and unforgiveness.) Sometimes it could be painful as it spread somewhat, but was not as serious as some, although any arthritis is not pleasant.

Now back to my son and his terrible hidden pain that was about to surface…

# 19

# *To Relate ... Or Not To Relate ...*

One particular day, I don't remember the actual time, but would guess it was late 1996 or early 1997, the lad came in a bit subdued and got himself ready for bed. I went to his door to say goodnight. "Dad, you know nothing!" "Err ... maybe you're right, Old Son, but I have been through quite a lot and sometimes I feel it's been more than enough." "No, Dad, you don't know anything - you don't know what happened to me." I replied, "I've been in leadership, had a counselling ministry for a good number of years and had a vast amount of life experience - nothing you can say to me would be something I don't know about." Now, they were the famous last words before I would eat humble pie! "Come in and shut the door; I will only tell you," he said. "Well," I said, "let your stepmother (saying her name) listen at the door." He nodded his head to say 'yes' and I went in, closed the door and sat at the end of his bed. He launched straight in to what he had wanted to say and offload for over ten years. "Do you remember that night when I was four and a half years old and Nana and Grandad took me away late in the evening to their flat?" "Yes," I said, and continued, "I remember that night and time, for it didn't make any sense to me." "When he got me to their home (that was the one-up council flat in Philip Place still standing in Newcastle 4 and, as mentioned earlier, his Nana had already mentally 'lost it'), he cuddled me in on the couch and it was my sleep time ..." My son continued on in graphic detail to explain how he was sodomised by his maternal grandfather. I listened carefully, though in shock myself, and let him talk until he could say no more, and so at last he had shared the horror, terrible burden, pain and guilt and begun to deal with the trauma of it all and this would be the very start of some healing.

When he stopped talking there was silence for a few seconds; then I said, "I feel sick ... so that's what happened? ... It was so late at night when you went, it didn't make sense ... and when you came back you were weeping and I couldn't console you ... a lot of things changed ... you were different ... you developed asthma ... you had fears ..." I paused, then continued, "Okay, I was head of the home and did not know or discern that could or did happen - and ask you to forgive me and your mother, even though she has been gone a few years now, that this terrible adult betrayal across the board by someone so sick and evil was allowed to happen." He stated that he did forgive us. I then said, "You need to forgive your maternal Grandad, even though he has been gone a while." My son said something like, "I know that, Dad." I further commented, "To help you sort out all the trauma, pain and memories, would you not consider going to Ellel Grange to either see them one afternoon or go on a healing retreat - they would definitely be able to help you to some extent?" "No, Dad," he replied, and went on, "I'll sort this out and deal with it in my own way. I'll be okay." "I could help you, but think it would be helpful if you go to someone else to get help on this occasion," I replied. He said, "No, Dad, I'll sort it out my way." "Okay, I won't say any more unless you bring the matter up, but am so pleased you were at last able to share all that you've just shared. If you want further help, just say." We gave each other a hug and I apologised again as I left the room, saying that I now understood a lot more of what had happened, especially to his Mum as a child, and now at last had the whole picture.

WRONG! I still didn't have the full picture. Fast forward a few years and my daughter suddenly told me this, so it is 'second hand info'. She said, "My brother was sitting in a bar drinking with one of his mates in downtown Newcastle and within earshot there was an Alpha Course (course in basic Christianity) going on." Now I realised my son would have known enough about the 'Christian Faith' to mock or 'take the mickey' and did so. My daughter went on to explain that a woman came out from the Alpha Course and went up to him and spoke a word to him … it was a 'word of knowledge' (that is, something she could not possibly have known with the natural mind as in I Corinthians chapter 12) and the words she spoke to him went something like, "You are doing this because you were abused as a young child and so was your sister," at which he broke down and started weeping. My daughter did not say any more and I did not pursue it or ask any questions, but took on board what she had said and said to myself, "I don't want to pursue or hear this."

Fast forward again … by now it was that golden age of around 40 years old (therefore 2003) when some will dare to share some terrible thing(s) of what happened in their distant past. It was in the kitchen of her home one evening - she was standing by the sink unit, her partner was two or three feet away and I had sat down on one side of the dining table chairs. She suddenly said, "I'll tell you what happened, Dad." "What happened *when*?" I asked. "It was in the summer of 1973 and I was 10 years old. Mum and I were at Nana and Grandad's old caravan at Edmund Byers, near Consett - the four of us were staying there. One day he (her grandad) took me into the woods and then said, 'Now I am going to show you how it's done' - he then raped me - that's what happened." I paused and said very slowly, "Is there no end to the evil that this man did? I went to RAF Aldergrove in the May of that year and did not get a married quarter until the September (as stated earlier) and was trying to keep my leave until I would be allocated one - if I could have got one earlier, this would not have happened. Just to think I was trying to serve Queen and Country and do my best for us as a family and *he* was doing *his* best to destroy you and therefore me."

I took the same line as I did with my son: I apologised and asked her to forgive her mother and myself - to try and start to forgive her grandad, which she said she had done. I also mentioned the healing retreat at Ellel Grange, but she also said "No", and that she would sort it out for herself; but that was still not the end of it. It was just two or three years back, as I write, my daughter and I were having a reasoned conversation about her being raped as a child. She said, "Dad, I've never told you, but *he* (her grandad) tried it on twice when I was a teenager and was visiting with Mum. One of those times was in the Philip Place flat and Mum had just gone out to the local shop to buy something and I was washing my hair at the wash basin in the bathroom and *he* came in and tried to get me. I managed to get away and run down the stairs and outside. I waited until Mum came back and said to her, '*He* has tried to get me again,' but she just looked straight ahead, walked by me and in through the front door, up the stairs and into the flat." I said something like, "That was sickening and somewhat strange, but whatever was happening, at least you stood your ground against evil."

I took time and thought long and hard about all of this. I thought about 'justice' versus 'loyalty to family', even a family ruined by terrible sin. Again I thought about social history and the old 'community spirit' in areas of extreme poverty, where they would often help each other when in great need if they could do so and, as stated, I had experienced the communities of both wealth and real poverty. I remember talking to someone much older than myself years ago, an honest hardworking man in his time and very much for justice, who told me that in the poor community there was much immorality under the surface, though he did not say anything further on that subject. Father God, though merciful and willing to give people the opportunity to put their lives right before Him, is certainly *for* and will always *bring* justice. I seriously wondered, if I had known of the incest years earlier and stopped at nothing until justice was done and my father-in-law was well and truly behind bars and named and shamed, would it have cost me my marriage to my first wife? Was that the strength of the 'soul ties' and allegiance and protection to her family tree, with all else coming second? My first wife got tuned into the Lord, but that could only have given her a conflict of interests. To seek help when it is available is a key, but *justice* must be over and way above *loyalty*, otherwise society will disintegrate!

The summer of 1997 came and my son was earnestly looking for work. I knew he had an admin. gifting, was a 'people person' and had a gift of leadership, but what I missed was that he had a gift of selling! I thought being an estate agent might be a good career for him, but he was offered a training in High Street retail travel and this was something he wanted and so it was right, of course, that he made his own choice - I gave him my full support, encouragement with positive words spoken over and written to him, along with prayer, and he was certainly in the right business! Slowly it began to help him - giving him some self respect, and he enjoyed his work which was, of course, very important - he liked earning money and in those days spending it! - he was not through his rebellion, but nevertheless it was a milestone.

Well, life ticked over, but something happened to me around that time. A man called Clive Corfield, who lived in the Lancaster area and had a leadership gifting (I heard later he joined the Elim denomination), with one called Steve Hepdon (they had both been, I was told, briefly in leadership at Ellel Grange, near Lancaster), organised for a speaker called Marc Dupont from the leadership of the Toronto Revival to do a conference of, I think, three days. The venue was a particular Church of England building in Lancaster. Late in the day on the Saturday of the conference, the only place I could find a seat was at the very back to one side, as the room was packed. Now, this might seem strange, but when Marc Dupont was in the area that I was in (and I had seen him at one or two different conferences), my 'spiritual antennae', if you like, would pick up an anointing from Heaven and I would become very much 'Pentecostal' in its original meaning and those few days of conference were no exception! That meeting was also no exception and I could neither see nor hear Marc Dupont, as people were standing towards the front and the acoustics were not good and there was a lot of noise in the area to the back of me from people talking and moving around. I noticed a couple immediately in front of me becoming very agitated (they wouldn't have been able to see or hear Marc Dupont either, as none of us at the back could at that point). With that background, I don't remember exactly what I did to upset them, but upset them I sure did, as I enjoyed praising and, yes, even shouting (as instructed to do so at certain times in scripture), to the Lord! After a while and some whispering, they stormed off towards the front, down the aisle and out of sight. "This may not look good for me," I thought, and so moved out of that pew and into the aisle a few feet from where I had been. My wife by this time was face downwards on the floor, praying, in the aisle. Then I noticed that the couple were in the 'train' of another man, 'Rich and Famous', who was obviously heading straight for me, with zeal. I stood my ground and gave eye contact. 'Rich and Famous' came right up to me and said, "You will be quiet," and at the same time put his hand right over my mouth and nose. I thought, "You must be joking, with all the noise from others going on around me!" Now, I'm not all that tall, but he was a very tall man. Then I quickly got to thinking, "It is very handy to get air into your lungs - this breathing business really is good for you," for I was not able to breathe at all!! I'm totally non-violent as such, but wondered if I was to kick him on the shin if it could be a sort of protest – no … for 'vengeance is Mine' says the Lord! He lectured me again about keeping quiet and it seemed like 30 to 40 seconds went by before he let go. "What do you think you're playing at - that was a vicious physical assault and the police should be called!" I exclaimed. He said, "No, you will shut up." "I would remind you that I have fully paid up the monies required to Clive Corfield to attend this conference" was my answer to him. Well, his gramophone needle was stuck, so no need to tell you what he said! I replied, "If you silence me now I will go straight out of the door and onto the streets and proclaim to Lancaster just what your game is!" At this point he said, "Be quiet" and, true to form, for all bullies and dictators are truly cowards at heart anyway, he turned and proceeded back down the aisle with his entourage. I was indignant and started to praise and worship the Lord in Heaven with every bit of breath and strength that was in me, and so a great anointing came upon me and I started to roar like a lion!! "What is this?" I said to the Lord in my heart and felt the answer was, 'It is *My* boldness from Heaven for *you*.' "I'll definitely 'buy' that one," I said back to the Lord. I later wrote to Clive Corfield, who I respect, but never did get an answer. That day made me realise that the battle between those who want everything from Heaven which God has to give to get the job done in fighting all unrighteousness, and those who limit Him and are self-satisfied with arrogance and religious nonsense, is not only still raging but intensifying. Why on earth would some who were so anti what had happened in the Toronto Revival (bringing freedom and power from Heaven) have any of the Toronto leadership anywhere near them? - that was crazy and asking for trouble. Are they so staid in religion they will never change? Their behaviour towards me, I would say, is what they would really like to have done to Marc Dupont!

The next morning I went to the small meeting in Lancaster which I had been attending and there were a few extra people present, as a pastor from Dumfries was the speaker. He was a livewire and really good. At a certain point in the meeting, a great anointing came upon me and I was pressed by the Spirit of the Lord onto my chair, but did not fall off - it was again the 'weight of God's Glory' and I prophesied out loud a powerful word of encouragement, etc, to this pastor and that God was pleased with him. It is the only time in my life I had no control over the words I was speaking, as they just tumbled out in real Pentecost manner and were not part of my thinking process. Now, the leader was sitting right in front of me and I sensed he was not happy. I was dead right! At the next Tuesday evening meeting, with only a handful present anyway - he told me if I continued to attend I must sit at the back and say nothing … "No chance!" I thought, and shortly after said goodbye and left. That was strange … as I had helped support his fellowship in one or two ways, such as door knocking in his area. Ah well, that's life, I guess.

In the late Spring of 1998, I felt it right and 'a nudge from the Lord' to move to the south coast of England. My wife and I had a talk and I stated I would have liked to have gone to Cramlington, but knew it was right to choose the mid-south coast. We went down and had a look at the New Milton area and sorted out a plan of action. The Heysham house was in excellent condition and that part of Berwick Way and Heysham Village were pleasant enough, but houses were not selling very well, possibly because Morecambe was not exactly the holiday resort it had once been and the house was a mile or two from the Heysham Nuclear Power Station, alongside the massive Heysham Port complex, trafficking whatever to the Isle of Man. The house did sell that summer, but not for what we thought it should have gone for. Slowly it all sorted itself out and came together. We found a flat in New Milton/Barton-on-Sea and had to do some work on it to put it into good condition. My son got a transfer in his work to that area and we stayed with a friend of my wife in the New Forest for a few weeks while sorting out the flat.

That was the time that Barry and Batya Segal, best known for their singing and musical gifting, along with their work among the poor, etc, in Israel, had their first England Conference on a fruit farm near Verwood - I think it was in the August - 'Be Not Silent Day or Night'; what a superb conference that was, with powerful praise and worship, teaching and ministry, etc, over three or four days, with real freedom to be yourself and totally enjoy the Lord.

Mahesh Chavda and other excellent speakers were there and it was highly organised by Anthony Malpas, and from it a video was made for the God Channel ... someone told me I was on it for a few seconds, though I never did get to view it. The doctrine, ministry and fellowship of that conference were totally on my spiritual wavelength! I've never known another conference with probably around 1,500 people where we all came away with a present of an excellent Christian book (couples/families shared), which was well worth reading, such was the generosity of Anthony Malpas; so it was all good stuff.

It must have been late summer when we moved into the New Milton flat and we were there about a year. I really liked New Milton and Barton-on-Sea and everything about it, including the fact that 75% of its population was said to be in retirement. In some ways it was like putting the clock back a few years. It was ideal for cycling and walking, with the shops, etc, all nearby. We soon made a lot of friends and contacts with believers in various Church fellowships covering that area. Time went by and my son was still not through his rebellious stage, though he did not have the group or 'gangs' of youths he had had in Heysham. He worked hard, but would still come in drunk on occasions and that was difficult. I suppose the age gap between us did not help any - and so we climbed into 1999.

One weekend night in the early Spring of 1999, he had not come home or made contact at all. I felt very uneasy and tired of it all and, of course, so was my wife. I was slowly getting into bed at about midnight and just at that moment the doorbell rang. I groaned, "Oh no", and went and answered it. A policeman was standing there. "Are you 'so and so'?" he asked. "Yes, that's me," I replied. " Have you a son named 'so and so'?" "Yes, that's him." "I'll go and get him," he said. A minute or two later he, with another policeman, brought the lad up the few flights of stairs and into the flat. The five of us were in the hallway as the police explained what had happened. We all went into the lad's small bedroom, then, with my son remaining in the bedroom, the rest of us moved back and were talking in the hallway. His bedroom door was still open and at this point one of the policemen was facing the inside of the bedroom and the window. Suddenly, like lightning, he moved forward and into the room and only just managed to grab hold of my son, who had opened the window and was half way out, and pull him back in, and after a second or two the other policeman helped him. The first policeman turned white and shouted, "Right, that's it, I'm taking you in!" and the two policemen without any further ado marched him out of the flat and down all the stairs of the stairwell of that property built around the later 'sixties and, as he must have been approaching the door to the outside, he cried out, "D- a-a-a-d!" ...but *Dad* could not help any more! ... and he was gone.

I can still hear that desperate cry for help ringing in my ears: so loud, then tailing off through the stairwell, as I closed the flat door and can still remember the emotional pain of that moment! I looked out of his bedroom window at the road, a cul-de-sac, around 50 yards away across lawns and a path, and saw they were holding him securely over the bonnet of one vehicle and there were police cars and a van all over the place. Perhaps I should explain that my wife and I had chosen his new bedroom double-glazed window to be exactly the same as the one in his bedroom in Heysham, only *there* if he got out of it he was onto the roof of the downstairs loo and it was possible to jump down the several feet to the front lawn. In New Milton, however, it was ground, first and second floors and, not only were we on the second floor, it was a straight drop down to the ground – true, it was a lawn - but immediately below his window, attached to the wall of the ground-floor flat, was an unused stone/slate window box and, even though he had had drink, in my opinion, it would have been highly unlikely that he would have survived the fall. I was certainly grateful to the two policemen for their quick action. I could not any more allow my son to go on with this type of behaviour.

I travelled up to the Southampton Courts, where he would appear in a Youth Court, and waited and waited all day, taking only twenty minutes or so for a lunch break nearby in case I missed anything. In the late afternoon, the whole building went quiet and empty and I realised they were keeping him to the last. I got talking to one of the court officials as things became quiet and asked him if I would be allowed to go in. He was telling me that, when he first started on the job a few years earlier, for a month or two it was interesting - then he realised it was the same group of people returning time and time again - I'm not saying that he didn't still find it interesting, but I think he found it disheartening and sad. We talked about a lot of things and eventually he said, "You are allowed to go in", and ushered me in and I sat right at the back. I was surprised at the dozen or so people sitting around the tables in a sort of horseshoe shape and it was quite informal. The lad was brought in and had to keep standing, of course, and I think he was horrified to see me there. Well ... it got worse for him ... for, much to my surprise, they more or less immediately asked me if I would like to say anything! I was totally unprepared for this, but far be it from me to turn down such an opportunity! I struggled to get my brain working and think what line I should take. I did not apologise for his behaviour, but I stated that I thought there was not enough help/support given to parents or whoever when they were struggling to get through as their children were difficult ... also that I thought it was more like a suicide attempt than anything else and so on. When I had finished, one or two of those present passed pieces of paper over to me with telephone numbers, saying to contact those people for help. I said, "Thank you", but I already had a plan of action in my thoughts. He was in the wrong, of course, but they did not come down too heavily on him. Outside, on our way to the railway station to get the train home, he was very angry indeed - he was desperate for a cigarette - so I gave him some money and he went straight to a newsagent and bought some. After buying some he did share his experience with me; then we got home and he had something to eat.

A few days later I said to him that we needed to talk and we did so. I stated it had always been my ambition to look after him until his eighteenth birthday, then my job would have been done. The situation was so serious and damaging now that I gave him an ultimatum. "Stop drinking and obey the rules of the house and you can still go on living with us." "You're not telling *me* what to do," he replied. "Fair enough," I said, "but that means you will need to leave home now, still a few weeks before your 18th birthday - we will help you find some 'digs' close to where you work and will keep an eye on you to make sure you get food, etc, but it's one or the other"; so he said he would find digs.

It didn't take long, just a week or so, and a room was found just a few minutes' walk from his work. He did a little bit of decorating and we helped to make his room as clean and comfortable as possible. We visited regularly, did some of his washing and made sure he had food in and was actually eating something.

Just a few weeks went by and his 18th birthday arrived. My wife and I had arranged for him to come over at a certain time in the early afternoon and had said we would prepare a really nice buffet/tea for him. My daughter and family were travelling down from Cramlington on that day - it had started off as a secret, but he found out!

I made a terrible mistake so far as the lad was concerned and it was regarding the small bedroom in our flat, which had been his room. My wife suggested that we get rid of his furniture and then I also agreed (although two or three years earlier she had stated to him that if he ever left home we would keep his room intact for him for a while, in case he wanted to come back) and we did this, but neither consulted him nor told him. Whatever had happened to me at around 18 years old, I had just sort of adjusted to it and got on with it. I knew well Psalm 15, especially in the NIV Bible, where it states we should honour our word, even when it hurts, and my conscience was working overtime, as this was not good. My son turned up on the day at the appointed time and immediately went into what had been his bedroom. When he saw it empty of his furniture, he just wept and broke his heart and tried to leave the flat, but I prevented him and tried to talk to him - after some time we did talk, but I felt terrible because I realised how important that room being intact was to him, even if he may never live in it again. I guess he saw it as cutting him out of our hearts altogether and a total rejection of my parental loving care for him. His mother had gone those few years earlier and now, in another sense, his father had 'gone' by 'rejecting him'. I had failed to understand the depth of that loneliness, pain, hurt and anger that he had carried over the years - I'm not saying that his bad behaviour was acceptable without some correction, but I am saying he was crying out to be understood and there needed to be trustworthiness on my part for him to reach maturity. I said I was in the wrong, would take my correction and asked him to forgive me.

My daughter and family arrived and we were all talking and having fun and enjoying the birthday tea when my son quietly came up to me and said, "Dad, I really forgive you, so don't worry about it; it's okay, and I've really enjoyed myself this afternoon" - we gave each other a hug and he thanked me and, though I felt a little guilty for a day or two, I knew he meant it! (By the way, of course he thanked his stepmother as well.) Then I said to my son, "We cleared the room out so your Big Sis and co. could put airbeds down to sleep there for the next couple of nights and you can sleep in the lounge. Also, as you know, we have started a fellowship up in Southbourne because the other one disbanded. We have decided to try to move to the Southbourne area, possibly to a one bed-roomed McCarthy & Stone flat." (This happened by the autumn.)

As I look back now, I realise that, as such, my job regarding the parenting of my son was finished on that day of his 18th birthday. We have kept in touch with contact whenever and been good friends – well, we have put our strong and sometimes stubborn characters against each other at least once anyway, but we still came back friends!! I'm not so sure his 'digs' went all that well for him, because a month or two later he transferred in his work back up to the Newcastle area and my daughter and family said he could live with them. Could it have been something like, "We'll show you how to get it right, Dad!" If so I thought, "I'll watch with much anticipation!"

When the day came for his move, we had the Citroen ZX packed full of his belongings, with him squeezed in on the back seat, and so we drove up to Cramlington. Time went by and, of course, I had normal regular contact with my family in Cramlington. About three months later, they phoned me up one day, "We can't take any more," they said, "we've had enough." "Only three months?… that's not long … it's not easy, is it?" was the gist of my reply, though I appreciated what they had done. My grand-daughter was going through some rebellion as well by then so, to be fair, they had their hands full. Well, my son landed on his feet again, for he bought a little modern studio flat close to where my daughter and family lived and they helped him to put it into really good condition - and his life continued on ...!! So what happened to my son? If he ever wanted to give his life's story from his own perspective, it would, I'm sure, be interesting - perhaps he won't or ... maybe he will, one day ... that is up to him! He *made* it into maturity, to being a responsible member of society and into higher-grade management in the workplace. Okay, work hard - play hard! Make some mistakes ... and life's a training ground for us all anyway - but *make* it ... he did!! The unconditional love, acceptance, encouragement, prayer, positive words spoken to and over him, the heartache of it all, etc, without my putting upon him any of the nonsense of any 'work ethic pressure' or 'you will meet the standards I expect from you ...' certainly paid off!!

Throughout the summer of 1999 I began, led and shouldered the responsibility of a fellowship in Southbourne. My wife and I shared evenly the preaching, leading the meetings and the pastoral side of things. I felt that if it didn't flourish within six months then it would not be likely to do so, unless the Lord said differently, of course. If it didn't do well, then it wasn't for the want of trying! We put a lot of work and effort into it - I would take the best part of a week to prepare a sermon - weaving in preaching and some teaching, then often 'act out' a part of it, sometimes in a humorous way, using simple props like chairs, etc, to help those present receive the Word into their inner beings. When I first started this strange preaching, I think they thought I'd lost the plot; then I knew, as time went by, they were really understanding what I was trying to get over each time I preached. I didn't have to answer to anybody as such - so it was fun and I could concentrate on whatever biblical verses I was communicating. We had no musician or music, so that was not helpful. The core group of us was six or seven, but the number of different people who attended or visited the fellowship, including holidaymakers, was just under thirty.

My wife and I did a lot of leafleting with info re the fellowship and door knocking in the streets around the area where we hired the building for each Sunday morning. We advertised in the Bournemouth newspaper each week and they once did an article on us, but the growth we were working towards was not happening. One or two visitors paid a compliment on the preaching and the way we tried to bring in and maintain freedom, though not so sure we ever did! Not only did I never make an appeal of any kind for money, but simply left a small plate to one side in case anyone felt led to give, and one or two would just hand me some money when they gave. Each Sunday I left a three-column cash/accounts book on a table with info on all the income and outgoings for each calendar month - all my wife and I took out was some admin. expenses and the money that was left over at the end of each month was sent, in its entirety, to a good evangelical charity ... I remember a visiting man one Sunday looking surprised to see the accounts book available for anyone to look at and he studied it carefully for several minutes, though he did not say anything ... the strange thing was that each month the monies given to the fellowship increased and so we were able to give away more as each month went by … there is a valuable lesson in that somewhere! Although the core group of that small fellowship did not want it to close down, I nevertheless decided, with sadness and my apologies, to close it, and did so by the early November. It was time to quietly wait on the Lord to seek some answers.

We had booked into the 'Father Heart of God Conference' in the Toronto Airport Church, where the controversial Christian Revival was with John and Carol Arnott. We went for one week and stayed in a B & B owned by a family heavily involved with Airport Church in a place called Brampton, several miles from the Fellowship. We managed to do a little sightseeing of Downtown Toronto at the CN Tower, also Niagara Falls; it was an incredible week and memorable fun - definitely an experience I would not have wanted to miss! The actual conference with the fellowship, meetings, teaching and ministry was quite something. The large building and its main meeting room obviously would hold several thousand, though for that conference it was not full; guess there would be around a couple of thousand or so at the actual conference, with thousands more attending the evening meetings. I was observing and soaking in everything I could that week in all that took place and was not disappointed; also, the times of personal fellowship were good, talking to all different kinds of people.

During one evening meeting, John Arnott said, "Let's have a 'wave offering'." Whatever could that be, I wondered? … with thousands present, it was effectively done, for, as most knew anyway, we were told that everyone was to sit down quietly, apart from those on the platform, and at the back the people in the very last row were to jump up to their feet and openly praise the Lord - as soon as they had done so, the next row down was to follow suit and so on all the way down to the front. I was seated at the front and when John Arnott gave the cue to start, it was like a powerful wave going down the meeting hall, from which the sound of high praise became louder and louder until it reached the front - it was another awesome experience, pleasing to the Lord God Almighty (Psalm 47 verses 1, 5-7, Isaiah chapter 42 verses 12, 13 and chapter 12 verse 6 … and wherever) - but when the momentum at the front hit the platform, one of the musicians was thrown back onto the floor with the power of God (ref John chapter 18 verse 6, NKJV and The Amplified Version) - he was not hurt! A few minutes later, there was another 'wave offering' and it was just as powerful as the first - talk about fun!

At times of ministry in Toronto, usually at the big meetings, several hundreds would line up, as directed by coloured tape on the carpet/floor, and ministry teams would come around praying for each one individually as they moved down the lines. On one particular evening, a very tall, well built Canadian man prayed over me and I was anointed in the Spirit, fell back and lay on the floor. I was just peacefully soaking in the Lord's love when, after nearly a minute or so, someone took hold of my ankle - I opened my eyes and looked up and it was the same man, who had then come back, and his prayer went something like, "Lord, give this man the capacity to channel your power," and he was gone. I thought, "I'll have that one, Lord" and was just starting to think and analyse what he had said, when I said to myself, "no, relax, and just keep receiving God's love and power into your heart," for at that moment that was certainly what was happening!

At one very powerful evening meeting towards the end of my time there, John Arnott had a lady brought to the platform and asked her what was wrong with her. She replied, "I was hit by a metal bar on the side of my face years ago and it damaged the bone, nerves, skin, etc, and I've been in a lot of pain since." "Who did it?" he asked, but she refused to say. "Will you forgive that person?" he said to her. At first she hesitated, obviously finding it difficult, and then forgave whoever. John Arnott touched her on her forehead and prayed for her (I did not catch what he said and it was difficult for me to see her from where I was sitting) and she fell backwards under the anointing, was caught by a 'catcher' and lay on the floor under that anointing. He started to deal with another person who had been brought to the platform when, after just less than a minute, the lady on the floor suddenly started shouting and screaming at the top of her voice, which startled me and made me think, "What's going on?" She was helped up onto her feet and shouted with great amazement, "I'm completely healed; I'm out of pain!" It was a 'creative miracle', as her face structure was put back to normal by the Lord. John Arnott touched her again on the forehead and she fell back under another anointing! I couldn't see the detail of her face from where my seat was, but have seen the Arnotts several times in England over the years since that time of Toronto - and have been prayed over twice by Carol Arnott and have no reason to doubt their power, love and authenticity in and from the Lord Jesus.

A man called Peter Jackson led the Saturday evening meeting of that week in Toronto. It was powerful and every time he encouraged us to drink in (metaphorically) from the Living Waters of Life so that we would be 'drunk' in the Spirit, I pretended to lift up and drink from a large container as he and many others were doing, and each time I did so I felt 'drunk' - we're back to Acts chapter 2 again! That was a superb meeting. The next morning, Sunday, I could hardly wait to get to the meeting, but on going into the main hall, all was quiet and I saw what must have been several hundred sitting only in one large block of seats, right in front of the platform, not talking and seemingly not moving - it was as dead as a dodo! "What is going on?" I wondered, "they've lost the plot; deadly creeping religion has taken over here and it's the same old story, help!" Peter Jackson spoke again that morning and said that the people had complained about this and complained about that. If *he* sounded sad, *I* was disgusted - so the battle for 'life and adventures in the Lord' still rages and on this occasion 'living death' had crept in to win the day, just like all the other times I had seen it happen in my life! When will the Church wake up and realise just Who, in reality, Almighty God is, what He has done and will do for us? - yes, we need discernment against the enemy, but the scriptures clearly say we are not to limit God or His power and love so as not to misrepresent Him, which is dangerous. We need to believe and receive the scriptures into our minds and hearts and also realise the gems there are in such classics as Your God is Too Small, by J. B. Phillips and Tozer's That Incredible Christian.

When I think of King David in 2nd Samuel chapter 3 verses 13-16 having his betrothed Michal returning to him as his wife, but then later despising him over his leaping, etc, before the Lord and the Ark in 2nd Samuel chapter 6 verses 13-23 - he was dancing in his underclothes to the Lord and she definitely, looking at the outward appearance only, missed the heart of what God was doing and what King David, her husband, was doing, as she was proud. There is a biblical principle in this: the religious folk, in their living death, can come against those who are free and love the Lord with all their hearts, but the price they will pay is barrenness (verse 23). Later, after thinking and talking with others, I soon realised that the people who had once visited earlier in the revival and had now returned to this Toronto Fellowship from other places or fellowships for this conference were carrying with them and therefore somehow bringing back the intensity of the original revival of that fellowship which had lasted from 1994 for about four years. The Sunday evening meeting was again 'abnormally normal!' ... superb and again anointed by the Lord - yet it was at the ministry time that something made me think - for John Arnott stated that all the Roman Catholics were to go to another room, where their leaders were to see to them, and hundreds and hundreds, so it seemed, gathered together and went out. That really ministered to me for John Arnott to be kind and mature enough not to exclude them from visiting the meetings, but big-hearted enough to let them go off to a room for ministry on their own!! I'm not saying there would not still have been some differences on both sides, but unity where possible and kindness and peace prevailed - well, that's the way I viewed it anyway!

There was some contention and fall-out over 'animal noises' emanating from the actual Toronto Revival itself and I just want to say a few words and make an observation. During one of those meetings at ministry time in Toronto, I heard a wolf howling noise. I went and looked around to find out more and found a team member delivering someone from demons - she was getting free and the demons were manifesting that noise through her. I once heard someone during a ministry/soaking in God's love time at the Grapevine Conference at Lincoln making duck noises like laughter. I laughed out loud and it was all infectious, as many others laughed as well - it was a tonic I needed that day to relax and be light-hearted, for even the scripture says that laughter (clean and righteous) is a good medicine. As I write, there are lots of ducks and other wildlife on the nearby river and I love to go down and have a look - it is a bonus when I hear at least one of those ducks quack as if it was laughing - I still laugh or chuckle and it's no different from that day at the

Grapevine Lincoln Showground. By the way, I heard on Radio 4 that it is nearly always the female duck that does all the quacking ... but don't quote me on that one! But the leader(s) of Ellel Ministries, with Derek Prince, wrote a paper against Toronto. Of course, we need to be spiritually alert and have discernment, but as already stated, I've seen Derek Prince, John and Carol Arnott in England and Toronto and Ellel Ministries' leadership in action a lot of times over twenty-odd years and they all had powerful ministries, loved the Messiah and had seen incredible signs and wonders, etc. If Derek Prince and possibly the Ellel Ministries folk had never been to Toronto in the mid-'nineties, were they qualified to write a paper of condemnation? ... I doubt it. Okay, Paul and Peter fell out in the New Testament and had to go their separate ways - two powerful personalities and, like those mentioned above they all are Heaven-bound (or are already there).

Back to Southbourne, Bournemouth: what a lovely place to live, right next to the miles of beautiful sandy beaches and promenade. I never tired of living there or seeing it in the different seasons and looking out from the cliff top across the bay towards Poole, Studland, etc, in all its weather moods, from clear skies to varied cloud formations. I still had many friends in that area and visited fellowships, but what did the Lord want from me and what would He yet do? Would he allow my wife and me just to drift on or would He guide or channel us in particular paths?

The end of the century came and the celebration plans we had made did not happen! First of all, my wife got a bad dose of flu and after a few days it affected her lungs - getting medical treatment at first proved difficult and that was not good. After two or three days, I also went down with flu: it was about the 2nd or 3rd of January ... Oh boy, just like in my childhood, was I poorly with a high temperature, pounding headache, etc, and it was incredibly painful to even try to swallow. It seemed to go on for ages into January, when I started to get back into the land of the living and normality.

Friends of ours, a leader called Tony Cassons with his wife, who at that time lived in Verwood, came down to visit and pray over us on 21st January 2000 after our being poorly. That was fine, but he also started to prophesy with some words of knowledge, first over me, and then over my wife. 'Strange why separately and not together?' I wondered, as I later digested what was said to me. My guess now is that the word given to me was about 65% accurate and it contained the words 'a new phase of experience' and 'a new time coming for you quite soon'. The relevant parts did not make sense to me at that time, so I didn't really take it on board. By the time we had gone into the spring/early summer, it became abundantly clear to me what was happening - accepting it as such was another issue! My wife slowly started to close the marriage down, wanting to go and visit people and places on her own, which more or less closed down the 'teamwork' that we had had in the Lord. She had gone back on what we had originally agreed before we got married - if the reasons why were clear to her, then they certainly weren't clear to me. Because of suffering some abuse in relationships much earlier in her life, she came to hate men and then could only remain in control, so far as they were concerned, by having, then throwing, those relationships away. I knew only too well by then where her love loyalties lay and where they did not. I presumed she had sorted that one out with the Lord, but perhaps not quite.

I would have had at that point somewhere around 35 years of marriage, but I did not believe in sharing the intimacies or secrets of a marital relationship outside of it as it would cheapen, weaken or damage it or start to cause much hatred, so I did not share locally with anyone, though one or two asked me to do so in order that they might help. To me it was not worth the risk of escalating the problems or causing more hatred than necessary if it moved towards a divorce. I did share one or two things briefly with my daughter in the summer of that year, as I felt she not only understood much of the situation anyway but had the gift to remain impartial as well.

I still believed things would yet sort themselves out, but as the summer went by, that was not to be so. I was cornered and isolated and the mental and emotional pain took its toll and I cried out to the Lord for help and prayed a lot - but things did not change and I was just given enough grace from Heaven to get me through it. I received a curse or two from my wife as the time came to leave. One of those was that all of my family would be wiped out in an aeroplane accident. I remembered Derek Prince, who, of course, was excellent when it came to spiritual warfare, saying that someone once said to him, "I see you in a car wrapped around a tree!" He in no way accepted or received this, but in spiritual warfare broke its power of the Jezebellic spirit over him through the name of the Lord Jesus and, of course, it never did happen to him. I set to to break those curses off myself and my family. She also tried to curse any future marriage I might have. She said of me that I was so heavenly minded I was no earthly good - I know though that the kingdom of Heaven will win over this world and its ways!

In the middle of September, I left on a direct train from Bournemouth to Newcastle. I was traumatised and could neither eat nor drink - it was a terrible experience - I seriously wondered if I would make it, as the rejection and stigma of divorce was underway and I knew the Church could be vicious with anyone unfortunate enough to fall into that state. This, for me, was worse than spouse bereavement.

As my daughter and family had no room in their house, I had arranged to stay with George and Libby (she was a medical doctor) and their family in Cramlington, and it was early evening when I eventually arrived, mentally and emotionally exhausted. They were not actually all that keen to have me, but had a roomy house, so they sorted something out for me. I was certainly grateful to them, as I wasn't sure I would have survived without their help. I can remember asking if they would just give me two weeks to sort some other accommodation out … and the miracle was that, by the following Tuesday, I had signed for a purpose-built one bed-roomed Housing Assoc flat near to where I had previously lived in Cramlington! At that point, George and Libby said that I could stay with them on a permanent basis, and pay my way, of course! I thought carefully, but decided I would be best on my own, but thanked them, for it was a very kind gesture. I was exactly two weeks with them before moving into the flat!

The Lord clearly spoke into my heart that I must not borrow or get into any debt whatsoever, even short term. In the past, if I had had an empty property and needed something, I would simply have borrowed, normally from the bank, and bought the essentials. I put some carpeting in the areas that I considered important and that was all I could afford to do. I already knew the value of keeping a lifestyle as simple as possible ... even though I liked the 5***** treatment as well! I borrowed camping equipment from my daughter and family and she gave me some bedroom curtains: all very basic! From that day to this, I have never again borrowed any money and that is a good place to be with and in obedience to the Lord ... if I had to do without something or live on basic food for a while, then I was content to do so.

I got, in early October, all of my personal belongings, desk, chair and microwave from Bournemouth. A little later, I cashed in a life insurance on myself and so was able by the turn of the year to finish furnishing the flat and it came together nicely. I was in the flat for five years and it was economical and pleasant enough.

As the year 2000 continued on and drew to a close, I made one or two friends and contacts and, as I was not really in a very good way, I looked for and received some necessary ministry, which helped me through. I was not able, because of what was happening, to 'give out' toward others and decided I'd just generally withdraw until I felt better and would be free from any real or perceived feelings of guilt. I would pray, of course, and my daughter also helped me through by listening, encouraging and some wise counsel. From approximately all the latter half of that year, I could not accept or come to terms with all that was happening ... not a good place to be! Because I wrote several letters to friends in the south, really as a cry for help, and this was not very bright as I look back!... (an appeal for prayer and to help save my marriage) ... it turned out that I lost all of my friends anyway. Of course, it would be foolish to 'take sides' in any case; therefore it would be acceptable to be neutral. Strangely enough, no-one answered any of my letters. I did receive one death threat given verbally through my wife from someone, so my name must have been greatly dishonoured; but I was disgusted with the stupidity of it all. I cleared it with the Lord as to what wrongs I might have done to these people and then gave it all back to Him for His vindication. It was Christmas morning of 2000 and I spoke for a minute or two on the phone to my wife. I think her anger and hatred by then had made her dangerous, for she was keen to know if my family were still alive; so I explained that on returning from their holiday in Turkey they flew into Manchester Airport

(11th Nov?) and there was a terrible storm with very strong winds and as the pilot landed the aircraft and touched down he only just managed to steady it from going over. My family said everyone had applauded the pilot when the plane finally came to a stop. After she had got the info she wanted, she just said, "I never loved you anyway!" and put the phone down. Those were the last words I heard her say. What game was she really playing?

About four weeks later, I received divorce papers from Bournemouth. I did refute what she said, but my solicitor said I couldn't fight it as such and that she would get her divorce anyway. It all went through in record time of ten weeks and six days to the decree absolute, and that was that. I deliberately chose to walk away from it all and not to pursue any possible financial gain. Just days after receiving those divorce papers, and their return through my solicitor, I at last fully accepted all that had happened - I would put it all behind me, learn from it, forget about it and get on with the rest of my life. At last I had grieved to the point of acceptance!

The Lord said to me, "Do you forgive her?" "Of course, Lord, but don't forget justice and vindication on both sides," was what I said back to the Lord in my heart. Then I got the nearest I could get to a 'vision', a sort of mind outline of a picture. It was a courtroom, somewhat dark, very posh, with a long, beautifully polished wooden 'bar', and I knew it was the Lord Jesus alone sitting there, though I could not see any details of Him. I was at one end and it seemed a long way to the other end, where my wife was standing. There were no other beings present. The Lord turned to me and said, "Do you forgive her full stop and give her to me unconditionally, and if you do so she will walk free from this court?" I thought carefully, "Are there no other options? ... and yet the Lord will always bring justice and also I could forget any 'rights' I might have." (We only have 'privileges' in the Lord anyway!) "Right, Lord," I said, "I totally and completely forgive her for every and any wrong she has done to me and mine and give her to You completely; she is Yours, You love her and that's that." The Lord in the 'vision' turned to her and said, "You may walk free into the daylight" (which I could then see a little of at her end of the bar) and so she did!!! Then, He turned to me and said something like, "And so to you, Henry ...", and He later gave me some incredible spiritual blessings. Guess what: from that day to this, I have never been bothered or concerned in any way by what happened regarding the relationship and the divorce. I can talk about it and have helped and encouraged some divorcees over the years and I have most certainly kept my peace!

That season ended and onto another one. I served the Lord in helping people whenever I could or it seemed right and made a circle of friends in the Newcastle area. It is worth noting that God likes 'hot' or 'cold' as extremes, but not the middle part! I've had yet another season since then and the good news is the Lord still lovingly corrects me (nothing to do with punishment!). By the way, I have learned as we get older that it is an affront for younger people than your age group (e.g. middle-aged politicians) to tell *you* how *you* should behave or what *you* should be capable of doing work-wise, etc. You see, getting older brings its own set of problems!

At this point I will draw a line under my life's story, except to say one or two things. My daughter said to me in 2002, "It looks like your grand-daughter (saying her name) is pregnant!" I took that one to the Lord immediately, and He said to my heart, "I'm giving you three generations of daughters!" "That's an honour, thank You," was my reply to the Lord. I had no doubt whatsoever on this matter. On 11th May 2003 my great-grand-daughter, Caitlin, was born! I later realised that my three generations of girls were not only 'first-born', but there was a pattern in the years from myself to Caitlin. I was born in Nov 1944, my daughter was born in June 1963, my grand-daughter in July 1984 and my great-grand-daughter in May 2003 - it spanned 59 years, with a 4-3-4-3 pattern in the last digit of the years of birth and a 19-21-19 year pattern between the years of birth. Also, now I have another two great-grandchildren, Josh and Paige.

And, oh yes, I got married again to a lovely Scottish lassie and later moved from Cramlington ... and as stated, it was with her help I finally got this book sorted out on to the computer from my earlier handwritten version... no easy task... but we got there... and life rolls on in all its colours...!!

# 20

# *What ... Good News ...?*

'In the beginning God ...' are the first words of the Bible and that says it all. He is the Great, Mighty, Sovereign God, King of all kings and Lord of all lords, and everything else comes after Him. No-one or no thing is greater than He is. He created all of creation and all that we can comprehend as we observe it, so He created all things, including the Garden of Eden, and mankind who He made in His own image, to live in it for eternity - and it was good: meaning, there was no evil, sin, sickness or any such thing - it was absolute perfection as the first couple lived in full contact, harmony and fellowship with, and worship to, their Maker God. They had no concept or knowing all about good and evil, therefore LIFE was total fun!

When the temptation to sin and be disobedient came from that evil serpent (created and subsequently fallen being) with his deceit, lies, cunning and smooth, empty words, Eve succumbed (by actually eating the fruit of the Tree of the Knowledge of Good and Evil which God had told them not to do), thinking it would be good, and so sided with God's enemy against God, and sin entered mankind via her heart and Adam quickly followed suit by doing the same as she had done. Purity of a holy life from Heaven did not now satisfy them and their relationships were now all damaged, first of all with God Himself, then with each other and within themselves and elsewhere across the board. They had been told that if they did eat that which was forbidden, they would surely die - first of all spiritually and *that* that death *in their spirit,* in its vital relationship to God, would cut them off from Him and so that meant death would permeate through to the physical and eventually they would physically decease, though their spirit would go on forever; but 'dead' towards and separated from God, unless God Himself intervened to sort it out. This would have applied to Adam and Eve (and therefore to all subsequent mankind) and they would be separated from God in that fallen spiritual state for all eternity because, as the Holy God, He could not have that which was sinful or impure constantly in His presence, so He could not be 'friends' or have 'fellowship' with them or look upon their sin.

Sin is a horrific thing and a book that I have by a man called Venning, with the title The Plague of Plagues, rams home to us its deadly corrupt and contagious work!! Sin (missing the mark, an archery term) caused Adam and Eve to try to clothe themselves best way they could, using leaves, and in great fear run and hide from the Majesty of the Lord. So when God came to them to confront them with what they had done, He quickly dealt with it to sort it out totally from His side. He told them the way things would be from then on with the curse of the ground, work, etc, as a result of their sin and He sacrificed an animal and He made its skin into clothing for them to wear. What God did would have to be done totally of Himself on their behalf, because of their complete helplessness to sort out the mess of it all and their mental, emotional and heart confusion of trying to cope with their newly acquired knowledge of 'good and evil' as a result of eating the forbidden fruit.

Why then was the death of an *animal only* required by and acceptable to the Lord God, and not an offering of 'leaves' or 'fruit' or the 'whatever'? The Lord clearly says that the wages of sin is death ... the Lord God cannot lie, so death there had to be!! With the likes of fruit or leaves there was no real cost involved to those who offered them, as it was 'man's way', an easy way out, an attempt to appease God by trying to sort out their own salvation, but there was no 'death' to cover their sins and take their punishment of death ... *that* death was still in place over them. But the Lord God could accept a substitute of His choice and look upon its 'death' to cover each one's sin. This is because the life is in the blood, so the blood that was shed by that which gave of its life to a sacrificial death would then be accepted by the Lord God as a substitute in the person's place, as long as 'the whoever' approached the Lord in the right way. With Adam and Eve, they accepted in their hearts for God to do what God *would* do and when He gave them the sacrificed (innocent) animal's skin for clothing, because their innocence had gone ... they were now back into a heart relationship and so, from then on, were able to walk in that relationship with their Maker and, no doubt, even by their clothing, would know the cost involved. Also, the Lord would look upon the animal skin and remember the price paid by its innocent blood.

I have included a bibliography in this book and, because I now wish to keep things as concise and as simple as possible, I do not propose to get into in-depth teaching.

Genesis chapter 3 verse 15 is a key verse because in it the Lord God indicated that He Himself would one day take on human form and would deal once and for all with sin and His arch-enemy, the devil. The plan, which was carried out nearly 2000 years ago, was to clothe Himself in human form and come to earth to fully identify with us and, although He would be tempted just as we are, He would always choose the good and not evil. He would lead a totally sinless life for thirty-three and a half years and then would offer Himself up as a human sacrifice - as a clean, spotless Lamb, and, once and for all, deal with sin, sickness, the devil, evil and the final enemy, death - overcoming evil with love and showing evil up for what it is and is capable of. The animal sacrificial system that the Lord God put in place in and after the Garden of Eden needed to be repetitive in order to satisfy the Lord and to keep reminding mankind of the cost, because all of creation as we know it was by then under the curse of sin.

The Way I See It

And so it is that in God's plan and purpose of things in history it's the Cross of Calvary that is central to everything, the place where He was personally involved and in much pain and distress. Why would He do this? The answer is simple - in His LOVE for us, all He wants is a people who will return His love and freely love Him for Who He is, what He has done and what He will yet do!!

Why was the Saviour's life and the Cross so effective? When the Messiah came to live on Earth with all that He went through in His first thirty years (e.g. was a refugee in Egypt with His parents as King Herod wanted Him dead), followed by His three and a half years of powerful ministry of healing, miracles and teaching, etc, *He was completely sinless* and in His being He represented both God and man. He showed such love that He willingly - though not easily, because of what it would entail - endured the most horrific tortures and pain lasting a day or even two (the Roman common beating itself was so horrific with its many lashings on the back and meant that for some you could even see through their body when it was finished and no wonder some did not survive it). This was as much as any one being could ever suffer or take. He was marred more than any other man and so took upon Himself all the worst of sin that man and the demonic in man could give out, then offered Himself up as a human sacrifice on a tree of crucifixion. At the moment when He accomplished what He had come to Earth to accomplish, He gave up His life - it was not taken from Him. The crucifixion was a most terrible torture in itself, but He still lived until He shed His pure sinless blood and all was accomplished to clean up and set men free and He said, "It is finished", meaning "*IT IS FINISHED!*" and no one can add to or take away from this now once for all Covenant that He made in His blood and sinless life and all this was totally acceptable to Father God.

He took upon Himself and was 'clothed in' all the sins of mankind and dealt a death blow to all the forces of evil and wickedness, in His perfect selfless love, showing them up for the wickedness they are. Because He was both divine and human, He *alone* is able to bring individuals of fallen mankind back to their Maker, Heavenly Father God, and to the Tree of Life and to harmonious right relationships, etc, etc.

The 'whole package' of His plan, if you like, is the most wonderful free gift (and a gift must be received, opened and become yours to be effective) of pure Love. This new or second Covenant includes His life, torture and sacrificial death on this Earth for you and for me, His body buried in a tomb, resurrected on the third day, His ascension to Father God and quick return, His being seen by many on Earth, His ascension to Heaven and the promise of His return at the appointed time, and the giving of His Spirit 'in' at salvation and 'upon' at the power given at Pentecost to help us make it through and serve Him in building His Kingdom. It is a bit like us being 'the glove' and He being 'the hand', so that the Holy Spirit, within us, can direct us.

He totally kept and fulfilled during His life on Earth all the laws that had been given. Every animal sacrifice required by the Lord (as stated in the Torah/first covenant scriptures) made from Adam and Eve up to the Cross of Calvary looks *forward* as a type of, and to the sacrifice of, Messiah. Of course, every true believer, since Calvary, looks back to the Cross of Calvary, which alone gives life from death. That the Messiah kept the 'law' and then gives His keeping of it as a gift to every true believer in Him, because he/she is 'in Christ' means genuine believers are free from legalistically keeping the law and that His 'law of love' is written in their hearts.

What I'm saying, in a nutshell, is this: it is God's creation - He made us and all that is around us - all was perfect in a beautiful garden - sin came in through the temptation by evil and the first man and woman completely failed the test - they then tried to sort out all this general mess of sin by/for themselves, but could not, as it was impossible for them to do so - God has said, 'the wages of sin is death' - God sorted it out for them with animal sacrificial death instead of the death due to them for their rebellious wrongdoing - He clothed them with the animal skin and this all pointed to the Messiah who would one day come to Earth to minister to mankind as a Suffering Servant and give His life for their and all of our sins, past, present and future.

As the winner and the victor in the fight against evil, that is life over death, Jesus the Saviour Messiah gives gifts to those who give themselves to Him, puts His love in their hearts, allows them to be part of His Kingdom (from and of Heaven), so they know they are Heaven-bound to be with Him for all eternity and not bound for the only other alternative, the lake of fire, a place of unbelievable torment for all eternity, originally made for only the devil and fallen angels. These are hard words, but they are clearly laid down in scripture, e.g. Revelation chapter 20 verses 10 and 15. If we reject Almighty God and what He has accomplished for us, we do so at our peril!

For me, even after the benefit of doing an in-depth study of this subject at BTI in Glasgow, it was Derek Prince who, in a short list on a bookmark which he simply called 'The Divine Exchange', gave an extremely helpful 'key' of understanding and wisdom by stating and so simplifying the full meaning and truth of what the Saviour Messiah suffered on our behalf, as our substitute, on and before Calvary's Cross. In this 'Divine Exchange', He gives to us all the perfection and good things of and from Himself and all the evil due to us He has taken upon Himself and so dealt with it by His finished work, death, resurrection, etc. It is an awesome enlightenment as we experience the reality of it and add to the list. Some examples are: the Lord Jesus died our death … that we might have His life; He was 'clothed' with our sinfulness … that we might be made righteous with His righteousness; He was wounded … that we might be healed; He was punished in our place … that we might be forgiven and go free; He bore our shame … that we might share His glory; He endured our rejection … that we might have His acceptance with the Father and the family of Heaven; He took our curses ... that we might have all the blessings of His Heavenly Kingdom; He took our poverty ... that we might have His riches. I sum it all up by simply saying that the Lord Jesus took everything bad about us and gives us everything good of Himself!!! No wonder this package, deal or free gift is just too good to miss!!!?

When the Lord said that we have all sinned and fallen short of His glory, that is exactly what He meant - everyone on this planet has 'blown it' through sin and we ALL need saving from the terrible consequences of sin and we are ALL in serious trouble. Almighty God is in the 'fishing business' for people to be 'caught' by Him and we all know you catch the fish first, then clean it ... well, we should all know that! To repeat what I said earlier, God in Heaven has no conscripts, but only volunteers. I am not responsible for you before the Lord for your salvation and you are not responsible for me or the one next to you! Each and everyone *must* give an account for and of themselves to God. If we live without Christ, we die without Christ - why should anyone spend their life or eternity with someone they don't want or love or like? Where does the blame for sin really lie? For all our sin, whatever has happened, we are still responsible. We must take the responsibility for our own sin and for being part of mankind's collective sin, i.e. we are all born as sinners because we are all descended from Adam and Eve; this is the 'doctrine of original sin'... let's face it, you don't need to teach a child to do wrong, but you do have to teach a child to be good ... would guess that something similar applies to adults - some more than others! You may be free to choose your sin, but you are not free to choose the consequences thereof!

In this light, consider the terrible sin (adultery and murder) of King David in Psalm 51, especially verses 5, 6 and 17, where he says that he was conceived in sin but also faces up to the responsibility of his own sin and eventually was seriously corrected and vindicated; unlike King Saul, who was demonised and only got temporary relief through David's music. Much of what the Lord Jesus did was deliverance ministry; that is, casting out demons from people - not least from 'Legion', of course, and deliverance from demons is still needed as and when people want to be set free from them. The Lord Jesus cast out every demon (where applicable) from all the people who came to Him and asked Him for help. The demonic that would still trouble and torment people here on Earth requires deliverance in order to free them.

Salvation itself has nothing to do with our 'works', 'good deeds' or 'being religious'. In fact, all these things are like filthy rags before God (Isaiah chapter 64 verse 6), especially if doing them before salvation is to try and 'earn' our salvation or try in some way to appease God. Don't misunderstand me, it is always better to do good works and deeds and be selfless and kind, as they are good for you and your soul, but they are no good as a means or substitute for salvation itself. But after salvation has taken place, there are good works and deeds for you to do from and for the Lord - but they are only for our own benefit within our giftings, e.g. to test our hearts, to help and mature us - there will be rewards in Heaven for them if we get them right, but we do them for the Saviour Messiah alone through love and give Him the glory. (Roger Price did an excellent talk on this subject ... 'Palaces or Mud Huts?', BBS 23).

God does not have grandchildren, but only one generation of His own children, and they are 'in Christ', which means we cannot rely on the fact that, after the age (relative to an individual) of being aware of sin or consenting to it, we have or had a Godly mother, father or any other relation who was saved ... they can only help you find the Lord, but salvation itself is personal between you and Him. God does not want 'robots' or the like in His Heaven, but only those who *really* want Him for Who He is and want to be part of His wonderful family - no sin, no pain, no tears, no rejection, no hate, no temptation or the likes of any of these, but only His perfect Light, Life and Love ... and this will be for all eternity!

Cold religion and big-stick legalism go from the outside in, based on fear and coercion, do's and don'ts. But love emanates outwards from deep inside the heart, a love that is free to love without fear or force of any kind. Jesus knocks on the door of our hearts (Revelation chapter 3 verse 20) and will never enter unless invited to do so ... I think the door handle to our hearts is on the inside! God is Love. God looks at our heart and not the outward appearance (1st Samuel chapter 16 verse 7). The Lord God will test our hearts and our motives and The Truth will set us free.

There is a matter of our completely flawed concept in whatever way we might have picked it up, be it cultural or otherwise, of who *we* think God is and how *we* try to contain Him as in 'a box'. According to the concept *we* hold, we then try to tell Him how to behave and what He should do ... when the reality is that few of us, if any, much to our shame, have grasped the concept of His incredible Might, His Power, His Ways, His Love, of all that He is and does and will do far beyond our expectations and understanding. (See Roger Price 'Character of God' series, excellent on this subject.)

Where then is the Fear of God? ... which is the beginning of wisdom. What I am saying is that *we* want to be in control and control God as you would a 'puppet', but it is *God* who is in absolute control anyway and He wants us as His wise subjects under His loving authority ... yes, we need discernment, as His enemies will get in the way and deceive us if they can!

How then do you (or I) get into this vital relationship with Father God so as to make it personal to you? It is *not* by the 'doctrine of universalism' or any other liberal stance or the like, which says something akin to, "If Christ died for the sin of all mankind, then all mankind will ultimately get saved; therefore, do anything or follow anyone you want, anything goes and all roads will lead to Heaven" ... Surely *scripture* does not bear this out and man would have no responsibility of partaking in the salvation God has procured for us ... licence to sin would be the result and therefore unrighteousness would somehow follow on and into God's Kingdom and then even into

Heaven, if that were possible. It is true that our sins are forgiven at Calvary's Cross (but *only* if we appropriate the death of the Lord Jesus, personally, on our behalf, as individuals, e.g. John chapter 5 verse 40); but if we love the Lord and know that He loves us by what He went through, it cannot be licence to sin deliberately, otherwise we disdain the torture and suffering of the Lord Jesus on the Cross. Yes, we may fall without meaning to, ask the Lord for His forgiveness and walk on with Him, but it is never a licence to practise evil or wickedness as a believer. (Remember, in the powerful prayer the Lord gave *us* to pray, 'Your will be done on Earth as it is in Heaven!') You must believe (trust and faith) that the Lord Jesus *is* who He says He is, the Messiah, the Christ and all that that means, who came as a Suffering Servant to give His life for us and will return victoriously to this Planet Earth, to Jerusalem, as King and Lord of All!!

In John chapter 3 verse 3 (in context and elsewhere), the Lord clearly says to Nicodemus, one of the rulers of Israel, "You must be born again," meaning that, as any one of us believes in Messiah and His death being a substitute for us in our place, the resurrection life, etc ... and we take it on board and receive it by faith into our hearts, then and only then can that 'rebirth' take place. So to verse 5, where the Lord Jesus clarified it by saying that unless one is born of water and the Spirit he cannot see the Kingdom of God ... 'of water' is from your mother's womb and 'of the Spirit' is by the power of God from Heaven when you truly ask Him into your heart. The 'Spiritual' is more real and more powerful than the 'natural', even if that does seem strange to us at first - it is the 'natural' around us that is temporal, changing and dying or contains death. In Heaven, I believe, there is a type of complete transparency (no sin, so nothing to hide), which is totally different from our lives here on Earth. You must believe in the Deity of the Saviour Messiah and make a firm and positive commitment to Him in repentance; that is, changing your heart's, mind's and life's direction from that of 'self' and the world's ways to Messiah's ways of and in His Kingdom (the rulership of God from His Heaven), also specifically ask Him to forgive you for all that you have done wrong and forgive all others who have wronged you in your life - not always easy, but always therapeutic if you mean it. 'Vengeance is Mine', says the Lord - and it really *is*, along with justice. But if the Lord has compassion and mercy on *you* to forgive all of *your wrongs*, should not *you* and each one of us forgive those who have wronged us? The key is to subdue the carnal nature and the world's ways within us that would pull us down! It is God's breath, His Holy Spirit Life in us at the 'rebirth', that gives us the power and strength to deal with our fallen nature as He cleans us up when we deliberately ask Him to do so. You cannot be born again - that is, be in a close relationship with the Lord God - by 'knowledge' or of 'the mind' or by 'intellect' or even by knowing the Bible (scriptures) or by knowing all about the Lord Jesus Christ, but only in and through your heart, even if there is some mental understanding as background. Of course, the 'will' is involved and God 'wills' to reach out to us and love us and hopes we will reciprocate and so in our response to His love there is an element of the will to love God and others.

For those who practise the ways and religion of the Pharisees (who were some of the leaders in Israel at the time the Lord Jesus walked on Earth), with their pride, arrogance, religious nonsense and control over men for their own means and selfishness, the Lord said it would be difficult for them not to be sentenced to hell and told His followers not to be as the Pharisees were. The likes of them are still around today, playing their games. The Lord Jesus, in Luke chapter 18 verses 9 to 14, in a parable, told of two men who were trying to get Father God's attention. One was thanking God he wasn't like other men and the Lord was silent about him but the other man cried out to God, obviously from his heart, beat his chest, and said, 'God be merciful to me, a sinner' - the Lord said the latter was the one who was heard and went away justified!

The response to the Gospel as preached and stated in Acts chapter 17 verses 22 to 34 was threefold and therefore happened in three ways. Which one of the three is yours? Some mocked, as shown in verse 32, and they just didn't believe or care. Others, again in verse 32, were interested in what they had heard, so said, "We will hear you again on this matter", as they were keen to hear more, but did not take action to make a decision there and then; but in verse 34, yet others were completely smitten, believed, and made that decision of belief and joined with the other believers!

It is giving Him your heart and life, as in falling in love with Him, living for and with Him and being a subject in His Kingdom ... this is what is required, because *what gets your heart gets you*, that's where your treasure is!

The Lord God will hear the *intense* cry of the sincere heart in humility and even brokenness, asking Him for help, and at that point He will most certainly help you. When you are in turmoil and your heart is broken, He alone is able to give you peace and put a new heart within you, soaked in His life and love and, as you quietly bow your heart and life in humility and give Him all that you are, good, bad and indifferent and open the door of your heart to let Him in, confessing you have 'blown it' in His sight and allow yourself to fall in love with Him, you will then realise how much He has loved you. Even if you have never known much real love, let Him gently pour His soothing Love into your heart, because you are *special* to Him, along with His Grace (undeserved favour), Mercy, Truth, Life and Peace. He then wants to show His loving kindness to and through you towards others. As you give Him *all* of your heart and live for Him, so He will give you *all* of His heart and give you LIFE in abundance! Even *today* His agape (Godly) love gift of His Mercy and Grace can enter your heart and change you forever to be like the Saviour!! It's your decision!

This is *the* GOOD NEWS *and* OH ... WHAT GOOD NEWS!!!

# 21
# *Why the Controversy Over the Jews and Israel?*

I have mentioned elsewhere in this book something of my understanding of the Jews and Israel, gleaned from various sources, and how this, for me, slowly began to come about. Though there may be some overlap, I will develop this a little further to answer the title of this chapter in the light of the precarious events of history we are now in and those which will shortly unfold and I will deal with the latter in the following chapter.

As my autobiography shows, I was born and raised a 'gentile' and that, in some ways, it was a survival course for me. The 'aloneness' which I experienced and took for granted through much of the '50s no doubt was due to the dysfunctional family and the 'institutionalism' of most of my schooling, where the whole of life was 'ordered' and 'regimented'. No wonder I longed to be an adult and 'happily married' and have some control over my life! I would say that no-one could go through what my siblings and I went through and not be 'damaged goods' to some extent, because the stable, happy, healthy family was non-existent. Destroy the family unit and soon you destroy the whole of a society. Life can be easy or it can be hard, as most of us know … we either survive or we don't survive and the rulers of a nation either do good to those less fortunate in their midst or work against them and oppress and/or badly use them, as they, the less fortunate, might struggle to gain normality, whatever that is! For most of my childhood I did not know or care what a 'Jew' was, or for any other nationality as such - mainland UK only was 'my patch' and I was content about that. My understanding of the Jews and Israel grew a little as I went into my teens and twenties - not least about some of the hatred towards them.

In my early years I did not see the importance of the link between the Church (my experience of which was only that of the Church of England/Church of Scotland), with its structure, its ways as in its brand of 'Christianity' and its lack of Jewishness in its relationship to the Jews, their Messiah and their land of Israel. I could not see the wood for the trees, you might say, i.e. that the Messiah was fully Jewish and belonged to the Jews; but reading some of the Bible in 1961 was for me the beginning of change and starting to go down the right road. My understanding of the whole subject had matured by the time I was in my late thirties, but the priority I placed on it was not high enough so as to take positive action.

Although the Jews were scattered amongst the nations for the last approximately 2000 years, they have, against all the odds, generally kept their Jewishness and their faith in the Lord God, with all that that means, and returned to the very place from which they were scattered and such a thing is unequalled in history by any other nation. Whatever the Jews had received from God, they ran with it, even if they stumbled more than a few times; but the main reason that their identity and separateness survived down through the generations and centuries was the strength (not necessarily perfection) of their family units, along with the 'tribal', where applicable, and 'national' family as well, and, of course, the way in which their scriptures, precepts, and their symbolic teachings (e.g. the feasts) were handed down. The (Jewish) family is spiritual, of the soul, and physical and when working in a righteous way should bring a sense of belonging that would bring order, stability and confidence. The 'nation' or 'people' which has strong family units - and this is not so much of a 'harsh legalism' or being overly strict, but with a caring, kind heart - whereby adherents are part of it on a voluntary basis, will be invincible, even if they do often need the Lord's help and protection!

My eyes had been opened by that small powerful prayer group with Alan, Roma, Pat and possibly others in Moldgreen, Huddersfield, who for years faithfully prayed for the Jews and Israel; but I still did not 'run with it', even though the Lord was speaking to me about it. When I went into the Bradford Church, the above little group - even if it was unknown to me at the time - prayed vehemently that I would leave that Bradford fellowship, which, of course, I eventually did. When I was put to one side 'spiritually' so that I would hear more clearly what the Lord was saying to me, it was then I came across and was influenced and challenged by the relevant teaching on this subject from Roger Price's earlier work; so for me it was in the early part of the '80s I began to listen to his tapes and my eyes were opened as I understood and saw clearly the Church and its relationship to the Jews and Israel. Finally, I woke up and made the decision in the mid '80s, so far as myself and the whole spectrum of the Jews and Israel was concerned, that I would 'run with it'!

Here in a 'nutshell' is a 'mix 'n' match medley' if you like of how my understanding of this subject came about and developed.

As already written, in the 'sixties, I had my encounters with the Lord and eventually got wonderfully born again, believing God to be a trinity of Father, Son and Holy Spirit, yet knowing He was (and is) 'One' God, and whoever said, "God is One in essence but Three in Personality" was correct ... so my simple faith, belief in and fear of this awesome God of Love persuaded me to then make my heart commitment to live, with all of my being, for Him Who I had received ... the years go by and I receive from the Lord His whole package, more intensive training in life itself ... and the Bible ... and that of being a disciple and so on ... go into leadership as a pastor/elder, having by this time more or less accepted the Church's concept of a sort of 'Gentile version' of the Lord Yeshua (Jesus), brought about by a Westernised cultural 'Christianity' which was somewhat influenced by the Roman and Greek Empires of long ago. This Westernised Church was not totally free from anti-Semitism, tainted with the traditions and structures (wherever) of man, sometimes wrongly teaching that the Church has replaced the Jews anyway (not so in the light of Romans chapter 11 and related scriptures) and even teaching by some that Great Britain had replaced Israel 'British Israelism' - "and did those feet walk on England's green and pleasant land?" - I think *absolutely not* and this in spite of His being a refugee when fleeing for His life and, as He clearly later said in Matthew chapter 15 verse 24, that He was only sent (the first time He came, as a 'Suffering Servant') to the lost sheep of the House of Israel. We rightly take the scriptures of the Old and New Testaments (Covenants), in the form that we have them, for the Old Testament, as we have it, contains that which is in the Jewish Bible, only with some differences in the order of the books, along with the complexities of translation, yet virtually all of the New Testament has its roots in some form within the Old Testament.

Now, continuing 'the medley' ... when it fully dawned on me that if I wanted an extra blessing as laid down in the scriptures (as I mentioned earlier in the book - Genesis chapter 12 verses 1-3, regarding those who bless Israel being blessed and those who curse her being cursed), then all I had to do was to bless Abraham, Isaac and Jacob and their seed, the Jews, along with Israel and Jerusalem, and I could not fail to indeed increase God's favour if I took positive action, though I thought that I'd better check that my motives were not merely selfish; but I would definitely and immediately buy and receive that one - I was not going to risk the curse of cursing them ... and so I did from that day forward in the mid '80s and wrote it on my heart, though it took a year or two to fully activate; but activate it did, and I did not look back with regard to this matter ... because of my gifting and upbringing and time available, I would be limited in the depth of what I could learn from the believers' Jewish roots (though there is a great deal of knowledge and good teaching out there today like The Jewish Feasts of the Bible and specifically C.F.I.'s www.keshercourse.org.uk and Barry and Batya Segal's music and ministries, plus much more) ... I would generally support Israel and the Jews, give financially whenever and go to any relevant meetings/conferences and, not least, pray ... I felt all of this was more important for me to do than even trying to go to visit Israel/Jerusalem ... so, for over the last twenty or so years, I can testify that I have known great blessings from Heaven in all the contacts and friends made at different times/stages, all of the meetings and conferences, repentance at UK meetings for what the Church and the nation had done to the Jews, teaching days by different people and participants from the borders of Scotland to the south coast of England (especially the 'Be Not Silent Conference' with Barry and

Batya Segal and team in the height of summer 1998 on a farm near Verwood, Dorset - this was 'the tops'!) ... I am amazed at what I have seen, experienced and learned over these years which was not planned but just happened and unfolded before me whenever ... I would not for anything have missed these superlative blessings - always for me with freedom and discernment as appropriate - pressed down and flowing over to the glory of God.

Key verses are found in Genesis in chapter 12 verses 1-3 (see above) and in chapter 15 verses 6-18. The Lord God owns the title deeds to our Planet and He does whatever He pleases and anything He wants, in keeping with His character, so it is His choice to give a land or allow a land to be given to this or that group. If God gives a word or a promise in the Bible and it is not, as such, cancelled or superseded, then it still stands to this day. A good example of this is with Noah and family after the flood, when they left the ark and God clearly said in Genesis chapter 9 verse 1 (compare with chapter 8 verse 17) to go forth, multiply and populate the Earth. Nowhere in the rest of the Bible does God go back on that general command. It is man's greed and corruption that does not feed the world. So it is in Genesis chapters 12 and 15 where God has stated and given something and has never gone back on it!

The verses of Genesis chapter 12: 1-3 are certainly important in order to understand what God is about in His history in dealing with mankind, and background information is found in Acts chapter 7 verses 2, 3 and much of that chapter as well, Genesis chapter 13 verses 14-17, Genesis chapter 15 verses 6-18 and, of course, in lots of other relevant scriptures. It is through the seed of Abram (Abram means 'high father' and becomes Abraham in Genesis chapter 17 verse 5, meaning 'the father of many nations'. See also Nehemiah chapter 9 verse 7, etc), Isaac and Jacob that God would make Abraham into a great nation and this was the line down to David and on to the Messiah: see Matthew chapter 1 verse 1 and relevant verses following.

Looking briefly at Genesis chapter 12 verses 1-3, verse 1 tells us that when God spoke to Abram he *listened* and was *quick to obey*, even if it meant a 'faith adventure'! The Lord, in verse 2, said He would make him into a great nation and not only to bless him - that is, give His favour to him - but also to make his name great and this has happened and will continue to happen. Then in verse 3 it becomes personal to us all as we react to this verse and so we can either receive a blessing or a curse, dependent on whether we give out a 'blessing 'or a 'curse'. This applies not only to ourselves individually and immediate families, but to groups, tribes, towns, cities and even whole nations as well! The nation that is cursed in this way will eventually suffer greatly (it may take some time) and this alone should bring about a healthy fear of God Almighty, for it is easily possible to reverse it and change the curse back into a blessing by repentance (Numbers chapter 24 verse 9 in its context is interesting!).

The last part of verse 3 in Genesis chapter 12 is also very important, for it shows what God is fully about. It was and is God's desire to have a lead nation through which He can bless all other nations on our Planet, a nation that He wants to represent Himself through and certainly not to 'be misrepresented by', and so this applies to the people and nation of Israel simply because that is what God wants, whether anyone likes it or not. Of course, He does not want *any* nation or people to misrepresent Him. He has given the people of the nation of Israel a lot of gifting and insight into His character; but, like all of us, they are not perfect and need the (their) Messiah to save them for we (apart from the Messiah) have ALL sinned and fallen short of the glory of Almighty God - in other words, once again without God's help we have all blown it!

The true Church (born again believers), whoever they are, have the opportunity in this age of grace to represent God and His love, as they should do, to the nations; but it also has sadly struggled to get this right, even in the first instance on the basics of 'having love for one another' within its genuine family, wherever they are. But God has definitely not finished with the Jews, Israel and Jerusalem on this matter for what is still left to unfold and happen on this Earth - they will yet fully represent God as He intends them to do and so give and show His loving kindness to all the families (tribes, peoples and nations) on Planet Earth.

So it is that Genesis chapter 15 verses 6-18 is also of great importance, for God Himself 'cut a covenant' with Abram (Abraham) by the said animals as they were halved (except the birds) and each half side represented one of the two making the covenant, in this case one half represented God and the other half Abram - note verse 12 and realise that God being gracious sorted it out from His side for Abram's side, because Abram should have walked between those carcases to make his side of the covenant, but God, Who knew that man was not good at keeping his side of covenants/promises, graciously put Abram into a fearful sleep and He sorted it out on his behalf (the relevant Roger Price's teaching on these verses is excellent). This leads to verse 18, after the Lord made the above covenant and He gave Abram the promise of all the land from the Great River Euphrates down to the River of Egypt (it's not my place here to get into the debate of exactly which river/sea that is, but it forms a boundary with Egypt) and the day is not far away when Israel will fully possess all of her inheritance; that is, the said land in its totality.

Why then does the controversy rage against the land of Israel and the Jews? In the natural it is akin to what happened between Joseph and his brothers in Genesis chapters 30-50. Joseph was the first-born to his mother, Rachel, and was especially liked and favoured by his father, Jacob. This caused a lot of trouble all round, but God was powerfully with Joseph in everything that happened to him and He sorted it all out, in the end, for the whole family. The problem for Joseph was the hatred of his brothers towards him, because of their jealousy (to understand the power of jealousy see

Proverbs chapter 6 verse 34 and Song of Solomon chapter 8 verse 6). The Jews and their land of Israel are like Joseph of old and are favoured by God in all that He has given *to* and what He expects *from* them. The nations of the Earth in their relationship to the Jews could be likened to Joseph's brothers in their relationship to Joseph with regard to their hatred and jealousy, resulting in persecution, and this has often been in horrific ways. Hitler, in his time, wanted to wipe out the Jews and murdered, as far as I know, approximately a third of them during the Second World War, and after that war even the British murdered some in preventing them from getting back to their land of Israel and our track record generally in dealing with the Jews at that time was not good. Even today, Israel's enemies state they *will* destroy her. I'm sure that no other nation on this Earth would tolerate such talk against it without taking or trying to take radical action to protect itself!?

The Biblical proverb asks *who* can *stand* against jealousy? (Proverbs chapter 27 verse 4) It implies 'no-one' - unless, of course, the Lord God is with them to fight for and protect them! Some have said that in these times of the last of the last days there would be an intensive spiritual warfare with Almighty God who is Light versus His enemies and that it would be like that of Elijah/Elisha (the men of God) against Jezebel (the epitome of witchcraft, evil and darkness), eventually resulting in victory over darkness (1 Kings chapter 17 to 2 Kings chapter 9). In this comparison it is the types of warfare and their scale, intensity and outcome that are important. Another issue tied in with this is that of the order of events that will unfold in *our times* which, as already mentioned above, I will state in the next chapter. Remember that behind the physical realm is the spiritual realm and what is going on in the spiritual realm affects what is going on in the physical realm and vice-versa. For example, prayer, praise and worship can affect the spiritual realm (see Daniel, where it is clearly stated in chapter 10 and in other chapters - and note the warfare in the righteousness and prayer of Daniel and what followed as a result in the Heavenly realms).

The battle between Elijah/Elisha and Jezebel was so intense that one side *had* to totally destroy the other. The nature, horror and pain of warfare on this Planet is all due to sin. Elijah won some of the battles in the beginning, e.g. Mount Carmel, then lost some due to fear, low morale, exhaustion, death threats (1 Kings chapter 19 verse 2) and whatever. What an exciting and incredible account is given in all that was involved. In 1 Kings chapter 21 verse 23, Elijah prophesied the fall of his arch-enemy, Jezebel, before passing on his work to Elisha and then being caught up to Heaven in a whirlwind.

The whole world, being now a 'global village', is in a theatre of war and we are on either one side or the other - it's hard to say it, but there is no neutrality. If not in deception, we are either truly for the Lord God Almighty and His armies or *for* His enemies, who will definitely deceive, pretend justice, peace and pacifism, but in reality are seeking to destroy all that is of God, belongs to God or is seeking after God. The Messiah/Saviour only is the Way, the Truth and the Life.

Those who truly belong to God and His Kingdom of Heaven are on a collision course of momentous proportion against all the people and nations caught up in the world system. God's enemies would seek to and must totally destroy the Jews and Israel at any cost if they are to try and destroy the plans that God has for Planet Earth and on into eternity (Roger Price, in his relevant teaching on this subject, helped me to gain a deeper understanding). God's arch-enemy is no pacifist, though when it suits him he will pretend to be one, and will go to any length of evil to try and save his soul from eternally going to the lake of fire (where he is destined in eternal judgement, Revelation chapter 20 verse 10), for then he would be allowed to live on Planet Earth, where he has been banished, as he would then have a legal right (if he could break any promise of God and make God a liar) to be here - how we need discernment in these times! God's enemies can only work through man and the physical of this Earth and the first Heaven (Earth's atmosphere) and now it is only *this area* that is the battleground. The battle is only possible because of man's freedom to choose and there is coming a certain point after which man's choice, if he has chosen the enemies of God, will be irreversible. Remember, though, Almighty God is All Powerful, Just and True and the God of Love and Life and His Perfect Love casts out fear!

In God's plan there is no such thing or doctrine as 'replacement theology' and no group, tribe or nation anywhere has replaced or ever will replace Israel and the Jews. How we need integrity based on the Word of God, as our nation *had* over the centuries until recently. The refusal to fight anti-Semitism and the forces of evil in the *spiritual realm*, through prayer, worship, etc, and in the *physical realm*, through the hierarchy of this land such as the politicians, forces, defence and so on, will be at our peril ... and ...

... oh, yes, all this sure is controversial!?!

# 22
# *Let the Last of the Last Days Unfold ...*

In the last days the most horrific times will come because of the fallen state of humanity in its deprivation, for people will only be interested in themselves, with love for money and wealth which will be 'over the top', disrespectful to parents and God, having brutality, full of pride and unforgiveness, traitors without wanting the good, only interested in pleasure, pretending to be godly but without the real power to be godly, and so on within that given list. The above list is my paraphrase of the powerful and prophetic verses, given in 2 Timothy chapter 3: 1-5, of the Bible, which I find to be so relevant today and would recommend for these verses the New King James Version, New International Version and the New American Standard Version ... and definitely the Amplified Version, which really brings out the full meaning in a frightening way regarding the state of the world as it is today.

Although the items listed in the above paragraph have generally been around on Planet Earth since the fall of man, it is the prophetic application of them in their quantity and intensity, for and in these last days, that should set the alarm bells ringing in no uncertain way! They were written in a letter from Paul to Timothy approximately 2000 years ago and their relevance and accuracy is unfolding before us all even as I write!

I had been a believer two or three years before I even heard that there was such a thing as a 'doctrine of the last days/things' (Eschatology) and I only found out about it in the very early '70s through the writings/teachings of Selwyn Hughes. I was puzzled as to why no-one had ever mentioned it in the circles (mostly C. of E.) that I moved in, and started to ask questions, but I immediately became extremely interested and fascinated by this subject and have continued to be so over almost the last forty years and, in fact, it became a pet subject of mine on and off during these years. I dealt with it in Bible College and again later with the Roger Price teaching - along with various books, charts and seminars over the years - and the first two just mentioned were fair in giving the different viewpoints/interpretations where applicable and, rightly, they left it up to the individual to make their own choices; though, when controversial, they themselves would usually state which view they held and why. There is no doubt that it is a very deep and complex subject and can be emotive, yet we dare not and must not 'brush it under the carpet', as it were, for the key is to get the many 'pieces' (the events that I believe will happen) in their correct order and with a right understanding -

only then does it all begin to make sense as to what God is doing in history and why.

Once again I'm not giving in-depth teaching here, but only a skeletal structure of the *order* of events as I understand and believe they will happen. Many in the Church would agree that these are the 'pieces' as such, but would place them in a different order and possibly with a different interpretation. Having said this, there is a move afoot that would deny and dismiss much of what I believe on this subject; yet what I do believe is backed up by scripture and by what is happening and no doubt is about to happen now on this Earth. An example of this was the Radio 4 "Beyond Belief", I think it was called, religious programme on Thursday afternoons, which I happened to be tuned into a year or so ago when out and about in my car. Suddenly, in what they were discussing, one man deliberately held up the evangelicals in derision, saying that they believed in a 'Rapture of the Church' whenever, but that the word 'rapture' does not even appear in the Bible ... no-one answered him or said anything and there followed a horrible silence. Meanwhile, I'm addressing the car radio in no uncertain terms, "Come on, someone, answer him!!", but they don't do silences on the radio as such, do they? ... so the Chair quickly moved on to another topic. The answer is fairly straightforward! The word 'rapture' doesn't appear in scripture and was coined by some of the evangelicals (as far as I know), but there are two relevant words that do appear. They refer to the actual return of the Lord to earth - that is, to Jerusalem - as King and Ruler to bring in His Kingdom reign which He will do at the very beginning of the (His) millennium, and to the 'catching away' of all true believers in an instant of time. The return of the Lord to Earth is called, in Greek, the 'parousia' and literally means 'a presence'. It is from 'para' meaning 'with' and 'ousia' meaning 'arrival and then presence', so it is the arrival/coming of and being with, by someone and could, in Greek, refer to the arrival of a leader. The 'catching away' refers to the believers in 1 Thessalonians chapter 4 verse 17 and is used elsewhere in the new covenant scripture and is the Greek word 'harpazo', which means to snatch or catch away and conveys the idea of 'force suddenly exercised' (see Vines New Testament Words). In the old covenant, two examples of this happening are with Enoch in Genesis chapter 5 verse 24, who 'walked with the Lord and was no more for the Lord took him' - what a privilege! - and Elijah, in 2 Kings chapter 2 verse 11, the prophet who was caught up to Heaven in a whirlwind.

Both of these above words and happenings - 'the arrival and the staying' and 'the catching away' - pertain to the 'tribulation period' and I will mention them in this context again below. It is worth mentioning at this point that the word 'rapture' was coined (to the best of my knowledge, by the evangelicals as in 'jargon') because it would save using words for the whole event from the Heavenly perspective - it is the two events in one of the Church being 'caught away' and the return of the Messiah to Planet Earth and to Jerusalem, yet when understood that it is paralleled to the Jewish Wedding of 2000 years ago it makes sense. At the end of this age of grace, all true believers will be called up to be with the Messiah Bridegroom and so will be with Him forever. We go off to the Wedding and return with Him in His 'train' of all believers to Jerusalem at the end of the seven years of tribulation on Earth and so the word 'rapture' covers these two events of the 'catching away' and 'arrival/return'. Before giving the 'order of events' that I believe must soon take place, I need to give some overall background information, general comments and deal with some scriptures that clearly show us what is happening right now on Planet Earth. In spite of the complexity of the subject, I will try to keep it as simple and as brief as possible.

With the Lord one day is as a thousand years and a thousand years are as one day (e.g. Psalm 90 verse 4), not least because God is eternal, infinite and outside of time! So far as the time span for mankind is concerned, this is all the time on Earth that God needs - so for us it is that of 7,000 years, but for Him it is just like 'seven days' and He will obtain and prove all that He wants in this time and get His remnant of people to be with Him in Heaven for eternity - this is clear from scripture in the last chapters of Revelation. I will break down these 'seven days' (as God sees it) into what some have already stated - 'three times two days and one day' - (Roger Price, in his 'Chronology Teaching Material', dealt in depth with this whole subject and I acknowledge and am grateful for virtually all of his teaching material, especially on eschatology, as it has helped me in furthering my understanding).

The first of each of these *two days*, or for us approximately two thousand years, was that of 'conscience', so that it was up to each individual to seek after God if each person chose to be guided by his/her conscience along with their will and heart. The next *two days* (for us approximately two thousand years) were those of 'law' as it was given to the Jews and, of course, the animal sacrificial system that culminated as such in Messiah coming to Earth as the Suffering Servant to give Himself up as the once for all Supreme Sacrifice, as previously stated. Each person had to try to keep the law, but had the back-up of the animal sacrificial system to deal with relevant sins of breaking the law. After 'the law', which *only the Saviour Himself* fulfilled and kept in its entirety, came the *two days* (again for us approximately two thousand years) of 'grace', thrown open for anyone to truly believe from their heart in the Messiah and His finished work for them on Earth, so that they could then become part of the family of Father God by and through His grace, mercy and loving-kindness ... and the '*final day*', the seventh day ...? ... well, that is God's 'Sabbath', for He *will* have one at the end of His 'week' for mankind here on Earth ... and it is yet future - but not far away! This

'Sabbath Day' is what is called 'The Millennium', the thousand years of His Kingdom reign from Jerusalem.

In God's history and time we are *now* at the end of 'day six', which is the end of 'six thousand years', more or less, in our time. In order to make the transition from the age of grace into the 'millennium', a terrible seven-year period must take place, referred to as 'the tribulation'(a time of unprecedented great trouble on Earth), which the Lord likened to the labour pains (sorrows) of a woman in the travail of birth (1 Thessalonians chapter 5 verse 3, Matthew chapter 24 verse 8 and Mark chapter 13 verse 8).

The Lord has several different ways of communicating with mankind and has His own reasons for this. Here are one or two examples. The Lord God may give some straight talking on occasions, as He once did, through a donkey, to rebuke a man and show him that the donkey was more sensible than he was! Also, when the Lord walked on Earth and gave a strong rebuke/correction as He sorted out the money changers in the Temple and those selling the doves, or whatever, for sacrifice, saying that they had made the Temple that was meant for prayer into a den of thieves (see Matthew chapter 21 verse 12, in context, Mark chapter 11 verses 15 to 18 and Isaiah chapter 56 verse 7).

In Proverbs chapter 1 verses 2-6, it is stated how valuable the book of Proverbs is. If you think you have some drawbacks and are not very bright, the proverbs will give you prudence! If you think you are really wise, the same proverbs will increase your learning! And so to verse 6, where it states you will not only understand the proverbs but also the puzzling things of the wise. It's almost as if the Lord is saying to some, "Hey, you like a good detective story or crossword or to understand life's trials - well, I'm giving you a few clues to help you on your way and make life a bit more colourful as you go on 'life's journey', as you will have to think and search and re-search in order to really find life's answers and help you get through … if you want to!" The Lord, when on this Earth, often spoke in 'parables' - that is, an account of something laid alongside of another to help you understand what that 'other' thing is or means. Even the 12 disciples sometimes struggled to understand and would have to ask the Lord to tell them what He meant!

Sometimes, Father God has a 'mystery' of something He wants to totally hide from all of His creation until the time He chooses to reveal it - 'the Church' in Acts chapter 2 was one of these where, in power, it ('the Church') was revealed. The prophetic, the visions (pictures), dreams and words of knowledge given in the books of Daniel, Revelation and in other scriptures are symbolic of what will happen from Daniel's time and on to and through the age of grace to the tribulation (which includes a big chunk of the book of Revelation), the millennium and on into eternity. The Lord also hides some things for a purpose and then reveals them when He is ready! One example was that the Messiah came unexpectedly as a Suffering Servant to Earth the first time, and not as the King to set up His Kingdom and deal with the cruel occupying forces of Rome ... surely this had to be so ... and when He returns at the end of the tribulation period, at His second coming, He definitely will set up His Kingdom and reign from Jerusalem!

In the book of Daniel in chapter 2 and again in chapters 7 and 8, which tie in with other scriptures too, is found, as mentioned above, the language of symbolism (that is, visual imagery and pictures), and in these same chapters is some of the interpretation of this symbolism given as required, directly or indirectly, to and through Daniel himself. Sound and reliable scholars have identified and dealt with these verses in the above chapters and so we now have a 'picture' of what they mean, even though part of the interpretation was future at the time of Daniel and company, when they were still in captivity - nevertheless, what Daniel saw caused him great fear!

As we now know, there have been six major empires in history so far that have in some way involved the Jews and Israel - Egypt with its leaders being the first and is recorded in Genesis with Joseph and on into Exodus with the account of Moses, then there was Assyria, Babylon - which is the 'head of gold' in Daniel chapter 2 - Media-Persia, Greece and then Rome. Some have said that in the British Isles we have been influenced by certain aspects of the above-mentioned six; for example, Babylon (as I understand it), for its materialism and pursuit of pleasure; Egypt, representing, as a type, the whole world system; Greece, with its emphasis on its common language, the mind and intellect and its resulting fluidity/instability with much emphasis on sport and its historical Olympic Games held every four years in the area of Olympia, traditionally home of the 'Greek gods', along with its supremacy of male over female and homosexuality over marriage, all of which is kind of interesting to the times we live in now and the reality of just what or who is mankind following anyway?!

The sixth, the historic Roman Empire, with its military might, roads and resulting communication and travel and its unbelievable evil, wickedness and cruelty as it generally subdued or destroyed everything in its way or what it could not control - has left its mark, as we know, to this day on mainland Britain. What eventually made the Roman Empire so different from the others is that each Caesar was given divine status and treated as 'God'. As history shows, some of them went/were completely mad and went beyond dictatorship and despotism into being above or outside of the/their law. I believe you cannot serve two masters: it's either mammon or the Messiah. If it's 'mammon', be alarmed whenever you see anything similar to the above, where someone sets themselves up as God, starting to take place, for a society's 'freedom' that is so precious for decent folk would be disappearing fast!! This proves to me that fallen mankind on this Planet cannot cope with power, wealth and control beyond what is reasonable and right and remain in normality, for they will soon want to make themselves as 'God' (Genesis chapter 3 verse 5).

The seventh and final major empire is yet to have its day! This empire is the one I need to further deal with here and is the last given in both Daniel chapter 2 verses 40 to 43, being 'the feet' made up of 'iron and clay' in a sort of mix, and in Daniel chapter 7 verse 19, where it is the last of the four 'animals'. These both refer to the same empire. This last empire of 'the feet' is described as an 'exceedingly dreadful beast', and is what concerns us all now, as it is forming and about to be revealed!

It is the re-emergence of the Roman Empire and will have the same boundaries as the historic one. In the UK now, as I write, the surveillance and near control of our lives (with most of it recorded as to our whereabouts and any electronic transactions) is almost complete - we have been duped and deceived with our countless laws, and our ancient boundary stones and cultural basis on our Godly Biblical heritage have either been removed or destroyed; we have certainly sold our 'birthright' for a 'mess of potage'; we have shouted, "Get rid of the Lord Jesus and give us Barabbas!" (a terrorist, an evil man) and our nation is now sick. Justice has fallen in our streets, the immature rule (see Isaiah chapter 3 verses 11 and 12) and smooth-talking lies and deceit are the order of the day, which is now far spent. The wicked tell us, "All is well"; they call it 'progress', not knowing that the storm is about to break where 'Jezebel', the epitome of full evil control, will rule. Nevertheless, God will have His remnant - those who will still choose Him and not bow the knee to the world's system or the antichrist, no matter what the cost!

Time-wise, the tribulation will start the very second the 'true Church' around the Planet is 'caught away' and thus removed from the Earth. I believe there will be a gathering of some of the nations for battle at this point; that is, just before the catching away of the true Church, in order to try and destroy Israel, but they will fail to do so. The tribulation will continue until the Lord Messiah returns at the end of the seven-year tribulation period, which must slightly be cut short at the Battle of Armageddon so that the Lord can save the Earth/mankind from total destruction. This is why the return of the Lord Jesus to Earth takes place in two parts, as mentioned above, and is based on the Jewish Wedding of around 2000 years ago. The then wedding procedure was that, first of all, a visit of the man to the woman's home took place to ask her for marriage and to sort out 'the whatever'. If she said "Yes", he went back home and they both prepared what was agreed between them for married life (on his part a place to live in, etc); then, preparations complete, he returned without warning of the exact time and when he did so she *had* to come out of her house to him (as it were, to the road or path); then they went off together, along with all the guests who were there at that point, to his father's home for the seven-day marriage celebrations and so on. It is worth noting that, when the woman said "Yes", 'betrothal' was legally counted as marriage from then on.

When the Church is caught away above the clouds to be with the Lord, the man of evil, sin and lawlessness will arise and pretend to be the Messiah and deceive many people and nations in his dictatorship and, as time goes by, demand to be worshipped, with no mercy on those who do not conform, as he will seek their destruction. He, the antichrist, will reign through this resurrected Roman Empire in Europe/Middle East because the European Union will have the *same* area/boundaries as the old historical Roman Empire and I believe that the whole Earth at that time will, broadly speaking, be divided up into ten sections in total, each with a leader; e.g. the EU is one of them, USA and Canada will be another, Latin America another, China, Russia, India, Africa and so on, so that the whole world, our now 'Global Village', can then be more easily and even totally controlled! As we know, just about all of the 'Information Technology' to do so is now available. The spotlight, as it were, will be on Israel, the Jews and Jerusalem and the last three and a half years of the tribulation will be worse than the first three and a half, and it is in the middle of the tribulation itself that all Israel will believe in their Messiah and no longer be deceived by the antichrist. At this time, the Jews will certainly have a fight on their hands, as much of the rest of the world will be against them to the point of wanting their total destruction - so God will give them supernatural help so that they survive.

As stated above, the empire is made up of 'iron and clay'. The 'iron' signifies the aggressive cruelty of the first Roman Empire that destroys everything in its path to subdue and get its own way - only with the forthcoming Roman Empire it will be much worse and, in fact, more intensive and unequalled in its evil cruelty than anything previously known in the history of mankind on Earth (Matthew chapter 24 verse 21). The 'clay' represents the parts of the 'Greek Empire' mentioned above, such as sport, the Olympic Games, emphasis on the mind, the down-grading of marriage, etc, and 'the clay' will be 'mixed in' with the culture of this future Roman Empire (that is, the aggressive evil hardness of the destructive capability of 'iron') and surely no one can deny that this is forming right now in front of our eyes!

The seven-year tribulation of this soon-to-be Roman Empire is further dealt with in the books of Daniel, Revelation, etc, and by the Lord Jesus in Matthew chapter 24, which is mostly addressed to the Jews/Israel about the actual time of the tribulation. Rome is called a type of 'Babylon' in Revelation and will be known for its decadence, its pursuit of the 'material' through the business world so that this control will mean no-one will be able to buy or sell anything whatsoever unless they have the 'mark of the beast', the 666 of Revelation in chapter 13, that will most likely be a barcode of 18 digits (3x6), whereby its aim is for everyone in the world to be numbered so as to be quickly identifiable and thereby totally controlled.

In the UK alone at this present time a massive amount of detailed data and information is being collected on every single one of us and stored wherever, and I believe this is in preparation for the fast-approaching 'tribulation time', for use then at the touch of a button, as it were, or in scanning, as at a checkout, as part of what will eventually be total control. The hierarchy of evil will know everything and anything about each person by that point - where you have been, what you have done and even what you have said - the surveillance will be complete and there will be no escape for those who have fully adhered to it. I believe that, even worse than this, they will be able to direct you to do what they want you to do and that is why people with the 'mark' will then not be able to come to a heart knowledge of Messiah. This tiny 'chip', I believe, will be planted in the area of the right wrist or the forehead in some way, leaving a mark, and will be supposedly 'voluntarily' received as in a democracy - but what will be the cost to force one to 'volunteer' in such an evil and God-forsaken world where no one without this mark will be able to sell or purchase anything at all … and where will one be able to hide from the 'Big Brother State' with all the modern-day technology anyway?

I believe, along with others, that the next step for us at this time (which will eventually lead to this 'mark') will be to purchase things through our mobile phones linked to our bank accounts. It will be a cashless society – it will all seem so good and plausible, but the reality is it will be a 'living death'!

What I'm writing may seem like something from a horror film, but according to Revelation, etc, in the Bible, it is the reality of what is *soon* going to take place. This will embrace the 'jezebelic spirit' of complete control and everything that is now going into 'one' will be controlled through a hierarchical system via IT, along with the vehicle of force and violence by the 'man of sin and lawlessness' at the top. The gathering of data on every individual is nothing new, of course; e.g. the KGB in the Communist Regime had a written file on much of the population in Russia and most dictatorships would be the same.

There are three important things that need to be mentioned as background to the above, which are all *absolutely relevant* to the time we live in. The first is that in Israel and the Middle East there are usually 'the first and latter rains' - the first to make the harvest grow and the second at the end to 'swell the harvest' for reaping. The 'first rain' is, in the very early chapters of the book of Acts, to get the growth and harvest underway of the outpouring of the power and love of God. At the end of the age of grace, there will be a similar outpouring of the 'latter rain' of His grace and loving-kindness from Heaven to swell out the harvest just before its ingathering. Almighty God in His righteousness always brings a measure of grace just before judgement to be kind and fair in His dealings with nations - to see if any nation/people-group will accept and receive what He offers! As the coming judgement will be horrific on an uncaring and unbelieving world, the outpouring of His grace beforehand will be quite something! This is so the Lord will get in His harvest at the close of this age just before the seven-year tribulation starts. I have believed since the early 'seventies that this harvest will take place and that in the UK it will be amazing! The true Church, whoever they are (there is an 'apostate Church' as well), will finally get its act together and will be very powerful, especially with 24-hour worship, with praise, healings, miracles, evangelism and so on, with all ages of people being used in powerful ministry - it will be awesome!

The second is that the Lord said in Matthew chapter 24 that, when you see famines, wars, rumours of wars, earthquakes, natural disasters, etc, that is only the beginning of woes and the general time He is going to return to Earth and these things will become more intense and frequent.

The third is that the Lord also said, "As in the days of Noah, so shall it be." Could it have been that in the days of Noah society was sophisticated? There are two things clearly stated in Genesis chapter 6 from verses 5 to 12, especially verse 11 (but don't forget verse 8 and put *your* name in there with Noah!), that show us what that society was like. These two things were 'corruption' and 'violence', so that the whole of the then world was *full* of corruption and violence, except for Noah and his family. Now let me see … does this remind you of anything? … ah yes … *definitely the world we live in*!? For then as now, God grieved in His heart for the state of mankind and the corruption and violence was not just a little here and some way over there, but permeated through all of society - from top to bottom - look at the unbelievable corruption/stinking rottenness and terrible uncontrollable violence that has spread through our world like apples rotting in a barrel! Again, in the book of Daniel chapter 12 verse 4, it pertains absolutely to the times we live in right now, where it says that many will move to and fro and knowledge shall increase. The way travel and knowledge have greatly increased in the last one hundred years alone is phenomenal. If those who are now 25 years or under could be transferred back to the early '50s, they would be utterly amazed at how completely different our society was then. Even in my lifetime, the increase in 'travel' and 'knowledge' across the board has sometimes been difficult to cope and keep up with! Has the vast increase in knowledge and IT simplified our lifestyle or necessarily been good for us or has it complicated it and unnecessarily absorbed and side-tracked us? When God mentioned these above, four things in His Word (violence, corruption, travel and knowledge), thousands of years ago, it was because each would be *extreme* in their happening now.

And so to list the order of events as I see and understand them from this time onwards …

We are fortunate to be in this age of grace still with some restraining power from Heaven released on all the forces of evil, even though the very dark storm clouds are forming around us. Nevertheless, the light of love from Heaven will get through and the 'latter rain revival' of the grace of God will begin to take place just before the true Church is 'caught away' and there will be serious warfare at the gathering of some nations against Israel to destroy her just before the 'catching away' of the Church, but this will fail. That will be when God has the full number of souls He wants from this age into His Kingdom, so He will call "Time!" and all true believers around the Planet will be 'caught away' in an instant of time (will just disappear from the Earth!) to be with Him forever, along with those believers who have gone on before - they are off to a Heavenly Wedding based on the format/order of the Jewish Wedding of approximately 2000 years ago and this is the 'key' to the understanding of why God is doing what He is doing regards the transition into the millennium …

The betrothal to the Messiah (Bridegroom) has been made by all those who have accepted or will accept Him throughout this present age of grace and what He did when He first came to Earth. The Jewish Marriage Celebration, when it took place, lasted seven days, but the Heavenly Marriage Celebration will last seven years …

On Earth the seven-year tribulation gets underway at the precise moment in which the Church is 'caught away' from the Earth and the 'man of lawlessness and sin' immediately begins to rule with his minions, setting himself up as the Messiah, and God gives man over to what he wants and his own counsels - 'Barabbas' they want and 'Barabbas' they get, yet many will resist the evil and the control, but at what price? All those who embrace, accept and worship the Antichrist and his system of 'buying and selling' will have sealed their own fate to be without Christ for all eternity. However, many will realise the great deception and con of the Antichrist and not follow this 'beast' or play his game of total rebellion against God in His Heaven and His Kingdom and will pay a terrible price of martyrdom …In the middle of the tribulation, at the end of the first 42 months, all the Jews in Israel will realise what is happening and fully turn to their Messiah in Heaven and, because the latter half of the tribulation is even worse than the first, God will fully supernaturally intervene to protect the Jews and their land, for most of the nations of the world and its system will be desperate to totally annihilate them *all*, and my own belief is that at this general time nuclear warfare will again take place …

The end of the tribulation must be cut short, otherwise mankind would totally destroy themselves and their environment and that would be that, for some of the great armies of the world will have joined forces to march on Israel and the Jews - who may only number around twelve million anyway - in order to try to annihilate them totally, and *that* is the 'Battle of Armageddon' … the most horrific battle of all time, where there will be deep rivers of blood. At this moment of great darkness (actual) on Earth, the true and real Messiah will return in magnificently brilliant light, to Jerusalem, and set up His Kingdom there and rule and reign for the 1000 years of His 'Sabbath Day'! At this point, the devil is 'bound' for the entire millennium…

This is the time that Messiah will sort out the 'sheep' and 'goat' nations/tribes in judgement, rejecting the 'goat' nations/tribes and allowing the 'sheep' nations/tribes to remain and populate the Earth, and Israel will be the lead nation to bless the other nations. I believe the Lord will change the Earth (whichever way He chooses) in such a way that it will be a place of perfection once again and mankind and the animals will live in peace and harmony and all will eat of that which grows, e.g. fruit, herbs, cereals, grass, where applicable, etc, and there will be minimum effort in obtaining our food for that which we need to live. So it is that the animals will lie down together and 'a child will play with a snake' (Isaiah chapter 11 verses 6 to 9; see also Hosea chapter 2 verse 18). Everyone on Earth will believe in the Messiah and sin will be minimal and dealt with accordingly, and people, like Methuselah of old (Genesis chapter 5 verse 27), will live to a very great age. Whichever way the Lord God works out all the details of this millennium age, it will certainly be an 'okay time' and very pleasant indeed. Yet God Almighty at this time will still be in the process of making an important point about the human heart and the helpless fallen state of man, in spite of the lovely environment man will then have …

It is at the very end of this millennium age that some of mankind will again rebel against the Messiah when the devil is released from his prison in the bottomless pit where he has been bound and held throughout the millennium. They will gather together to make war on the Messiah and those who belong to Him when the devil is allowed to go forth to deceive the peoples once again (see Revelation chapter 19 verse 19 to the end of chapter 20 and, of course, other relevant scriptures), but God will intervene and draw the Universe, as we know it, to a close - the Earth will be destroyed and the whole Universe will literally be wrapped up, for the scripture says that God will wrap it up or change it as a garment (Psalm 102 verses 25 to 27, especially verse 26 in Amplified Bible) …After all this, in Heaven, will come the Great White Throne Judgement, whereby the Messiah Saviour will sit on His Great White Throne and judge everyone who has ever lived and our Sovereign, Just, Holy, Righteous God, in all truth, will make sound and just judgement and no-one will be able to answer Him back and say He is wrong - so everyone will either go down to the torment of the Lake of Fire to be forever with all those who have totally rebelled against God or, if they have believed in and sided with the Messiah and lived for Him and their names are written in the Book of Life in Heaven, they will go on to the New Heaven, New Earth and New Jerusalem, very specially and wonderfully prepared and incredibly beautiful, to be with the Lord Messiah for all eternity in that 'Eternal Day' of His Light and Love.

# 23

# *Suffering in the Day of Battle ... for our Freedom*

As a nation, we must defend ourselves militarily from being overrun by an aggressor, as any nation that has failed to do so has not lasted many years before losing its freedom and possibly its identity. Evidently, battles fought up to a few hundred years ago were generally fairly straightforward - each side would line up their armies facing each other and attack and the one to destroy most of the other and cause them to flee or surrender won the land and whatever. The Battle of Flodden Field in 1513 at the English/Scottish Borders only lasted approximately a couple of hours with much bloodshed (the stream ran red!). With modern armament, the First and Second World Wars both went on for years, containing many battles with untold pain, bloodshed, death and destruction, to say nothing of the knock-on effect of trauma afterwards. Certainly, in recent times, Planet Earth has never been free of warfare going on somewhere. Almighty God is no pacifist and neither are His enemies, though they may try to pretend 'pacifism' to obtain a false peace and gain the upper hand by whatever means.

The *total war effort* of the two World Wars, as far as the UK is concerned, was important for us to win over evil, but at what cost? As already stated, volunteers are always better than conscripts and to have incentive and a heart for 'the cause' is better than coercion. The trouble is that warfare means violence and it is horrific to and for us all. There is a violence which should be minimal to fight the righteous cause and there is also a destructive violence where cruelty and bloodshed and the like are the vehicle for aggression and destruction and are unstoppable until effectively dealt with. Of course, in warfare men will be sacrificed, but if life becomes 'cheap' to those in authority, then where would the destructive force of violence end? Just look at any full-blown dictatorship and you will see the answer! The trouble is that violence and bloodshed as a learned behaviour do not know where to stop, for violence mostly begets violence, with all its after-effects - remember that its effects can be directed outwards and inwards, with both being destructive. Many who saw/experienced much violence in the Second World War were not able to adjust, handle the trauma of it all within or relate in a right way afterwards, so there were then dysfunctional families, relationships, etc. The 'ripple effect' of the violence of the Second World War is still causing havoc even to this day. Here are some interesting Second World War accounts that I've come across over the years. Unless stated, these are from memory only, going back over thirty years, so I trust I've remembered them with a good degree of accuracy and apologise if anyone knows differently.

I got to know John Hepworth and his wife, Flo, when I first went to Huddersfield as a pastor and, in fact, stayed in their house as their guest when he was not too far away from retirement age. I had a lot of respect for him, for he was a gifted man with intelligence and common sense and was a hard worker. Their home in Huddersfield only had a small 'postage stamp' back garden, yet some could not believe the amount of fruit and veg he was able to grow from it. One day he shared with me, though not easily, something of what had happened to him. The Germans captured him and some of his fellow soldiers fairly early in the war - as far as I remember, it was in one of the Mediterranean countries and the first thing they were made to do was to run naked through the village to subdue and humiliate them. Speaking of his German oppressors, he used words like 'brutal' and 'cruel' and there was no way that anyone would have been able to stand up to them - as I understand it, they were almost totally devoid of mercy. John, who would only have been in his early twenties, was taken to a PoW Camp in Austria, where he and those lads with him spent most of the war years. "Do you realise that they broke your will and your spirit?" I said to him. "I know that," he said, and after a pause continued, "we were given hard labour day in and day out (possibly they had a day off once a week), but we never had enough to eat and we were never free of body vermin." He mentioned something about them being made to go out on parade at any and all times, which would have meant sleep deprivation and near exhaustion. Another pause and, with tears slowly coming down his face as he shook his head as in saying 'No', "You would never believe what some of the lads would inflict on themselves in the way of injuries just to get some respite!"

As a year or two went by, John got hold of an old tea towel and something with which to write on it, having 'escape' in mind, and started to make a map of the surrounding countryside on it. One day, the Gestapo Camp Leader found the hidden tea towel and called a parade. "Whoever did this, own up!" was his command, but there was silence and great fear, as all knew the Gestapo were a law unto themselves. I don't remember how long in minutes or hours it was that John held back, but eventually when on parade he had to take courage - I suspect to protect his fellow PoWs - and own up to the fact that it was him. To his utter amazement, the Gestapo Leader of the prison commended him on doing such a good job of the map and John didn't say if there was any punishment, so I presumed there wasn't; but I have no doubt that that was a miracle!

I asked him what happened as the war came to an end and he said it got a little bit easier and the guards just wanted it to be over. Again I asked him what happened when he was finally freed. "We were brought back to England and given three months' leave to recover and get our strength back." "I would have thought you would have been given an instant discharge," I said. "No, no ... after the three months we had to report back to duty and the first thing they did was give us a route march/run with full backpacks on." "That sounds a bit hard," I said. He quietly answered that a lot of them collapsed and they were given an instant discharge. He continued with tears, "A lot of them did not live to be any real age at all." John also told me he was on a troop ship on or near the Med when they had to do some burials at sea. When on parade during the actual time of the committal and prayers, everything went eerily totally quiet until it was over, then the normal noises you would hear and expect at sea on a ship returned - that experience was one of the reasons why he later became a believer in the Lord Jesus Christ.

John has gone to Heaven some years ago now, but some time before doing so, I was told, he went on a holiday to Austria and to the area that the PoW Camp was in and, although it was very difficult for him to do so, he further came to terms with the dreadful pain of all that had happened. He was just one out of countless millions, one 'salt of the Earth man' worthy of respect ... what a privilege to have known him, albeit only for a short while!

I first met Roy Wood in the summer of 1988 when looking at and taking over the rented flat at Eastbourne Gardens on the Beacon Lane Estate in Cramlington. With my then wife, we had no choice but to take it and I liked the flat and the area, but on the actual day of going up to view the property I thought I'd knock on a couple of doors to speak to a neighbour or two to find out more of what the area might be like. One happened to be Roy and he invited us into his flat for a few minutes and that was one of the few times I ever met his wife, who was not in good fettle. Roy was a born leader - a leader of leaders - and in his seventies was still a strong, hefty man. He had been in the Middle East Desert War Zone fighting the Germans and had been a Sergeant-Major. We were 'neighbourly - polite friends' for the next four or so years and only once or twice did I get to talk and question him on his early life and his Middle East war years, where he told me he was known as 'Woody'! "The men always volunteered to come out with me on scouting trips or whatever," he said. I replied, "Were you popular then ...?" "Not so much that," he said, "but they had worked out that I always came back!" He told me he would sometimes go behind enemy lines in vehicles and go through the actual German Camp to see what was going on ...! I thought, "Talk about dangerous! How did they get away with it without getting caught?" I asked him, "Did you get enough to eat then?" "We usually would find a 'desert chicken'. " I wondered how they managed to cook it ...!

He told me what happened once when all the men were out on parade with a certain Commissioned Officer in charge, who he described with disgust as 'still white behind the knees', though he never did give me any further information on that officer, so I could only guess that because of his lack of experience in the theatre of war he was unnecessarily sending men to their deaths or putting them in great danger. Right in the middle of the parade,

Roy, as the Sergeant-Major, marched up to that Commissioned Officer and punched him so hard he knocked him to the ground! Now Roy had been into boxing, so no doubt that would have been some punch! "Whatever did you do next?" I gasped, without any idea whatsoever of what would happen next! "Oh," he said, "I just turned and marched myself back to the guard room tent and stood to attention just outside the entrance." Reasonably quickly there was a Court Martial and he knew beforehand what they were going to do, for they took off his badges of rank and put them back on with a couple of loose stitches. At the actual Court Martial they stripped him completely of his rank, ripping the badges off his clothing - he was down to the rank of Private. I knew in peace time later that he got his rank back, but still exclaimed to him, "Surely that must have been the end of your career!" "Why no," he said in a somewhat Geordie accent with a grin on his face ... "I was back up to Sergeant within three months ... it was wartime!!" I was trying to get my brain cells around that one and think it through, but I didn't know enough about that situation. He confirmed to me he did go back up to the rank of Sergeant-Major. I asked him what happened to the Commissioned Officer. Roy stated, "They removed him forthwith and sent him elsewhere."

I was talking to Roy one day about discipline, family discipline and justice. He paused and said, "Some of my upbringing was in a village in Devon and there was a lad who was a real nuisance in the community, always in trouble ... until one day they took him into the Police Station and he got birched ... from then on he was very quiet, as was the community, for there was no more trouble from him!"

It's well worth repeating that all of the combined war effort whatever and whenever that made up the 'whole' that fought and won against horrific evil was important and valuable to give us freedom as against a dictatorship. To get into what was 'righteous' or 'unrighteousness', so far as all that effort was concerned, is not for me in this book, but the aim, vision and morale was for and towards a free society in our fast-changing world from 1945 onwards. Some had a more colourful and adventurous time than others and one such person I have known as a friend for the last four years, now in his mid-eighties, definitely comes under this heading! He, Norman Lusher, a Yorkshire man (as in Bradford!), a Barber/Businessman by trade, experienced more than most. I asked Norman a lot of questions, which he answered, but I never made any notes, though I did say more than once, "If only we had taped that conversation just as it was, it could have gone out on Radio 4 or the like!" Below is some background info, along with one or two of his stories of what he saw and experienced and an essay account written by him which is included here with his permission.

He finished his hairdressing apprenticeship early and joined the army to do mobile electronic signalling (morse code) - a box machine fastened to the upper front of his body to allow mobility. Of course, it would now be considered archaic, basic and primitive, but in those days it was quite something. Interestingly enough, he once received enemy fire that went into his machine, putting it out of action; so, in one sense, that was one time out of two or three when his life was spared - the enemy considered it more important to put the machine out of order in the first place rather than kill the man! I asked him what happened about getting another machine to continue doing his job, to which he replied that he was able to go to where the stores were kept and replace it within a day.

Shortly after his 18th birthday, he was trained as a soldier and qualified for his duties on signals and was down in the New Forest and Poole areas with the English contingent being prepared for, and who then made, the D-Day landings on 6th June 1944. Just a few years ago, I saw one of those areas in the New Forest that held some of those D-Day troops and another at Poole Harbour, so it helped me to imagine something of what it must have been like. Here in Norman's own words is a transcript of the actual Normandy landings from his personal experience.

Date 6th June 1944
It was 5am when we came in sight of the Normandy Beachhead. I was only 18 at the time and like the rest of the soldiers did not know what to expect; then, with a sudden thump, the front of the landing craft dropped down on the beach itself. For what seemed an eternity, nobody moved! Then the officer shouted, "Move!" and we all ran out onto the beach. I was expecting heavy machine gun fire, but there were just four German soldiers, who took one look at us and fled! It wasn't until some days later we were told that the troops who had been guarding that beach had been sent to defend a bridge which our paratroops were attacking. Up to the first three miles, not a shot was fired; then suddenly all hell broke loose, machine guns - shells - rifle fire - we got the lot! However, it was soon cleared by our fighter planes; good old RAF!

It wasn't so bad for me. I was the unit radio operator and had plenty to keep me occupied, not like the other young lads who were waiting for the next bullet to hit them … it must have been nerve-racking for them …!

Same day, time 5pm
We had been under heavy gunfire from the German heavy guns for over two hours; just then the Sergeant came over and asked me to contact HQ and ask if we could have air support. Twenty minutes later, I called the Sergeant and told him that some air support was on its way. At 6.30pm three of our fighters zoomed overhead towards the guns and within five minutes all was quiet!

Same day, 8pm
Apart from the sniper fire, all was quiet … too good to be true! It all happened around 9.30pm, when German tanks came over the hill towards our trenches

and just then ten of our bombers came overhead, saw the tanks and went for them, knocking out five and the rest turned and fled!

6am 7th June

We were all waiting for the German counter-attack, but for some unknown reason it never came. The Sergeant came over to me to say that he had to pick six men to form a special squad and, of course, with me being the radio operator, I was one of those picked. There were two snipers and two demolition experts making up the squad. Our Sergeant spoke German. We were pulled back, where we were given instructions of what was expected of us.

7am 8th June

Last night we were told that our assignment was to go into no man's land, blowing bridges and railway lines to try and stop the enemy from sending down reinforcements. My assignment was to report back everything we did ... from that day we were a team to be reckoned with. For the next eleven months we were mostly in trenches or behind enemy lines, with just an occasional 24, 48 or 72 hour break where we would get a shower and change of clothing, a good meal and plenty of sleep! During the following eleven months it was real adventure and many things happened to me.

So, as described above, Norman took his part in the D-Day landings, then went up through France and into Germany and on into the northern part of Germany, which covered for him the eleven months of fighting in the war before it was all over in the May of 1945. It was no picnic, as the life expectancy of that front-line warfare was only an average of three months. Norman experienced much danger and, with one or two escapes from certain death, it's miraculous he lived to tell the tale!

He told me he learned as 'gut reaction' in a fraction of a second - no time to think or reason - that a situation was very wrong or dangerous and he would shout, " Booby trap!", and the team would stop, identify and if needed put a marker, as another team following on behind would deal with booby traps as the team Norman was in had to move on. They came across a dead German soldier by the side of the road. It was Norman who instantly shouted, "Booby trap!" and the team carefully checked out the situation. Sure enough, there was a trap as there was wire from the dead soldier leading across the road to a petrol station - it would have been some explosion! I said to Norman, "How did you know?... There must have been something ..." "Oh," he replied, "I worked it out ... he was propped up a little, but it was his right arm that was deliberately showing with a wrist watch on it ... it was virtually unheard of to wear a wrist watch on the right arm!!"

He told me they came across a derelict-looking house and he shouted, "Booby trap!", but a young Commissioned Officer came on the scene, took issue and disagreed with the team; so he, on his own, went through the front door and sadly that was the end of his life. I asked Norman that question again, "How did you know?" "It took me a little time to work it out," he said, "but if you were escaping from a house in danger and in a hurry, you would not stop to even close the door - that front door was firmly closed!"

Norman said he and his Sergeant were on one of the famous bridges over the Rhine on the side near where there were some American soldiers and German soldiers were there too, just a little further back. The bridge was blown up, but it did not totally collapse into the water at that point. I think Norman did or was trying to send a signal, but his Sergeant, viewing the whole situation, shouted, "Let's get out of here!" Norman said he had never sorted his signalling stuff out so quickly so that he could run for it ... which they did, across the damaged bridge, somehow, and onto safety. He told me the Americans tried to go another route, but unfortunately most of them lost their lives.

Another time he said, "One day we were in our group and coming towards us, a little way off, were two German soldiers, each with their hands up, one walking behind the other. The Sergeant, like lightning, weighing the situation up, said to one of his snipers, "See those two German soldiers walking towards us - do not harm the man in front but shoot to kill the one behind."

"BANG!", it was done! "Okay, Norman," I said, "sock it to me before I ask the question!" It turned out that the man behind was one of the cruel SS men and he was wired up to the ordinary German soldier in front of him who was forced to have explosives on him which would be detonated when they got close enough to the British soldiers, to kill them ... but the soldier in front was so nervous he was shaking and walking abnormally. Without the quick and wise action of the Sergeant on that occasion alone, none of them would have made it!

There were some light-hearted things as well, but I guess I'll have to keep some of them to myself!? ... okay, maybe not all! Norman told me things like they used to get a tot of rum each day. I said to him that I thought that was only for the Royal Navy, but he said it was for those in the front line of the army as well. I thought for a moment and realised, of course, it would provide a tiny bit of nutrition, kill some of the bugs in the stomach and gut and warm up body and soul!

Now Norman calls himself 'crafty', though actually he has used much stronger language than that once or twice to me! I don't think the war was quite over when he said a Sergeant-Major came along and said that the lads' hair was generally too long. He asked if anyone could cut hair and Norman said that he could. A day or two later, he came back with some 'hand clippers' and whatever to cut hair and so Norman got the job! It wasn't long before he was asking the lads if they wanted a 'special' or 'ordinary' haircut! When they asked him what was the difference, he said the army haircut was free and very short all over and the 'special' was more as they would prefer it, but would cost them two or three pennies (army tokens' equivalent). This was fine until he stopped drawing his wages and he was asked why ...! Well, he sharp got that one right ...! Now, I would only dare tell that story because I complimented him on his business acumen and I had to admit that if I had been there to have my hair cut I would have definitely paid to have a 'special'!!

One time he was talking to the famous singer Vera Lynn, 'The Forces' Sweetheart', at the top of some steps and, as he turned around, lost his footing and fell down them all. He lay there for a moment or two and suddenly a young attractive German female rushed over and asked him if he was okay!? He opened his eyes and it was love at first sight, so he pretended not to be okay for a few moments so that she would give him more attention and sympathy?! It took him two or three weeks to track her down where she worked and he got a date with her, then two or three years later he married her!! Although she is gone now, I did a year or two ago get to meet her once or twice. They had over sixty years of marriage!

The 'old soldier' had to think and use initiative to stay alive in warfare, to judge every situation differently and break out of 'military-ism', not in rebellion but in mature 'thinking for yourself', to do the job, as in 'stay alive' and win, going up a notch from 'blind obedience'!

Here is Norman's own account of the worst thing he ever went through.

BELSEN HORROR CAMP
MY FIRST-HAND EXPERIENCE
A TRUE ACCOUNT OF WHAT WAS SEEN
NEVER TO BE FORGOTTEN
Norman Lusher     Printed 2010
We were looking for snipers and booby traps, instead we ...?
Now READ ON

I first encountered Belsen at 3pm 13th April 1945, just one month before the end of the fighting. It was a cold, wet day when we entered the camp and we found over ten thousand unburied corpses and a further forty thousand sick and dying prisoners! Entering the camp was the worst experience of my entire life. The stench of dead bodies was unbearable and it wasn't long before each of us was violently sick. It was an extremely traumatic time and I would never ever want to go through that again.

The first person we came across was Josef Kramer, the camp commander, and he came towards the sergeant with his hand outstretched, but the sergeant just turned and said, "How could you do such a terrible thing?" Kramer was a huge man, with the bulk of an elephant. Brutality and arrogance were written all over his face. He tried to excuse the state of the prisoners by saying that the Germans, and not only the prisoners, were also short of food.

Later we had the task of rounding up the camp guards and taking them to the camp gates, where they were put on trucks and taken away. That night the shock of what we had seen got to us all. Each time we tried to eat something, we began to vomit and shiver; in fact, we were so traumatised that we had to be relieved there and then and taken directly to hospital. We were there for a few days before they sent us back to our unit.

At the beginning of September we were told that we were to be posted to Luneburg for the period of the war trials which were due to start soon and it was a mad rush to get organised, but we managed with time to spare. The trials were conducted by a British Military Tribunal in the converted gym of the cavalry barracks at 30 Linden Strasse, Luneburg, Germany, and commenced on 17th September 1945.

President Major General HMP Bercly Ficklin headed the panel and four military lawyers handled the case for the prosecution. The accused comprised of sixteen men and sixteen women plus fourteen former prisoners. They were all tried together and sat in a large dock, each with a number fixed to their chest. For the first few days it was somewhat technical and, as all of the charges were put to each prisoner, they each in turn pleaded, "Not guilty".

Eventually, the trials stepped up a notch where witnesses gave their account of what had taken place. Suddenly, one of the witnesses told the court that he knew where a thousand bodies were buried! He said that the Americans had bombed the railway line and a train load of men and women destined for Belsen could not be taken there, so the guards took everybody into the woods (Lunberg Heath), where they were made to dig large holes and were then shot. This was verified by another witness. The trials continued and eventually, on 14th October, the court adjourned to deliberate for two whole days before resuming.

When the court convened again at 10am on 17th October, it started with the lesser charges and, out of the forty-six accused, fourteen were acquitted, eighteen were given between five and twenty years and the remaining fourteen were given the death sentence, which was to be carried out on 13th December.

The Belsen nine given the death sentence were named as follows:
1. Josef Kramer, Camp Commander
2. Fritz Klein, Camp Doctor
3. Peter Weingartner
4. Franz Horsaler
5. Karl Franchioh
6. Wilhelm Dort
7. Juan Burmann
8. Elezabeth Volkenrath

9. Irma Grese, Female Commander (Author's note: She was the one called the Beautiful Beast of Belsen.)

There were five others from Auschwitz who were to hang at the same time, so all these prisoners were taken to Hameln, where the death sentence would be carried out.

A few days later, we were informed that we were to go to Hameln to perform guard duties, guarding the accused until the sentences were carried out. The guard duties were numerous, but Norman, the crafty one, got himself a cushy number driving the CO around. On 11th December, the CO told me to drive him to the airport at Buckeburg to pick up a VIP, who I was told to look after until all his duties were performed and, of course, we now know the VIP was Albert Pierrepoint, the British hangman. I had a good few days with him and he gave me a few pointers on the official way to carry out the sentences.

On 13th December 1945, Pierrepoint and his assistant began the preparation for that day. There were to be seven double drops, with each drop side by side, and Pierrepoint and his number two, O'Neil, would work both drops at the same time. The first two would be the females, Elezabeth Volkenrath and Irma Grese. There should have been another female, but she was put back to a later date. Three days after that, Albert and Richard returned to England; but for the next four years they would continue to return to Hameln for further hangings. In all, they hanged two hundred war criminals, the last on 6th December 1949, a man called Jerzy Anndziak.

(Please Note: Some people 'in the know' tell me that the British forces didn't go into Belsen until 14th April and not the 13th. True, the British went in on the 14th, but remember, we were a special unit and our orders were to go in on the 13th looking for snipers, booby traps and land mines.)

This was written to give you a true account of what I saw and did during those few months of 1945. I owe my thanks for the information received from persons on the internet, and also to the Holocaust Memorial Museums.

In memory of all of the people who never came out of this atrocity alive.

## RIP

EX SOLDIER NL

There is no doubt in my mind that part of Norman's suffering, through his horrific Belsen experience, included some post traumatic stress for several years after the war which, though never recognised as such, he simply had to sort out for himself as time went by and as we talked it through one day he agreed that this was so.

He showed me a picture of his Sergeant and his wife in Civvy Street taken years later, after the war. I said to Norman, "You do know that your Sergeant was Jewish!" But Norman would not continue that conversation. Such was the way it was, I don't think he would get into this kind of controversy. I stated that I was pro Israel and the Jews. He showed me another picture of his Sergeant plus Bride on their wedding day with 'the team' around them and, of course, the men were all still in uniform. "Which one is you, then?" I asked Norman. "That's a bit of my shoulder at the back, as I was behind that woman standing up a few inches in front of me just to one side behind the bride and bridegroom, who were sitting down facing the camera." "Very strange," I said. "Ah well," he said, "the bride had been a prisoner in Belsen." He showed me a picture of her taken in Belsen to show those appalling conditions, but she had a sister who was taken to another concentration camp and survived - she was tracked down and secretly brought to the wedding and Norman moved back to let her stand in his place - so at the very moment that photograph was taken the bride didn't even know whether her sister was dead or alive, never mind standing three feet to one side of her … good old Norman, the 'Recycled Teenager', as he sometimes calls himself … mind you, that must have been some reunion of those two sisters …?!!!

# 24
# A Breath of Fresh Air ...

I first started doing open-air preaching/evangelism in the early part of 1975 and was immediately 'hooked' and have continued on and off ever since. Below are just one or two of my experiences in the fun and heartache of it all! To 'preach the Gospel' just as it is in its truth and purity and to exalt and lift up the Saviour Messiah in all His Love and Glory for all that He has done and will do is wise, beneficial and honouring to Him and is one of the greatest things we can do - it is about Him and His Kingdom - so when this is done in the open air, that is a 'breath of fresh air to our lungs' in a dark and putrid world!

I was at 'The Monument' (Earl Grey Monument) in the heart of Newcastle-upon-Tyne, which is a place for 'public speaking' and where people can gather to have their say, socialise or whatever. So long as there has been freedom of speech in the UK, this has been good, but as our freedom of speech is being diminished through 'politically correct nonsense', fear and various other means, this is unfortunate to say the least, for the day when our freedom to speak out and have our say is outlawed will be the day of the start of great persecution. I have often used and still have in my possession a simple cloth banner with the words of John chapter 14 verse 6 in red on a beige background and have had various tracts and leaflets over the years which I've given out. This particular day at The Monument was a lovely summer's day and the whole of that area was absolutely packed with people, some standing, some sitting down on the steps of The Monument and some passing by. Two local Newcastle Fellowships were working together for about an hour with only their two leaders preaching alternately for several minutes at a time and some members of their fellowships handing out tracts and talking to folk. That day I got down there for about 11.30am and talked to people. About an hour later, the preachers stopped preaching and the witnessing group started to leave to go and have a meeting in one of their buildings. I decided to have 'a preach' on my own while two or three of the group were still around, but soon they gave me a wave as they went off one by one.

I don't know how long I preached for that day - there was no 'amplification', just speaking out, so it could be hard going at times, especially with the general noise of the city centre with all the people, traffic and the hustle and bustle of it all! My guess was I spoke for about twelve to fifteen minutes, by which time I was certainly ready for a drink of water. I stepped off The Monument between people who were sitting down on its steps facing south towards Grey Street and it was totally uneventful - nobody seemed to take a blind bit of notice! Suddenly, a man came up to me, taller than myself and quite well-built. "Can you tell me where I can buy a Bible?" he asked me, as if he did not have two moments to spare. "Yes … that's no problem … and in seconds," I replied, and also added, "Did you just hear me preaching?" "No, I didn't," he said. He was obviously asking me because of the banner. "Do you know the Lord Jesus as your Lord and Saviour?" I asked him. "I don't think I know Him in the same way that you seem to," he replied. "I have a prayer that you can repeat after me and it will clarify things for you and help you." "I haven't got time, I have to be somewhere in just a few minutes," he said, rather excitedly. "Just give me about two minutes very quickly to say the prayer and we will still have time to get the Bible," I said. "Yes, go on, but very quickly." I went through that prayer like lightning and he followed it through and I knew he meant it. "How do you feel?" I asked. "Fine … different …," he said. "I will just touch lightly on your forehead with one drop of the oil I use for anointing." "Yes!" he said. I did so immediately and prayed a very short prayer over him for the Lord's favour and help. I heard a lady say to her friend as they passed by, "I think it's some kind of new religion?" "No, I thought, it goes back to the Biblical Old Testament times!" But the man was under such an anointing, he said, "I'm falling backwards … help me!" "That's God's grace and anointing from Heaven … wow … but I can't catch you or hold you up, there are too many folk around!" I replied, so I stopped and rolled my banner up … he looked different, for the better, and without delay I shouted, "Follow me!" As quickly as I could, I ran down the alleyway, past the Tyneside Cinema entrance, turned the corner and went straight into what was then the Bible Society Bookshop, heading quickly for the back of the shop, found a New King James Version of the Bible and handed it to him. "Not a red but a black copy," he said as he exchanged it … we went quickly to the front of the shop where he paid for it, and we went outside onto Pilgrim Street, where he firmly shook my hand, thanked me and was gone … the whole encounter took less than five minutes and I felt it was the Lord who impressed upon me to go for a cup of coffee and then go home … so I did!

I was standing at The Monument once on my own with my banner unfurled and not a lot was happening - in fact, there were not very many people around. A man pushing a pushchair with a little girl in it had come along Grainger Street and was making straight for me. When he got close enough, we gave each other steady eye contact and no doubt we were weighing each other up. I thought to myself, "You are obviously well to do and probably have a good job." He said to me that his wife had been very sick, but he had made a bargain with God that if He spared his wife he would acknowledge Him and as he had come across me he could now put that one right. I immediately reached for the prayer in my pocket and, unfolding the paper it was written on, said, "I can deal with this right now and all you have to do is repeat this prayer after me, a few words at a time." Then, after a pause, I said to him that it would be good if he said those words and meant them and it would be a step in the right direction, but that it was only he who could mean them from his heart and then walk the walk with the Lord Jesus, for it was a heart matter. We went through the prayer and nothing spectacular happened and he agreed with what was said. As I remember, I did say a short general prayer over him and one for his wife and his daughter. I gave him some literature and, would you believe, mentioned about him getting a good version of the Bible! He was not volunteering any further information about himself and so, of course, on that occasion, it was not right for me to probe any further. What I did say though was that it would be good if he could find a suitable Evangelical/Pentecostal Fellowship where they generally really loved the Lord. He said goodbye, thanked me and was gone.

It happened a good number of times that, though there were no plans or organisation, the Lord would tie in the timing and whoever He wanted to be in a particular place! I once missed three buses going into Newcastle from where I lived in Cramlington and another bus just didn't turn up. It then seemed pointless to go in as it was mid-afternoon and the time had gone; but go I did and eventually got into Newcastle and was walking down Northumberland Street and there was Alan Wharton, one of the other Street Evangelists, walking up. "I was late, I've only just got here and there's nobody else around that we know of," said Alan. I replied, "I've only just got here as well." So he preached that day for a little while right there in Northumberland Street and then we went for coffee. For us that was a special God Appointment, as we *never* met in Northumberland Street or that late in the day. Another time, a similar unplanned thing happened whereby Alan and I ended up outside of M & S on Northumberland Street. He had some tracts to hand out and I had my banner open - neither one of us preached, we were just talking and there were not all that many people around. I noticed a young lady walking ever so slowly, just a few inches at a time, up Northumberland Street and she then seemed to be heading directly towards us. This she did and I realised she was probably one of the 'Street People'. "See *you*," she said, and continued, "two weeks ago I had no time for any of you, but then I jumped off a bridge to end it all … I'm still here, but now I know differently because of that near-death experience!" She showed us her arms, which had been badly scratched/lacerated and in a terrible state, but were now healing. "What a mess!" I exclaimed, and questions to be asked were queuing up in my mind. "Can we buy you a cup of coffee in M & S and talk a little?" I asked her. "No … I'm just going to that church up there", pointing towards the Haymarket, and no doubt she meant St Thomas's C. of E. church building.

"Will you take some literature?" Alan asked her. "No," she said, starting to slowly move off, and was definitely very weak. I said, "We'll pray good things for you ...", but she was gone!

One clear, crisp, sunny summer's morning a few years ago I was at The Monument and an off-duty policeman I would sometimes team up with for an hour or so at a time, was preaching - he was a 'born' Evangelist/Street Preacher! He was on the west side of The Monument and more or less facing down Grainger Street as he preached. It was a normal mid-week working day, with only a few passing to and fro. I was not on the actual monument itself, but just handing tracts out to anyone who would take one, and had my banner open for all to read. Not a young man, possibly in his fifties, had just walked by me and stepped up onto The Monument behind the preacher. Realising what was going on, he was noticeably furious and, looking at me, in a loud outburst shouted, "I'm going to kill you!" and so I shouted back even louder, "You're not going to kill me at all!" Around his neck he had some kind of 'necklace' with what looked like pieces of small bones attached to it and he immediately started fingering each bone in turn as he muttered his 'prayers'. I thought to myself, " I dread to think what bones were sacrificed to make that necklace!" The preacher turned round to look at what was going on, as if to say, "Do you mind, I'm preaching!" I said to him, "If you want to continue preaching, I'll deal with this", so he turned and continued preaching, whereupon the man, from about five feet away, spat at him and just missed the back of one of his shoes! I guessed he had had a lot of practice, but not quite enough, which was just as well! ... so he turned his attention back onto me, still sorting out his necklace and muttering as he slowly took two or three steps backwards. He stopped, and, still facing me, very loudly shouted curses, blasphemies and foul language. Now it was my turn and I too shouted for all to hear, "I don't know how far down the road of evil you've gone ... but it's only the blood of the Lord Jesus Christ that can save you, so repent and give your heart to Him ...!"; at which he became very agitated and upset and, shouting in words I did not know and wailing, he turned and fled! A lady from one of the large Newcastle Pentecostal Fellowships who had been watching came up and said, "Well done", and shook my hand, which was kind of her!

It was late afternoon one day down at The Monument with hardly anyone about as it had turned cloudy and cold. I was on my own and thought it was time for me to go home. A mature man walked across The Monument towards me, looking directly at me and the banner, then sat down facing Grey Street. We started talking and he shared where he was at. He had been an alcoholic and that had caused problems for him and he was trying to dry himself out and put his life in order, but he was a 'Street Person'. I said that I couldn't help him to find anywhere to live as such (from that time on, for a year or two, I began to carry details of 'Betel of Birmingham' and 'Teen Challenge', which could offer some safe help), but explained where I was coming from and the Gospel, also the fact that the Lord Jesus sees and knows everything - and He most certainly can help! So I slowly went through my 'salvation prayer' with him and when I finished he said he felt 'good' and 'different' and I said to him that he looked different too! I apologised that the genuine true Church had not got its act together as regards helping people like him to find a rented small property that was 'safe' and 'pleasant to live in' (but I know now, of course, that he could have applied for sheltered accommodation and that one or two of the believers have owned properties to let). I prayed over him, crying out to the Lord to help him urgently, anointed him with oil and gave him some tracts and, if I remember correctly, a booklet of one of the Gospels, I think it was Mark's Gospel. We said goodbye and, as he started to walk away, he said, "I'm nearly sixty years old now and I'm getting too old to cope with being on the streets ...", and he was gone! I don't ever remember seeing him again and prayed for him for a while, but was heartbroken that we, the Church, were not giving enough help to people like him with regard to suitable accommodation.

A few years ago now ... I didn't even know his name and don't remember talking to him, but I knew his face and as far as I knew he was a 'Street Person' and may have had a drink problem. He was mature and looked to me as if he was tough and would most likely be able to handle himself in a fight if needs-be. I was walking down Northumberland Street one warm day and everywhere was packed with people. He came up to me from out of the throng and said, "Can I have a word with you?" "Yes, fine," and we found a seat and sat down. He very carefully got some photos out of his 'wallet' and said to me, "Do you want to see photos of my four children? - I haven't had contact with them for a while." "Yes, I would - that would be an honour," I replied. I only spoke to him for a minute or two and chose my words very carefully. He shared a few things and there was no doubt he had a really nice family. I encouraged him, for he was heartbroken, as he had had no recent contact with them. Okay, I didn't have the 'full picture' of all that had happened, but inside I was weeping as 'with those that weep' and I said goodbye and that I would remember him and his family each day before the Lord for two or three weeks and ask the Lord for a miracle for him to have contact with his family and put his own life in order. I saw him once or twice shortly after that, but then I presume he was gone, as I didn't see him around again.

There was a tall Scottish man who would occasionally be around The Monument and said he was 'a believer' and knew some 'Christian doctrine'. My guess was that he was in his early thirties - he was an alcoholic and I wondered if there were other addictions as well. Normally on seeing him I

The Way I See It

would simply be polite but keep my distance from him. One day when I went to The Monument he was sitting down as in semi 'laid back', isolated from other people and a little worse for wear. He saw me and said curtly, "Pray for me" and nothing else. "That sounds fair enough," I thought, and said to him, "Okay." I paused and thought for a few seconds and then launched into a prayer - to be positive yet not sure what direction it would take! The latter I would never find out, for after only a few seconds he became furious as in hell-bent on violence. I have no idea what I said that could have caused such hatred, so I said to him, "Listen, Mate, you asked me to pray for you ..."; but he was nearly to his feet and still breathing violence. At that point I walked away from The Monument and realised that this man could destroy much good work that was being done by the believers in the centre of Newcastle and I went home and cried out to the Lord to sort it out, praying until I knew I had got an answer in that the Lord had heard me!... so I kept my peace and forgot all about it and weeks and months went by.

I don't remember how long in time it was, but fairly early one morning in warm weather when I was on my way somewhere I decided to walk down Northumberland Street past The Monument and down Grainger Street. There were few people about, but as I passed by the north-facing side of The Monument, I noticed someone sitting on the ground, leaning back on the actual monument with his head down - it was the tall Scottish man, but I knew immediately there was something not right! I went over to him and, calling him by his Christian name, asked him if he was okay. Raising his head, he looked at me and said soberly, "I was stabbed last night!" He was obviously in pain and I could see some blood on his chest and clothing, though he was not smartly dressed as I'd seen him at other times, but had a white T-shirt on. Without hesitation, I started to take control of the situation and said, "Right, you need urgent help. I'll go and phone for the police and an ambulance so I'll have to go and find a phone that works." (I didn't have a mobile phone, but that day made me go out and buy one within a week.) Much to my amazement, he strongly protested and said, "No! No! I'll be okay, don't do that ... I'll get out of Newcastle and go to Sunderland!" My mind was now in overdrive. Was he in his right mind to make such a statement? In spite of the pain he was in, I gave him the benefit of the doubt. If he could make it down to below where he was sitting, he could get the Metro train straight to Sunderland. Now I'm not exactly 'street-wise', but I thought that this must have something to do with the sinister world of gangsterism and the fear and all the evil that goes with it, so I double-checked that he meant what he said and thought that to summon help could make things worse for him. A year or two later, I was down in Newcastle and some of my friends said to me, "You remember so and so? (saying his full name)". "No, it doesn't ring a bell," I replied once or twice, but they persisted that I knew him. They described him to me and, though I never knew his surname or much about him, the penny dropped - it was the Scottish fellow mentioned above. "He was murdered over on the north-west side of England," they said, and added that the word going around was that it happened when he was in prison. All I could think of was that he at one time must have had so much going for him - looks, personality, brains and so on … what a tragic waste of a life!!

At The Monument, similar to the above, late afternoon, cool and cloudy with few people around. One of the Street People came by, accompanied by a younger female, and he said, "Here's Henry, he'll look after you," and continued, "Henry, this is Kim," and he did not even stop walking as he went off down Grainger Street. She sat down on The Monument. I said to her, "I'm not so sure about being able to help you in a practical way as it's not my department, but I can help you spiritually." So I talked with her about the Gospel and the spiritual side of life and she readily talked back and agreed to repeat the salvation prayer after me and did so and I believe she meant it from her heart as much as she was able to that day. She was a pleasant enough young lady, but she did not say much about herself or her background. I prayed over her and asked the Lord to sort things out for her, though I apologised that I could not give her a lead on finding herself somewhere suitable to live, and she went off down Grainger Street to try and find the other Street Person. Some months passed, then one day she came by The Monument when it was busy - she was smartly dressed and had one or two friends with her. We started talking for a couple of minutes and she said she was going for an interview for a trainee post at a hairdressing salon. I said I would pray that she got the job as I was sure it would suit her. Again, time went by - at the least several months - it was the onset of winter and just after 6pm and three of us had been for coffee in the Tyneside Cinema Café and I had just left to make my way home. I was just about to walk across the road and go up Northumberland Street when, from out of nowhere, in the dusk, a man was walking beside me! I wondered, "Whoever are you?" but then he said to me, "I've got Kim in my flat." A few questions came to mind, but no doubt he was not going to volunteer any more than minimal information, so I asked him more or less immediately, "How is she?" He replied, "She's well." "As long as she's getting fed and looked after … that's good," were my thoughts that I spoke out to him. I paused, as I had been taken by surprise and wasn't sure what I was supposed to say or do. "Send her my regards and tell her I'm asking after her and that I'll pray for her situation and good things for her." He said he would do so, paused and then his voice changed slightly and he started begging for money and so, having my return bus ticket home, I emptied out the little bit of change in my pocket (normally I would not have done so) and gave it to him and I've never heard of Kim from that day onwards, though I did pray earnestly for a month or two for her protection and all round provision. Some time after that, I was talking to the Street Person who had originally left Kim with me. "I'm not street-wise," I said to him; "I don't understand, I don't get the picture about Kim." "Henry, you don't get it!" he exclaimed in amazement, and went on, "not one of us knew anything about her at all and not her age or even if that was her real name ... she looked very young!" "Fair enough, I get it now, but even I looked younger than my years in my later teens and I was married with a child, so you can't always go by looks for a person's age, but now I understand your fear of the authorities in this situation!" Perhaps the Street People had a rule that they should not 'shop' each other, but it looked to me as if this situation worked in such a way that they protected Kim from many evils on the streets and if that was the case the Lord certainly answered the prayers for her protection and well being!!

One summer's day lunchtime, again at The Monument, in 2005, a petite young lady came by who was a 'Goth' and we started a conversation. She had the black clothing on and 'bovver boots' and right around her neck was a neckband with big 'spikes' as in 'sharp' and so her whole message to everyone was, "Don't mess with me or I'll sort you out!" By about 45 minutes later I had talked and then slowly gone through my salvation prayer with her, though she struggled over some of the forgiveness issues she needed to sort out to get free, but she got through. She was called Petra and was a down-to-earth person and quite outspoken. She accepted some literature, said goodbye and she was gone. It was the following year or maybe a bit longer in time and I was standing at The Monument one afternoon when she came by; only I didn't recognise her and had forgotten her name! She quickly reminded me and it all came back to me of the previous time I had met her. This time she was dressed in light/casual, colourful summer clothes and her whole demeanour and looks were different for the better! She said what a lot of people had said to me on helping them to get born again, that it was not sensational that day but that she slowly and positively had gone on with the Lord since that time. She said she had had people praying for her for some time and she was in a Fellowship in Dumfries. I said it was highly likely that her pastor was the visiting preacher that day when I prophesied to him when he visited Lancaster on the weekend when Marc Dupont came to town. She showed me his photo on her mobile phone, but as I had only seen him for an hour years ago I could not be absolutely certain, but the 'Ulf Ekman' (a well known man of God who knew the pastor) link would confirm it to her that it was so. We talked and she asked me if she could stand with me and say some words of testimony from The Monument. "No problem," I said, and continued that I would read a Bible verse, start preaching, then hand it over to her quite quickly to say what she wanted to say, then for her to hand back to me when she was ready to do so and I would stand beside her with my banner and Bible and keep an eye on what was happening as support and in case of any danger. This we did and she fearlessly and clearly spoke out for several minutes, telling everyone that she had been abused, saying it as it was, and telling some of the problems she had had and how she gave her heart to the Lord; then she handed back over to me. The amazing thing was, as she spoke straight from her heart saying it as it was, a crowd gathered, most of whom were ladies, and without any heckling or the like they listened intently to her every word ... and it was fun that afternoon!

Once again at The Monument on a hot summer's day ... the place was packed and Dougie March, the Street Evangelist, was preaching and another two in our group, as I remember at that point, were handing out tracts and talking to folk. Suddenly, a man who I had seen only once or twice before in that area and who was a Buddhist and was in the crowd listening to Dougie, became very agitated and started doing some physical exercising and heckling at the same time, then began having a loud open conversation with the preacher, Dougie, which went on for a minute or two. Many had by then stopped and were watching to see what would happen next, so it was some crowd. Dougie paused and, as I was standing nearby with my banner unfurled, I decided in my mind that this could be a 'three-way open conversation' for all to hear, so I went straight onto The Monument next to Dougie and started out loud to join in the conversation with the man in the crowd - well, it was more like taking over! Now, those of us who were open- air preachers and friends, had an unwritten rule that we would not take over another's preaching unless they were finished or possibly had asked for help, so I did offer an apology to Dougie a little later on that day. But as the public conversation with the man who was still angry continued and he must have felt that he was losing some ground anyway, he suddenly shouted in a derogatory negative way, "Who is interested in YOUR GOD anyway?", and immediately a positive, great and loud instantaneous, enthusiastic shout came out of the crowd, "WE ARE!", in what I would describe as a mark of high praise, joy and respect to the Lord! I don't know how that happened at that moment, but happen it certainly did and the whole situation was defused and deflated in an instant of time and everyone seemed relaxed, even the Buddhist, who started talking to one of the believers, one to one! In fact, I began to count in the crowd those believers who were involved in the street work or otherwise and remember reaching a total of fourteen - where did they come from just at that moment?! As I looked around, just about every one of those fourteen, as far as I could see, was in conversation with someone else, no doubt about the Lord Jesus. God's appointments that day were quite something!

I had successes, and, of course, some failures and weaknesses that were unfortunate and were 'learning curves', and there was much that was heartbreaking, not least in what people would share of abusive situations that they found or had found themselves in, and even others who were the abusers and their lives were not in a good way, to put it mildly. Several times I was asked to pray round people's homes to spiritually cleanse them. This happened in one of my neighbour's flats in Cramlington a few years ago.

"Feel free to go from room to room," the lady of the house said, and so I did. It only took a few minutes as I prayed around the flat and anointed it with oil as I felt led and I then said to her and her partner, "It's done!" "That's funny," she said, "it feels warmer." "That's right," I replied, "it's the warmth from Heaven and you can have that warmth in your hearts if you will say a prayer and so give your hearts to the Lord Jesus." "I will," she said, but the man overruled and said, "No", so I felt it right just to leave it.

Three times over the last twenty years I volunteered or was asked to go in to visit terminally ill patients in hospital and that with very little warning. The first was Roy Wood's wife (mentioned in the previous chapter). I had just gone to catch a bus on my way to shop in Cramlington Town Centre, but ended up going with Roy in his car to the North Tyneside General Hospital to see his ill wife. I wasn't sure where they stood with regards to the Gospel and 'chickened out' of confronting them or even praying for them, my only excuse being that I was not too well myself. In retrospect, I'm nearly certain I was wrong, for I think they would have listened and responded, as they were looking for me to take a lead. She died the following week. About a year later, I lost my wife and several months later there was a knock on my door: it was Roy! He said that we had both lost our wives, but that I was coping much better than he was; also, he told me that he had gone to a small Gospel Hall Sunday School as a child in the village in Devon where he lived for some time and that he wanted the faith that I had. I invited him in, so he came upstairs, into the lounge and got on his knees - and so I led him in a prayer to accept the Lord Jesus ... it is sometimes strange how things work out and it was a rebuke to me!

Another time I found myself visiting one evening in one of the Newcastle City hospitals, but the person who was not well, I felt, definitely did not want me to pray over her, though her close family did. I thought, rightly or wrongly, that I'd best not minister to her against her will; I wanted her permission or agreement, or at least some co-operation, so I did not take authority in the situation - it was heart-breaking, as she only lived a week or so after that.

Another time I went with a friend to the RVI Hospital in Newcastle, where there was a man around 30 years old, as I remember, who had been poorly and was in a coma, and three close relatives were present in that side ward. I weighed up the situation and realised there was some disunity and unbelief in that room and understood why the Lord Jesus put people out of the home concerned on some occasions in order to minister to people. I got my anointing oil out, but did not feel free to minister as I wanted to in the situation. It was not my place to ask anyone to leave, but I might have been better to have done so. I put some oil on my finger and was bringing it down towards his forehead, praying quietly as I did so - suddenly, although his eyes were firmly closed, and he was in that coma, both of his hands reached up to try to prevent my hand from lightly touching his forehead. I knew I needed to take authority and cast out the demonic and more in order to bring him out of the coma … but sadly I didn't do it. As I look back now, I think I should just have got on with it regardless, but within a minute the Medics came into the room, en masse, to see to him and that was that. He never came out of the coma and he was gone the following week.

A woman came by The Monument: she was quite slim, tall and very smart and as we spoke she said she had been on drugs but that she would give her heart to the Lord Jesus. As I led her through the prayer, she struggled to forgive someone who obviously had wronged her in no uncertain terms and as she struggled one single tear rolled down the right side of her face - I wanted to weep as well, for I understood the pain and difficulty of her forgiving whoever had wronged her, but she did so and there was a quiet and definite release that was awesome, as was the fact that in the spiritual realm God had put that tear in a bottle in Heaven as it was so precious. When I had finished, she said she felt very peaceful … something that many I had prayed over said they had felt. We have a God Who cares and loves us so much!

Someone shouted, "Henry!" to me one day at The Monument and came over - I knew his face, but had never really spoken to him before. "My mother was taken into hospital and it doesn't look very good - would you pray for her?" "How old is she?" I asked. "Mid-eighties," he replied. "I'm going to say a short prayer now and ask for a specific time in years of restored health to be given to her and will pray tonight at home as well." So I prayed and took authority right there and then and straight after that he was gone. The following week I was at The Monument one day and the same man rushed up to me, shouting again, "Henry! Do you see that lady over there walking down past The Monument towards Grey Street? That's my mother." "Well, the Lord certainly answered that prayer," I said, as I watched her walking briskly. He was grateful and then he was gone!

One busy hot summer's day at The Monument I spoke to two young ladies who were friends and, I guessed, around the age of twenty, sitting side by side, and they immediately agreed to receive the Lord into their hearts. They went through the salvation prayer together and I anointed them with oil individually and prayed over them. "How do you feel?" I asked, "Well, that's funny," said one, "I had a headache when you started and now it's gone." "That's good," I said, and asked the other how she felt. "That's strange," she said, "I didn't have a headache, but I've got one now!" I thought to myself, "Get out of that one", but said, "I think it's back to the drawing board!", so I anointed her with oil again and prayed over her and she said she was okay!

It was not all that often, but I would preach in other towns with some of the other Street Evangelists/workers and a man called Andy Gray and I would usually sort it out between us with the minimum of fuss, as to the who, when and where and the lifts to get us all wherever. The maturity, the teamwork and the quality of preaching of that group was, in my opinion, second to none - it was never about 'controlling' or 'organising' anyone else, but we just worked as a friendly team in hearty fellowship with real unity one with another until one day something went wrong as the forces of evil put their big guns on us to destroy the unity and scatter us. I remember that nearly every time I, with some of the others, preached in Northallerton, the police were called - we were obviously upsetting some folk, but the police were friendly and never stopped us preaching! The team was preaching once in Middlesbrough and I was preaching when the police were called and they tried to curtail my method of preaching, as I would walk up and down but, as someone told me later, they had no legal right to do so at the time. I felt the Lord say to me in my heart, "Are you going to obey Me or them?", so I just freely preached on as I normally did and the Lord honoured that obedience - Marjory, who was on the team, led someone to the Lord!

From over the years I once, from memory, counted a total of just over 50 Street Preachers that I had seen who had preached in the centre of Newcastle - men, women, young and old, the good, bad and indifferent! Many would build up the work and some would destroy it. They were preaching from all different kinds of backgrounds, motives and reasons, some preaching freedom and others not so free (!), some with their past not dealt with so that it got in the way of the present and some with sound doctrine and others with a mixture of demonic doctrine and religious nonsense. Yet Newcastle-upon-Tyne city centre is a very privileged one to have had the truth of the Gospel preached in it over many years by so many in the recent and the distant past. If I remember correctly, it was John Wesley who preached in the city centre slums in 1749 and saw an incredible revival. Also, all of the preaching over the last sixty years and no doubt before at The Monument and Bigg Market has been quite something. The forces of evil and wickedness would still seek to destroy the city, but the Word of God and the praise to Him that has gone out on the streets of Newcastle will, and indeed must, bear much fruit and will not return to God void, for it will have a special visitation from Heaven in the soon-to-be-awesome Latter Rain Revival of an incredible outpouring of mercy and grace from Heaven and, of course, that Latter Rain Revival will touch all of the United Kingdom. When this happens, God alone will definitely have all the praise and glory - not one single person or his 'grouping' will share that. The established churches and other groups have generally treated the Street Evangelists as despicable and I can sometimes understand why, but the reality is that God is so often patient and merciful to us all, no matter who we are, in spite of our sinful state/carnal nature that refuses to die, though God's patience does run out. Of course, John the Baptist no doubt looked a bit wild and rough as he powerfully preached the Good News and gave the prophetic word in the wilderness, but the Lord Jesus said that there was none born of women who was greater than he (Matthew chapter 11 verses 11-19). The Lord Jesus had a massive chunk of His three-and-a-half-year ministry in the open air! Peter kind of 'blew it', then did well even on his first open-air preaching at Pentecost and Paul was definitely an open-air man with all the rest of his amazing ministry and suffering for the Messiah. Whatever the Church thinks of me matters little when the times I have got it right, in obedience to the Lord, have brought blessing to people. The Street Evangelist Preachers are not a people who can be 'controlled' by man as such, due to the very nature of what they face on the streets, such as hostility, rather like the old soldier who knows how to survive.

Ken was a powerful and fearless Street Preacher in his late sixties. He had been a Royal Marine and had his own small business, but had, as a believer, been back-slidden for 15 years earlier in his life and wanted to make it up to the Lord, which he was doing in his street preaching. I knew him for two or three years as part of the preaching team. He was poorly but made contact and asked me if I would take him into Whitby to preach with him once again. My wife and I went down to his home near Whitby and after lunch took him in our car to where he preached for just a few minutes, after which I preached for only a short time as well and my wife talked to folk. He asked me if he could preach again and, as he did so, he had to hold onto a post to support himself and was obviously not at all well and in discomfort, but was determined to continue preaching – however, after two or three minutes he stopped. We just managed to get him back to the car and home and, although unwell, he was content that he had preached. We talked for five minutes in the car outside of his home and one of the things he said was that he would go on preaching even if they put him in prison for doing so and when they let him out he would go immediately back on the streets and continue preaching. We said our goodbyes and he slowly went into his bungalow. The Lord had something else for him, for he was gone to Heaven later in the following week. That was an honour to be with him for the last time he preached on this Earth, as it is people like him who made this nation great in its time.

A few years back now, one autumn day, a couple of others and I had been helping at someone else's outreach over lunchtime in Darlington. We decided on our way home to go to The Monument in Newcastle, then go for another coffee somewhere. It was late afternoon, quite cool and the light was just starting to fade. There were still one or two people about, but not many. I got into a conversation with someone and the others were talking to folk as well. Richard, one of the team, came up to me and said, "Henry, someone is not in good shape over there, sitting on The Monument steps, and it might be good if you spoke to him." I replied, "Okay, just give me a minute or two." Several minutes went by and Richard came over to me again. "Are you just about ready? He's not in a good way." I finished off the conversation and Richard told me the man waiting was suicidal. He said, "Look in my anorak pocket." I looked and there was a small cellophane packet of white powder. "What's that?" I asked. "It's heroin and he's just given it to me to destroy. He's addicted and wants to get off the stuff," he replied. "So that's the menace that kills ... You gotta get rid of it straight away, down a drain or somewhere," I said. I went over to the man, who was smartly dressed, and my guess was that he was somewhere in his thirties. He was sitting with his head/face in his hands. I started a conversation with him and he shared some of the terrible things that were happening to him, his addiction and that he couldn't take any more. He just wanted, now, to end his life. I said to him, "It would be much better if you gave your heart to the Lord ... but really, what have you got to lose anyway?" So he agreed. I thought I would get him to repeat some of the salvation prayer and when finished I'd take authority and pray specifically into his situation for it to be sorted out. "I'll say just a few words at a time and you repeat them after me; see how you get on and take your time." So I said a few words only and then over to him. He threw back his head and at the top of his voice started to sing those words out aloud!! "Errrr, that's not what I had in mind," I thought, not knowing if I should laugh or cry! It would have to be one short sentence only - not long enough really, but never mind, so I asked him if he could quietly say these words after me and he did. "Stand to your feet," I said to him, "I'm going to minister to you with power from Heaven and break addictions and curses off you. Okay?" He said, "Yes." I paused and tuned into Heaven in my spirit and then with every bit of Messiah's power and strength within me spoke out and broke off every curse, negative and addiction from him and cast out every demonic spirit in him that was troubling him, in the Saviour's name through His sacrificial shed blood. I stopped and he went almost still and very quiet. A few seconds went by as I watched him intently and then he rather excitedly shouted, "I've got a spirit of lust, pornography, lust ...!" "That's no problem for my Lord Jesus," I said out loud. "I'm going to take two steps back then move quickly towards you, put my right hand on your heart area - only lightly - I won't hurt you in any way, and I'll say some words as I do so. Okay?" He said, "Yes." I took the two steps back, then quickly moved forward and, as my right hand fell lightly on his chest, I just shouted, "The blood of the Lord Jesus totally cleanse you!", removed my hand and stood back. He went quiet and started to sway backwards and forwards and I thought momentarily, "Is he going to fall over?" ... absolutely not, for he suddenly raised his hands to Heaven and shouted - I think the exact words were - "It's Jesus, Jesus, it's all about Jesus!!" as he started jumping up and down, obviously for joy! "Well," I thought, "he spectacularly came through. Thank You, Lord!"; and I turned to see where the others were in the dusk. As I turned round, and much to my utter amazement, there was quite a large crowd quietly standing and watching the events. I was aware that the Lord Jesus when on Earth would hastily carry out deliverance if people were running to watch, as in 'forming into a crowd'.

Well, it was too late and sorted, so I thought, "I'll preach to them"; but on The Monument was the one we called Big Jim, a man in his later sixties who was from Seaton Delaval near Cramlington (he has since gone to be with the Lord) and he would normally work on his own anyway, having one of those bag/containers on wheels with a handle which could also be turned into a seat and he would sit on it and read aloud from the Bible, which he had been doing all the time I was ministering and still was doing and that was okay. "Would you give way to me to preach?" I asked him. "No," he said. I asked him again, but he answered again in the negative. "That's fair enough, Jim, you were there first, I'll leave it", and we didn't fall out over it or anything like that. I remembered the man who had just been set free and prayed for him each day in my prayer time for some time after that as I felt led. It was getting on for about nine months later when Alan Wharton said to me, "Someone came by the other day and asked me if I knew you. I said I did and he said to tell you that (saying his name) he was going on with the Lord and attending a small Evangelical Fellowship in the Newcastle area." I knew immediately this was the man mentioned above. "That's good news," I said … God is Love and All-Powerful. There is nothing impossible for Him …!!

# 25

# *And The Lord God is Shaking All Things ... including The Church!*

The concept held by the majority of what the Church is, is nowhere near the reality of what it should be, from a Godly, New Testament, Biblical perspective. Let me make some comparisons.

The first, of course, is the word 'church' itself. Ask people what they understand by the word 'church' and the majority of times the answer would be 'such and such a building over there or wherever'. They might also say it is a particular denomination, as in 'the Church of England' or 'the whatever' that they are referring to. A lot of years ago I found out that The Church in the New Testament was never a building or a denomination or the like as it is understood in our Western culture and I was flabbergasted as to our gullibility over this matter. At last there is a greater awareness now that in the New Testament it is the Greek word 'Ecclesia', which simply means 'God's called- out people' (as mentioned elsewhere in this book).

In God's sight, as laid down in the scripture, in the present age of grace, the 'true Church', whoever and wherever they may be found, with, as stated before, a heart/life relationship with their Maker in freedom and truth, is not something you attend, become a member of, join, swear allegiance to, go through membership (or the like) classes in, blindly adhere to or any such thing - it is something you are 'born into', a special *family* with a very special King who rules and reigns, a very special King who is in Heaven and has a special interest in Planet Earth - not least to get a certain people for Himself to be with Him forever - a redeemed people who will be like Him when He has got us ready and made all the preparations (training and testing, etc) and taken us to His Heaven. Buildings may have or serve a temporary purpose, but they are not and never will be 'the Church'. The only buildings mentioned for the Church in the New Testament were the believers' houses, in which they met. It's not the 'buildings' that are important, it's the 'people'! Yet it is the Saviour Messiah Himself who is the most important of *all*.

The Lord God does have His 'building' in this age of grace and He calls it His 'temple' and 'spiritual house' - not made by the hands of man or as and when found in Jerusalem, but a spiritual temple made of 'living stones', of which each true believer on this Planet, no matter who or where, is one. Again, God is clearly into 'nations'; after all, He made, formed, started and/or brought or will bring to an end all the empires, nations and tribes of the Earth throughout His history with the character, boundaries and all the diversity of each. God has His 'nation' at this time - a 'holy nation' consisting of all true believers on Earth, wherever they are, who form this nation - only the Lord God knows who, in total, is in this family and where they are because He has spiritually sealed them as His, with His special loving-kindness. Israel still has her special place on Earth at this time as well. As human beings we are all special to the Lord, but it is how we respond to Him that matters!

In the times of some or great persecution, the Church is 'there' but 'underground', therefore not seen and certainly with no buildings or the like - yet so often, as in China, it has thrived. The word 'Christian', that was originally meant to be derogatory in its application, is mentioned two or three times in the New Testament Scripture, but not as such used as we use it today; but the words that *are* frequently used are 'believers' and 'disciples' as terms for those who believed fully in the Messiah and His Kingdom of Heaven and who had entered into a once for all never-ending relationship with Him on His terms. It follows then as 'believers' that we should have been 'discipled' and hopefully should understand something of the 'who, what and why' we believe along with sound doctrine, so as to translate it into positive action in our daily walk.

The 'systems' that run our world are followed by many who tune in and adhere to them and so often, so it seems, without questioning or discerning whether 'who' or 'what' around them may be dubious. The believers are told that they will hear their Messiah speaking to them and guiding them and are told to question and discern! It's nothing to do with *intelligence* in either group, but rather the way each group would approach life.

Believers are called 'ambassadors' here on Earth. Ambassadors amicably represent their own country and ruler(s) in a foreign land, having their own culture and ways represented through a small piece of land and property which is totally allowed to be, without interference, as they want it to be. This 'home from home', if you like, is there to relate to the authorities of that land they are in, as needs be, and assist their own nationals, etc … this works because of the link and input from the 'homeland'. In a time of warfare or another serious issue, as we know, ambassadors are recalled or sent back to their country of origin. So it is with believers here on Planet Earth, for this is a parallel of how it actually is. The Lord will see to it that we, as His ambassadors, have all that we need in order to do His will and bidding, so long as proper contact is made with the 'homeland', i.e. with Heaven. Also, this is why I believe the true Church, as His ambassadors, will soon be taken away at 'The Rapture' when relations between Heaven and Earth totally break down in enmity. Israel as an actual nation and land must, during the time of the seven-year tribulation period, see *their* place in all of this for themselves and respond accordingly to their Maker.

It is clearly written in New Testament Scripture that *all* believers are not only a 'priesthood' but a 'royal priesthood', because of our standing in Messiah and His Kingdom and that the Lord is our 'Great High Priest'! A 'prophet' hears the Word of God and passes on that word to whoever it is for and a 'king' is there to rule from his throne, which is the ultimate place of authority in a kingdom, and a 'priest' is there to represent men to God for men's well-being. In the Church, because of the once for all supreme sacrifice of the Lamb of God on Calvary's tree for all of our sins, the Old Testament priesthood requiring animal sacrifice is not now of itself applicable or required. This means that *every true believer* in Messiah is *not* required to *attain* to the/a 'priesthood' ... for the office of priesthood has been *conferred* upon each one of them as a gift when 'born again', so that they can *of themselves*, as part of His Royal Family, approach Father God in His Heaven on behalf of themselves and also pray for and petition God on behalf of others! So it follows that those who 'elevate' themselves into a 'priesthood' in the literal or pastoral sense, as in a place of authority and power that would usurp what God has done in the 'priesthood of all of His Church' and attempt to blot out or make God inaccessible and not allow the true Church to be what it should be, especially if this is for the leaders' own and/or selfish means, are causing something to happen which is not only dangerous but disgraceful in God's sight.

Generally, and however it has happened, the Church has developed into a 'hierarchical structure and system', but what kind of message (and the results that follow from this) does that send out in the light of the above on both sides of the 'divide', and is it Biblical? The 'World's Systems' in commerce, etc, normally have a strict hierarchical system and chain of command structure by lording it over others in an authoritarian way, but this is not the way God intended it for His Church.

The hierarchical structure in the Church has created a 'them and us' situation amongst believers as they copy the world's system, instead of mirroring the Kingdom of Heaven which should be here on Earth. Whenever or wherever there is a strict system of rules and procedures of going about things within the context of a 'fixed structure', it can become so rigid and controlling that in that controlling it will kill all life, spontaneity, creativity and freedom - not to mention leading up to a possible dictatorship! Whether or not God was really in a move of His power and Life working with and through man in any particular situation and then, subsequently, if something appeared to go wrong, man has put his hands on that work to 'steady and control it' (2nd Samuel chapter 6 verses 6,7), in order to try and sort it out *his* way, it will die - if man still then continues it on regardless and God has said, "No", it may look and seem good, but will be 'empty' and devoid of 'Life'. At this point, when the world and liberal establishment infiltrate the Church and get into its 'ranks', exercising their 'power and authority', operating in the area of the mind, intellect and knowledge with emphasis on status, certain types of clothing, qualifications and titles that represent 'authority' as it builds its empires, then it loses any supernatural power it may have had within any group, denomination or the like and will become man's very own 'do it yourself/ourselves religion', which results in religious nonsense and 'death', as Life only comes through repentance and the Cleansing Blood shed on Calvary's tree, which alone allows us to feed on the Tree of Life.

As stated, it is the hierarchical system in the Church that bolsters a 'them and us' situation, making it the same as that of the world and its ways. This is called 'hierocracy' and means being ruled by a body of priests and is a type of 'heavy shepherding'. But hang on a minute, we need to get all this into its right Biblical perspective and it will all make sense. Every human being on this Planet is 'equal' in sin/wrong-doing along with every other human being and we are *all* sinners and in need of the Messiah and His finished work of salvation! In James chapter 2 verse 10, it says that if someone could keep the whole Biblical law but were to fail in one tiny point only, then he/she would be guilty of breaking all of God's commands in His sight and is therefore totally helpless. But those of us who have truly accepted the Messiah are *all* equal in Him and, at the point of rebirth itself, good things happen to us, not least that, as previously stated, we are each given 'giftings' to help us and to build and further His Kingdom here on Earth. We are in God's family first, and out of that relationship we serve. But man has not changed with regard to wanting 'a leader' since the days of Samuel in Israel, when they shouted, "Give us a king!", for they wanted to be like the nations round about them and have a king to display as well as having God in His Heaven - Samuel was somewhat dismayed and God knew it was Himself they were rejecting in that it was His direct rule so far as His Kingship was concerned - and so God gave them kings and this certainly was not all beneficial by any means, just as they had been warned at that time.

*All* believers form a royal priesthood to God and this is a 'theocracy' rule by priests with the Messiah as the Great High Priest, constantly interceding/praying for us to Father God. This is equality for believers!

But the 'them and us' mentality has meant that the 'them' are in some ways superior to the 'us' and so, in their privileged positions, they will have various perks, and the 'us' must be subservient to the 'them' - this is definitely 'first and second class status' for believers, which is not found in the New Testament. The 'them' nearly always turn it into a 'rich man's club', exercising a power and authority through status and money which is not theirs to exercise and goes beyond their brief. The 'us' can only fit into the 'them's' rule, 'vision' and 'empire building' and do as they are told and are only allowed to operate in that which would fit in with the group's leadership, regardless of what giftings they have. Because in the UK the 'us' have been kept down for so long as mere numbers to make things look good and as 'pew-fodder', and 'leaders' who are unable to cope with the power they have laid hold of (surely none of us can cope with this kind of power and remain in both reality and humility) and the Church hears preaching and teaching for evermore, in its blatant immaturity and introversion it can do little or nothing about this situation, as it has been rendered infertile and useless.

On Radio 4's 'The Moral Maze', it was clearly stated fairly recently, "The Church is of no consequence", and with little or no fear of God or His power and love from Heaven or the prophetic word, or sharing of the treasures and life that it has at its disposal - it is sadly regarded as a laughing stock in our society. But the reality is, the Church plus God, as He gives of His Heavenly power, is a mighty force to be reckoned with! In Heavenly unity with our eyes firmly fixed on the Lord Jesus and as He works through us all there is no enemy in our land that we cannot rout! With its 'eyes' no longer on man but firmly fixed on God the Saviour, man will then no longer get in the way, the Church will then indeed hear God and obey Him and not try to control God, but will loose Him through His Word and His Power and so, not working under the world's system of Information Technology and all its electronic control, etc, the Church would then not be engineered by man but would function primarily in the supernatural realm. God is not mocked and will not share His glory and praise due Him with any other.

Of course, there are leaders - that cannot be denied for one moment and, because of the deceit and wiles of the enemy, they are needed, but how does the Lord expect them to operate during this age of grace? In the body of Christ there should be unity, but not uniformity, because of all the different giftings and personalities therein. Within the context of freedom in Christ and furthering the Kingdom of God in humility, love and a good measure of maturity are needed for all to be in the likeness of the Messiah. This means not being selfish, greedy or authoritarian or putting oneself forward to be prominent, but simply as another one of the believers; if one finds they have a gift to lead, knowing that that gift does not make them superior to anyone else, for within the Church their authority is *certainly* limited and not across the board.

Many of the early believers and others throughout this age 'loved not their lives unto death' and would not compromise in their love for, and life in, the Messiah. Doing the Tunisia tourist trail, which many have done, to the Atlas Mountains, Salt Lake, Sahara Desert and so on, included, for me, a brief early morning visit to the amphitheatre in El Jem, built by the cruel Romans in the third century AD, where the believers, who would not conform to the authorities and would not denounce their faith in Messiah, along with others, would be given over to death by wild animals for the sport of the people. One illustration I saw showed a small group of believers in the arena with their 'leader' standing tall, fully clothed and immaculate - I think there must have been a five-star hotel nearby! - with a few other believers at his feet gazing up at him with great admiration and a lion was just standing looking towards them! Nothing, of course, could be further from the truth. Those to be sacrificed would have been used, abused, starved and filthy and any ravenous animal would have been at them within a second or two. Hopefully, a leader would try and encourage the others, but surely they would all also have encouraged each other, keeping their eyes upon the Lord and worshipping only Him as He would have been close to their hearts and to them at that time.

But in Acts chapter 5 from verse 1, Ananias and Sapphira, his wife, lied to the Lord, and this in front of the Church Fellowship, regarding the money they had sold their property for in order to make themselves look good. When they were challenged by the leaders, they each, respectively, fell to the ground and died, resulting in great fear. The leaders could only rightly operate in what God was showing them and, as shown in verse 4, the property and money were there for the couple to use entirely as they wanted to - they didn't have to play any silly games! Nobody, certainly not any leaders, could tell them what to do with their property or money, but the deliberate lie the man and his wife told was 'not on' and would have misrepresented God, who was having none of it, as His judgement fell to purify the whole Church!

These days not everyone who says he/she is a believer *is* one - so that needs discernment if it's not to cause havoc! Within the true Church, single honour should be given to all, but double honour to those who do have some leadership gifting, and that is respect and hopefully preferring others above oneself; but *worship* should be given to the Messiah alone!

In Ephesians chapter 4, it tells us that gifts have been given from the Lord to His Church and not least the gift of the measure of grace. Although there are various other gifts given in the New Testament, e.g. the gifts in Romans chapter 12, there are five ministry gifts as stated in Ephesians chapter 4 verse 11 - apostles, prophets, evangelists, pastors and teachers. These gifts are not 'offices' but 'functions' of eldership overseers and, though they may occasionally speak with authority, it is definitely not so that they can lord it over anyone, for clearly in verse 12 they are there to *equip the Church*, and why is this to be so? It is so the other believers along with those younger in the faith can be equipped to get on with their own ministries for the edifying of the whole Church - that means being built up to do what you need to do for the Lord, as shown in verse 13, i.e. to be Christ-like with His stature. This then is loving-kindness and maturity, with our carnal natures needing to be subdued; but for it to work well within the true Church each of us needs to be walking with the Lord, in His direction, no matter what stage we are at or which season each of us may be in.

When I joined the RAF a little over 40 years ago now, as I write, and as far as my memory serves me, I received my equipment and clothing from a building with a large room and a long solid counter where the new recruits would line up and receive whatever, with the process of visits to this room lasting a week or two. But I did not receive that equipment and stay all the time in that room for my five years in the RAF, bored to tears and just looking at and thinking about the equipment ... of course not! ... I went out and used it and did further training, etc, and served in my rank as best I could and that meant moving on and having adventure! This in Ephesians chapter 4 verse 13 onwards is what Paul is saying: not to be *children* in the Lord, but rather get equipped, grow and grow up and be mature in the things of God as mentioned, not by the cunning, deceiving trickery, etc, of men, but being yourself in Christ, using your own gifts, reaching for maturity and having adventures! The qualities to have are Godly love, wisdom, knowledge and understanding as they are found in Christ and if and when you work at them, to make them your own, you will be on a winner and as stable as a rock. I'm not so sure you can dissect 'love, wisdom, understanding or maturity' and the like found in scripture. You can learn about them, such as 'the fear of God is the beginning of wisdom' or that 'God is Love' as shown in 1 Corinthians chapter 13, but you have either got these qualities or you haven't ... we apply ourselves and hopefully with determination reach out for and receive them and thus get the right 'keys' for living, for they are to do with God's grace.

With regard to the titles of 'elder', 'deacon' and so on, for leaders, as mentioned above, and without going into any detail or deep teaching, I think the Baptist Denomination and the Assemblies of God Pentecostal Denomination both get a lot right in the way in which they approach the order of their autonomous fellowships, where each person who is a member can have a say. Of course, it needs the freedom and the power of God and maturity for it to work as God intends.

With a union of fellowships and if there is a strict area overseer a 'denomination' may emerge where the fellowships become all exactly the same as each other, but then autonomy and spontaneity may be eroded, along with the power and freedom of God. It is not about being 'rebellious' and 'everyone doing what is right in their own eyes', but rather about an order directly from God that gives life and freedom in the supernatural. It is so important that people function in their right giftings.

The present important move within the Church for it to get back to its 'Jewish roots' (not legalistically but foundationally), as against the 'Gentile roots', must continue along with our supporting of and standing with the Jews and Israel.

The way I would work now if there is time for me to do so would be to disciple a group of a dozen or so believers (meeting in homes) and teach/share something of what I know and have experienced in my life as a whole and my walk with the Lord. I would use some of the teaching material that Roger Price left, as my basis of what and why I believe, and other material as well, of course, and would meet regularly for up to two or three years, teaching, discussing, asking questions, identifying gifts, etc, in friendship and fellowship and what the Lord may direct and all with a very loose/minimal leadership by me. Throughout this time I would co-ordinate things and give some direction, then afterwards I would disband the group totally so that each one, in their own walk with the Lord, could go on to serve Him to the best of their ability and gifting and some would go on to disciple others and I would repeat the process with another group. Of course, wider fellowship in the area would be ongoing in homes and elsewhere and I would not neglect witnessing and evangelism!

If and when there is any form of 'heavy shepherding' by leadership exercising authority and control beyond their remit (over-control will never allow *you* to be *you* or do what *you* want) and clouding out the Lord's communication to those around them, then this really is wrong. The catalogue of wrong-doing, the attacks upon and the infiltration of the Church by 'dubious believers' and others, some of which I have experienced, observed and heard about over the years, have caused serious problems and much sadness, which could often have been avoided if 'nipped in the bud' through discernment and action, as the Lord always gives warnings - we learn our lessons and then move on, as stated in Philippians chapter 3. Interestingly enough, in the light of powerful spiritual discernment, one leader who pastored a fellowship of 6,000 people said that he had 1,000 preachers in his flock, but how many did he have who could work in signs and wonders ... ? ... he said he had only 5!

One area in which something has gone wrong and has permeated through most of the UK Church so that they have 'lost the plot' is that of 'spiritual warfare'. I mentioned earlier about the ministry of Derek Prince and how he was second to none when it came to spiritual warfare action. It was a few years back now in his teaching that he stated that the warfare that would unfold (an overall view) would be like that of Elijah versus Jezebel in the scripture! I totally agree that he was absolutely right and that it pertains to the end of this age of grace which we are now in and that it will intensify continuously as it unfolds before us all. This time, leading up to the seven years' tribulation will affect the true Church everywhere, along with the Jews and Israel, but the actual seven years' tribulation (sometimes known as 'Jacob's Trouble') will affect the World but centre on the Jews/Israel. Elijah, the prophet and miracle-worker, represented the Jews and Israel and those who genuinely belonged to God ... and Jezebel was the epitome of what the world system stands for in its evil, deception, manipulation and control - the intensity of the fight was, and had to be, to the death of one or the other. As stated earlier, all of Israel will come to its senses in the actual Tribulation time.

The Church has been 'comatosed' and rendered almost useless and somewhat ineffective as it has failed to be like the Messiah, has not got its act together and has failed in such things as discernment and the art of spiritual warfare - not least deliverance ministry and using spiritual authority over its enemies instead of subduing its own people who are 'pew fodder'. It knows how to run a 'nice, comfortable, prosperous club' and how to make nice polite prayers, but where is the desperate cry of the heart for a lost, suffering and sick world and a Church in the UK that is generally still on 'milk', having little idea of who or what it really is? Remember the saying that it is not the 'dog in the fight' but the 'fight in the dog' that counts. Well, in one sense this applies to the Church. Where is the fight in the Church for the warfare it is in, a fight unto the 'death' for one side or the other from which there is no escape? It is 'spiritual warfare aggression' that is needed by the Church and that's what I mean by the 'fight in the dog'; it's a spiritual fight against God's enemies who would seek to destroy us as they show their full true colours working against the Church and, sadly, almost all of this battle has come through the political arena in recent times. We need the nation's leaders to show justice and physical aggression to combat the forces of evil in order to restore the Godliness that the nation has lost and given away. The Church fights in the spiritual realm and our nation's leaders should be fighting in the physical, in justice, policing, etc, to bring order once again into our society. The Church should be a powerful entity of God's Love, filled with His Power and Life and glorifying Him!

Because of the state of the world, as it is now, being a sort of Godless 'global village' with all its I.T. Communication and knowledge and just as Elijah and Jezebel could not in any way mix so the true Church wherever (and the same does and will apply to the Jews in their land of Israel) and the world are in total opposition to each other, so their systems can never mix. This means we, the Church, (and Israel at some point) are heading on *a catastrophic collision course* with the world and its ways, for it is impossible we could ever integrate because of the types of spiritual 'push' on either side and therefore we, the true Church, will ever only worship and serve the Messiah and build and further *His Kingdom* here on Earth and will never, ever, ever bow the knee to the world system in its evil and wretchedness and to those in authority over it.

God is judging, in His displeasure, the nations and will yet judge; but first of all, as stated earlier, will come the 'latter rain' of His grace that will be poured out to give people the opportunity to repent and to experience His merciful loving-kindness and Life! But here in the UK, and it will soon take place, there will be a mighty revival awakening as prophesied by such people as Ern Baxter, Jean Darnell, Clifford Hill, Mahesh Chavda, Tom Inglis, etc, and I believe fully with them that it will affect the younger ones, the youth, the teens and twenties of the nation, that being moved by the Lord God, they will rise up in their hundreds of thousands, if not millions, in the UK. From the top of Scotland southwards and with awesome power, cleansed in the blood of Yeshua and keen to do His will, with an amazing freshness and zeal, they will subdue and rout the enemies of God in this land, supported by us older ones, who have walked with and love the Lord Messiah and have laboured in building His Kingdom for years. When we all, as believers, join together in our prayers and praise of and to the Lord, *no corrupt entity* in our land will stand (some of the forces of evil and darkness will go temporarily underground) and certainly not the politically elite class that has short-changed the nation in so many ways or those who have been/are guilty of treason in our land (remember, the word 'treason' is from the Latin root meaning 'to hand over' and fits all those in authority who have simply handed us over to the evil of the horrific European Union and destroyed the nation's Godly heritage; that is, its 'ancient boundary stones'). It is once again our nation, this time through our youth, who will go over to 'The Continent' in Europe and win many for the Messiah! After this blaze of glorifying light from Heaven - God's latter rain to swell the harvest - the lights will go out and the darkness of unrestrained horrendous evil will be a deep darkness indeed!

God is definitely shaking *all* things everywhere on Earth in these important days of His History which we live in and this pertains to both the Church and the world and will continue for the next several years and God has His own reasons and purposes for doing so. So far as the Church is concerned, there is a measure of judgement, and that means correction, a sifting and sorting out and an alignment to His will in order to purify the Church and make it fit for His purpose.

Many in the Church cannot see that the pain and hurts of their past, if not dealt with and sorted out, can go on to do all-round damage both to them and to others. Likewise, what a believer was before salvation, he/she may bring into the Church in a 'sideways move' and simply continue on with it in a different guise within the Church and if this is something negative, e.g. violence, bullying, controlling or anything else that is detrimental to the Kingdom of God, then much damage may be done if not checked. Further examples would be all those who have been in positions of authority and leadership of any kind or those who have used their wealth to influence whatever, those who have been seriously abused, those with uncontrolled anger, those who have been in immorality or those who have charismatic personalities which will attract people to them regardlessly … and pride is one of the most deadly sins of all.

As God's intense shaking continues, all that is not of Him will cease, fall and be destroyed. When the shaking is finished, only that which is of Him will be left standing … only that which is and those who are *on The Rock, The Foundation* that is the *Messiah Saviour … will stand and never be shaken*!!

# 26
# What in the World is Wrong ...?

The Lord God is a God of extremes! Clearly from Revelation chapter 3 this is so and He is not normally pleased with the 'pussy footing' or, as it states, lukewarm middle ground that is neither something nor nothing. I'm reminded of King Ahab in the Old Testament who had really 'lost it' to evil, but when he repented somewhat (1 Kings chapter 21 verses 25-29), God stated that He would 'buy that', as it were, and forgave the particular matter - in Ahab's extremes of evil and then of 'a good', at least God knew where He stood with him and so dealt with him accordingly.

As mentioned earlier, there are two things in the book of Daniel that would be a backdrop, if you like, to these end times which we live in, i.e. *travel* and *knowledge*, and two things in the book of Genesis (chapter 6 verse 11) regarding what the world was like before it was flooded at the time of Noah, which also pertain to the times we live in, i.e. *violence* and *corruption*. Surely no one can deny that the increase in each of the above is phenomenal. God stated that these four above-mentioned things would happen - so it is now that each one listed is totally relevant to the time we live in! It is not just a 'little' of whatever. *Corruption* is not just some over there and a little over here and we can cope or deal with it - it is epidemic, permeating everywhere in its deception, greed and destruction. *Violence* also has reached horrific proportions. In recent years *knowledge* has increased almost beyond what we can comprehend and the increase of *travel* far exceeds what was imaginable even in my lifetime, never mind further back. God has allowed the extremes of all this in their own way as He prepares to give the world over to what *it really wants.*

We're back to Derek Prince and Lance Lambert! Derek Prince, as stated, was part of the Florida Five when they wrote New Wine Magazine, back in the 'seventies, which occasionally, as I remember, touched on some teaching against 'humanism'. Later, Derek Prince wrote an excellent teaching letter in August 1994 with the title 'No 3: Humanism - Forerunner for Antichrist', wherein, because of his background in Greek philosophy as a university lecturer and his subsequent knowledge of the Bible along with his involvement and understanding of spiritual warfare, he was certainly well equipped in his authority to counteract the subject of 'humanism'! He mentions the image of the man as in the book of Daniel (referred to elsewhere in this book) depicting a total of five important empires, with each being a part of the image of the body of a man, and zooms in on the Greek Empire being the third empire out of the five, and so, using his knowledge of Greek philosophy, shows that he saw this third empire being in the area of the 'reproductive organs' and thus was and is able to 'reproduce itself in other cultures'! So that is why we have the idolatry of the human mind, the emphasis on 'athletic conquests', the downgrading of the marriage relationships between a man and a woman and instead the elevation of the view of a homosexual relationship between two men being more important, as considered to be more 'intellectually fulfilling' and so on. He goes on to state that the so-called 'gods' of Greece lacked any binding moral code, etc, and relates it to the times we live in and to the fact that in 1992 in the USA and Israel was the time that 'the spirit of humanism launched a major new offensive on each' that is of pure undiluted humanism (and it was, of course, from 1997 the UK succumbed to this great evil deception). He also states that, when carried to its ultimate, 'humanism will believe anything but the truth' and will tolerate anything but righteousness and said it is 'not spiritually neutral but is an anti-religious religion'.

Lance Lambert gave teaching/prophecy in his 'update' tapes and I still have the one from 1990 where he stated (my words from memory) that just as communism was the ideology of a demonic spirit from hell that would cause rivers of blood wherever it went, so it would go out again, only this time with the doctrine of humanism (with its claim of equality for all and all having the same 'rights', which would be believed by many round Planet Earth, and this also would cause much suffering and bloodshed).

Humanism, as Derek Prince states, is a 'deliberate denial of God's power and authority'. Mankind then is very keen to totally deny God's existence and to keep God out of His own Creation, as it were, and try to get by on his own. The dictionary meaning of 'humanism' given by Derek Prince is 'the denial of any power or moral value superior to that of humanity; the rejection of religion in favour of a belief in the advancement of humanity by its own efforts'. The recent Oxford Dictionary definition centres on humans being of more importance than divine or supernatural matters. Humanism is centred only on the human race itself and claims its rights and equality for all along with unity and justice. But what is happening as we are all being conditioned to accept this nonsense and what is the package it is being sold in?

God has a completely different view from that of mankind, as shown in His biblical perspective. What is the sum of 'humanism' in which it needs to operate in order to convey its deception and lies? The sum or equation is 'evolution' + 'humanism' = 'pantheism'! The enemies of God, in order to achieve the result of this sum, have sought desperately to force it upon peoples in order to bring about a total 'control' across the board and they will not give up trying to do so in these days! Humanism could not exist or have even got off the ground in the UK without its backdrop of *evolution*. I will deal briefly with each item in the above 'sum'.

# Evolution

Surely it takes more faith to believe in the theory of evolution than ever it does to believe in the Lord God's Creation?! There was nothing and then, "There was a big bang", they say, as they desperately set out to prove at any cost their theory ... but all you get from a 'big bang' or 'explosion' anywhere, apart from a headache and deafness, is noise, chaos and destruction! The choice is simple ... it's either 'nothing ... made something ... out of nothing' and of its own accord it somehow developed into what we are and see around us!? ... or ... 'In the beginning God ...', then follow it through from Genesis to Revelation for the big overall picture?! Now, in the first choice, let me see ... there is 'absolute nothingness' and from this total nothing at all vacuum (devoid of matter or anything) ... suddenly there is space and something within it that can somehow ignite itself into matter ... then over a period of time develop into the vast Universe with our Planet Earth somewhere in it ... this with all the unbelievable complexities and order for life to *just happen*! ... surely not! Do you know what I think? ... I think someone's taking the mick good and proper?!

With no artistic designer creator, how could anyone ever believe, unless duped, that from moisture or water, slime or mould came about and decided of itself it would grow into marine or plant life, animals or birds of the air, never mind human beings that have a spiritual side to them! The incredible complexities of creation as we see it are all interdependent with the sun, moon, stars and planets all in their courses - the roundness of the sun, moon and earth ... we can tell the time to the second from them! To kick-start life as we know it in any of its forms is totally impossible without a Designer Creator who knows what He is doing! So, we are told to believe by 'them' that a bit of slime or mould forms and says to itself, "Oh good, in a billion years I'll just grow into a hen, no ... no ... make that a human being, okay ... I'll grow into a toe ... but I have no blood or food to feed the cells to make up the toe ... no ... I'll grow into an eye instead so I can see ... but what's an eye? ... oh, my brain hurts ... silly me ... I haven't got a brain ...?!" *Exactly*!! (Please note Psalm 94 verses 8-11.)

At school in the later 'fifties I would get the usual C. of E. Morning Assembly, as mentioned earlier. Then one day, there it was in the biology textbook ... an ape or chimp and in about seven following different 'pictures' it's grown into a man ... not a *woman* ... ! ... because if they had done so the publishers and scientists no doubt would never have lived very long to tell the tale!? Now someone/some people somewhere must be really confused, or is it all the push of much deception and a great big lie propagated by certain educationalists, certain politicians, some sectors of the media and definitely in recent years by BBC Radio 4 ... in fact, wherever the cap fits ...?

No, God tells us in scripture what we need to know of how He designed and made His creation, each grouping after its own kind with much variety therein, their procreation and programming - everything needed was provided at the outset and it was all perfect - no violence, corruption or any such thing and food was in abundance for all! The sin of mankind, as stated previously, brought chaos and God counteracted it with justice, order and whatever ... God was 'on the ball', if you like! Global warming, carbon footprints and the like are nonsense! Because of mankind's polluting of the Earth and for our own safety, common sense tells us this pollution should be dealt with to eradicate it - we are supposed to take general good care of the Earth under God. But we all know God made certain things cyclical, did He not? Obviously the water ... yes, we should gather it into reservoirs, etc ... also the salt in the sea with the paths and tides of the sea bring purification to the Earth, acting as a preserver ... the seasons have been given for rests, growth and harvest. He who totally flooded the Earth can do anything He wants and scripture clearly says He uses the elements to bring forth His judgements. In Psalm 104 verse 30 is a 'key' which positively states that He, God, *renews the face of the Earth*!

The Lord Jesus said, in Matthew chapter 6 verse 27 and in Matthew chapter 5 verse 36, that we cannot change, of ourselves, our height by mere mental or willpower and that even every hair on our head is numbered - in other words, you are not going to develop or change yourself into anything other than a human being created in the image of God Himself. If the lie of evolution could be true in any way, then surely its process would still be continuing ... so where is the sort of dog-like self-creating animal with 15 eyes, 5 legs, etc, trying to form into something?! When mankind gets proud and too big for his boots, then God would say to him/her what He said to Job and indirectly to Job's 'friends' as well in Job chapters 38 and 39, especially chapter 38 verse 4 (my paraphrase), "Now, Job, mate, where were you when I created the Heavens, the Earth and ...?", as God goes into all the various details. Job could give no answer back to God and neither can any one of us!

## Humanism

As stated above, with regard to the roots of humanism, it is simply pure Godlessness and is the pride and rebellion of man against his Creator so that man can cast off all restraint and do what is right in his own eyes! With the 'push' of the spiritual forces of evil behind and working through mankind towards a powerful revolution of disobedience and rebellion against God, in order to deceive and trap as many of the whole of mankind as possible onto their side, to try and make God out to be in the wrong according to what He has said will unfold in the world, the sides are lining up against each other for the showdown.

Let's get one thing into its right perspective then. God, in His Heaven, does not look down at the state of mankind and all that is happening in His Creation and His plans and then go to pieces and put His head in His hands and shout, "This is terrible! ... I can't cope! ..." On the contrary, He is not surprised by anything, for He knows everything, though His heart may ache in His love for us all and the rejection of Him that is taking place. No, the Lord does not waste words and though He knows good from evil He, of Himself, is not negative. So in His Word, such as Psalm 14 verse 1 and related verses, He doesn't deal with the countless negatives of mankind, but simply states that the fool in his heart will say that there is no God and this is to do with corruption, etc, and also that they do no good ... and so it is ... but we do not have to be foolish towards God!

I'm just going to give a few brief comments about the pitfalls of humanism. Humanism is seeing things from and through man's perspective alone - but his vision is distorted because of his proud, selfish, fallen and depraved state (contrast with seeing things from the Heavenly Kingdom of God's perspective and we start to see things clearly). Human rights may mean 'rights' for the evil and the wrong-doer ... but unrighteous people do not care about the wrongs they do and exploit their 'freedom' for their own wrongdoing and selfishness, whereas the righteous ones will normally want to go on doing what is kind, good and right.

Humanism has no fear of God as it throws off all Godly restraint and chooses not to acknowledge Him and tries to reinvent created life without Him ... but God does not have to answer or justify Himself to His creation or to mankind, so it is the most dangerous thing that could happen to an individual or group to have the Lord go silent on them and so give them over to their Godless desires, selfishness and their own ways ... for who is there left to help them for good?

The smooth 'politically correct' evasive words of humanism are both empty and 'hard to nail down', for it is so often only by their fruit you will see what humanists are ... and this is poisonous ... for in the multitude of their words sin is not lacking and Almighty God is kept at bay. Humanism is only for the chosen few and only for 'the survival of the fittest', for it is exclusive in its nature and therefore cannot give equal rights to all ... how can it when all or part of 'the victims' rights' have been lost/taken away at the cost of much suffering and/or bloodshed and the biblical moral code and *real justice* are sacrificed on the altar of our 'human rights', regardless of those left alive and well enough to continue in their wrongdoing and who will still do so ... all this is at the expense of the victims' rights ... and God is certainly not given *His* rights!

With humanism it all stops with 'man', who 'they' say is just a part of all the 'animals' anyway and is still presumably 'evolving' (into what I dread to think!), so animals have a certain 'equality' with man and so it follows man is not then responsible or accountable as such ... anything goes ... however, *reality* is that it is God alone who is able to bring stability, order and righteousness, but in humanism He and His Word are no longer wanted or required ... any man or 'think-tank' of men/women goes, no matter who, what or where they are coming from! ... who cares so long as it looks, seems and sounds good ... if this is not man pressing the self-destruct button then *nothing* is ...! Only God (not the Deceiver) can make a way to sort out the mess that mankind has got itself into!

In the eyes of the world, humanism is now 'the tops'. It is the be all and end all and has been substituted in the place of the Lord God Himself and so it requires a form of adherence that is 'worship', whereby this 'cancer' is spreading worldwide and will sacrifice, at great peril, real freedom, integrity, justice, etc, through its own countless controlling laws. Humanism leads to control and not maturity and it shouts, "democracy!" and "peace!"; but in its outcome is, or will be, neither, for it is a new type of 'pacifism' of the masses, but will turn out to be no pacifism ... it is the human race turned in on itself guided by the spiritual powers of darkness (see Ephesians chapter 5 verses 6 to 8).

## Pantheism

Pantheism, as stated above, is the result of evolution plus humanism and its modern-day global movement that is 'religious' in essence boldly embraces several forms or types under its umbrella with headings to cover several occult or other terms for 'Godlessness' that are 'humanistic' and 'green' in the sense of being emotionally at one in 'worshipping' the physical in the Earth's environment and beyond, where they 'fuse together', if you like, their idea of God as the 'spiritual Creator' with the physical and so this may lead to a type of 'idolatrous worship' of the physical. Its perpetrators believe that this life is all there is (how they state what they believe is somewhat complicated and in one sense anything goes within its framework of that belief and, in contrast, two biblical answers are found in Hebrews chapter 9 verses 27, 28 and Revelation chapter 20 verses 10 to 12).

The literal meaning of pantheism is: 'pan' = 'all', meaning everything or everyone; the Greek 'theos' = 'god'; 'ism' = that which would denote an action or its results. To simplify, the complete meaning of pantheism as given in various dictionaries, etc, is to say, as they do, that God and the universe are both 'one' and it is a doctrine saying that 'God' is only known in and through the Earth and the Universe and is the worship and tolerance of all 'gods', or as someone said, the 'self-deification of man'. A few years back, some would have put 'Pantheism' under the heading of 'New Aquarian Age Rainbow Teachings', which would include items or headings such as feminism, superstition, drug abuse, drunkenness, etc, and quite right, but now I would say that Pantheism, in spite of *many other types of things* that are there to keep people from finding the truth of God's salvation, has taken the lead in its above context. Biblically there is a list in Deuteronomy chapter 18 verses 9 to 14 of that which must be avoided in order to please God and keep ourselves safe and again in 1st Timothy chapter 4 verse 1 God shows us that there are 'deceiving spirits' and 'doctrines of demons' which churn out their never-ending nonsense to try and trip mankind up. Humanism/Pantheism and the like can smooth-talk anything up or down but, in doing so, will never arrive at integrity or the truth and without the Lord God cannot win.

It's back to Scripture and to Genesis chapter 3 verse 5, where, in the Authorised Version, it says not to regard eating the fruit from the Tree of the Knowledge of Good and Evil ... and as God said ... "You will be as gods."...? If the names of people are important to us, how much more the names of God, for there is a good number of them and they give us colourful meaning and some understanding to mankind of just who God is. When you get into an in-depth study of names in the Bible and, though it can be difficult to understand this vast subject, as long as it is based on sound teaching in truth it can be rewarding to have that understanding for those who have the time and the desire to do so. I am not a Hebrew scholar, but I will try to briefly simplify the point I'm making!

In the Old Testament one name for God is 'Adonai', where it is used to show God as the Lord and Master and is therefore used to show great respect, as a servant would to his/her master.

In the New Testament you will find other words like 'Abba' which refer to God (e.g. Romans chapter 8 verse 15), used by a little child to a loving father, and shows that you can have an intimate, special relationship with God!

Back to the Old Testament, the word 'Lord' has different meanings in Hebrew, but the English language does not always show this. One such word taken from the Hebrew is now something of a non-word 'YHWH' (e.g. Exodus chapter 6 verses 2 and 3), as the word itself or the enunciation/pronunciation of it was deliberately dropped and lost in both writing and speaking by Hebrew scholars, out of respect, in case they misused or blasphemed the name of God. It means the 'self-existing one' and more, and is translated as, 'I AM', e. g. Exodus chapter 3 verse 14, where God gives a double emphasis of Himself and it shows that God has always existed and will always do so! The Hebrew word 'Yah' (Psalm 68 verse 4) is a translation of the word 'Lord' in Exodus chapter 6 verse 3, which is tied in with the Hebrew word 'YHWH'.

God is a Spiritual Being outside of time, space and the finite, as He is in Eternity, He is infinite and so it is impossible for us in our created state on Earth to understand this - yet in the depth of our heart/spirit surely we know there is something of us that will live on throughout Eternity.

Elohim is a Hebrew word for God and is found thousands of times in the Old Testament. There are two ways it is used in the Old Testament, though it may be written as God or gods. The first of two meanings of Elohim is 'as an object of worship' and that is the word used in Genesis chapter 1 verse 1 . "In the beginning God ..." and also again at the beginning of verse 5 in Genesis chapter 3. The second time Elohim is used, it is used as meaning Gods or gods and my guess is that that appears over a couple of hundred times in the Old Testament.

In the New Testament, 'Theos' is translated God or god(s) and is to do with being an object of worship. This word appears in John chapter 10 verse 34 and also in several other places in NT and refers to the point the Lord Jesus was making about the 'gods' in Psalm 82 verse 6, where He is speaking of the Elohim as in 'mighty ones' who were 'the judges' in the land, appointed by and under the Lord God with power and status, but were not judging righteously at all and so God was angry - their privileged authority, status and responsibility were not being denied by God.

So keeping the above in mind, it's back to Genesis chapter 3 verse 5, when the second time the word for 'Elohim' is used, where it then goes on to say, "you will be like 'Gods' or 'gods' ", and the latter is correct, for when taking the forbidden fruit they would become like God but *not actually Him*, of course, but like 'gods'. This then is the downfall of the human race and what 'Pantheism' is about - mankind cannot cope with the knowledge of good and evil, for he is not meant or designed to take it into himself; but as he tries to cope with this, in his sin and wrongdoing, without God but as a 'god' (mighty one … remember we are made in the image of God) and becomes all puffed up and proud, in spite of all the good and bad he may do - then he has got himself into a tragic mess/state! We were made to worship the Lord God *alone* and serve *Him*, but that worship has been directed elsewhere, anywhere in fact, and not least to the self-deification of man. We have made ourselves 'Elohim', just as it was stated we would do, in Genesis chapter 3 verse 5 … as gods or God … and mankind, in his arrogance and pride, threw away his innocence and, since the fall, we could say has become far too big for his boots! Salvation is humility, giving back to God His worth. No wonder we need to 'die' to ourselves and be 'born again' and 'alive' in, to and with … the Saviour Messiah in His Resurrection Power Life!

Hedonism, which is the going after and exaltation of pleasure in selfishness at any cost, along with Pluralism, which believes that there can be more than one absolute authority of divine or philosophical principle, are both included in the 'sum' with Pantheism … so we are back to the false plurality of 'Gods' or 'gods' …!

If I was to give a brief prophetic word to the nation in order to bring us back to being a God-fearing people through Biblical repentance … it would go something like the following:

Woe to those who call evil 'good' and good 'evil', embrace lies and are far from the truth, those who would do away with the Lord Jesus Christ and welcome 'Barabbas'!; Woe to the nation where innocent bloodshed on our roads and streets cries out to the Lord for justice, but that justice has fallen on our streets; Woe to the younger people who party and party, sacrificed on the altars of commercialism and greed - male and female young adults who do not ask those who are 'returning' from further down their road what it is like up ahead and they do not know that recompense of their account will be required sooner rather than later!; Woe to you 'shepherds' throughout the land of the ilk of Ezekiel chapter 34 verses 20 to 22, whoever you are, for you have mistreated the sheep and you think, because you did not see the Lord act straight away, that it was 'a wink and a nod job', but when God moves in His anger to sort it all out it will be a terrible day; Woe to those leaders who have deceitfully 'handed over' and signed away, without legal warrant, our nation, giving us over to all kinds of evil and to a corrupt budding dictatorship of a European Union, for they will not go free unless they mourn and repent with real change of heart and action to put it right. Know that the Lord God does have the last and final words in every matter.

The UK needs to be like Nineveh of old, when God said through Jonah, an Old Testament prophet, that He would judge to destroy that great city; but when the people of Nineveh, from the king downwards, fasted and prayed in repentance for three days, God had mercy on them and withheld their destruction. *Come on UK* - let's make our stand for and take this land for the Lord Jesus - it's time for repentance - a change to move towards God in heart, mind and action and ask Him for His mercy and loving-kindness to come upon us!

I'm reminded of Jeremiah chapter 9 verses 23, 24 and Isaiah chapter 1 verses 16 to 20.

It has taken me a little over four years to write this book, so the time and the acceptable space allowed for doing so have gone! I will simply list or reiterate, with some comments, a few of the things and the order of events over recent years which have completely changed our society - certain politicians and others would call it 'progress', but it is *'regress'*, leading the nation away from its Godly Heritage and Truth and from the way, over the centuries, we have, as a nation, generally stood on the Bible as the Word of God, which has resulted in special favour and has then somewhat influenced other nations for good.

I would say that the UK brought itself under a curse around t h e time of 1948 because of how we treated the Jews and the land previously allocated to them and though no doubt we were exhausted by the two World Wars within the previous thirty-odd years, we can trace from then the beginning of the loss of the British Empire. The laws and actions passed regarding how we treated the Jews and their land of Israel have since taken us away from our Godly Heritage in Messiah with its stability and values. In my lifetime I was just able to see and experience, as a child, something of what it was like in this nation, with its very low crime rates, safety in our streets and neighbourhoods, etc, but have since seen its demise to the dreadful state we are now in, being almost the complete opposite of those far-off days. In my opinion, based on scripture, certain laws passed brought about detrimental changes. In 1951 we saw the abolition of the law prohibiting witchcraft and it was up until that point the nation had stood on the scripture of Deuteronomy chapter 18 verses 9 to 13. In 1959 the Obscene Publications Act was changed in favour of immorality. In 1965 the Death Penalty for murder was abolished … 1967 saw David Steele's Abortion Act passed, legalising abortions, and whichever viewpoint any one of us might take, I see it as murder and at the least that it is the cruel termination of potential life and several million babies in our land have been dealt with in this way since then. Also in 1967 was the Sexual Offences Act and a further change to the Obscene Publications Act; then in 1968 the Theatre Act, all no doubt bringing their own consequences. Of course, in the 1960s the Pop Culture brought into this land Eastern religions along with the drug culture in a big way and the laws of divorce and homosexuality were changed and so on.

It is true that some of these things above have for some time now been legal in our society, but that does not make them 'righteous' if they are not so according to God and His Word, the Bible, or the Kingdom of Heaven. We may get to choose our sins, but we certainly do not get to choose the consequences of them!… but let me state there is forgiveness available through the Lord Jesus Christ. When those in authority in our land in recent years have 'bowed the knee' to the likes of 'Pantheism', however it is portrayed, it has meant that the above laws have been put on a par with the Gospel of the Messiah and if you believe this is not so, they have, in my opinion, certainly been elevated above all that the Lord Jesus did, leaving the way for 'believers' to be sidelined and silenced where possible. In the 'fifties it was normally safe to walk on our UK streets even in the dark - there was no fear! … and so to the times we now live in … it did not exactly get better, did it? The UK is not a safe place any more and crime has reached unmanageable proportion, with much fear.

This is all a deliberate plan and strategy of the enemies of God to oppose Him and try to live without acknowledging Him on Earth as in trying to bring a curse upon mankind through lawlessness, etc. It is all moving towards a 'one-world' everything, including a 'one-world' dictatorship coming through the vehicle of I.T., leading to a complete control of each and every individual who eventually adheres to this above dictatorship in its cashless society, whereby no-one will be able to 'buy or sell' without the electronic chip implantation, and obviously mobile phone technology is leading us into this time that will supposedly solve everything … but nothing could be further from the truth!

The time in that season is short, as already stated, so the authorities will not tolerate any 'dissenters' or anyone who will not conform to their control in what will be the worst 'dictatorship' ever! All this is based on fear, lack of trust, 'snooping' and furtive tale-telling on fellow members of society and, with the destruction of the family unit, along with total greed, selfishness and immorality, spells disaster. Society has been programmed by the likes of I.T., television, electronic (violent/sordid) games and propaganda with an unhealthy dependence upon those utilities that were once provided by the State, e.g. water, gas, electricity. (I realise there is a provision that comes through 'State' or business help, but I'm referring generally to the fact that, without the way we are now organised in society, we could not manage in our daily living unless the provisions and help were forthcoming from food, to heat, to water, etc). There are some people out there who can hardly communicate without various branches of I.T. and again there are many who are soaked in violence. Look at the way 'Work Canteens', Public Houses, Social Clubs and the like are starting to disappear in the UK - it is so that personal social communication is being minimised and this is bad news so far as decent communication amongst normal friendly folk is concerned!

A change, in whatever, is brought about by God's enemies in order to try to alter something from good to evil and seems to happen so often as follows:

## Stages of change

From ... anti (not allowed) ...
to ... neutral (neither punished nor allowed) ...
to ... tolerated (officially allowed) ...
to ... celebrated (allowed and considered to be 'wonderful') ...
to ... if you don't agree you will be persecuted if not criminalised, so
  you had better conform, regardless of beliefs or conscience ...

In applying the above 'stages of change' to various issues, 'creation to evolution' is a case in point. As an example of this, BBC Radio 4 has almost totally portrayed 'evolution' as a fact/truth and it is now considered to be 'wonderful', whereas 'creation' until the summer of 2010 was seemingly scarcely mentioned at all. Capital punishment, corporal punishment, gambling, pornography, freedom of speech due to humanism with politically correct nonsense would continue the list. With regard to homosexuality, I can clearly remember my mother in the early 'fifties saying that 'homosexuals' went to prison and then a neighbourhood friend, when on school holidays from Fettes Public School, trying to 'inform' the group of friends about 'homos'. Fortunately for me, I didn't know what they were on about and thought they had 'lost the plot'. From then till now it has been completely turned around so as to now be totally in the favour of homosexuals (ref. 'Stages of change' above). At the risk of repeating myself, it was Roger Price, somewhere in his teaching material, who stated that it was homosexuality that destroyed the armies of and, subsequently, the mighty Roman Empire! If homosexuality is linked to paedophilia, then I would not even dare to think what might be next.

The family unit based on Godly principles is the basis of a stable and healthy society. Our UK society is now divided between the 'royalists' and the 'EU-ites', if you like, and it is interesting, as the above 'stages of change' would apply in how this has come about and has happened without the lawful consensus of the British people, it is almost incredible! I am amazed and astounded ...! It is a universal Godly principle that we cannot serve two 'masters'; it's either one or the other, so the choice is either to be totally integrated into the EU or to remain independently with the British flag and stay under our monarchy, with its Godly principles and oaths to God to defend The Faith of the Lord Jesus Christ and the version of the Word of God as authorised by King James in 1611 (and the updated version of the New King James). As long as our Queen defends The Faith according to her Coronation Oaths and she is still our Queen, then that is definitely what stands!! There has been no mandate for any politician or anyone else in this nation to minimise our monarchy, drain away the nation's finances and substance over the years and sign us over, giving control of our nation to a dubious (if not corrupt) group of people from other lands of Europe ... it is happening to our peril! If nearly all the politicians and their 'parties' are pro-Europe (???), they still have no right whatsoever to take *us* into Europe without the British people's consent ... (*in God's sight and in democracy this is not lawful*) and definitely not while we have our monarchy, who will defend The Faith. Obviously I'm a royalist so far as defending *The Faith* and our *Godly heritage* goes! The British Nation has a choice between curses or BLESSINGS!

The Earth and everything in it is all of the Lord God Almighty's Creation and so it all belongs to Him and He knows what plans He has for it and the reasons why He has those plans. God is in ultimate and overall control and will yet show Godless man, in his total depravity in its various forms, that which he is capable of descending into, even down to 'the gutter' ... yet in HIS Wonderful Love there is still the way of escape ...

# 27
# *So What Then ...?!*

The conclusion I came to with regard to the opening words of this book, and as I progressed in writing it, is that my parents did not really want me or my siblings. My father was a provider when he had to be and tried to sort out the education side of things, but he was not able to form close relationships or keep them as such and no doubt he was damaged by the Second World War and at other times in his life - he was not cut out for normal healthy family life. I suppose he had sixteen or so years of being with my mother, so this out of his total of 84 years was only a fraction which he seemingly wanted to forget. My mother certainly had the capacity to relate, had common sense and showed loving kindness, but sadly turned in on herself and into 'escapism' and was greatly damaged by her self-abuse, not least at the end of her life. There are stages and seasons to our lives, some good and some bad, and people come in and go out of our lives over which, at times, we have no control. My parents' time together was a terrible tragedy is my conclusion and the children born to them would not totally escape the damage and consequences of this. Yes, hopefully we forgive as needs be, and put it behind us and there is real freedom in doing so; then we can get on, unhindered, with life!

It was interesting to write this book, though not without some emotional pain, of course, and see my 'life's picture', and I hope I'm not afraid of the odd 'reality check' and to seek correction and realignment as necessary. I hope I will always 'call a spade a spade' and say it as it is! Okay, yes, I know I'm damaged goods to some extent and take responsibility for mistakes made, wrong reactions and for the times I've been part of the problem and not the answer. To survive all the rejection and abuse in my upbringing it is no wonder I at times became something of a loner. Even now I'm still misunderstood from time to time, which is a bit of a nuisance when condemned without being allowed to have my say. If my experiences of life have helped me to help some other people and show compassion, then it was definitely worth it all. I know from my counselling and sharing ministry over the years that many of you will say, reading this book, something like, "Hey, mate, you think you had it rough, you want to hear what happened to me," and yes, no doubt I would agree, as and when your secrets come out of the abuse, etc, suffered and I would wonder how each and everyone of you coped with it all as you carried much pain and grief along with any roads of 'escapism' you might have taken.

The bottom line of all sin is broken relationships and so success in all of life is measured by the healing of relationships that are then good, kind and righteous! I'm grateful that I was able to have and receive the measure of loving kindness that my mother was able to give and grateful for the kindness of others to me in my childhood, even if this was only at certain times and in spite of the various negatives also experienced. The music of the 'fifties which I liked with regard to 'love' helped me to express and be in touch with my emotions and gave me a 'dream', if you like, for adulthood. Sadly, we live in a day of 'easily throw-away relationships' and so these are shallow or tainted because of sin and its 'ripples' and, of course, they are not always easy! But 'true love' is of the 'heart' and then the 'will', it is not of the 'mind' or the 'intellect'. It is something that just 'happens'; it is a free commodity that cannot be denied, forced, analysed, contained or explained. The love of God cannot be quenched if let loose and so it goes with 'freedom'. It is not 'love' but something else if it is cold, controlling, manipulative, mechanical with 'do's and 'don'ts', legalism, selfishness and greed or squeezes you into what it wants you to become. Those who experience real love/loving kindness in mature and righteous relationships are really well off and usually the most content, in spite of life's problems.

We cannot 'give love' if we have not 'received love', or indeed if there are 'obstacles' blocking it that have been caused in some way by life itself. It is amazing that you can really receive God's love from Heaven, that special 'agape' Godly love, which only He can give, and that straight into your heart when you believe in Him and cry out to Him in your brokenness. Isn't it the sick who need the doctor? In the same way it is the 'sin-sick' who need the 'Divine Physician' Who alone can help, save and bring healing! When He touches your heart and His love and His life flow into you, you are also able to give His love out and away to others and there is no measure in His giving, though we might curtail Him! As we receive His Love, then worship, praise and thank Him, it all makes sense - nothing else seems to matter in comparison, as all else is secondary - this is exactly the same as finding true love on Earth, only more so. Someone has said, "God has many servants, but not many lovers," and it is true. I serve because I have known and know God's Love that cannot be equalled on this Earth and I worship, praise and honour Him just as I am, 'warts and all', and could never, ever deny Him or His Love, come what may, and I know I will spend eternity with Him in His Heavenly Kingdom. If God has shown *me* His Wonderful Love and Favour, how much more will He do so for *you* if you will but ask Him?!

Sadly, our world is in deep trouble as it wants/seeks to go on its own way without God in deception by God's enemies. It was James Dobson, a believer and doctor from the USA, who, years ago, said something akin to the fact that the world will love you if you are tall, good looking, intelligent and if things look okay … and this may be so, of course …! And again a song sung, with great gusto, by Marilyn Baker, contained some words saying that all the world loves a superstar who loves to play the part but I'd (God) rather have a poor man who opens up his heart ... and the words of this song are also true ...!

As the world and the UK, that are in dire trouble, rush headlong towards the 'finale', if you like, at the end of this Age of Grace in which we now live, the time of the 'Latter Rain Revival' which will result in an unprecedented harvest of souls worldwide for God's Kingdom of Heaven, followed by the seven years of horrific tribulation, surely there is an urgency *now* to question, search, evaluate and to find out what is really happening here on Planet Earth?!

When my father was resting after his lunch on that fateful day on the Lancastria looking at and weighing up the lifeboats, he realised they were not ready to be used and mentioned this to someone at that time, but nothing was done about it and *this was just before the troopship was bombed by a German Bomber that very summer's afternoon, taking only twenty minutes to sink*! The Captain stated to all on board, "It's every man for himself!", and so it was they would all have to swim or whatever to escape ... shame about the lifeboats! If that ship had so many people on it, possibly up to 9,000, and therefore it could not move, then if this was so, several thousand people died, making it by far the worst single maritime disaster ever. It is more or less the same right now on Planet Earth: we are in a *terrible, terrible warfare of good versus evil*, with no holds barred by the enemy, and from the intensity of this warfare there is no escape - we are all either on one side or the other – and 'our ship' (Earth) is in trouble on the sea of the stinking filth and mire of sin as we are about to be 'hit' by the enemy, which means it is 'every one for themselves to escape' ... We have been warned, but will we heed that warning? Now is the time to prepare for that escape. There is plenty of room on 'God's Lifeboat' and that is the finished work of the Lord Jesus Christ!

Believe Him, cry out to Him to be saved and washed clean in His blood, giving Him your broken and contrite heart, your life and your everything, and walk His Way with Him! It's *your* choice! All power and authority is and has been given to Jesus (Yeshua) and He will supply all of your needs and more and will help you every step of life's journey. When your heart feels the Saviour Messiah's gentle touch from Heaven, you can't deny, even if you try, His True Love when it starts and you will always want more! *Nothing* can match this Love and Life of Father God through His Son, the Lord Yeshua Messiah. It is wonderful, He is Wonderful, Great and Awesome and He loves you so, so much you cannot fail overall ... what are you waiting for ...? Give Him your heart ... He is only a heart's gentle whisper away ...

HE is THE WAY ... I see it ... DO YOU ...?!

The Way I See It

# *Three Items contained in the following pages*

I The words only taken from my previously printed booklet as it stands, minus "The Creed (revisited)" by the Evangelist, Giles Stevens

II The account given by my father with regard to his experience in the sinking of the troop ship, Lancastria, on June 17th 1940, as printed in The Loss Of Lancastria, compiled by John L. West (pages 32, 33 and 34) and published by Millgate Publishing Ltd., Rossendale, Lancashire. I understand that John L. West is now deceased, as is my father, and could find no trace of the publisher.

III Some important books/material from my life's 'bibliography'

Henry preaching at Grey's Monument, Newcastle

*I The words only taken from my previously printed booklet as it stands, minus "The Creed (revisited)" by the Evangelist, Giles Stevens*

LIFE'S TROUBLES, CRISES, HEARTACHES -
WHATEVER LIFE'S JOURNEY BRINGS - WHERE
DO YOU TURN?


    THE
    HEART OF
    THE
    MATTER

IS….

    THE
    MATTER
    OF YOUR
    HEART
            WHERE
               WILL
                  YOU
                    STAND
                      WHEN
                      YOU
                        ARRIVE AT
                          ETERNITY'S
                        DOOR?

HENRY A. FIELD - NO REGRETS - THE LORD JESUS
IS THE ANSWER

DRUGS....PORNOGRAPHY....
CLUBS....T.V.....VIOLENCE....OCCULT.... RELIGIOSITY.... LOVE
OF MONEY....GAMBLING....SPORT.... WORKAHOLISM....
ALCOHOL.... COMPUTERS.... MUSIC.... NEW AGE....
MATERIALISM....IMMORALITY....


.......these and many more are things we may 'escape' into, there is a way
that seems right .......but it ends in death. See Proverbs chapter 14 verse 12
and Romans chapter 6 verse 2.

Hi, we all have a testimony to give on life's journey. Briefly, here is
mine.

Deep calls to deep. I was born in Newcastle upon Tyne in the second
world war, the son of a GP and the middle of five children. I had a
middle class upbringing and for most of it lived in Carlisle. All was not
well. Home life was very unhappy and my father left home when I was
about 11. My parents got divorced in the later `50s. My school life from 5
to 10 years old was spent at boarding schools - horrific militaristic
regimes, not nice places to be. The last one was a catalogue of evil. I
saw everything from sadistic torture to the whole school running riot.
Though from about the age of eleven I went to an independent day school
which was bearable, fear was the thread running through my school life
until near the end. The total freedom I had in the school holidays was
compensation. I smoked throughout my teenage years - often heavily -
and though not a problem, would drink alcohol as well. I lived for the
romantic rock'n'roll music of the later `50s....with passion! I got on well
with my mother - she was good to me and had a godly influence upon me.
Though still young I stood by her the best way I could through her
divorce and afterwards, yet she sadly turned to alcohol which eventually
ended in tragedy. So for the latter part of my schooling years I was largely
left to my own devices and was prone to be a loner. I did not have a
Christian or 'religious' upbringing, it was all Radio Luxembourg,
Sunday newspapers, television (very different in the `50s) or whatever. I
never disbelieved in God and held Him in respect. I have had many
adventures in, and experiences of, life, have moved house many times
and had a lot of different work experiences that included, largely, training
for hotel management, shops and offices, being a weaver (the world's
slowest!), serving in the Royal Air Force partly in the Far East and
Northern Ireland, and working for British Rail. I have been to Bible
College and in full-time Christian Pastoral Ministry and have done the
work of an Evangelist. I have one daughter, and - with an 18 year gap -
one son, one grand-daughter and now two great grandchildren.

Towards the end of the '80s I experienced burn-out. In my 28 years of marriage to my first wife we had love, loyalty and faithfulness. Sadly latterly she had some serious sicknesses. After she went to Heaven in 1991 through leukaemia I was left a one-parent family and home-educated my son for a while. After 3 years I married again and though everything seemed to be okay after a few years the marriage suddenly disintegrated and all the trauma of divorce followed. In some ways this was harder to bear than spouse bereavement, and a time of severe testing yet The Lord lovingly took me through the dark night of pain and anguish and walked with me in it, giving me His comfort, promises and hope for the future. Proverbs chapter 3 verses 5 to 8; and 2 Corinthians chapter 1 verses 3 to 5. It did not fully make sense to me. *I let God be God.* He is in the business of healing broken hearts and broken people. He simply closed lesser doors to open greater ones. Psalm 30 verse 5 says that joy comes in the morning after the night of weeping. *This is always so for those who know their Father God.*

So it was a few years later I married again.

In late 1961 I got hold of my grandfather's Bible and started reading Proverbs, Psalms and some of the Gospels. I secretly believed in God as my Heavenly Father and acknowledged God as a Trinity of Loving-Kindness; Father, begotten Son the Lord Jesus Christ, and Holy Spirit - as I know now, *'One in Essence and Three in Personality.'* I loved Proverbs and the Book gave me a great fear and respect for God. In Psalms I saw the more emotional side of God's love and care and the Gospels of Mark and Luke brought some of this into focus. I had had a real encounter with God but did not know what to do next or how to take it further. Something within me began to change.

In the May of 1962 I met my first wife, fell in love, made her pregnant in the September (yes, all true Christians are sinners saved by Grace and the Blood of the Lord Jesus Christ) and married her in the December - we were both 18 - and had a lovely baby daughter the following year! In the material sense life was sometimes very hard. We knew times of very real poverty yet we were incredibly happy. We had times of prosperity as well. As the years went by in the '60s I began a spiritual search once again, mainly through reading. I got involved with hypnotism - not wise. I said, 'No'. I eventually read books like 'When Iron Gates Yield' and 'God Holds The Key' by Geoffrey Bull that explained about The Lord Jesus Christ and miracles which had happened to the author in his coming out of Communist China as a missionary. I was totally hooked! This was not the norm 'religiosity'. This was exciting and for real!! So it was that in October 1968 I bowed my knees and stiff neck to the Lord Jesus Christ and gave Him my heart on condition that He would use me!! Something instantly happened in my heart and life - I came into a living relationship with the Lord Jesus. What joy filled my heart! I learned later that I had been 'born again', everything about life and eternity started to come into perspective and my marriage was even better if that were possible. My wife was totally with me and asked Jesus into her heart at that time as well. Spiritually speaking, I have never looked back to this day.

*I knew God was my Heavenly 'Dad'* and, unlike my late earthly father, I had to learn I could easily approach Him. I knew the Lord Jesus as my Friend and Saviour. It was *awesome.* Could there yet be more? I did my best to believe the Word of God as it stood as I love God's Word. What was this 'Baptism in the Holy Spirit' in Acts chapter 2? For years I searched and refused to take 'No' for an answer. Then suddenly in September 1973 when visiting London, I was taken to St John's Hainult where I knew there were revival meetings happening with the then Vicar, Trevor Dearing. It was awesome in the meeting with the singing, love and power of God - I felt as if I had arrived in Heaven!! Later that evening I was powerfully and totally baptised in the Holy Spirit along with my then wife, through Trevor Dearing's ministry of the laying on of hands, as God filled me from head to toe with His mighty power from Heaven. I was 'drunk' in the Holy Spirit and praised the Lord all night long. This was even more power to praise, worship, love and serve Him. This is the start of the 'Full Gospel'.

*If this was all it would be enough but there is much, much more!* However I have no space left here. Please don't miss out on all the wonderful adventures of the true Christian Walk in Life. Many times since, I have experienced powerful anointing of the Holy Spirit including being under the 'Weight of His Glory' and the 'Lion's Roar'. It is about the Kingdom of God and Heaven here with us on Earth. It is all about forgiveness, deliverance, relationship, holiness, loving- kindness and so much more.

God has put His love into my Heart through the Lord Jesus and.....*He will do the same for you no matter who or what you are.....if you will let Him.*

## *A Prayer to Pray*

Two cannot 'walk' together in harmony unless they agree! The Lord Jesus is perfect and sinless and He has made The Way through His shed blood and finished work on Calvary's Cross. Those who want Him, as an act of their will, must give Him their heart and life in all its wrong-doing and sinfulness and come into a living relationship with Him that will last forever - The Bible calls it 'being born again' (John chapter 3 verse 3 and verses 16 to 18) and 'being a new creation in Him'. It's a fresh start with the eternal life and love of The Lord Jesus deep in one's being.

It is good to say a prayer to start the relationship off - the unrighteous with the Righteous God. Every journey starts with the first step to go somewhere and every true friendship starts with something in your heart and soul saying 'we get on well together, let's be friends and go on in life together as such.' It is my desire to be as thorough as possible even if you are not fully aware of what step you are taking - it is a matter of faith, trusting Him at His word. If you do so you will be very pleasantly surprised. Now you can say a fairly brief prayer, a cry of the heart, such as 'Heavenly Father, Lord Jesus, I trust You are there. I have had enough of all wrong-doing and sin. Forgive me all my wrongs against You and, God, be merciful to me, a sinner. I give You my heart and my life, I surrender to You all I am and I come into Your loving arms. Amen and Amen.'

I have a longer prayer that I have used many times which people have repeated after me, little by little, and nearly always with powerful effect, sometimes quite quickly and sometimes with great difficulty as The Lord would help me to help them get through and even at times 'counsel' them completely through it. Sometimes those who repeated the whole prayer were already 'born again' and that's okay. And for others it would 'bring into focus', if you like, what they needed to understand more clearly as they got going on their journey with Him. Sometimes they would be wonderfully set free from that which was hindering them and nearly always they had a joy and peace inexpressible. May it be so for you! Amen!
Here it is:-

## *A Prayer for Salvation –*

## To Know you are Going to Heaven,
## To Know God's Love          Henry A Field

Heavenly Father, Lord Jesus (Yeshua) Christ, Holy Spirit - I may not fully understand at this time, but I acknowledge You as The Trinity of God and believe in You so help me now as I put my trust in You. Please help me as I pray this prayer.

I know I have sinned/done wrong in my thoughts, words and actions. There are so many good things I have not done....there are so many sinful/wrong things I have done. I am sorry for my sins - please help me and I will turn from everything I know to be wrong. I renounce all meaningless, empty and damaging religion, any and all occult and any cult involvement and ask for Your total cleansing. I yield myself to You - my pride, anger, hurt, pain, selfishness and any bitterness, everything. I give it all to You. Please forgive me. As an act of my will I forgive all others, no matter who, when or where, who have done wrong to me, and break/release the emotional pain of the abuse from me, both conscious and sub-conscious. I forgive myself.....Soul and Body, I forgive you. I give You my guilt, real and perceived. I break off me all wrong inner vows and curses. As You gave Your life, Lord Jesus, upon The Cross for me, by and through Your sinless, perfect, shed blood, and died my death and give me Your life - Your blood come into my life and cleanse me from every sin.....gratefully I give my life back to You and ask You to come into my heart and life as my Lord and King. Come in as my Saviour to cleanse me. Come in as my Lord to control me. Come in as my Friend to be with me. Come in by Your Holy Spirit and flood me and baptise me with Your Holy Spirit Love. I will do my best to love You as You have first loved me, to have a close relationship with You and serve You as You give me the gifts to do so. And let me walk in that serving in obedience to You and fellowship with You all my days on Earth.

Thank You and I praise You Lord Jesus that You will take me to Your Heaven to be with You forever. Thank You Heavenly Father that You are now my Perfect 'Dad' with unconditional love for me. Thank You Holy Spirit that You are my Comforter and much much more. Clean me up, mature me and let me be like You, Lord Jesus. Free me from all demonic activity and teach me in Your Way and let me be Your disciple and a Kingdom of God/Heaven believer/builder.

I confess that Jesus Christ is God and walked in the flesh on this Earth. Thank You that my salvation is totally dependent upon You.

JESUS IS LORD! I love You Heavenly Father/Lord Jesus and praise You. AMEN and AMEN

### *Helpful Hints Now I am Saved*

Okay, if you have understood something of Who The Lord Jesus is and the Way of Salvation by His shed blood and finished work on Calvary's Cross and His resurrection from the dead and have made a decision of some kind to follow Him as you have given Him your heart to trust Him and live for Him and you know a joy and peace as His loving-kindness and mercy fill you - this is very good. Praise The Lord! Is there any useful advice that could be given you as you start to walk with The Lord Jesus that will be of help to you so that you know what you are looking for? Yes, lots!

As I look back in hindsight over the many years, since the sixties, of being a disciple of Jesus and think of what advice I would like to have been told then that I know now, and what would have helped me at that time to adjust more quickly from the world and its ways to The Kingdom of God, laying aside every weight that might hinder and keeping my eyes firmly on The Lord Jesus Christ and somehow attain to maturity in Him, the following is some of what I would like to have been told when starting out.

It's not about man, his ways, quest for power, greed, structures, restrictions or empires that he builds as he exalts himself in his pride and natural strength - it's all about The Lord Jesus - He is truly God, so in gratitude worship and serve only Him. Begin to see just something of The Awesome, Almighty and Incredible God we have - infinitely so beyond words. Don't let any man put you down, that is, demolish your esteem, dignity and worth in Christ - look and search to see all that He has given you - you will be amazed! Only Jesus owns you - no man does - and The Lord always has the last word. If something binds, controls or oppresses you, you are not free .....so let no man take away your real freedom in Christ - The Truth will always set you free. Don't be afraid to be real, to be who you are - only allow the process of your Father God making you like His Wonderful Son. Love Father God with all your heart - your aim is to grow up and so be mature in Christ for love never fails. Measure yourself up with Scripture - when you fall short cry out to God for help. Life is all about change, sifting all things, and wisdom is keeping that which is good and relevant for you, it is knowing when and having the courage, to say 'No'. Keep it simple with godliness and contentment. We give The Lord God His rights and we only have privileges. Seek a Godly, mature mentor and be discipled 'for a season'. You are in a living, loving relationship with Him. *Religion* is Satan's ace card except in James chapter 1 verse 27.

Remember there are Godly universal Biblical principles that apply in your life. For example: what you sow you will reap, usually in another season; the reality of what you write on your heart is what will determine the direction you take and will affect what happens to you e.g. Proverbs chapter 3 verses 3 and 4 where it is for good; if you submit totally to Jesus and give Him your everything He will give to you His everything and you will walk powerfully for and glow for Jesus; God has a tendency to give people over to what they really want or persistently strongly desire.

*Don't compartmentalise your life into 'secular' and 'sacred'.....your life is all one in Him.* The promises of God are always true and totally kept in His time as He cannot lie and cannot fail.

Prayer (in its different kinds) is basically you and Him.....simply addressing Almighty God in your mind, thoughts, heart, words, motives and vision. So talk or share with Him naturally as you would a close, good friend - respectful pillow talk - He knows and sees everything about you anyway, and still loves you - every thought you have is open before Him. Although He will lovingly correct you He loves you unconditionally. He will prune you and, as needs be, lovingly give correction and may test your faith or teaching received at any given level - all these things are to mature you. Listen to Him and learn to do so, to recognise His voice from all the other sounds in your life. The Lord speaks in several different ways e.g. through His Word the Bible, an inner witness, circumstances etc.

It is not about becoming 'a leader' or having titles, status, exams or credentials for we are all precious and equal in Christ. It's not about 'professionalism', 'intellect', 'the mind', a type of self-condemnation so often found within a 'church class system' (for example where you feel of no consequence) or the world's values and ways when they have infiltrated the church - it *is* about being real, knowing that we are *all* totally lost *unless* we feed from 'The Tree of Life' through feeding on the 'Lamb of Calvary's Cross' in our hearts. We are *all* sinners saved by grace and not one of us has or can do anything without Christ - it is about serving and finding your God-given gifts which you received in the natural at birth, and spiritually at salvation, along with the anointings of the Holy Spirit and exercising those gifts for the benefit of 'all' and leaving the rest to Father God. Remember The Truth will always set you free and lead you to Jesus - the rest will bind or oppress you.

Don't neglect to meet together for fellowship (not 'services' or 'churchianity' but simply true believers meeting together, always centred around the Lord Jesus). This fellowship may take various forms - the very early church in Acts met together in their homes. Building-centred church fellowships with an emphasis on buildings, attendance, systems, structures with man's control and insistence on legalistic financial giving, and denominations with their man-centred hierarchical structures and doctrines to be adhered to (where some may be suspect and the questioning of them will not be tolerated), are not found in the New Testament after Pentecost. You are free to seek a good fellowship that suits you where the full gospel is preached, power of the Holy Spirit demonstrated, where the people love Jesus and it is real 'family' with their eyes firmly fixed on Jesus and on building the Kingdom of Heaven, His Kingdom. Every Kingdom has a territory and a ruling and reigning monarch. Yours is Heaven and …..your Ruler is The Lord God Almighty, King Jesus, The Messiah. There are genuine leaders of course in Fellowships - they will never 'lord it' over you or control you but are there to equip you, encourage, guide, protect and within right bounds to admonish you and so are there *for* you to stand mature in and for Christ. The Christian walk should be a 'life- style' for all of your life as a disciple for Jesus. This is all about discipleship and maturity in Christ. The Christian walk as a disciple for Jesus and growing up in The Lord can be difficult at times but as we walk through it with our eyes fixed on Jesus we will do so victoriously, for our Heavenly Father always delivers us. It is an adventure with such fun and joy!

Get into the Word of God, The Bible, in any sound version such as The New King James Version, the New American Standard Version or possibly The New International Version. A paraphrase ( i.e. not a literal translation from the original languages) such as 'The Message' may be helpful for some or for reference. Beware of the many bad translations that are available. Find out what your favourite books or verses of the Bible are and keep with them to get started. For me it was Psalms and Proverbs and parts of The Gospels.

Take the bread and wine (or non-alcoholic juice that would remind you of wine so as not to offend anyone) as often as you will - The Lord's Table - hopefully fairly regularly. See 1 Corinthians chapter 11. This is to remind you of the Cross of Jesus, to examine your heart, look forward to His return, say sorry - 1 John chapter 1 verses 8 and 9 - and much more to keep us in fellowship with and centred on Him. You, as a true believer, can never lose your salvation which is dependent on Jesus but we can be out of fellowship with Him on our journey here on earth.

Get baptised by total immersion - it is believers' baptism and the correct thing to do if possible. Ask The Lord until you receive the Baptism of The Holy Spirit from Heaven as in Acts chapter 2 - His wonderful anointing love, grace and power from Heaven and then seek further anointings whenever possible - no matter what - and they will come your way.

We are in a spiritual warfare of the spiritual forces of good and evil battling in the heavenlies and the battle is intense - of which the results are being outworked in the physical realm for good or evil. We play our part through passionate prayer, spiritual authority and deliverance ministry - Daniel, Ephesians and Revelation are keys but it is in all of scripture. Remember Satan seeks to destroy that which he cannot control. There are two choices. We either knock out the enemy or the enemy will knock us out if we give way or legal right to him, until God delivers us - hence the prayer 'Give me victory over my enemies!' Tune into Jesus and it will be done for you.

## Doctrine

Very briefly, I just want to say something more about the word 'doctrine' as it is far more important than many realise. Some are frightened of the word and rightly so, for it does bring division. Even a little understanding and wisdom about this will be of much help. We nearly all have and are following doctrines - but in each case what is their source?

Definition of the word:- 'doct' is the root of the word as in 'doctor' and means teach, teacher or teaching so in the New Testament the word doctrine means 'that which is taught' or 'the act of teaching, instruction'. In the letters of Paul to Timothy and to Titus where the word 'doctrine' appears several times is of interest. For our word 'doctrine' there are two words in the original Greek. One shows an emphasis on the substance and authority of teaching and the other the act or action of teaching. The dictionary meaning is: a set of beliefs or principle(s) held and taught by a church, political party or other group; what is taught; a body of instruction.

To paraphrase:- it is a belief system or systematic set of ideas, thoughts, words, phrases, statements etc put or strung together methodically into an ideology or credo (a statement of belief or aims of the Church) that may be believed in, taught and acted upon.

So what does all this mean? As stated, we are in an intense warfare between good and evil. Though there are many 'doctrines', according to the New Testament there are only two types of doctrine: sound doctrine or demonic doctrine! We soak ourselves in the Word of God to begin to know which is which. By the fruit, also, you will know them for the Holy Spirit will lead you into all truth.

Some examples of how Satan has twisted the truth:- take the doctrine of 'The Church'. Ask almost anyone today in the UK and they would reply, "Oh, that's a building down the road of such and such a group or denomination". The meaning of the word never meant 'a building' but is the Greek word 'ecclesia' which means 'the called out people' and refers in the New Testament to the true people who belong to God and *never* was a building in which people met! The only New Testament recorded places where the early believers met, apart from the open air, was in their homes!

The word 'Christians' was only used three times in the New Testament and not in a nice way. Sound Bible doctrine would or should use the words 'believers', 'disciples' or 'brethren', which all pertained to the Lord Jesus. The doctrine of financial tithing, as laid down legalistically, if not extortionately when taught and practised by some is not found in the New Testament after The Cross. What *is* found is a secretive, cheerful, from the heart-giving to *people,* usually when very poor or going through hard times and a sharing of what they had overall. There is a right and fair giving, between you and The Lord, which will not just favour the rich so they get richer - motives count. I think it is safe to say you cannot out-give God especially in the light of eternity. ( The Roger Price tapes /CDs on 'Giving' are excellent and a must on this subject.)

The doctrine of 'infant baptism' is not found in the New Testament yet many adhere to it. Believers' baptism, though, is clearly taught in the New Testament.

The list goes on, of course, but generally I would not refuse fellowship with other believers just because of any differences in the above-mentioned doctrine(s).

'Humanism' with its backdrop of 'evolution' and with its 'human rights' and 'politically correct' nonsense (which is designed to kill freedom of speech as 'they' demand perfection from us ) is anti-God and anti-Bible and it refuses to acknowledge either, along with sin and the like, and is atheistic as it will only recognise the physical. It is totally demonic, akin to its predecessor, 'communism', that has always resulted in a blood-bath of violence, slavery and terrible oppression wherever it goes. Through Information Technology humanism is now being taught and believed by much of the world or certainly by most of its leaders. It can never succeed and no good will ever come out of it for it has no absolutes and neither is there equity, justice or the like within it. It knows nothing of God's rights, ways or righteousness etc. We remove or water down the 'ancient boundary stones' of our society/culture set up by our ancestors, based on good Biblical foundations, and replace them with every kind of humanistic and pluralistic insanity *at our peril.*

## Eschatology

'Eschatology' is the doctrine of 'The Last Things' or the things that are about to unfold at this crucial and important time in God's history as He allows His plans and purposes to come to fruition. It is a massive and complicated doctrine and has been my 'pet subject' on and off for thirty odd years now as I have sought to unravel the whys and wherefores - to find the truth of it all. It has its own 'jargon' of course and I have found over the years that with all its variations of belief, few people would seem to agree together on all the main points and it can be very emotive and divisive because of this. Again, I have found the teachings of the late Roger Price on this subject to be excellent and a must - certainly on his 'unfulfilled prophecy' material. I will only be very brief here in what I write.

Dealing with this subject with all its various aspects is so important for if we get it right it will give us wisdom and understanding as to what is happening on Planet Earth at this dangerous time and if not and we are on the wrong track, and there is great deception, then who knows where we will end up. Unsound doctrine is a deceptive counterfeit of the enemy and if we fall into it or believe it by taking it on board how then can we be prepared for what is about to happen? Yet, Almighty God will do what He is going to do anyway - the enemy who is allowed to work for a short while will desperately *try* to destroy God's plans, promises and purposes. Many evangelicals would have no problems in the *events* themselves that are about to take place but the problems start in the reality of where they fit in order, one after the other. I would liken it to a jigsaw puzzle. You have the pieces but putting them in the right 'order' and 'place' to get the whole right picture is what it is about. Hammering the pieces in in their wrong place, in exasperation, just to make them fit can create more problems than it solves - get them right and you will see the genuine picture. All I am going to do here is list the main 'pieces' of the subject in the order of events that I believe and understand they will happen. I would hope that this may whet your appetite for more Bible study/research and further information. Scripture is our final authority and if we get the interpretation correct it will all make sense.

Here is a brief overview of God's history for Planet Earth. We are in the 'church age' that is fast drawing to a close. In God's seven day plan (for a thousand years is as a day and a day a thousand years with Him) He is going to get a people for Himself and a 'Bride' for His Son. This is to be 7,000 years in total from Adam and Eve at the start, in a perfect garden environment, to the end of day seven after which the fixed eternal state starts. One of several simple, broad but good ways to look chronologically at the first six days is that the first 'two days' (two thousand years) were the 'age of conscience'. This is followed by the next 'two days' (two thousand years) which were the 'age (or dispensation) of the law' and the keeping of it, pertaining to The Jews in the first instance. The next 'two days' (two thousand years) is the 'age of grace' whereby Salvation is equally thrown open to all. The final 'day' (one thousand years) is called 'The Millennium' and is God's 'Sabbath', the 'Rest Day' of the human race on Planet Earth as we know it - and will be a perfect environment (just as it was in the very beginning of time in the Garden of Eden) with The King, Messiah Jesus, ruling and reigning from Jerusalem through Israel and The Jews. At that time human beings will again live to be several hundred years old. But at the end of this time, in spite of all the kindness God has shown and delivered for man's good, man will once again rebel against God, calling on Satan so as to begin to make war against The Lord and true believers - and God at that point will wind up and destroy the Earth and the Universe as we know them - He will have made His point! This is followed in Heaven by 'The Great White Throne Judgement' of The Lord Jesus Christ who will judge everyone who has ever lived - either to eternity in the Lake of Fire, a Christ-less eternity, *or* to be with Christ in His new Earth and Heaven, a place of total, perfect bliss, for all eternity (because they trusted in the finished work of Christ who took their judgement and death, due for sin, on their behalf and gave them His Life). How we responded in heart-reality to the love of Christ on this Earth determines where each one will spend eternity. There is consciousness for all after death but there are no other places than the two just mentioned.

We are in an important transitional time. It is 2006 and we are fast approaching the close of the 'two days' of the 'age of grace'. To get from now to the 'Sabbath Day' ('The Millennium') certain things must take place. The nations of the Earth, under the sway of Satan, will go into more and more turmoil - keeping, to their utmost, God out as they follow their own devices with more and evermore control and manipulation and untold evil. There are several signs clearly mentioned in the Bible of this e.g. adverse weather conditions and destructive natural phenomena (tsunami, earthquakes, tornadoes etc), lawlessness, violence and with travel and knowledge greatly increased and so on. The time of this 'transition' on Earth is to last seven years and each half of the seven years has meaning. This seven year period is called 'The Tribulation' and in fact the last three and a half years of it is called 'The Great Tribulation' - a time unequalled in evil and 'The Tribulation' is referred to as the 'Birth-pangs' leading into 'The Millennium'. There are two levels of what is happening during 'The Tribulation' - one in Heaven and the other on Earth.

The first one is that at the very moment 'The Tribulation' starts all true believers everywhere on Planet Earth will be caught up in the air ('The Rapture') to meet with The Lord above the clouds in a moment of time, forever to be with Him, and are going to the Marriage Supper of The Lamb (The Lord Jesus) to be, collectively, His Bride. At the end of the seven years the believers will return with The Lord Jesus to the Earth, to reign with Him from Jerusalem throughout the 'Millennium'.

The second one is regarding all other people on Earth for whom these seven years are a time of unequalled troubles, evil and wickedness not known in Earth's six thousand year history. The antichrist i.e. satan personified in the flesh being revealed at the time of 'The Rapture' as it is so called of 'The Church' will immediately arise and call himself 'The Christ' and with almost unrestrained evil and often along with the supernatural will do whatever he wants to try and subdue the peoples and nations - especially Israel which he will still seek to destroy as her people will not all worship him. At this time the whole Earth is divided up into ten kingdoms for this purpose. The European Union is just one of these kingdoms that will be within the boundaries of the Old Roman Empire.

Please understand that I emphatically believe that the Second Return of The Lord Jesus is in two parts, the first is in the clouds to call all the believers up to Himself (The Rapture) and the second at the end of The Tribulation period, returning from Heaven, literally, to the Earth, to Jerusalem. (It is interesting to note the similarities between the ancient Jewish Wedding and the above order of events). There are two relevant major battles, in what I am saying here, against Israel, one leading up to The Rapture with mainly the armies of The North descending on Israel to destroy her but finding they themselves will be totally destroyed at that very point. When The Church is taken out of the equation - the spotlight once again fully goes onto The Jews and Israel. The other battle is The Battle of Armageddon just before the Lord Jesus returns to Jerusalem and intervenes to save The Planet from total destruction by man. People will be able to become true believers during The Tribulation period providing they do not give their allegiance to the antichrist and his system..... but at what cost?

## The Jews and Israel

It took me from the sixties to the mid-eighties to fully understand the basics of this very emotive yet important subject of The Jews and Israel. A doctrine in itself, of course, and the soundness thereof will help give light to the doctrine of The End Times mentioned in this booklet. Again, the relevant tapes, coming out of Chichester Christian Fellowship, Bognor Regis, in my opinion are an absolute must.

'The Church' on the one hand and 'The Jews and the Land of Israel' on the other are two separate entities in God's history and plan - yet they are totally one in their roots. When someone asked the question, "What proof have you that the Bible is true?" The answer was given, "The Jews" (with Israel of course). No other nation has ever survived after losing its land and its structures, the people being scattered and often persecuted for nearly 2000 years and then brought back to their land of origin to set up their original political structure etc - this could only happen by the Hand of The Maker of Heaven and Earth - it is without doubt one of the most incredible signs of the End Times and God's Biblical prophetic fulfilment!

In Genesis chapter 12 verses 1 to 3 God chose Abram (Abraham) and also said that anyone who blessed him and his seed would be blessed and anyone who cursed him and his seed would be cursed. Now this important statement has never been cancelled or superseded to this day and therefore still holds true. We curse in this context to our peril. The Jewish Nation came out of Abraham and she was given certain giftings and responsibilities. She was birthed as a favourite nation out of the world systems and set apart to do God's bidding and to be a 'show-piece' . Why did God specifically choose the Jews? Simply because He chose them - just like choosing a favourite chocolate from a box of chocolates. He could have chosen any nation or peoples - it was His prerogative because He is God! He wants to use them to bless all the nations and the families of the Earth. So it follows that if we too bless them so we will be blessed - a very good deal - and applies to individuals, families and nations.

The nation of Israel got it wrong quite a few times even to the point of being quite severely corrected as they sometimes misrepresented God but they also sometimes got it right and found great peace and prosperity which was the way God intended. They will get this right as a nation throughout the entire Millennium and greatly bless all the nations of the Earth. He entrusted His law and sacrificial system to them for this would show the difference between good and evil. The most important reason for God to make His choice was to have a people, a nation with a land that would contain the Messianic Line for The Messiah. He is God manifest in the flesh, to be the supreme blood sacrifice, above any of the animal sacrifices, the Perfect and Sinless One likened to a Perfect Lamb, to live and work and give up His Life by the shedding of His blood once for all for the sins of the human race to make a way back into fellowship and close relationship with Father God. This He did. He defeated Satan and all evil at Calvary's Cross. Now, if we are spiritually in Christ, and He lives in all true believers - that makes us also the seed of Abraham and 'Messiah ones'. Israel as such missed their Messiah because they were looking for something different, something with a worldly 'victory and fanfare' to it and not to *crucifixion* though *that* is clearly prophesied in Isaiah and Psalms etc. Salvation was then readily thrown open for anyone, yet that door will close and when it does so, with The Church gone, Israel will come back into her own to be used of God again.

So why such hatred against Israel and the Jews called 'anti-Semitism?' Even with some jealousy and hatred it does not make sense at a human level to want to persecute and totally destroy them. But at the spiritual level behind the physical is the warfare of the forces of good and evil. Satan and his forces want to destroy Israel at any cost in order to prevent God from keeping His promises and plans and so try to make Him a liar. The time period that is left on this Earth is Satan's last chance to do this - but he will fail along with all those who belong to him.

And why is there anti-Semitism from some branches of The Church that originates from a demonic doctrine called 'Replacement Theology' and though it has been around for a while may have some of its roots in something called 'British Israelism'? In a nutshell, 'Replacement Theology' says that The Church has replaced Israel and that the Jews and their land of Israel are now irrelevant in God's plans and so The Church is all that matters. Is this a form of spiritual elitism and pride to deny the end-time truth of Scripture? Whatever the reason for it.....surely it is a disgrace!

*So you are invited to the Greatest Banquet ever* - the Marriage Supper of The Lamb of God, the Heavenly Bridegroom, to His Bride, soon to take place in Heaven. Read all about it in Revelation chapter 19 verses 5 to 9 in context and Luke chapter 14 verses 16 to 24.

On your life's journey it is time to board God's 'Hallelujah Special' as it were, Heaven-bound. All tickets are still available and free, a gift of His Mercy and Grace, paid for by The Blood of The Lord Jesus at Calvary's Cross.

*The result of sin is death.* Because we are eternal beings, it is a 'living death' of separation from our Maker, Father God. (Don't confuse God in all His goodness with the works of Satan and all his lies, wickedness and deceptions. We are all in a battleground). It is only the Blood of God's only, perfect, begotten Son that is fully acceptable to Him. Hebrews chapter 5 verses 5 and 9 and verses 11 to 28. At Calvary's Cross - and in His death, resurrection and ascension to Heaven - an incredible divine exchange takes place. The Lord Jesus gives you everything good of

Himself and takes everything bad from you upon Himself as He took your death and died in your place for all your sins. He took your punishment, condemnation and eternal separation from God and gives you His life, abundant life, and much more and you will know His love now and in all eternity with the Trinity of God in His Heaven. Get the Full Gospel, everything good He has got to give, at any cost e.g. Acts chapter 2.

*God's gift of salvation is free.* You can't earn it, give money for it, be religious for it, study, do works or be good for it, or anything - you can only trust and accept His Gift with humility and give Him your heart. He can soften even the hardest of hearts. Matthew chapter 11 verses 28 to 30. He is the Perfect Gentleman and is knocking at your heart's door. You need to ask Him into your heart and let Him be your Lord and King and He will take up residence by His Holy Spirit. Psalm 34 verse 8 and Revelation chapter 3 verse 20.

*To receive His awesome forgiveness*, He is only a repentance prayer away. I would implore you to say a prayer such as the one included in this booklet or, in humility, the sincere cry of your heart will do to begin with, 'Lord, have mercy on me and forgive me' Luke chapter 18 verse 13. He will change your life completely from the inside out and I promise you will have no regrets.

Kind regards, all the best,

Henry


THE LORD JESUS SAID "UNLESS ONE IS BORN AGAIN HE CANNOT SEE THE KINGDOM OF GOD" JOHN 3: V3

Note: You will find, as I have, virtually all of the teaching and doctrine of the late Roger Price is excellent and a must – certainly the Basic Bible Study audio cassettes /CDs and books. For further information and a catalogue please contact: CCF Tapes, 35 Crescent Road, Bognor Regis, West Sussex PO21 1QO.

Finally completed and published December 2006.

## II *The account given by my father with regard to his experience in the sinking of the troop ship, Lancastria, on June 17th 1940, as printed in The Loss Of Lancastria*

**Account No. 9 - Capt. N. Field, R.A M.C. (Retd)**

From a letter to Major Petit:
Herewith a few notes which may help you in writing your book about the sinking of the "Lancastria".

I note that a certain survivor "Ron Evans" seems to have forestalled you with an article in the 'Empire News and Sunday Chronicle', date 31st August last, but perhaps this will be a source of information to you. I travelled across from Dieppe, the Medical base sub area, with 24 men and another Officer. As I had been P.A.D. Officer for Dieppe I brought with me an ambulance and two trucks each towing a trailer fire pump. We drew rations and petrol from the local DIDS and got across the bridge at Rouen 24 hours before the French blew it up to arrest the Germans. In this connection we were very lucky not to get caught on the Dieppe peninsular by the Germans advancing down the Seine, etc., we drifted down to la Boule and decided that we would get out, so joined the queue at St Nazaire docks and were all ferried onto the "Lancastria". As I set foot on board I was given a 'life jacket' which saved my life, and told my cabin number. A placard asked us to submit nominal rolls, but I never got this done. It was a glorious day and I went below for luncheon, after leaving my gear in my cabin. I had a good meal but presently we all felt a bomb explode, not ours but I learnt after, one on the "City of Mobile" ( I was told). Some officers jumped up to go, but later sat down again. This bomb saved the City of 'Mobile', because her Captain (I was told) took his warning, pulled up his anchor and started moving around, whereas the 'Lancastria' still remained at anchor! I felt sick with dread. I wanted to go to a quiet part of the ship and took my Sorbo Lifejacket for a pillow with a book to read (a book of P.A.D.)!! To the extreme stern, where being an Officer they left me alone. I had a chat with the master of arms about P.A.D. arrangements for the ship, because I had noticed life-boats roped still to the decks, but he said 'Don't worry, she would take a good twenty minutes to sink'. He was soon to be proved wrong! I lay down on the deck and presently heard the troops shouting 'Look there he is', a small white silvery plane hovering high up in a small white cloud. There were two 'Spitfires' skimming over the water near the ship. Then I heard men shout 'here he comes', and he started to dive on us out of the sun. I heard the troops trying to tell a gunner where to shoot but he kept saying 'where, where'. Soon the scream of the bomb replaced the noise of the diving plane, louder and louder, as we all lay flat cowering on this 'after deck', then suddenly the sound of impact, like someone bursting a child's tin kettle drum with a hammer, then clouds of steam and smoke and fragments raining down. I felt that she was mortally wounded, and the next bomb was also a direct hit as the bow was going down there being a slight slope forward on the deck. I sat perched like a bird on the extreme stern of the 'Lancastria' (taffrail? is it called), going higher up into the air as the bow went down. I could not get away from this rear deck, I forgot why probably joined bulkheads and packed troops. I was intently sitting watching the two Spitfires waiting for a good aerial battle but they never noticed the 'Boche' and to my intense disappointment flew away. I saw many things then such as soldiers struggling to release the captive rope fixing a life boat to the deck and one shouted 'can you not cut it' (the rope). I saw a boat being lowered full of civilians, and one end too fast spilled them all out and one fat old lady having fallen into the water like a plum having nothing to do but sit pretty in the water with her life jacket on, gave a dreadful scream and put her head under the water and drowned herself. Such is the power of panic.

The Naval personnel poor fellows, were our worst enemies. They did what they had been trained to do. They threw overboard everything floatable, presumably to avoid them being pulled down by the ship. Unfortunately they had not been trained to think, and a three knot tide carried everything away to St Nazaire, the ship being at anchor. I was unable to see what sort of a party was going on at the fore part of the ship, but the stuff drifting past told its own story. Bodies & oil, bodies some with life jackets on, presumably hit under the chin jumping feet first, crack swimmers, one with his steel helmet on to protect him, then floating flares and a soldier shouted "Good God, surely he's not dropping those things" but he was and I saw one drift past but it didn't seem to be igniting anything. I noted decks packed with soldiers laden with rifles and equipment, just waiting for a miracle to happen, with here and there a crack swimmer diving away in his underpants. What a pity all soldiers are not trained as "Marine Commandos", so as to rise to an emergency such as this one was.

By this time there was a considerable slope forward and downwards of the deck and I had no desire to be sucked down with her, she having given no hint yet of capsizing. The bows would be under the water with the stern sticking right up. To show how we go a bit mad under the strain, I remember taking all my money out of my trouser pocket before the jump and putting it against the rear of the hatch cover to save it from rolling down the deck! As I decided to 'git' a soldier came and said 'you'd better jump now sir, she's going', so we both clambered out over the rail and jumped feet first about seventy feet. I was saved from being stunned by my life jacket (as even though a Sorbo one, it would have been a killer from that height) by landing on my side, but when I eventually broke surface blood was pouring out of my throat like a hose pipe and the other chap who had jumped and came to help me just turned away and gave me up as finished. I

The Way I See It

shouted 'I've got T.B.' thinking that I had had a cavity in my lung which had burst under the shock of the fall into the water. However to a young man life is sweet and I contrived to swim away from struggling bodies until I got about 200 yards away from the ship, when I was all in from loss of blood, but my life jacket kept me up. I could only gaze at this great ship, now beginning to capsize. I thought to myself, this is the end, what a lonely place to drown. 'Lancastria' after a severe list to port capsized slowly in this direction and as long as I live I shall never forget the sight of thousands of soldiers scrambling along her hull side down towards the keel as it came out of the water, all screaming, or shall we say shouting and yelling.

So many men had run across her hull as it lay level with the water, that the keel was plastered with them. *But these men came out of a race which had over run the earth and soon the shouting stopped, to be replaced by 'roll out the barrel', with the 'Hun' peppering them from the air and a destroyer peppering the 'Hun' from the sea.* The song stopped slowly as the keel went down and more men were drowned, and soon there was silence with one or two life boats making away. My haemorrhage had stopped and the cold water was reviving me, so I took off my trousers and swam for a mile or two (I had been a Lakeland swimmer in a small way) and eventually caught up with a raft and attempted to get on board, but as it was level with the water, I was politely told there was no room for me but in my efforts to climb up they saw the three 'pips' on my shoulder, so decided that as I was an officer they would pull me on board! Once on board I felt an agonising searing pain in my left chest, and no wonder I had smashed my lung, due to the fall onto the water on my side and this had set off a burst blood vessel. I was put onto a ship full of wounded, which ran for it that night and landed at Plymouth next evening. I had a fortnight in hospital and then went back to duty after sick-leave. An incident occurred during my transport as a stretcher case from Plymouth Hospital to the Royal Masonic Hospital at Hammersmith, when an M.O. got into a flap about letting me go when he saw the label on my notes Haemoptysis 'spitting blood', however he decided in the end to let me go and then putting the note into my hand he said 'hang on to that, it's worth five pounds', he not knowing me to be an M.O. also, and so it was, I got a whole month's sick leave!

• At 1400hrs the anchored Lancastria, seen here in background, was attacked by enemy aircraft

• At 1557 she was struck by bombs below the waterline which ruptured the boat's fuel tanks

• Others were burnt as oil was ignited by flares from the few lifeboats. By 1615hrs it hadsunk.

• Rescue boats picked up survivors under fire from enemy aircraft.

• Exhausted and covered in oil, many were loaded onto ships bound for the UK.

• Of the estimated 6,000+ people onboard the Lancastria, less than half survived

• The Lancastria troopship in its final movements. Those who managed to escape overboard were engulfed by huge quantities of leaking fuel oil

"Latitude 47.09, Longitude 2.20. I shall never forget that position that marks her grave. Of the five thousand souls aboard her less than half had been saved; she sank like a stone and hundreds could not swim."
**Harry Grattidge, personal account**

• The Lancastria memorial on the sea front at St. Nazaire

"Opposite this place lies the wreck of the troopship Lancastria sunk by enemy action on 17 June 1940 w British troops and civilians during the evacuation of France. To the glory of God, in proud memory of more died and in commemoration of the people of Saint Nazaire and surrounding districts who saved many wounded and gave a Christian burial to victims. We have not forgotten. HMT 'Lancastria' Association. 17 June 1988."

### III Some important books/materials from my life's 'bibliography'

As I understand it the renditions were sound across the board, from the original translations, of the following two versions of The Bible, giving accuracy for personal reading and study:
*New American Standard Version (N.A.S.V.)* (Creation House)
*New King James Version (N.K.J.V.)* (Thomas Nelson)

Price, Roger. He left a wealth of material of books, tapes/CDs, dealing in *Basic Bible Studies* of the important doctrines regarding our faith and walk with The Lord and many *Special Topical Studies* clearly dealt with so that even the difficult is made easier to understand and apart from some, mostly minimal, negatives this is a goldmine of complex subjects simplified often with revelatory insight of sound doctrine and therefore a foundation for maturity in Christ…..a must!
CCF TAPES of BOGNOR REGIS, PO21 1QG, ENGLAND
www.ccftapes.co.uk

Andrews, Ian. Has a powerful healing ministry, with his wife, giving important teaching on this subject, designed to equip and help others to move in this much neglected area with a vast insight and revelatory knowledge of his walk with the Lord Jesus.
Various CDs and the book: *Equipped To Heal 2003.* PO BOX 28, CHARD, TA20 1LT, ENGLAND
www.citadelministries.com

Richards, James B. The only material I have to date comprises of 8 audio tapes entitled '*Prayer that builds self-worth*' - an excellent resource.
IMPACT INT. PUBLICATIONS, 3300 N BROAD PLACE,
HUNTSVILLE, AL. 35805.
www.impactministries.com

Sandford, John and Paula. They have a counselling ministry and I'll mention just three of their books that I found both interesting and helpful.
*Healing The Wounded Spirit*
*The Transformation of The Inner Man*
*Restoring The Christian Family*
(Victory House)

Bennett, Dennis, J. *Nine o'clock In The Morning* (Coverdale, London) 1971. A classic!

Phillips, J B . *Your God Is Too Small*
(Epworth Press, London) 1952. Definitely a classic!

Grubb, Norman. *Rees Howells Intercessor*
(Lutterworth Press) 1952. A classic - what a challenge!

Samson, Steve. *Listening to The Holy Spirit - Expecting The Miraculous*
(Sovereign World) 1986. A readable, excellent work.

Cook, Faith. *William Grimshaw of Haworth*
(Banner of Truth) 1997. A brill book - what a testimony, what a challenge!
The social history is fascinating.

Chavda, Mahesh. *Only Love Can Make A Miracle*
(Kingsway) 1991. Powerful testimony.

McClung, Floyd.
*Living On The Devil's Doorstep*
*The Father Heart of God* (Kingsway) 1985.

Tozer, A.W. *That Incredible Christian* (Christian Publications) 1964. Surely
this book is a classic?

Shakarian, Demos. *The Happiest People On Earth* (Hodder and Stoughton)
1975. A very powerful, readable testimony.

Baker, Marilyn. *Another Way Of Seeing* (Word (UK) Ltd.) 1988. What
courage!

Buckingham, Jamie. *Where Eagles Soar* (Kingsway) 1980. A must - an
excellent book.

Wilkinson, Jim (and Chris Spencer). *Miracle Valley The Story Of Hollybush
Christian Fellowship* (Marshalls) 1984. A great read!

Ericson, August (with Noel Davidson). *Sign of The Fish An Adventure in
Faith and Chips* (Ambassador) 2003.

Woodworth-Etter, Maria. *A Diary of Signs and Wonders* (Harrison House)
1916.

Frodsham, Stanley Howard. *Smith Wigglesworth Apostle of Faith*
(Gospel Publishing House) 1948 - 2002. Any of these type of several
paperback smaller books published a number of years ago giving accounts of
the miraculous of Smith Wigglesworth and Kathryn Kulman are classics and
faith builders.

Seamans, David A.
*Healing For Damaged Emotions* (Scripture Press) 1986.

Seamans, David A.
*If Only...* (Victor Books) 1995.

Allender Dr. Dan. B. *The Wounded Heart Hope For Adult Victims Of
Childhood Sexual Abuse* (CWR) 1991.

Lockley, Dr. John. *A Practical Workbook For The Depressed Christian* (Word (UK) Ltd.) 1991.
Gems in this book - helpful for freedom from the tyranny of legalism etc.

Prince, Derek. *Blessing Or Curse: You Can Choose* (Word Publishing) 1990.
*God Is A Matchmaker* (with Ruth Prince). (Chosen Books) 1986.

Campbell, Ross, Dr.
*How To Really Love Your Child* (Victor Books)
*How To Really Know Your Child*
*(Also sequel on the teenager)* Valuable reading.

Torrey, R.A. *The Power Of Prayer* (Zondervan) 1971.
(From 1924 and 1955 original editions).

Bounds, E.M. *Praying That Receives Answers* (Whitaker House) 1984.

Crispin, Ken. *Divorce The Forgivable Sin?* (Hodder *and* Stoughton) 1988.

Duty, Guy. *Divorce And Remarriage A Christian View*
(Bethany House) 1967.

Robertson, Norman K. *Understanding End Time Prophecy*
(Sovereign World) 1989.

Paine, Frank, L. *Miracle Of Time* (Shiloah Ministries) 1994.

LaHaye, Tim and Ice, Thomas. *Charting The End Times*
(Harvest House) 2001.

Liardon, Roberts. *Breaking Controlling Powers*
(Whitaker House/ Roberts Liardon Ministries) 2000.

Dupont, Marc. *Walking Out Of Spiritual Abuse* (Sovereign World) 1977.

Waller, Sue. *Let No Man Deceive You* (New Wine Press) 1986.

Lee, Robert (with Lee David). *Beware The Devil* (Marshalls) 1983.

DeHaan, Dr. M. R. *Chemistry Of The Blood*
(Zondervan) 1943 and 1971. Maxwell

Whyte H.A. *The Power Of The Blood* (Whitaker House) 1984.

West, John L. (Editor). *The Loss Of 'Lancastria'* (Millgate) 1988.

Conner, Richard and Joyce. *Marriage Alive* (Diasozo Trust) 1986.

Saxon, Sue. *Table For Two* (New Day Publications) 2002.

Lightning Source UK Ltd.
Milton Keynes UK

171252UK00001B/10/P